Ann Sophia Stephens

High Life in New York

A Series of Letters to Mr. Zephariah Slick

Ann Sophia Stephens

High Life in New York
A Series of Letters to Mr. Zephariah Slick

ISBN/EAN: 9783744687409

Printed in Europe, USA, Canada, Australia, Japan

Cover: Foto ©Thomas Meinert / pixelio.de

More available books at **www.hansebooks.com**

"Come, now, s'posing we strike up a trade. I've took a sort of a sneaking notion to that are new-fashioned side-saddle. So, if you'll throw in the tackling, I'll give you ten dollars for it, cash on the nail."—*Page* 150.

"I wish you could a seen that Astor House chap when he read the name; he looked as if he didn't know what to du, but at last he stepped back, and made a bow, and sez he—"—*Page* 184.

HIGH LIFE IN NEW YORK.

BY

JONATHAN SLICK, ESQ.,

OF

WEATHERSFIELD, CONNECTICUT.

A SERIES OF

LETTERS TO MR. ZEPHARIAH SLICK, JUSTICE OF THE PEACE, AND DEACON OF THE CHURCH OVER TO WEATHERSFIELD IN THE STATE OF CONNECTICUT.

EMBELLISHED WITH ILLUSTRATIVE ENGRAVINGS.

Philadelphia:
T. B. PETERSON AND BROTHERS,
306 CHESTNUT STREET.

JONATHAN SENDS A PREFACE.

A letter was dispatched to Weathersfield requesting Mr. Slick to forward a preface for his volume of epistles, but that gentleman instead sent the following letter, which is so full of his own peculiar humor that his friends will no doubt gladly accept of it in lieu of one.

THE PUBLISHERS.

WEATHERSFIELD, CONNECTICUT.

GENTLEMEN, SURS:

Your letter got tu the old humstead last night, nigh upon bed time, and it eenamost upsot me to think that a feller that's printed so many smashing books, had got a notion tu print my Letters tu, and asked my consent jest as mealy mouthed as a feller asks the gal he's been a courting to yoke in with him for life.

Now about the price of them are letters when they are all fixed out in a book. I ain't much acquainted with that sort of trading; but I reckon you'll have to go a notch higher yit. I never yit heard of a Slick's taking the fust offer for any thing, and I've cut my eye teeth as well as the rest on 'em, if I du write. Say ten or fifteen dollars more now, and mebby it 'll du, providing you give in a set of them are stories of the Revolution with picters, and some of the smashing novels that have got your names tu them, for my book-shelf in the back-room. Come up tu the mark on this point, and I'll agree tu sign off any time you want me tu, and I hope the book 'll go off like a flash of lightning down a forked rod.

But you want me to write something with a pesky new fangled name that has eenamost upsot me. Write a preface! What on arth is a preface? I can pull an even yoke with any York chap yet, at writing a letter; but when you come to talk of prefaces, darn me if I know what the critters are. Your letter kinder riled me up. The first thing I did was to get down the old goose quill and ink-bottle and go to work. I was a'most tuckered out a grinding cider all day, but the thoughts of having my name on the kiver of a smashing book with picters in it, sot my genius to working like a yeast pot; but then how tu begin with this new-fangled consarn—there it was agin. I got the old dictionary and tried to find out what a preface was; but I might as well have tried to make timber out of pine shavings. "Something to go before a speech, or a book, or an essay, to tell what they're about." Now if it had said an old hoss leading off an ox-team with a cart behind, I could have sent the animal at once, fresh and chirk from the cider mill; but how to tackle an idea on a book and make it pull, is more than I am up to, without knowing more about the sort of literary animal you want to use, and the harness that fits him. I ain't rusted out yit, by no manner of means; but I don't mean to make a coot of myself by tackling in with any strange animal till I know what he is. Now take a pen in hand tu once and let me know what it is that you want, and you can depend on me, fodder or no fodder; but keep dark about my having to ask about it. I don't want all the literary chaps in York a poking fun at me.

Wal, yes, I ain't ashamed to own it, I am tickled eenamost tu death with the idee of my letters being printed in a harnsome book with tip-top picters in it. But about my likeness, taken for the *Morning Express* when I first come tu York, with the corn-colored coat and pepper-and-salt trowsers and old bell crown—gauly, how I sot by that old hat! Wal, as I was saying about that are likeness, I han't no objections tu its going inside the kiver jest as it was. But like all great literary characters, I reckon there's been a pretty considerable improvement in me since I began to write, and, like our old barn that's been shingled and clapboarded over, I'm the same critter yet, timbers and all; but I reckon you'll find that I've slicked up the outside a few, and grown a little more pussy since the old pepper-and-salt saw the day.

Now I'll tell you jest how you'd better manage it. Put the picter you speak on inside the kiver ; but on the outside jest have me pictered out in a bran new hat, that Mr. Genin sent me jest afore I left York. It's about as near like the old one, as a son ought to be like his par. Don't forget my velvet vest, finefied off with curlecues, and my blue coat with the shining buttons ; and if you don't git a picter that'll make the gals' eyes water, your artists down there in York don't know a good looking chap when they see him, or can't paint him if they du.

Now about writing another book, I raly don't know what tu say. Them letters of mine eenamost tuckered me out at the time ; but somehow I'd give all creation to be at 'em again, and one of these days I may pluck up grit and take a trip over tu England. If I du, by the living hokey, you'll find John Bull in a tantrum by the time I've got through with him. That are English lord that I writ about in my letters, gave me an invite tu come tu England, and mebby he'll see a good looking chap about my size on t'other side the fishing pond some day or other. Who knows ?

You want to know if I feel content to give up life among the big bugs in New York, and settle down here in the country. Wal, now, between you and I and the post, I du feel a trifle melancholy now and then. Foddering cattle, going tu mill and chopping ovenwood ain't jest the thing tu rile up the poetry in a feller's bosom ; and onion tops and garden sars generally ain't considered the sort of greens that a literary chap wants put round his head, though they're awful refreshing to the stomach. But then again, my par, the deacon, is getting to be a purty old man, and Judy ——; but what's the use of talking arter a feller's under the harrow?

Wal, if I ain't contented, I sartinly ought to be, if the women folks are judges, and it's quite a considerable time since I've thought it worth while to have a tussel for any opinion of my own. But tu own right up, I du hanker awfully tu get off into the world agin; but, for gracious, sake, don't say a word about it. I should never hear the last of it, if you did, for Judy hates city gals like rank pisin, and is allfired jealous that I'm hankering to git among 'em again.

I don't know how I ever cum to write this ere long letter, but somehow, when I set down, pen in hand, the old natur will bile up and run on.

Now about that are consarned preface, jest set down tu once and describe the way it's to be done, and I'll undertake it, for I want tu make the book first chop; and if you want more team, I'm the chap tu hitch it on, the minit you let a feller know what's wanted. So, hoping you'll be particular about the preface,

I'm yours tu command,
JONATHAN SLICK

P. S.—Don't forget to have my watch chain and things a hanging outside of the vest, and put my two big rings with stones in 'em, on my left hand. I say nothing, but there may be gals in New York that would like tu see them are rings agin, but take them off from all the kivers you send into these parts now, I tell you.   J. S.

CONTENTS.

LETTER I.

First Impressions of New York—Visit to the Counting-room of a City Cousin—Advice to his Clerk—Description of a City Residence and its Inmates.................................... 13

LETTER II.

The Family Dinner and Effects of July Cider................. 23

LETTER III.

Jonathan visits the Express Office—Sensations on seeing himself in Print 27

LETTER IV.

The Political Meeting and its Disasters...................... 33

LETTER V.

A Little of Jonathan's Private Love Affairs.................. 39

CONTENTS.

LETTER VI.
Jonathan's Opinions of Ministerial Interference—A Card of Invitation, and an Evening Party at Cousin Beebe's, in which Jonathan makes some Mistakes and a Lady Acquaintance.... 44

LETTER VII.
Scenes in Broadway—Jonathan's Interview with the Count and Flirtations with Miss Miles......................... 69

LETTER VIII.
The Morning Call—A Coquette's Dressing Room............. 78

LETTER IX.
A New York Parvenu—Jonathan's Account of his Cousin Jason Slick, and how Jason was too lazy to work, and got rich on soft sodder—The dinner of a Connecticut Coaster—A New York Coat of Arms, lions couchant and levant—Yankee Ancestry—The way a Yankee speculates, and gets up States, Railroads and Banks, by soft sodder...................... 87

LETTER X.
New-Year's Calls—A real Yankee's New-Year's Treat of Doughnuts and Cider—Jonathan's ideas of the real difference between a real lady's House and Furniture and the House of a stuck-up Parvenu—Jonathan's ideas of Love and Ladies.. 99

LETTER XI.
Visit to the Park Theatre—First Impressions of the Poetry of Motion, as written on the air, in the aerial feats of Mademoiselle Celeste—First shock at the exhibition of a Ballet Costume accompanied by the "twinkles" of Celeste's feet—with her pigeon wings, double-shuffles, gallopades, and pirouettes, 117

LETTER XII.
Jonathan receives an Invitation to a Fancy Ball—Dilemma about the Dress—Choice of a Character, &c................. 129

CONTENTS.

LETTER XIII.

Jonathan Slick and the Grand Fancy Ball—Jonathan in the character of an Injun, and Cousin Beebe in the character of Jonathan—Cousin Mary as Jonathan's Squaw—Jonathan among Kings and Queens, Spaniards, Turks and Jews—Jonathan meets his pussey Cousin in the character of a Turk—Jonathan cuts his pussey Cousin.................... 133

LETTER XIV.

Advice to Jonathan from the Humstead—Jonathan's Criticism on his Brother Sam's book—The Ennui of Jonathan in good Society—Jonathan's entree into a Milliner's Establishment, and sad mistake about a Side-saddle.. 143

LETTER XV.

Jonathan visits the Milliner Girl—Reflections about her Situation 154

LETTER XVI.

In which Jonathan shows up the Hardships of Sewing Girls—Describes a Tammany Hall Ball—Milliner Aristocracy and Exclusiveness—Informs the reader how Miss Josephine Burgess took a tall man with whiskers into her Establishment, who took her in in return—The desperation of a little Apothecary—His Marriage, and the Ascent of Miss Josephine Burgess from the front store to a work room a little higher up.. 156

LETTER XVII.

Jonathan gets Ill and Homesick—Resists all entreaties to go to Washington, and resolves on going back to "the Humstead" with Captain Doolittle................................... 173

LETTER XVIII.

Jonathan's Arrival in New York from the Onion Beds at Weathersfield—Jonathan puts up at the Astor House—His notion of that great Heap of Stones—Jonathan's Ideas of a New York Cab, and the usual quarrel of a Stranger with Cabmen—A Sensation is created at the Astor............. 180

LETTER XIX.

A live Yankee and the Parisian Danseuse—Fanny sends her Card and Jonathan makes a call—Down East Yankee and French-English rather hard to be understood—Jonathan quite killed off by Fanny's Curchies and Dimples—A little sort of a Flirtation—An Invitation to see Fanny in Nathalie, which is accepted 188

LETTER XX.

Jonathan goes to the Express Office—His Opinion of Zeke Jones and the "Brother Jonathan" Newspaper—Explains his Absence, and enters into a new Agreement with the Editors.... 197

LETTER XXI.

Jonathan Visits Mr. Hogg's Garden and gets a Bouquet—Puzzled about the propriety of Paying for it—Purchases a Ribbon, and starts for the Theatre......................... 202

LETTER XXII.

Jonathan gives a Description of the Theatre, Private Boxes, Drop Scene, &c.—His Ideas of *Miss* Elssler's Dancing, and Dancing Girls in general—Jonathan mistakes Williams in his Comic Song of "Old Maids and Old Bachelors to Sell," for an Auctioneer who is knocking off, "La Belle Fanny," to the Highest Bidder—Jonathan is indignant that she is not his, after so much hard bidding, by winks, &c.—He flings his Bouquet at Fanny's Feet—Jonathan's Visit Behind the Scenes, and his Idea of Things seen there—Gallants Fanny home to the Astor House... 206

LETTER XXIII.

Jonathan gets out of love with Fanny Elssler—Doctors the Ague in her Face and Leaves her—Receives an Invitation from his Pussey Cousin to a Thanksgiving Dinner, with a three cornered Note for Lord Morpeth—Jonathan's Opinion of the Travelling Lords and Democratic Hospitality.............. 220

LETTER XXIV.

Description of Cousin Jason's Equipage—Figure cut by Mrs. Jason Slick and her Daughter—Manners of a Noble Lord—The Dinner—Jason boasts of his Birth, Heraldry, and Coat of Arms—Jonathan creates great Consternation by proclaiming the Head of the Family as a Shoemaker—Makes a Speech.. 224

LETTER XXV.

Jonathan rides to Mill—The Millerite Excitement—His Marm waits for the World to come to an End—Letter from New York—The old White Horse............................ 244

LETTER XXVI.

Jonathan arrives in New York—Travels on the Deacon's Mare—Has Trouble with the Colt—Embarks from Peck Slip, on Capt. Doolittle's Sloop, to meet the President—His Introduction—Jonathan's Idea of the Cold Collation—The Reception—Landing at Castle Garden—Review of the Troops—The Procession, &c....................................... 252

LETTER XXVII.

Jonathan attends the President at the Howard House—Visits the Park Theatre with the President and his Handsome Girl—Goes with Mr. Robert Tyler to have his Hair Cut at Clairhugh's—Takes Refreshments with the Ladies at the Howard House—Bed-chamber Scene with the President—Serenade, &c. 268

LETTER XXVIII.

Jonathan goes to see Mr. Macready—Description of the Theatre—Introduces himself to a Handsome Girl at the Theatre—Enters into a Flirtation—Promises to Visit her—Jonathan takes a Novel Method of providing himself with a Fashionable Dress—Quarrels with Captain Doolittle—Is reconciled, and starts off to make a Morning Call on the Handsome Girl..... 273

LETTER XXIX.

Jonathan Visits the Handsome Girl—Describes a Gambling-House in the Morning before it is put to rights—Visits the Lady's Boudoir—Describes the Furniture, the Lady, her Dress, and Conversation—Is Interrupted by the Gentleman of the House—And leaves with a promise to return and escort Miss Sneers to Mad. Castellan's Concert...................... 275

LETTER XXX.

The Gambling House—Jonathan is taken in with Cards........ 285

High Life in New York.

LETTER I.

First Impressions of New York—Visit to the Counting-room of a City Cousin—Advice to his Clerk—Description of a City Residence and its Inmates.

To Mr. Zephania Slick, Justice of the Peace, and Deacon of the Church, over to Weathersfield, in the State of Connecticut:

DEAR PAR:

I arrived here safe and sound, arter a long and tedious voyage down the river and along shore to this place. The Captain left me to navigate the sloop purty much alone. The lazy coot did nothing on arth but eat raw turnips and drink cider brandy all the way down. I'll be whipped if he warn't more than half corned the hull time. Now it's my opinion that the best thing you can do with that chap is to send him eend foremost about his business jest as quick as he gits back. He don't arn salt to his porrage, nor never did. The first thing I did arter the sloop was hauled up to the wharf at Peck slip, was to go down to the stores about Fulton market and peddle off the cider brandy and garden sarce. Captain Doolittle wanted to go with me, but you sent me down here as a sort of a supercargo, and I warn't likely to let him stick his nose into my business.

By gracious, if it didn't make me stare to see the purty gals and the harnsome married wimmen a walking up and down the market among the heaps of beets and cabbages. They looked around mighty knowing, and I rather guess I get my share of attention; but somehow it made me feel kinder streaked to have them a looking at me so steady, for I hadn't nothing on but my every day clothes, besides, the stock that marm made me out of her old bombasine petticoat, propped up my chin so that I couldn't a stooped to look into a woman's face if I'd a wanted tu ever so much. I do believe marm and Judy White must a put more than a peck of tatur starch into the lining. It's allfired stiff, that's a fact.

Wal, I sold out the lading to purty good advantage, considering the times. Then I went down to the sloop, and slicked up in my Sunday clothes, and started off full chisel to go and see cousin John Beebe. They told me that he kept store away down Pearl street, eenamost to the Battery; so I went on, as fast as I could git along through the boxes and barrels that lay in the street, till I come to a great high brick store that had cousin John's name over the door. It seems that John has gone into partnership with a Mr. Co, for that feller's name is on the sign arter his'n as large as life. I knew that he and John Wheeler went into company together, but I suppose they wanted more chink than either on 'em could raise, and so engaged this Mr. Co to help 'em along.

I swan if it warn't enough to make a feller dry to see the hogsheads of rum and molasses, and the heaps of tea boxes and sugar barrels, piled up inside the store; it looked like living, I can tell you. I went through clear to the other eend of the store, for they told me that cousin John was in the counting-room, away back there.

Wal, I got into the counting-room at last, and a harnsome little room it was, all carpeted and fixed out like some of our best rooms in Connecticut. I hain't seen so purty a store scarce ever. John wasn't there, but I could see that he hadn't got over all his old tricks, for a lot of chestnut shells were trod down round the stove, and there wasn't a few empty bottles standing round under the table and back of the desks. It was enough to turn one's stomach to look at the spit box; it was more than half filled up with pieces of segars, and ends of tobacco, that looked as if they had been chawed over a dozen times or more. I don't see where cousin John got that trick of smoking and chawing; I defy any body to say he larned it in old Connecticut. They needn't talk to us about the Yankees, for these Yorkers beat us all holler in them things; I hain't forgot the time when John would a turned up his nose at a long nine, as if it had a been pison, but now he's sot himself up for a gentleman there is no knowing what he hain't taken tu.

There was a chap standing by one of the desks, with the edge of his dickey turned over his stock—like an old-fashioned baby's bib, put on wrong side afore—and with his hair curled and frizzled up like a gal's. I knew in a minit that this feller couldn't be cousin John, so I went up to him, and sez I:—

"Friend, can you tell me when Mr. Beebe 'ill be in?" The chap took a watch out of his vest pocket about as big as a ninepence, and sez he—

"I don't know positively, but I s'pose in the course of half an hour or so. It's about time for the banks to close."

"Wal," sez I, "I s'pose I may as well wait for him, as I ain't in much of a hurry jest now." So I sot down in a chair, and arter histing my sole leather onto the top of the stove, I begun to scrape acquaintance with the chap, as I went along.

"Tough times with you marchants, now, ain't they?" sez I, a looking over the top of the paper.

"Very, sez he, a mending his pen. "It's as much as we can du to make both eends meet afore the bank's shut up days. Mr. Beebe's out a shinning now."

"A what?" sez I.

"A shinning," says he—"borrowing money to take up his own notes with, and if he don't get it, I don't know what we *shall du*."

"Oh!" sez I to myself, "this is the new partner, Mr. Co; he must have a good chance of money in the consarn, or he wouldn't feel so oneasy."

"We was doing a beautiful business," sez he, a shaking his head, "till some of the banks stopped specie payments. I wish they'd a been sunk."

"No," sez I, "that ain't fair, but it's human natur, I s'pose to give banks as well as people, a helping kick when they're going down hill. I don't understand much of these things, Mr. Co."

"My name isn't Oo," sez he, a staring; "it's Smith."

"What," sez I, "have they got another in the company?"

"No," sez he, kinder coloring up; "I'm the assistant book-keeper."

I couldn't but jest keep from giving a long whistle right out, the stuck up varmint! "Wal," sez I, arter a minit, "Mr. Smith, let me give you one piece of advice—don't be so ready to say *we*, and to talk over your employers' business with strangers next time. Such things do no good any way, but they may do a good deal of harm. It's the duty of a clark, among us, to attend to that he's paid for, and if he attends to much else, we purty ginerally find out that he ain't good for much in the long run."

You never saw a feller look so mean as he did when I said this; he turned all manner of colors, and acted mad enough to eat me. I didn't seem to mind him, but took up a newspaper and begun to read, jest as if he wasn't in the room; and by-am-by I got so deep in the paper, that I forgot all about him or cousin Beebe either.

Look a-here, Par, if you hain't seen the New York *Evening Express*, jest stretch your purse-strings a leetle, and subscribe for it. It's a peeler of a paper, I can tell you. You needn't take my word for it though, for I've made this letter so tarnal long, that it'd cost more than the price of a paper a hull year to pay the postage, so I've a notion to git the editors to print this for me in their primest evening paper, and so you'll git my letters and paper tu, all for five cents. I'll jest give you a little notion how they make the *Express*, for I read it eenamost through, afore cousin John come. The editors get all the papers in the country together, jest as we pick out our apples in cider time, and they go to work and git all that's worth reading out on 'em, and put it all in one great paper, which they sell for two cents; so that a feller can know what's said by every editor North and South, on one side and t'other, without the trouble of reading but one paper;—jest as we can git the juice of a bushel of apples all in a pint of cider, after it's once been through the mill. I raly think it's one of the best plans I ever heard on, and I'm so sartin that every body will take it by-am-by, that I've a notion that if you'd jest as livs let me throw up the onion trade, I'll try and get in to write for it, but we'll talk all that over by-am-by, arter I've seen the editors. Major Jack Downing is writing for them already, and perhaps—but I hain't made up my mind about it yit, though I kept a thinking it over all the while I was a reading in the counting-room.

Wal, I was jest taking a dive inter the advertisements, when cousin John came in. I raly believe you wouldn't know the critter, he's altered so. He's grown as fat and pussy as old lawyer Sikes in our parts, but I raly think he looks better for it. I tell you what, his clothes must cost him a few. He had on a superfine broadcloth coat, that didn't cost a whit less than ten dollars a yard, I wouldn't be afraid to bet a cookey. You could a seen your face in his boots, and his hair was parted on the top of his head, and hung down on the sides of his face and all over his coat collar, till he looked more like a woman in men's clothes than any thing else. I thought I should a haw-hawed out a larfin, all I could du, though it made me kinder wrathy to see a feller make such an etarnal coot of himself. I thought I'd see if he'd know me agin, so I on'y jist crossed one foot over t'other on the top of the stove, and tipt my chair back on its hind legs, and kept on reading as independent as a corkscrew, jest ter see how he'd act.

Wal, he cum right up to the stove, and took his coat tail under his arms, and begun to whistle as if there warn't nobody in the room. Once in a while as I took a peek over the top of the paper, I could see that he was a looking at me kinder sideways, as if he couldn't exactly make up his mind whether he knew me or not. I felt my heart kinder rising up in my throat, for it put me in mind of old times when we used to weed onions and slide down hill together. At last I couldn't stand it no longer, so I jumped up and flung down the paper, and, says I, "Cousin Beebe, how do you du?"

He stared like a stuck pig at fust, but I raly believe the feller was glad to see me when he found out who I was, for he shook my hand like all natur. Sez he, "Mr. Slick," sez he, "I'm glad to see you down in the city; how's the deacon, and aunt Eunice, and the Mills gals? You see I han't forgot old times."

With that we sot into a stream of talk about Weathersfield people, and so on that lasted a good two hours, by the town clock. Arter a while cousin John took out his watch, all gold inside and out, and sez he,

"Come, Mr. Slick, it's about four o'clock—go up and take a family dinner with us."

I rather guess I stared a few, to think of being axed to eat dinner at that time o' day; but as I hadn't eat any thing but a cold bite aboard the sloop since morning, the thoughts of a good warm dinner warn't by no means to be sneezed at.

"Better late than never," sez I to myself, arter I had put on my hat and stuck my hands in my pantaloons' pockets ready for a start. But jest as we wur a going out, there come a feller in to talk over some bisness matters, so sez Cousin Beebe, sez he—

"Here, Mr. Slick, is the number of our house—supposin you go along and tell Mrs. Beebe that I'll be home as soon as I can get through a little bisness—she wont make a stranger of you."

"I rather guess she won't," sez I, a taking the little piece of paper which he'd been a writing on; "if she does there must a been an almighty change in her since we used to go to singing school and apple bees together."

John looked kind a skeery toward the stranger, and begun to fidget about; so I told him I could find the way and made myself scarce in less than no time—for I thought as like as not the feller cum to git him to put his name to a note, or something of that sort; so I thought I'd give him a chance to say no, if he wanted tu.

By gracious! Par, I'd give a quart of soap if you and marm could a been with me in Broadway as I went along. I couldn't help stopping eenamost every other minit to look into the winders.

Some of them was chuck full of watches and ear-rings, and silver spoons spread all out like a fan, and lots on lots of finger rings all stuck over a piece of black cloth to make 'em shine. I'll be darned if it didn't make my eyes ache as if I'd been snow blind a week, only jest to look at 'em as I went along! I stopped into one store jest by the Park, and bought a silver thimble for marm, and it was as much as I could du to keep from going into one of the stores where I saw such a heap of calicos, to git her a new gown tu. But I can't begin to write more than a priming of what a feller may see as he goes up Broadway. It fairly made me ashamed of our horses, old Polly in perticlar, when I saw the harnsome critters that the niggers drive about them coaches with here. I tell you what, they make a glistening and a shining when they go through the streets chuck full of gals all in their feathers and furbelows! That Broadway *is* a leetle lengthy, and no mistake. I believe I footed it more than two miles on them tarnal hard stun walks, afore I got to Bond street, where Cousin Beebe lives, I swan! I thought my feet would a blistered.

Wal, arter all, I thought I never should a got into the house when I did git to it. It was so allfired high, and a heap of stun steps went up to the door, with a kind of picket fence made out of iron, all *curlecued* over on the sides. I looked all over the door for a knocker, but couldn't find nothing in the shape of one, only a square chunk of silver, with cousin Beebe's name writ on it. I rapped with my fist till the skin eenamost peeled off my knuckles, but nobody seemed to hear, and I begun to think the folks warn't to hum, and that I should lose my dinner arter all. I was jest beginning to think it best to make tracks for Peck slip agin, when a feller come by and kinder slacked tackle, and looked as if he was a going to speak.

"Look a here, you, sir," sez I, "can you tell me whether the folks that live here are to hum or not? I can't make nobody hear."

"Why don't you ring the bell?" sez he, a looking at me as if he never see a man afore.

I went down the steps and looked up to the ruff of the house, but it was so darned high that I couldn't a seen anything in the shape of a belfry if there'd been a dozen on 'em.

"I'll be darned if I can see any bell," sez I to the man, and then he kinder puckered up his mouth, and looked as if he was a going to larf right out.

"You seem to be a stranger in the city," sez he, a trying to bite in, for I s'pose he see that my dander was a gitting up.

"Yes," sez I, "I am, and what of that?"

"Oh, nothing," sez he, a hauling in his horns quite a considerable. "Jest pull that little silver knob there, and I rather think you can make them hear."

With that I went up the steps agin, and give the knob, as he called it, an almighty jerk, for I felt a little riled about being larfed at. It warn't half a jiffy afore the door was opened, and a great strapping nigger stood inside, staring at me as if he meant to swaller me hull, without vinegar or gravy sarce.

"Wal," sez I, "you snowball you, what are you staring at? Why don't you git out of the way and let me cum in?"

"Who do you want?" sez he, without so much as moving an inch—the impudent varmint.

"What's that to you, you darned lump of charcoal?" sez I; "jest you mind your own bisness and git out of the door." With that I give him a shove and went into the entry-way. When the nigger had picked himself up agin, I told him to go and tell Miss Beebe that her cousin Jonathan Slick, from Weathersfield, Connecticut, wanted to see her.

I wish you could a seen how the feller showed the whites of his eyes when I said this. I couldn't keep from larfin to see him a bowing and scraping to me.

"Jest step into the drawing-room," sez he, a opening a door; "I will tell Miss Beebe that you are here."

By the living hokey! I never stepped my foot in such a room as that in all my born days. I raly thought my boot was a sinking inter the floor, the carpet was so thick and soft. It seemed jest like walking over the onion patches, when they've jest been raked and planted in the spring time. The winder curtains were all yaller silk with a great heap of blue tossels hanging round the edges, and there was no eend to the little square benches, about as big as marm's milking stool, all kivered over with lambs and rabbits a sleeping among lots of flowers, as nat'ral as life. The backs of the chairs were solid mahogany or cherry-tree wood, or something like it, and they were kinder rounded off and curled in like a butter scoop turned handle downward. Then there were two chairs, all stuffed and kivered with shiney black cloth, with a great long rocker a poking out behind, and on the mantle shelf was something that I couldn't make out the use on—it was a heap of stuff that looked like gold, with a woman, all kivered over with something that made her shine like a gilt button, lying on the top. I wanted to finger it awfully, but there was a glass thing put over it, and I couldn't; but I hadn't pecked about long afore I found out that it was one of these new-fashioned clocks that we've heard about; but it's no more like them clocks that our Samuel peddles, than chalk is like cheese.

There were two other things, kinder like the clock, on both eends of the mantle shelf, but they warn't nigh so big, and they hadn't no pointers nor no woman on the top, and instead of the glass kiver there was long chunks o' glass hanging down all round them, like icicles round the nose of our pump in the winter time. I give one on 'em a little lift jest to find out what it was, but the glasses begun to gingle so that it scared me out of a year's growth, and I sot down agin mighty quick, I can tell you.

Wal, arter a while I begun to grow fidgety, so I sot down on a settee all kivered over with shiney cloth like the chairs, but I guess I hopped up agin spry enough. I never saw anything giv as the seat did, I thought at first that I was a sinking clear through to the floor, clothes and all. It makes me fidgety to be shut up in a room alone, so I begun to fix a little; but all I could du, them new cassimere pantaloons, that Judy White made for me, would keep a slipping up cenamost to the top of my boots. I don't see how on arth the chaps in New York keep their trousers' legs down so slick; one would think they had been dipped into 'em as marm makes her taller candles, they fit so.

Wal, arter I'd worked long enough on the tarnal things, I went up to a whapper of a looking-glass, that reached cenamost from the top to the bottom o' the room, and jest took a peep at a chap about my size on t'other side. I tell you what it is, the feller there warn't to be sneezed at on a rainy day, if he did cum from the country; though for a sixfooter he looked mighty small in that big looking-glass. I guess you'd a larfed to a seen him trying to coax his dickey to curl over the edge of that plaguey stiff bombazine stock that marm made, and to a seen him a pulling down them narrer short risbands so as to make them stick out under his cuff, and a slicking down his hair on each side of his face with both hands; but it wouldn't stay though. Nothing on arth but a hog is so contrary as a feller's hair, when it once gits to sticking up, I du think.

I'd fixed up purty smart, considering, and was jest sticking my breast-pin a leetle more in sight, when the door opened and cousin Mary come in. If I hadn't expected it was her, I'm sartin I shouldn't a known her no more than nothing, she was so puckered up. She had on a silk frock ruffled round the bottom, and her hair hung in great long black curls down her neck, eenamost to her bosom, and she had a gold chain wound all round her head, besides one a hanging about her neck, and her waist warn't bigger round than a pint cup. I never was so struck up in my life, as I was tu see her. Instid of coming up and giving me a good shake o' the hand or a buss—there wouldn't a been any harm in't as we were cousins—she put one foot for'ard a little and drew t' other back kind o' catecornering, and then she sort o' wriggled her shoulders, and bent for'ard and made a curchy, city fashion. Sez I tu myself, "If that's what you're up tu, I'll jest show you that we've had a dancing school in Weathersfield since you left it, Miss Beebe." So I put out my right foot and drew it up into the holler of t'other foot, and let my arms drop down a sort a parpindicular, and bent for'ard—jest as a feller shuts a jack knife when he's afeard of cutting his fingers —and keeping my eyes fixed on her face, though I did have to roll 'em up a leetle—I reckon I give her a purty respectable sample of a Weathersfield bow to match her York curches.

"Pray be seated, Mr. Slick," sez she, a screwing her mouth up into a sort of a smile; but when I saw how she was stuck up I warn't a-going to be behind hand with her, so I puckered up my mouth tu, though it was awful hard work, and sez I, "arter you is manners for me, Miss Beebe."

With that she sot down in one of the rocking-chairs and stuck her elbow on her arm and let her head drop into her hand as if she warn't more than half alive, and sez she—

"Take an ottoman, Mr. Slick."

I guess I turned red enough, for I hadn't no idee what she meant, but I sot down on one of the foot-stools at a ventur, and then she said,

"How do Mr. and Mrs. Slick du? I hope they're well."

I felt my ebenezer a gitting up to hear her call her husband's own uncle and aunt sich stuck up names, and sez I,

"Your uncle and aunt are purty smart, so as to be jogging about, thank you, Miss Beebe." I hadn't but jest got the words out of my mouth when there was a bell rung so as to make me jump up, and in a minit arter cousin John come in·

Your loving son,
JONATHAN SLICK.

LETTER II.

The Family Dinner and Effects of July Cider.

DEAR PAR:

"Wal, I see you've found the way, cousin Slick," sez he. "Mary, my dear, is dinner ready?"

She hadn't time to speak before two great doors slid into the partition, and there was another room jest as much like the one we was in, as two peas in a pod. A table was sot in the middle of the room, all kivered with rale China dishes, and first rate glass tumblers, and a silver thing to set the pepper box in—you hain't no idee how stilish it was. But as true as you live, there stood that etarnal nigger, close by the table, as large as life. I didn't know what to make on it, but sez I to myself, if cousin John's got to be an abolitionist and expects me to eat with a nigger, he'll find himself mistaken, I'll be darned to darnation if he don't! But I needn't a got so wrathy; the critter didn't offer to set down, he only stood there to git anything that we wanted.

"Do you take verminsilly, Mr. Slick?" says Miss Beebe, biting off her words as if she was afraid they'd burn her. With that she took the kiver off one of the dishes, and begun to ladle out some soup with a great silver dipper as bright as a new fifty cent piece.

"No, thank you," says I, "but I'll take some of that are soup instead, if you've no objection." The critter was jest beginning to pucker up her mouth again, as if she'd found out something to poke fun at, but cousin John looked at her so etarnal cross that she was glad to choke in. I s'pose cousin John see that I felt dreadful oneasy, so he said, kind a coaxing,

"She meant vermin-silly soup, cousin Slick. Let her help you to some, I'm sartin you'll like it."

"Wal," says I, "I don't care if I du." So I took up a queer looking spoon that lay by my plate, and tried to eat, but all I could du, the soup would keep a running through the spoon into the dish agin. I tried and tried to git one good mouthful, but I might jest as well have detarmined to dip up the Connecticut river in a sieve, and the most I could git was two or three sprangles of little white things that I stirred up from the bottom of the plate, that didn't taste bad, but to save my life I couldn't make out what they were made out on. Arter I'd been a fishing and diving ever so long, a trying to git one good spoonful, so that I could tell what it was, I looked up, and there was the nigger showing his teeth, and rolling about his eyes, like a black cat in the dark. It made me wrathy, for I surmized that he was a larfing to see me a working so hard to git a mouthful of something to eat. I couldn't hold in any longer, so I jumped up and flung down the spoon upon the floor, as spiteful as could be, and sez I to the nigger, sez I,

"What do you stand a grinning at there, woolly head? go and git me a spoon that hain't got no slits in it, I'd as lief eat with a rake as that are thing."

"Ha, ha, haw," larfed out the etarnal black varmint, "I thought you would not make the fork hold."

With that Miss Beebe giggled right out, and cousin John looked as if he would a burst to keep from larfing too.

"Stop your noise, sir," says he to the nigger, "pick up the fork, and give Mr. Slick a spoon."

I begun to feel awful streaked, I can tell you; but I sot down agin, and took up the real spoon, which lay on a kind of towel folded up by my plate, and I begun to eat, without saying a word, though I'd gin a silver dollar if they would a let me got up and licked the nigger.

Wal, arter I'd got a good mouthful of the soup, I couldn't

make out what it was made of, for I couldn't remember of ever seeing the name Miss Beebe called it by, in the dictionary. Maybe it's Latin, says I, to myself, and then I tried to think over what it could mean, and if nobody had told me what the definition was in the Latin school which you sent me to there in Weathersfield. Verminsilly! Verminsilly! Verminsilly! kept a running through my head all the time. I knew what silly meant well enough, and then it popped into my head, all at once, that *vermin* comes from the Latin *vermis*, which means worms. Worm soup! my gracious, the very idee of it made me feel awful bad at the stomach! But I might have known it by the looks, and I should if I'd ever heard of sich a thing, for the little slim critters swimming round in the liquor, looked as much like angle-worms biled down white as could be. Arter I found out what it was made of, I rather guess they didn't catch me a eating any more of their verminsilly soup; so I pushed it away half across the table, and wiped my mouth purty considerably with my pocket handkercher. The nigger took the whole on't away, and I declare I was glad enough to get rid of it.

"What on arth have they put this towel here for?" says I to myself; and then I stole a sly look over to cousin Beebe, to see if he'd got one, or if they only gave towels to company. Cousin John had one jest like mine, but he'd spread it out on his lap, so I jest took up mine and kivered over my cashmeres with it tu.

Considering there was no onions on the table, I made out a purty fair dinner. I was a beginning to think about moving when the nigger brought a lot of blue glass bowls about half full of water, and sot one down by each of us. What they could be for I hadn't the least notion, but I kept a bright look out to see what cousin John did, and when I saw him dip his fingers into his bowl and wipe 'em on a sort of red towel which the nigger brought along with the bowls, I jest went over the manœuvre as natural as life.

Wal, while we were talking about the banks, and old times, and Weathersfield folks dying off so, that coot of a nigger cleared the table right off as slick as a whistle, and afore I hardly knew what the fellow was up tu he come along and sot down a set of decanters, and two cider bottles with the necks all covered over with sheet lead, and then he brought two baskets made out of silver, one on 'em was filled chuck full of oranges, and t'other was heaped up with great purple grapes; I declare it eenamost made my mouth water to see the great bunches a hanging over the edge of the basket. I'd jest put a whopper of a bunch on the little Chena plate which the feller set for me, and was considering whether it would be genteel to cut the grapes in tu with the cunning little silver knife which was put by the plate, when all tu once, pop went something, eenamost as loud as a pistol, close by me. I jumped up about the quickest, I can tell you; but it was only the nigger a opening one of the cider bottles; he poured out some for me in a great long glass with a spindle neck, and I drunk it all at a couple of swallers, without stopping to breath. By jingo! but it was capital cider! arter I'd drunk one glass I begun tu feel as spry as a cricket.

"Here, snowball," says I, "give us another; these glasses are awful small; now, I like to drink cider out of a pint mug."

"Take care," says cousin Beebe, "I'm afeard you'll find the cider, as you call it, rather apt to get into your head."

"Not a bit of it," sez I, "I can stand a quart any day. Here, cousin Mary, take another glass, you hain't forgot old times have you? though I s'pose they don't have applecuts and quiltings here in York, du they?"

I don't remember what she said, but I know this, my eyes begun to grow allfired bright, and afore I got up tu go hum that nigger must have put more than twenty baskets of grapes on the table, and the oranges seemed to grow bigger and bigger every minit, and I know there wur more than three times as many glasses and decanters on the table, as there was at fust.

I ruther think it was purty nigh tea time when I got up to go back to the sloop agin. I insisted on giving cousin Mary a buss afore I went; and I won't be sartin, but I kinder seem to remember shaking hands with the nigger, consarn him, jest afore I went down the steps.

I don't feel very bright this morning, and I begin to think tha' maybe I shall come back to Weathersfield arter all. The York cider don't seem to agree with me. I've felt dredful peaked over since I drunk it, and kinder hum sick tu boot.

Your loving son,

JONATHAN SLICK.

LETTER III.

Jonathan visits the Express Office—Sensations on seeing himself in print.

DEAR PAR:

Since I wrote my last letter there's been no eend to the things that I've had to du. Arter thinking about it eenamost two nights, I about made up my mind tu settle down here in York a spell, and send you a grist of letters now and then, which I mean to git printed in the New York Express, the way I told you of.

I've been up to see the editors, and they want me to stay properly, and I don't think I shall ever git so good a chance to take up this literary way of gitting a living, as they call it, if I don't snap at this offer tu once.

I thought at first that I'd try some other newspaper, and see if I could git a higher bid, but somehow I'd taken a shine to the Express, and thought it wasn't worth while. It warn't because there wasn't papers enough, for you can't step three steps here in York, without stumbling over a little stuck up newspaper office. Besides, there's no eend to the papers carried round in the streets. You can't go any where but some little dirty shaver or other, about knee high to a toad, will stick a paper out under your nose, and ask you to buy it, as crank as can be. Somehow, it kinder seemed to me that the New York Express took the shine off the papers that I'd seen among 'em all, though they was as thick as toads arter a rain storm. I had a notion to write for it from the first, because, think sez I, that prime feller, Major Jack Downing, writes a good deal for it, and I rather think we shall hitch tackle like any thing.

Wal, jest as soon as I made up my mind about it, I went right off, full chisel, to the Express Office. I'd been round there once afore to put my t'other letter into the Post Office, and so the minit I come to the corner of Wall and Nassau Street, and saw a house with the "New York Express Office" writ on the eend, I knew it was the office without asking. So I crossed over, and kinder hung about a leetle, jest to make my heart stop a beating so, afore I went in. I swanny if I ever felt so in my life! I was so anxious about that long letter that I sent to them to get printed for you, that I was dreadful loth to go in, and eenamost made up my mind to turn about and make tracks for the sloop agin!

Wal, sez I to myself, it won't do any hurt jest to take a look about the premises afore I go. A feller can find out a good deal about a man's natur, by the looks of things about the place he lives in; so I drew up before a board, all stuck over with picters, and pieces of old newspaper, by the eend of the building, and putting my hands in my pockets, I stood still, and looked up'ards to see what I could make out. But instid of taking an observation of the premises, I begun to think about the cattle and the spring shotes that Judy White used to take sich care on, till the tears eenamost cum into my eyes, I was so humsick.

Wal, I was standing there on the stun walk, with both hands buried considerable deep in my trousers' pockets, a looking up at the sign writ out on the eend of the office, when a feller cum up and begun to read the pieces of paper stuck on the board jest outside. So I wiped the tarnal tears away with the cuff of my coat, for it made me feel kinder cheap to have anybody see a fellow of my size boo-hooing in York streets because he happened to think about hum and old times; and I got up a leetle grit, and went right straight down into the office, for it's half under ground. A chap that sot back of a sort of counter, where there was a lot of papers folded up, lifted his head once, and went to writing agin as if I warn't nobody.

"Do you print the Evening Express here?" sez I kinder low, for I felt so dreadful anxious about the letter, that I was eenamost choked.

"Yes" sez he, a gitting up, "do you want one?"

"Wal, I don't care if I take one," sez I, a forking out a fourpence-halfpenny from my trousers' pocket. "Anything particular—that is purty smart in it to-day?"

"Nothing very remarkable to-day," sez he, "but if you cal. to-morrow we shall print a capital letter from one Mr. Jonathan Slick of Weathersfield."

I swanny if my heart didn't jump like a rabbit at the sight of a piece of sweet apple in snow time! "You don't say so," sez I, and I tried not to look tickled all I could, but somehow my mouth wouldn't stay still; and I hain't the least dout but that I kept grinning in the feller's face, jest like a monkey over a hot chesnut. It was as much as I could du to keep from jumping over the counter and hugging him, I was so allfired glad.

He didn't seem to mind, but sot down and begun to write agin as if nothing was the matter, and so I took up the paper and went off; but, I ruther guess I stepped high, for I kept thinking what you and marm and Judy White would say when you saw yourselves all in print as large as life.

When I went out, there stood the chap a reading the pieces of newspapers yit. I wanted to go up and shake hands with him and tell him all about it, I was so full of what the chap inside said about my letter, but I didn't though. I went down to the sloop, and I wanted to tell Captain Doolittle about it. But, sez I to myself, I'll choke in to-day, but if his eyes don't stick out to-morrow I'll lose my guess.

I ruther think that I didn't let the grass grow under my feet, when Thursday cum, but up I went at the Express Office like a house a-fire. It raly seem'd as if my heart would bust, I was so dreadful anxious to see the paper. I didn't stop to ketch breath but went right into the office, and there sot a couple of fellers that looked as stiff and knowing as could be, back of the counter. Sez I to myself, I guess I've found the editors this time any how.

"I want to get five papers right off," says I (laying a quarter o'dollar on the counter); with that one of the editors got up, as mealy-mouthed as could be, and he put the quarter back in my hands—sez he,

"Mr. Slick, we shan't take money from *you;* here are the

papers—come, take a seat back of the counter here—we want to have a little talk with you."

Wal, I went back, and the tallest of the two chaps got up, and gin me his chair, and says he, "Mr. Slick, we've printed your letter, and should like to have some more on 'em."

I hitched a little in my chair, and sez I, "Wal, if we can agree about the price, I don't care if I send you a few more now and then."

"What subjects do you mean to take up, Mr. Slick?" says the shortest one.

"Wal," sez I, "I hain't made up my mind yit, but I reckon a'most anything that turns up."

"Supposing you try politics," sez the tall feller. "Major Jack Downing has done purty well in that line. The 'lection comes on soon, and it'll be a good time for you to begin."

"Wal," sez I, "ill go about a little, and see how I like it."

"That's settled, then," sez t'other. "Now, Mr. Slick, if we ain't making too bold, I should like to know how long you have been in New York?"

I kinder larfed in my sleeve to hear the sly coot try to come round, and find out who I was and all about me. Sez I to myself, I ain't quite sartin about the tall chap there, but I'll be blamed if you've the least bit of Yankee in you. Now a feller of rale ginuine grit would cum up to the mark tu once, and would a jest asked a feller right out who he was, and where he cum from, and how much he was worth, and how much he owed, besides some cute questions about his wife and children, if he wanted tu. Wal, thinks I, the man hain't been brought up to these things, and he ain't to be blamed for not knowing how. So I put one leg over t'other, and sez I,

"Wal, gentlemen, it ain't of no use to go circumventing round the subject, as old Deacon Miles used to in his exhortations, that had neither eend, middle, or beginning. So I'll jest up and tell right out who I am, and what I mean to du.

"I s'pose you've heard of Samuel Slick, that feller that wrote that tarnal smart book about Canada, wooden clocks, and matters and things in gineral?"

"*Sam* Slick, you mean," sez the tall editor.

"No, I don't," sez I, setting up straight; "he was baptized Samuel in the old Presbyterian Meeting-house in Weathersfield, and nobody but the newspaper chaps ever thought of calling him Sam. It's too bad this notion of cutting off the latter eend of a feller's name; it's a whittling things down a leetle too close, and looks as if a feller's father was so awful poor, that he couldn't afford to give a hull name to his posterity. Wal, Samuel Slick, Esquire, is my own natral born brother—I hain't no idee of bragging about my relation, because it's my notion that in a free country every feller ought to cut his own fodder; but when a man's relations is getting up in the world, it's of no use to be mealy-mouthed about owning 'em."

"Yes," says the tall chap. "Mr. Samuel Slick is a relation which any man might be proud to own."

I larfed a little. "Sartinly," sez I, "Samuel has contrived to come his 'soft sodder' over you newspaper chaps about the nicest. I've a notion, too, that they'll find out that I haint much behind hand with him; but I mean to write something about my life in Weathersfield one of these days, and send it to you to print.

"Now, I tell you what it is, I've a notion to hire an office somewhere down in Cherry street, and if you'll print my letters, why, I reckon I can make out to get a living out of these Yorkers, by hook or by crook. I mean to du things above board, and in an independent way, jest to see how the experiment 'ill work, but if I find that it won't do, I'll take up Samuel's plan, and go the soft sodder principle; his mode 'ill work tarnation well, and if they don't find Jonathan Slick, your most obedient servant to command, a chip from the same block, I'll lose my guess, that's all!"

When I said this, I got up and put on my hat, and then I happened to think about the fourpence halfpenny, and I turned to the chap that sot writing, and sez I—

"Look a here! I believe I forgot to take change for fourpence t'other day. I'll take that three cents now, if you've no objection." The feller handed over the three coppers, and I pocketed 'em as I went out of doors. "A penny saved is worth two arned," says I to myself.

The very minit I got into the street, I couldn't hold in any longer. So I jest stopped on the walk by the Post-office and opened one of the papers. By the living hokey! if the first thing I see wasn't a picter of my own self, as large as life and twice as nat'ral, a standing up on the top of the paper as crank as could be. There was the Express office jest as it was when I fust see it. I swan! if I didn't haw-haw right out loud in the street! Down I went to the sloop, about the quickest, and I up and told Captain Doolittle all about it. I thought the tarnal critter would a gone off the handle, he larfed so when he saw how nat'ral the picter looked; but he larfed on t'other side of his mouth, I reckon, when he read what I'd said about him in the letter. He got awful wrathy, but I only sot still and took it as if nothing had been the matter.

"Look a here, Captain Doolittle," sez I, "aint Editors and Lawyers always abusing one another in print? Don't they call each other all kinds o' names, and then don't they shake hands and come soft sodder over each other when they come face to face? If you have the honor of going about with a man that writes for the newspapers, you must be an etarnal coot if you git mad because he prints that you love cider-brandy and eat raw turnips. I can tell you what, you wouldn't find many newspaper chaps that'd stick to the truth as close as I did. So jest haul in your horns, and I'll write a private letter to Par, and tell him all I said about you was 'poetical license,' as the editors call it when they've told a whopper, or a leetle too much truth— for one's as bad as t'other now-a-days."

"Wal," sez he, "if you'll du that, I'll make up; yit it's allfired hard. But I say, Jonathan, you'll stand treat, won't you?"

I felt sorry for the critter, and so I went to a grocery with him, and I guess the long nines and the New England rum that I called for sot all things tu rights in less than no time.

Your loving son,
JONATHAN SLICK.

LETTER IV.

The Political Meeting and its Disasters.

DEAR PAR:

Wal, a few nights ago, I thought I'd try one of them politicn. meetings the Editor's wanted me to attend and see how they carried on there. So Captain Doolittle and I went to one of the great halls hired for caucuses and crowded in by degrees, for the hull building was jammed full of human live stock long afore we got there. Arter a good deal of scuffling, we got up by one of the winders where we could see purty much all that was going on. I never in all my born days saw such a lot of horned cattle together. Some on 'em was barefooted, and a good many hadn't more than a coat and a pair of trousers among four or five on 'em. One feller close by me had the rim of his hat ripped off till it hung down on his shoulders: the top was stove in, and he had a black eye, besides another that wouldn't see straight. "Look a here," sez he, to me, "why don't you shout when we du?"

"Because I aint a mind tu," sez I; "how are you going to help yourself?" Jest then a leetle pussy lawyer cum a crowding through the gang, and at the sight of him they all sot up a noise that made my hair stand on eend.

I never heard anything like it; they yelled and hollered enough to split the ruff of the house. The chunked feller, with his hat knocked into the middle of next week, poked about with his elbows till he got room to draw his fiddle bow across a rickety fiddle, that had two of the strings broke off and was cracked from eend to eend. Squeak, squeak, went the fiddle close to my ear, like a pig when he's being yoked. With that, a lot of fellers, some with their coat tails tore off, and some with their trousers held up with a piece of list instead of galluses, and every one on 'em as ragged as year old colts, begun to dance up and down the room, but such double shuffles and pigeon wings was enough to make a feller die a larfin. Our old white cow used to dance twice as well when she got into one of her tantrums. "Hurra for our side! hurra! hurra!" yelled out a tall feller close by the fiddler, with a mouth that twisted one way and his nose curling off on t'other side, as if they hated each other like cats and dogs; and with that he took off his old straw hat and shied it off into the middle of the dancers. It lodged on the top of a feller's head that was jest then trying to cut a pigeon wing over one of the benches.

"Helloa, you feller you, jest toss back that hat, will you?" sung out the tall feller, a pitching for'ard head over heels arter his hat.

"No I wont, I'll be rumbusticated if I du;" sez the t'other chap, a pushing toward the door, holding the hat down with both hands, as if he warn't used to them kind o' things; "all fair in 'lection time. Hurra for equal rights!"

Jest then there cum in a grist of fellers a yelling and a kicking up their heels like all possessed. They'd brought in some more 'lection news.

"Who on arth can these critters be?" sez I to Captin Doolittle.

"Oh that's a squad of Irishmen; don't you see how the hair's all worn off their heads a carrying brick hods on 'em?" says the Captin.

"You don't say so; now by gracious how they du blather out their words, dont they?" sez I, but I might as well a been talking to a stun fence, for jest that minit the hull on 'em sot up a noise that was enough to make a feller's eye teeth jump out of his head.

Did you ever hear four hundred thousand wild cats, and bears, and wolves, and screech owls, a squalling, and a howling, and a squeaking together? If you haint, there's no use trying to make you have the least idee how that etarnal crowd of critters did hoot and yell. There they were a screaming, and a stamping, and a dancing, and a fiddling, all in a heap, till a feller couldn't hear himself think, and wouldn't a known what he was thinking about if he did hear.

Now says a leetle man by the winder, clear your pipes, feller citizens; let's give 'em a song. I've got one printed off here so that you can all jine in. Them that can't read or don't know the tune can sing Yankee Doodle or Hail Columbia.

With that he flung a hull grist of papers among the crowd and begun tu raise his ebenezer rather strong afore the rest sot in. By-am-by they all got a going, and the way they roared out the song was awful, I can tell you. Some of 'em sung in one tune and some in another—every man went on his own hook. The pussy little feller pulled away on the fiddle like all natur, and the chap with the skewed nose made a plaguey squeaking with a split fife that he had. The feller that hadn't no crown in his hat bellered out Auld Lang Syne, and I see another chap holding his paper upside down, and blowing away at Old Hundred like all natur. When they begun to drop off, for it warn't to be expected that sich a heap of critters could stop all together, the pussy feller with the fiddle yelled out, "Hurra for the song! —Three cheers for singing!" And then they went at it agin, a hooting and tossing up their hats—them that had 'em—as if Old Nick himself had kicked 'em on eend. By gracious! I don't believe such a lot of white Inguns ever got together before, or ever will agin. There was one great feller, as pussy as a bag of bran in harvest time, that roared out his words like a hog that had been larned to talk.

"That's a Yorkshireman," sez Captin Doolittle, "I'll treat if it aint."

"Wal, who on arth is that feller there a talking to that little stuck up chap with the peaked nose? What in the name of natur does he mean by his *sprucks* and his *yaws?* If I was the little feller, I'd jest thank him not to bark in my face that way; he opens his mouth as if he was a going to swaller the poor critter hull, every time he speaks—du tell, who can he be, Captin?"

"Wal," sez the Captin, "I don't know sartin, but I ruther guess he's one of them Dutch fellers, by his lingo."

"There, now, look a there," sez I, a pinting to a feller that had jest come up to the Dutch chap. He wasn't over clean, anyhow, but he had a great brass handkercher-pin stuck in his bosom, and he strutted so that a common chap couldn't a touched him with a ten foot pole. I poked my elbows into Captin Doolittle's ribs, to try and make him tell me what he was; but he was a looking t'other way, and wouldn't mind me. By-am-by the feller begun to talk to the Dutch chap. He kept a flinging his arms about every which way, and a jabbering over a mess of lingo that was enough to make a man larf in his face. The words all run together like marm's curd when the cheese gets contrary and wont set. The Dutch feller kept a opening his mouth, and once in a while a word would come out full chunk right in t'other's face. Think sez I, if this aint a touch of the dead languages, it ought to be, that's all—for it's enough to make a feller die right off to hear it. He seemed to be ashamed of himself at last, and begun to try to talk genuine American, but he made awful work on't. By-am-by I found out that he was a Frenchman; for a tall laathy feller, that I'd a took my Bible oath cum straight off the Green Mountains, went up to him, sort o' wrathy, and sez he, "Hold your yop, you tarnal Frenchman; if you don't like this country and what we're a doing, you'd better go back hum agin. I haint no doubt but you can git enough frog soup without coming here to run us down."

The French feller turned as red as a turkey's topping, and he began to sputter away as mad as he could be. But t'other chap jest put his hands in his pockets and sez he—"you go to grass." I don't know what else he said, for that minit they all sot up one of their almighty roars and yelled out—"a speech, a speech." Then a feller with spectacles on, got up to make a speech, and arter rolling up his shirt sleeves and spitting on his hands as if he was going to chopping wood, he went at it shovel and tongs.

I'll be darned to darnation if it didn't make my blood bile to hear how he went on. Sich a stream o' talk I never did hear cum from one human critter. At last I got so wrathy that I couldn't stand it no longer, and bust right out the minit he'd got through.

"Feller citizens of New York," sez I, a mounting myself on the winder sill, and sticking my right arm out as stiff as a crowbar, "I aint much used to public speaking, but I must say a few words."

"Hurra for the Yankee—go it green horn—tip us a speech, a rale downright Roarer!" sung out more than a dozen on 'em, and all the men about me turned their jaws up, and opened their mouths as if I'd been histed up there for a show.

"Feller citizens," sez I, "I've been a listening to you here this night (they kept as still as mice now), and the rale American blood has been biling in my heart to see sich carryings on and to hear sich things said as that feller's been a talking," ("Hustle him out," sez they, "throw him over; go it ye cripples;") but when they got still sez I, "Since I've cum here to this city I've almost made up my mind that there aint a ginuine teetotal patriot among ye all, on one side or t'other, and that the least shake of a truth would suit a downright politic feller as well as water would a mad dog, and no better!" ("Hurra for the Yankee," sez they.) "Now," says I, a sticking out both arms tu once, "In revolutionary times it was worth while to a public character to turn solger, or patriot, or politician, for in them times folks found so much to du that they couldn't git time to lie so like all natur as they du now-a-days. In them glorious times a feller could shoulder his bagonet and write out his politics on the heart of the enemy, and there warn't no mistake in the handwriting. (What a clapping and stomping they made here!) When they sung out liberty, I reckon the British knew the meaning on't." ("Three cheers for the Yankee," sez they again, "Three cheers for the Yankee,") and then they hollered and yelled and whooped and stomped, and whooped and yelled agin and agin, like so many Injuns jest broke loose,—then sez I—for I *was* skeered by the noise they made, and my hair stood up on eend I felt so dandery. "Feller citizens, as true as I live, it eenamost makes me cuss and swear to think on't, though my par is the deacon of a church. When the people of these times sing out liberty, a feller can't tell whether they mean to tear down a flour store or roast a nigger alive." (But don't you think, that when I got as fur as here, as much as two thousand on 'em was taken dreadful sick all tu once, and groaned out in rale agony,) "but," sez I, " I don't wonder the old Revolutionary Patriots die off so. What I've seen of politics is enough to send every one on 'em into the grave with their tough old hearts broken and their foreheads wrinkled with shame at the news they have got to carry to Gineral Washington in t'other world!"

I stopped to catch a little breath and was jest poking out my arm agin to go on, for I felt as bold as a lion, and the words cum a flowing into my mouth so thick, I couldn't but jest find room for 'em. But the etarnal pack of varmints set up a yell that would a frightened any man out of a year's growth; and afore I knew which eend my head was on, they got hold on me and pitched me down stairs, and left me a wallering in the gutter. The first thing I knew I felt something floundering about under me, and a great black hog that had been lying in the gutter give a grunt, and pitched me for'ard on my face and went off squaling a little as if he was used to being driv up by company any time of night in them quarters.

Wal, I picked myself up as well as I could, and I went down to the Express office like a streak of chalk. I found the tall editor a setting there counting up some 'lection figgers, and he looked eenamost tuckered out. Sez I, "Mister Editor, look a here," and with that I showed him where they'd bust out the back of my coat a flinging me down stairs, and how that plaguy hog had kivered my new cassimere trousers all over with mud. Sez he, and he couldn't help from larfing, "don't mind it, Mr. Slick; I've got wuss usage than that many a time."

"Yis," sez I, as wrothy as all natur, "but I guess you haint been pitched head for'ard into the gutter with that tarnal hog."

"Wal," sez he, a trying to keep from larfin all he could, "try it again, Mr. Slick, you'll get used to these things by-am-by."

"I'll be darned to darnation if I du, and that's the eend on't!" sez I, a doubling up my fist. "If I can't find nothing but politics to write about, I'll go back to Weathersfield about the quickest, I can tell you that."

Wal, the long and the short on it was, I got back to the sloop and turned in awfully womblecropped, and as sore all over as a bile. I can't go out to-day, so I have writ this letter.

From your loving son,

JONATHAN SLICK.

LETTER V.

A Little of Jonathan's Private Love Affairs.

To the Editors of the Express:

Wal, you see I'm as good as my word. I hadn't hardly read t'other letter through, afore I sot right down and begun this right off the reel. By the living jingo! how it makes the blood bile and tingle in a fellow's heart to see his writing printed, and to hear people a talking about it. I wish you could a seen my office the morning arter that fust letter cum out. I thought my neck would 'v got the cramp, I had to bow so much to the folks that cum in to give me advice about my letters. One feller got awful wrathy about what I writ about politics, but I jest told him to mind his own bisness, for I guessed my eye teeth was cut if I did cum from the country. He begun to git a lectle imperdent, so I got up and showed him the door; and when he wouldn't go peaceably, I jest give him a specimen of Weathersfield sole-leather, but it's no use writing about such varmint.

Now you know who I be, you won't think it very odd when I tell you how awful womblecropt I felt to think what a chance the old folks gave Samuel to see the world, while they kept me tied down to the onion beds as tight as marm Jones used to be to that leetle squalling youngen of hern, that was so cross that its teeth couldn't cut straight, but stuck out catecorning all round its gums.

It made me choke awfully to see Samuel drive off with his wagon chuck full of wooden clocks, all painted and varnished up as neat and shining as one of your New York gal's faces on a Sunday. I could bit a tenpenny nail right in two without feeling it a morsel; but it was no use quarrelling. The old man said I hadn't got my growth yit, which was true enough, for it kinder stunted me to be always a bending over the darnation onion patches. It was awful hard, I can tell you. I do believe, if it hadn't been for the resting spells I got in the winter, I should a been as bow backed as an ox yoke. I'll be darned, if it didn't take me from fall till planting time to get the kinks out of my back.

Wal, I grinned and bore it purty well, considering, and, to own the truth, it wasn't so terrible hard while Judy White lived with marm. For a hired gal, Judy was a tarnal smart critter; there wasn't a gal in all Weathersfield could pull an even yoke with her a stringing onions. Nothing on arth puts a feller to his stumps like pulling in the same team with a purty gal—and between us, it aint no ways disagreeable to sit down in the middle of a patch of onions all running to seed, to work with a gal like Judy. I say nothing, but, by gracious! if my heart hasn't beat like a partridge on a dry log, sometimes when I've catched her a looking at me from under her great sun-bonnet; but as for courting or anything of that sort, she kept a feller at a distance, I can tell you. I ruther guess my ears catched it once, but I reckon I won't tell of that though; it's better to think about than talk over.

I don't mean to say that Judy had anything agin sparking in a regular way, on Sunday nights in the east room, when the paper curtains was all down, and the old folks had gone to bed. It cum kinder nateral to set up till two or three o'clock, and Judy warn't by no means old-maidish. But by-am-by the old woman began to make a fuss cause we burned out so many of her candles. She needn't a made such a rout, for they warn't made of nothing but soap grease with tow wicks; and I'm sartin it wasn't my fault if we burnt so many. I'd a been glad enough to have sot in the dark, but Judy wouldn't hear a word on't.

The old woman got into a tantrum one Monday morning afore breakfast. She called Judy all sorts of things but a good gal and a lady, and twitted her about being poor and setting her cap for me. At last Judy got her grit up, and I ruther guess she finished off the old woman in fine style. I suffered a few between them, I can tell you. The old woman began to brag about Samuel, for she's felt mighty crank about him ever since he had that great dinner give to him down on the Canada line there—and sez she to Judy, sez she—

"I don't see how on arth you aim to think of such imperdence as sitting up with my Jonathan. Why, aint my Samuel one of the biggest authors in the country, aint he hand and glove with all the judges and lawyers, and the New York editors, and all the big bugs fur and near? I'd have you to know my boys aint men of the common chop, and I guess any on 'em will look a plagney sight higher than to take up with a hired gal. Why, who knows but Jonathan will be as illustrated a man as his brother one of these days!"

I couldn't begin to give the least idea of the stream o' talk the old woman let out on the poor gal. But, by gracious, I rather guess she missed it a few. I wish you could a seen Judy White's face, for by the living hokey, if it didn't turn five hundred colours in a minit. I raly thought the critter would a jumped out of her skin she was so awful mad.

"I don't care that for your son, Miss Slick," sez she, a snapping her fingers in the old woman's face, "I can marry his betters any day. I wouldn't have him, not if every hair in his head was shining with diamonds; no, not if he'd go down on his knees to me; you make a terrible fuss cause Sam's gone sneaking about among decent people, but, after all, what is he but a wooden clock pedler, and as for you, you old vinegar-faced good for nothin——."

She was a going on to give poor marm an awful drubbing, but I always think a feller must be a mean shote that 'ill stand mum and hear any body call his mother names, whether she desarves them or not. So I stepped up and stood right afore Judy, and I looked her straight in the face, and, sez I, "Miss Judy," sez I, "I don't want to hear no more of this ere; come now, you and marm jest hush up, and don't let me hear another darned word, for I won't stand it."

With that marm put her linsey woolsey apron up to her face, and begun to boo hoo right out, and, sez she, "It comes awful tough to be trod on in one's own house; I won't bear it, so there now."

"Now, Judy," sez I, kinder coaxing, "jest go and make up; marm's a good-hearted critter, and you know it's kinder nateral for wimmin folks to git a little crabbed once in a while."

By gracious, if I wouldn't rather break a yoke of steers any day, than try to make up a quarrel between two wimmin when they once get their dander up; and of all horned cattle Judy White did take the rag off the bush when she once got agoing.

"Git out of my way, yeu mean, snaeking critter you," sez she, hitting me a slap over the chops that made my teeth rattle; "I won't make up, nor touch tu; I only feel sorry that I ever demeaned myself to set up with you; I'll leave the house this minnit."

Out of the room she went like a she-hurricane, and after she had picked up her duds she made tracks for home, without as much as bidding one of us good by.

It's curios how men will git used to eenamost anything; now I don't purtend to say that I hadn't a kind of a sneaking notion after Judy White, but somehow when I seen the tears come into the old woman's eyes, dimming her old steel-bowed spectacles, the water always would start into my own eyes, spite of all I could do to keep it out; so it wasn't to be expected that I should not feel disagreeable when the two got their dander up, and went into such a tantrum with each other. But there sot the old man a chonking an apple, and kinder larfin inside of him all the time, jest as he'd a looked on to see two cats scratch and spit at one another. I axed him how he could du so, and he tossed the apple core out of the winder, and puckered up his mouth and said, "I hadn't got used to the wimmen folks yit; the best way with them kind o' things was to let 'em alone."

Now it wouldn't a been much of a chore to have gone over to old Mr. White's two or three times a week, and if Judy had done the clean thing toward the old woman, I don't know but I should a gone to see her over there, but somehow a gal kicks over the milk pail when she lets her ebenezer git up before a feller, jest as he's beginning to hanker arter her. I couldn't make up my mind to tackle in with a critter that had shown such an allfired spiteful temper, so the next Sunday night I let her go home from singing school alone. I saw her look back kinder anxious two or three times, and jest for the minit my heart riz up in my throat till it eenamost choked me. But I kept a stiff upper lip, and went on without seeming to mind her;

and then she tossed up her head and begun to sing, as if she wanted to show me that she didn't care a cent for all I could do.

I felt awful bad for a day or two, but a feller must be a saphead if he can't make up his mind to give a gal the mitten when he thinks she desarves it. Now if Judy had had the small-pox, and had been pitted all over like a honey comb, I'd a stood by her to the last minnit; but somehow I couldn't git over the awful basting she gave marm. I do like to see old folks treated well, let 'em do what they will, and a gal can't be fit to bring up a family if she doesn't know how to keep her own temper. Besides, she hasn't much true ginuine love for a chap, when she won't try to put up with the faults of his relations for his sake.

Wal, the long and the short of it was, I gin Judy White the sack right off the reel, without stopping to chew the matter a bit.

Wall, arter this, working alone grew awful tedious, and I begun to hanker to see the world. So as father was loading up a sloop to send down to New York, I came a little of Samuel's soft sodder over the old man, and told him how much better I could sell off the onions and red cabbages, than eenamost any body else; and at last he said I might come down as a kinder supercargo. So he filled up the hold with potaters, real blue noses, I can tell you, and piled up a whole crop of garden sarce on the deck, and we sot sail down the river.

Now, I'd made up my mind to stay in the city when I once got clear of the humstead, but you may guess I didn't let out a word to the old folks, for it al'es hurts my feelings to see marm take on, and I didn't like to make the old man rip out *too* much, for he was a deacon of the Presbyterian Church. We was three days a coming down the river, and it made me awful wrathy to see that lazy old critter, "the Cleopatra," go by us on her way to the city and back agin before we got into the East river. We give her two cheers each time, but neither on 'em come from below the palate, I can tell you. We got into Peck slip at last safe and sound, and if I didn't jump on to the wharf as spry as a cricket, then there's no snakes on the green mountain that's all.

    I am your humble servant to command,
             JONATHAN SLICK.

LETTER VI.

Jonathan's Opinions of Ministerial Interference—A Card of Invitation, and an Evening Party at Cousin Beebe's, in which Jonathan makes some Mistakes and a Lady Acquaintance.

DEAR PAR:

I have just received your letter, and so I sot right down to answer it; for what you writ about my treating Captin Doolittle, and using sich bad language, made me feel bad enough. I don't know the reason on it, but when a feller's away from hum, it makes him feel awful oneasy to think that he's done anything to hurt his par or mar's feelings.

Now, about that Captin Doolittle business, I don't think arter all, I was much to blame. What I writ about him hurt the critter's feelings a good deal, and I didn't know of any way to make up but to treat, and so I did give him a drink of New England and a long nine or so, but I didn't drink any myself, not a single horn, and it warn't more 'an half fair for the minister to begin at you about it arter meeting last Sunday, and to tell you that you hadn't brought me up in the virtue and admonition of the Lord, and to say that "you be darned" and "darnation," is jest as bad as cussing and swearing right out. For him to take it on himself to twit you, and say that, "jest as the twig is bent the tree's inclined," is consarned mean, and I wouldn't bear it nor a touch tu if I was you. He knows as well as can be, that if I warn't bent right it wasn't no fault of your'n, for I'm sartin it wouldn't a been in the natur of things to have twisted me any other way than head for'erd, if you calculated on my weeding the onions as they ought to be.

Now, the truth on it is, I begin to think that your ministers there in Connecticut pull the bit on the church members a leetle too tight sometimes, and instid of giving you good holesome doctrine, right pure out of the Bible, and taking the potaters and apples and wood and chickens and turkies that the deacons and old maids send to them as part pay, they sometimes contrive to make their being ministers an excuse for poking their fingers into every body's pie as well as their own.

I am afeard you won't like to hear me say so; but it does make me awful wrothy to hear that the minister threatened to turn you out of the church if you let me go on so—but you needn't be a bit consarned about that. He'd no more turn you out of the meeting than he'd strike his own granny, not as long as you own the best farm in all Weathersfield, and send him a fat turkey every thanksgiving day, besides paying pew tax and all the other taxes, as you du. I don't know what he might du if you was to fail and bust up; for as soon as a man begins to get poor, the ministers grow awful particlar about his morality and religion; but there's no fear of that; so jest tell him the next time he threatens to church you for what I'm a doing down here in York, that you'll serve him as the parliament in England used to fix their King when he begun to grow obstropulous, and as they would sarve that little skittish Queen of theirn if she wanted to have a way of her own. Tell him you'll "stop his supplies." Don't send him a turkey next thanksgiving, and tell marm not to carry a single doughnut nor a skein of tow yarn to the next spinning-bee that his church members make for him. I ruther guess that this will bring him to his senses. As for me, tell him to go to grass and eat bog hay till's he as fat as Nebuchadnezzar. I aint one of his church members any how, and if I was, I shouldn't ask him to take care of me. I know what I'm about, and he needn't be scared on my account. I know as well as he does that York has a tarnal sight of bad people in it; and I know, too, that there's a good many rale down right honest, hullhearted fellers here, tu. As for the wimmen, though they are dreadfully stuck up, and eenamost ruin their husbands with dressing fine and giving parties, there's some of them that aint to be sneezed at in a fog, I can tell you. I don't want to say any thing to hurt the minister's feelings, but he needn't cum his church threats over me, for it won't du no good, I'll be darned if it will.

Wal, now that I've gin the minister a piece of my mind, tree gratis for nothing, I may as well write what's been a going on down here in York.

One morning a little black boy cum into my office with a heap of letters, and he give me one without speaking a word, and went off agin. I opened the letter, and there dropped out a square piece of white pasteboard, and on it was printed, in leetle finefied letters, "Mrs. Beebe at home—Thursday evening."

Wal, sez I to myself, if this don't take the rag off the bush—cousin Mary's got to gadding about so much, that she has to send round word when she is a going to stay at hum one evening. I do wonder how Mr. Beebe can stand it. I shouldn't blame him if he took to drink, or got into bad company, if his wife goes on so; for if a woman won't stay to hum nights, and keep every thing nice and snug agin her husband comes away from his bisness, a feller must have an allfired good heart, and a good head tu, if he don't go off and git into scrapes on his own hook.

I sot down and histed my feet on the top of the stove, and begun to think it all over, till it seemed to be my duty to go and talk to cousin Mary about the way she was a going on. I remembered what a purty, smart little critter she used to be when she lived in Connecticut, and how kind hearted she was; and then I thought of her queer stuck up ways since I'd seen her here; and it was as much as I could du to keep the tears out of my eyes, for if cousin Mary had been my own sister, I couldn't a liked her better than I did when she was a gal.

Wal, arter thinking it all over, I made up my mind to go and ask John if he didn't think it best for me to go and talk to her. for I felt kinder loth to meddle with his business, if he didn't want me tu; and anyhow, I didn't expect much thanks for giving her advice—for when a feller steps in between man and wife, it's like trying to part a cat and a dog, and he is lucky enough if he don't git scratched by one and worried to death by t'other; but I looked at the piece of paste-board agin, and made up my mind that something ought to be done, and if John didn't take it up, I would; for if there's any thing I du hate on arth, it's a gadding woman—and I didn't feel as if I could give cousin Mary up quite yit.

Wal, I took my hat, and put my hands in my trousers' pockets, and walked along kinder slow through Cherry street, till I cum to Franklin Square. I did'nt seem to mind any body, for my heart felt sort a heavy with thinking of old times. I kept a looking down on the stun walk, and felt eenamost as much alone as if I'd been in a Connecticut cramberry swamp; yit there was more than fifty people a walking up and down the Square. I'd got jest agin the old Walton House, that was built afore the revolutionary war, but was so busy a thinking, that I forgot to look up at the arms and figgers carved out over the door, every one of 'em put up there by a British tory family afore Gineral Washington drove them out of house and hum—when all to once somebody hit me a slap on my shoulder that made me jump eenamost into the middle of next week. I looked up, and there was cousin Beebe a larfin like all natur because he'd made me jump so.

"Hello, cousin Jonathan! sez he, "what the deuce are you thinking about?"

"About that," says I, a forking out the piece of pasteboard from my trousers' pocket, "a little stuck up nigger jest gin me that ere."

"Wal, what of it?" says cousin John, "it's all right I see, I suppose you'll come of course?"

"Yes," sez I, "I was a jest a going down to see you about it, and if you'd jest as livs I'll go right straight up and talk to her now; I feel as if I could say enough to break her heart, if it has got ever so tough."

With that Cousin Beebe bust right out a larfin. "That's right," says he, "you're coming on bravely, don't talk about one heart, I havn't the least doubt but you'll break a dozen—you literary chaps carry all before you in that way."

I felt kinder unsartin how to take his meaning, for it seemed as if he was a poking fun at me, for wanting to give his wife some good advice; at last I spoke up, and sez I—

"If cousin Mary has got *one* good sound heart left to break, since she came here to York, she's a good deal better off than I took her to be."

With that John begun to stare, and at last he bust out a larfin again.

"Why," sez he, "you haint no idee of getting up a flirtation with Mary, have you? upon my word, cousin Slick, you are a shaking off all your steady habits in a hurry. It generally takes a feller, though, some months' training, in fashionable society, before he can bring himself to make love to another man's wife."

"Now," sez I, "cousin Beebe, what on arth do you mean? as true as I live I shall git wrathy if you keep on in this way. Aint my father a deacon of the church? Aint I sot under Minister Smith's preaching since I was knee high to a toad? It's an allfired shame for you to talk to me as if I was a going to demean myself by making love to anybody, much less to another man's wife. When I du make love, sir, I can tell you what, it will be with a hull heart and an honest one tu; I'll never be afeard to look a girl in the face when I ask her to take me, or to let her look in mine for fear she'll see villain writ out in my eyes. As for your married women, they needn't be afeared that anybody, I don't care how imperdent he is, will make love to them, without they begin first. Now, Cousin Beebe, seeing as we've gone so far, jest look a here, see what your wife has sent to me!"

With that I give him the paper which the pasteboard was done up in, where Cousin Mary had writ, "Mrs. Beebe hopes Mr. Slick will not fail to come."

Cousin John read it, and sez he, "Wal, what harm is there in this? I'm sure it was very thoughtful of Mary, and I'm glad she did it. You will go of course; there will be a good deal of company, and they are all anxious to see you since your letters come out in the Express."

"What," sez I, "is Miss Beebe a going to have a party—why didn't she say so then?"

"Oh it's only a *swarry*, she often has them," says ne.

"A what?" sez I.

"A *swarry*—a *conversationanny*," sez he. I couldn't think

what he meant, but I remembered that jest afore Mary was married she used to have hysteric fits, now and then, and I thought they give them things some other name down here in York.

"Dear me," sez I, "I'm sorry, but if I can do any good I'll come up, I s'pose you'll have a doctor."

"Oh yes," sez he, "there'll be two or three, besides lots of lawyers, and poets, and editors."

"You don't say so," sez I, "why what will you du with them all?"

"Oh Mary will take care of them," sez he, "she does those things very well, indeed, considering she was brought up in the country."

"But I thought you wanted us to take care of her," sez I.

"Why, of course you will all make yourselves as agreeable as you can; there will be lots of harnsome winnmen there, and I haint the least doubt we shall have a pleasant party."

"A party!" sez I, "is Miss Beebe a going to have a party?"

"Certainly," sez he, a looking puzzled; "didn't you understand that by the card and the note?" I felt my heart rise up in my mouth, and I could have begun to dance on the stun walk. I do believe nothing on arth makes a feller feel so happy as to find out that somebody he can't help but like, but has been a thinking hard things about, don't desarve them. Cousin John kept a looking at me, and I begun to feel awful streaked, for it seemed to me as if he suspected all that I'd been a thinking agin his wife. Arter a minit, I up and took my hand out of my pocket, and I took hold of his'n, and, sez I—

"Cousin John, I've been making a darned fool of myself; I didn't know what this ere piece of pasteboard meant, and I"—

"Never mind, Cousin Jonathan," sez he, all of a sudden shaking my hand, "you know what it means now—so come up on Thursday. Now I think of it—you had better git a new suit of clothes; that blue coat and those shiny brass buttons did very well for Weathersfield; but here something a little more stylish will be better—supposing you go over to the Broadway tailors and let them fit you out."

"Not as you know on," sez I, a taking hold of the edge of

my coat, and a dustin off the buttons with my red silk pocket handkercher. "The picter that they printed of me in the Express newspaper was taken in these clothes; and if you'd jest as livs, I'll keep 'em on."

Cousin John warn't to be put off so, and at last he cum his soft sodder over me, till I agreed to get another suit of clothes, New York cut, for parties and meetings. So we shook hands, and he turned and went back to his store agin, for he war a coming up to my office; and I jest turned into a narrer street, and took a short cut across to the Express Office. The Editors give me some money, for they aint no ways mean about paying me for what I write for their paper; and they put on the soft sodder purty strong about my letters. They said that everybody was a reading them and a trying to find out something about me, and that lots of young ladies had seen my picter and were a dying to git acquainted with me. I warn't much surprised at it. Arter putting the poetry into my letters so strong, I was sartin that all the gals would be a talking about me. Nothing takes with them like poetry. I had my eye teeth cut when I wrote that, I can tell you. I couldn't help but feel tickled to hear them praising me so; but somehow one gits used to being puffed up, an_ arter a little while a feller don't seem to care so much about it.

Wal, I pocketed the cash and went to the tailors' store; it was a plaguy harnsome place, and there were two or three sprucelooking chaps standing about; but they looked at me kinder slanting, as if they thought I didn't want to buy anything; and I could see one on them looking arnestly at my coat, as if he didn't like the fit on't. I declare I begun to get ashamed of the old blue, when I cum to see the harnsome coats and vests and trousers hanging around.

"Have you got any first rate superfine broadcloth coats and trousers to sell here?" sez I, a chinking the loose change in my trousers' pocket a leetle, jest to show them that I was as good as the city banks, and held out specie payments yit.

"Yes," sez one of the clerks, a bowing. "What color do you wish to look at?"

"Wal," sez I, "I ruther think I'll take that color that looks so much like burnt coffee, or else a rale indigo blue, I aint particular, only I want it in the tip of the fashion—a rale harnsome fit, and all that, for I'm a going to a swarry and a conversationanny, and I want to shine like a new pin."

While I was a talking, a knowing sort of a feller cum out of the back room, and when he see me a looking at a coat that I seemed to take a notion tu he cum up and begun to talk about it—he pinted out the silk lining and the way it was stuffed and quilted under the arms, and would have me try it on. So I stripped off the old coat and put the new one on. I can tell you it sot as slick as grease; there warn't a wrinkle or a pucker in it, from the top of the velvet collar to the eend of the flap. I looked as trim and as genteel as could be in it—when it was buttoned over tight it seemed to me that I warn't bigger round than a quart cup.

Sez the gentleman, sez he, "that's a capital fit, sir, you won't lu better than to take it."

"Wal," sez I, "I don't know as I shall, I kinder seem to like myself in it—how much do you ask, hey?"

"Why," sez he, "that's a fust rate coat, superfine cloth and beautiful trimmings; but the times are hard, and I'll let you have it low for cash;" and then he sot his price; "but," sez he, "you mustn't tell how cheap you got it, for I couldn't sell any more at that price."

"Wal," sez I, "I ruther guess I'll take it; now let us look at some of your vests and trousers. I shall have to beat you down a leetle on them, for I'm raly afeard my money won't hold out."

"Not much fear of that," sez he, and he opened a drawer and took out an allfired heap of trousers. Arter I'd tumbled 'em over awhile, I picked out a pair of rale harnsome checkered ones, and then I bought a black vest with yaller stripes all over it, and between us, I ruther guess it made a considerable hole in the money that I got from the editors of the Express, to pay for 'em all The man had done 'em up, and I was jest a going to take them bum under my arm, but sez he—

"Where will you have them sent, sir?"

"Wal," sez I, arter thinking a minit, "you may direct them to Mr. Jonathan Slick, and send them round to the Express office, if you've no objection."

I wish you *could* a seen the feller! he seemed to be all struck up into a heap when I said this, and the clarks looked at each other, and cum toward us as if they had never seen anybody that wrote for newspapers afore.

"Mr. Slick," sez the head man, making a bow eenamost to the ground, "I'm much obliged for your custom, and I hope you'll cum agin. If you find the clothes suit you, perhaps you'll send any of your friends to our establishment, who happen to want any thing in our line. We shall always be happy and proud to sarve Mr. Slick or any of his friends."

Here he made another bow, and I stepped back, and bent for-'ard a trifle, jest to let him see that his soft sodder warn't put on at all coarse; and, sez I, "Wal, I'll try the clothes, and if they turn out fust-rate, mebby I'll mention where I got them in one of my letters. There is a good many chaps jest a going to be married about Weathersfield, and it won't do them no harm to know where to come for the wedding clothes."

With that the tailor bowed agin, and, sez he, "Mr. Slick, where shall I have the honor of sending you one of my fust-rate vests, or a pair of harnsome pantaloons? I'll take your measure, and have them made on purpose for you."

"Wal, now, I don't know as I can afford to buy any more jest yit," sez I; "but when these are wore out, I think as likely as not I shall cum agin."

"Oh," sez he, a rubbing his hands a little, and a smiling and bowing agin, "let us take your measure, and we shan't quarrel about the pay, we shall be most proud to supply you with a good article; and if you will accept of them, the honor"——

"Oh," sez I, a bowing, "you are very obliging, I'm sure, Mr. ——."

"Where shall we send them when they are done?" says he.

"Direct them as you did the others, to Mr. Jonathan Slick, to the care of the Editors of the Express. And look a here, Mr. ——, I wish you'd try and make the trousers so they wil. stay down, and not keep a hitching up to the top of my boots, if you can."

"Depend on it they will please you," sez he, a follering me to the door, "Good morning, Mr. Slick, I'm very much obliged to you for calling;" and with that he made another bow, and I give him one back again, and made tracks for Cherry street, as tickled as could be.

Wal, when Thursday cum, I begun to feel mighty anxious about the party; I had all the clothes sent down to my office, besides a prime hat, which I got, and a pair of real dandy boots that sot to my foot like wax.

As soon as it was dark I shut myself up and begun to fix. I declare I never did see anything fit as them checkered trousers did; they sot to my legs like the tin moles to a pair of tallow candles in freezing time, and I felt as if I'd been jest corked up in a junk bottle, foot foremost. Arter I got them on, and all buttoned up tight, I begun to think that I should have to go to the party in the blue mixed socks that marm knit for me, the last thing afore I cum away from hum; for my feet had got hung in a slip of leather, that was sowed across the bottom of the trousers' legs, and how to get 'em out, so as to put on my boots, I couldn't tell. I pulled and kicked till I eenamost bust off my gallows' buttons but they wouldn't give a morsel, and at last I jest took hold on the leathers, and I give them an allfired jerk till they slipped over my heel, and arter that I made out to roll up the trouser's legs till I could pull my boots on. When I pulled them down again the leathers stuck out from the heel of my boot behind, as if I had got spurs on; I didn't exactly like the feel of it, but "Who cares," sez I to myself, "a feller may as well be out of the world as out of the fashion, especially down here in York."

As soon as I'd got my trousers purty well braced up I put on the vest, and it sot like a button, for there wur holes behind and strings that laced up like a gal's corsets, and I girted up purty tight I can tell you. I snuggers, them yaller sprigs did glisten, and arter I'd put on the new stock that I bought along with the clothes, I ruther guess I cut a dash. It was all bowed off and curlacued over, with red and yaller sprigs, and it made my neck look as slim and shiney as our big red rooster's used to when he stretched his head out in the sun to see how many old hens and spring pullets he'd got about him.

I swanny, if I hadn't been in such a hurry to git on my new things that I forgot to wash my hands and face till jest as I was a putting on my coat! I peeked in the little looking-glass that I've got hung up in my office, and my hair was standing out every which way; and somehow my teeth looked as yaller as if I'd been chawin tobaccy a hull week. What to du I couldn't tell, but I picked up the Express, and looked into the advertisements to see if I could find out anything to make my grinders white—there warn't nothing there ; but I happened to think that I'd seen Doctor Sherman's tooth-paste puffed in some of the papers : and though I don't mean to patronize anybody that don't advertise in our paper, I thought, seeing as I was in a hurry, per'aps it would be as well to go out and get some of it. I slipped on my old coat, and down I went into Nassau street, eenamost to the corner of Fulton street, and I bought a little cheny box full of red stuff, about as thick as hasty pudding, and as sweet as honey, and back I went again to the office like a streak of lightning.

I didn't know how to use the stuff, but think siz I, they must rub it on their teeth somehow, so I spread some on the corner of my towel, and began to polish away like all natur. It warn't two minits afore my teeth was as white as a nigger's; so I jest washed them off in the hand basin, and went at my hair, tooth and nail.

How on arth these York chaps make their hair curl so, I can't guess—I tried to coax mine to twist up a little, on each side of my face, but it warn't of no use. I combed it out with a fine tooth comb, and I put some hog's lard scented with some of the essence of peppermint that marm give me to use if I should git the stomach ache down here, and I twisted it round my fingers, but it wouldn't stay curled a minit ; so at last I gave it up for a bad job, and put on my new coat as mad as could be.

I ruther guess you couldn't have found a better looking chap of my size anywhere about, than I was, when I put on my yaller gloves, and fixed my new red silk hankercher in my coat pocket, so as to let one eend hang out a leetle, arter I'd put a few of the peppermint drops on it—and the way I pulled foot up Pearl street and toward Broadway, wasn't slow I can tell you. It takes a feller forever to fix here in York---I'd ruther slick up for twenty quiltings and apple-bees, than for one swarry, I can tell you. I was a'most skared to death, for fear I should be too late, for it was eenajest dark afore I left the office, so I didn't let the grass grow under my feet on the way to cousin Beebe's, you may be sartin.

When I got to cousin Beebe's door, I pulled the silver knob kinder softly, for I felt a sort of palpitation of the heart at going into a room chuck full of quality ; and I jest pulled up my dickey a little, and felt to see if my hankercher hung out of my pocket about right, afore the nigger opened the door. At last he made out to cum, and when I asked if all the folks was tu hum, he begun to show his chalkies jest as he did afore, and sez he,

"Yes, but they haint come down yit."

With that I pitched in, and, sez I, "Look a here, Cuffy, none of your grinning at me, but jest mind your own bisness. I've come to see the swarry that Mr. Beebe's been a buying to treat his company with ; so jest shut your darned liver lips, and show it to me."

"Oh," sez he, a trying to choke in, "the swarry is going to be in the drawing room there, walk in."

"What, haint it come yit," sez I, "and where's all the folks ?—I thought he was going to have a party, too."

"Wal, so he is," sez the nigger, "but they haint begun to come yit."

"Wal, now," sez I to myself, "If this don't beat all creation. Now, in Connecticut it would a been eenamost time to go hum agin ; these Yorkers du beat all for laziness." With that I went into the room. By the living hokey, I never see anything like it! It was enough to dazzle one's eyes ; the two doors were slid back into the partition, and it seemed like one great ball-room ; and, besides that, there were two great winders at the further eend, that opened into a place that seemed kinder like a garden. I didn't know what to make of it, for it was chuck full of posies that looked as bright and as green as if it was the fourth of July, and yit it was a freezing like everything out of doors. I went down the room and stuck my head through the winder, and as true as I live it was a little room all full of bushes and roses sot up on benches ; it had a glass ruff, and the sides were one all-fired great winder, with little vines a hanging down over it, and a great tree chuck full of something that looked like oranges, a standing up agin it.

There were five or six cages full of little yaller birds a hanging among the bushes, and right back of the tree stuck over with oranges, stood a marble woman a holding up a bunch of grapes cut out of marble, with a lot of green leaves twisted round it as nateral as could be. It was awful harnsome, but I swan if it didn't make me feel streaked to look at her a standing there among the bushes, for she hadn't the least rag of kivering on, and it raly was enough to make a feller blush to see her a holding the grapes over her head, as if she wanted to make people look at her.

Think sez I, is this the swarry that Cousin Beebe has bought to show his company: I reckon he'd better have bought a calico frock or something of that sort to kiver over it. I couldn't bear to look at it, and so I jest turned about and stood still by the winder with my eyes wide open, for at the t'other eend of the room was another garden with a naked swarry and bushes in it, as much like the one I'd been a looking in as could be. I went toward it, but stopped short, and burst out a larfin all by myself, for it was nothing but the same garden a shining in the great big looking glass, that I wrote to you about, that hung up right afore me.

Arter I'd stole another sly look at the orange tree and the swarry, I jest stuck my hands in my pockets as well as I could, considering they were so tight, and stickin out one foot, leaned back agin the winder frame and looked around the room. A hot sweltering sun in dog days could not have been brighter than everything was. There were two great things hung by chains from the middle of both rooms, with hundreds and hundreds of chunks of glass a hanging all over them; and they were stuck full of candles as white as curd, all a burning and blazing, till they looked like a heap of ice and snow hung up to melt in a fire. Both the mantle shelfs were kivered over with them things that I told you about that looked so much like gold; some on 'em were lamps, and some had great white candles stuck into them; and there were lots on lots of flowers set in among them

"Think, says I, is this the swarry that Cousin Beebe has bought to show his company: I reckon he'd better have bought a calico frock or something of that sort to kiver over it."—*Page* 56.

that smelt as sweet as new hay, and such a shining and glistening I never did see. The best on it all was, that the whopping looking glasses on both eends the rooms made them seem twice as long, and as if they had a great many more things in them than they raly had. There were two round tables made out of some kind of cloudy stun, about as large as marm's cherry-wood tea-table, a standing at both eends of the rooms, all kivered over with leetle picters and all sorts of play-things, besides heaps of books with morocco backs and sprigged off with gold, all lying among them every which way, as if somebody had been in a hurry, and had pitched them on the tables without staying to pile them up.

Besides all that, they had brought in a whole heap more of them footstools that I told you about, and they had put square kind of back pillows all tossled off and kivered over with flowers at the eends of the two settees, besides a good many other things that I haint time to write about. "Wal," sez I to myself, "if Cousin Beebe don't take the shine off these New Yorkers in his party I lose my guess; but I wonder where on arth he contrives to raise money to do it with these hard times, for all this must have cost him a few, I'm sartin."

Jest as I was thinking this, the cuffy come into the room, and sez I—

"Look a here, snow ball, when is the party a coming, I've seen the swarry all I want tu, and I'm eenamost tired of standing here and doing nothing."

"Wal," sez he, "I s'pose they'll be here in an hour or two,—it aint mor'n eight o'clock yit."

"I rather guess I shan't stay here all alone any longer," sez I, and with that I buttened up my coat, and jest took a walk into the Apollo gallery to see the picters, till it was time for the party to cum. I haint time to say anything about the heap of harnsome picters that I saw, and besides, I mean to write you all about them some day afore long, for they are curios I can tell you. I felt so much pleased with looking at 'em, that it was long after nine afore I thought of it. So I jest started off agin for Cousin Beebe's. When I went in this time the rooms were brim full of people, and I was eenamost scared to death. I unbuttoned my coat and pulled up my dicky a leetle, besides giving my hair a brush—and then I went in with my head straight up, and my new fur hat in my hand; jest as I used to go in the singers' seat, there in Weathersfield. Think sez I, I'll jest let 'em know that I haint been to dancing school for nothing. So I held my hat a leetle afore me by the rim, and I made a genteel bow, first to one side and then to t'other. Arter that, I went and sot down on one of the settees, and I looked round for cousin Mary, for I felt kinder awk'ard; and I hadn't the least idee that she wouldn't have come up, as she used to in Weathersfield, and put out her hand and ask me if she should take my hat. But there I sot with it between my hands, a fingering it over as if it had been a hot potater, and she never cum near me. I felt dreadfully, for there was a lot of harnsome gals a staring at me, and a puckering up their purty leetle mouths, as if they would a gin the world to larf right out. Arter a minit cousin John cum up to me, and sez he,

"Cousin Slick, I'm glad you've cum, step in the next room and take a glass of wine with me. Mrs. Beebe is so crowded you won't get near her jest yit."

I got up, and we went into the entry way together, and then says cousin Beebe to the nigger, "Here, Ben, take Mr. Slick's hat."

The nigger took my hat and carried it off up stairs, and, arter a few minits, cousin John went back into the room where the company was, without saying another word about the wine.

"You had better go up and speak to Mary, now," sez he, kinder low; "there she stands by Count ——." I didn't hear the name, but it was some darned crabbed word, that was enough to choke a feller.

I hadn't looked round much when I cum in before, for somehow my head didn't feel steddy; but arter cousin John cum and spoke to me, I didn't seem to mind it, so I jest looked round as bold as could be. I declare I never did see any body dressed out as cousin Mary was. She had on a frock of shining satin, with harnsome pink sprigs all over it, and there was a great wide ruffle round the bottom, made out of something that looked as white and thin as a gal's veil the day arter she's married; and that was hitched up on one side half way to her waist, with a pink rose, made out of ribbon with long eends, that fell down eenamost to the floor. A heap of some kind of shiney thin stuff was ruffled round her bosom, and hung down round her arms, for her frock sleeves were short, and made like a little gal's; and she had on a pair of white gloves, with ribbon tops to 'em. One on 'em was fastened round her wrist with a wide piece of gold, and three or four bands set full of shiny stuns wos on t'other arm, which was pluguey white, or else I suppose she would not have let folks see it.

Mary al'ers had a tarnal purty little foot, but I never see it look so small as it did in that glistening white shoe of hern, and to own the rale downright truth, she didn't seem to be much ashamed to show it, but kept it stuck out from under her ruffler, as if she'd made up her mind to be ready to make a curchy any minit. There was one thing that kinder puzzled me a good deal; Mary's skin never was over white, but somehow it looked like wax work, that night, and you never see a meadow pink look brighter than her cheeks did; but instead of coming into her face and going away again, as every man loves to see the color in a gal's face when she's a talking, and knows that he's a looking at her, Mary's always kept jest so; it didn't seem as if an earthquake would make her turn pale. The hair hung in long curls down her cheeks and on her shoulders, jest as it did the other day, and she had a great white rose stuck in among the curls, on one side of her head, that looked as if it hadn't but jest been picked off the bushes.

I looked at her putty earnestly, I can tell you, and I do think she would have been a critter that John might be proud of, if it warn't for that stuck up way which she's got since she cum down here to York. She don't du nothing on arth natural, and as she did when she was a gal in Connecticut. Instead of standing up straight, and speaking to her company as if she was glad to see them, she stood with one foot stuck out and her hands jest crossed afore her, and kinder stooping for-ard, as if she couldn't but jest stand alone; I never see a critter's back stuck up as her's was, I raly thought she was a getting the rickets, and I felt so anxious about it that I turned to cousin Beebe, afore I went up to speak to her, and sez I, a sort of low—

"Cousin John, how did your wife hurt her back so? I declare it makes me feel awfully to see what a great hump she's got a growing since she cum away from Connecticut!"

With that cousin John looked at her and larfed a little, but I could see he didn't feel jest right, and arter a minit he said, sez he,

"Hush, cousin, you must not speak so loud; it's true Mary has put on rather *too* much bustle, but it's the fashion, you see." I looked round, and as true as you live there warn't a gal in the room that hadn't her back a sticking out jest the same way. Such a set of humpbacked critters I never did put my eyes on, and yit they all stood about a smiling and a talking to the fellers as if nothing ailed them, poor things! I never see a set of folks dressed out so much, and so awfully stuck up as they were. Some of the gals had feathers in their hair, and some had flowers or gold chains twisted among their curls, and I didn't see one there that wasn't dressed up in her silks and satins as crank as could be. As for the men, I thought I should have haw hawed right out a larfin to see some of 'em; there was one chap talking to Miss Beebe with his hair parted from the top of his head down each side of his face, and it hung down behind all over his coat collar like a young gal's just before she begins to wear a comb; and there was two bunches of hair stuck out on his upper lip right under his nose, like a cat's whiskers when she begins to get her back up. Every time he spoke the hair kinder riz up and moved about till it was enough to make a feller crawl all over to look at him. Think sez I, if it wouldn't be fun to see that varmint try to eat. If he didn't get his victuals tangled up in that bunch of hair, he must know how to aim allfired straight with his knife and fork.

When I cum to look round there were more than a dozen chaps, rale dandy-looking fellers, with their lips bristled out in the same way. Think sez I, there are some men that would be hogs if they only had bristles, as we say in Connecticut, but these chaps needn't keep out of the gutters for want of them, they are ready for sarvice any time. There were two or three ruther good-looking chaps, that didn't let the hair grow on their upper lips, but it come up in a pint like a letter A from the tip of the chins eenamost to their mouths. These fellers had great hairy whiskers that made them look as if they had run all to head like a seed onion. I swanny, I never did see such a set of infarnal looking coots in all my life—a tribe of ribbed nosed babboons would have looked ten times as much like men; and yet they did't seem the least bit ashamed of themselves, but strutted round among the gals as large as life, showing off with their white gloves on and white cambric handkerchers, that I s'pose they borrowed from their sisters, stuck into their pockets.

I wouldn't go up and speak tu Miss Beebe till that ninnihammer with the brustles went away from her, for I was afeard that I couldn't hold in, but should haw haw right out in his face, if I got tu looking at him too stiddy. I raly didn't know which looked the worst, men running about among decent people with dirty brustles under their noses, or women a trying tu make themselves look humpbacked so as tu be in the fashion.

At last the chap with the brustles went off with a young gal into the room where the bushes were, to look at the swarry, I s'pose, and so then I went up tu Miss Beebe and I made a bow, and sez I—

"It's a pleasant evening, Miss Beebe."

"Yes," sez she, "it is very pleasant."

I didn't seem tu stand easy, so I put t'other foot for'ard, and wiped my nose a little with my red hankercher.

"Any news a stirring?" sez I.

"Nothing particular that I know on," sez she.

I changed feet agin.

"I ruther thought it was a going tu rain, but I guess it won't now," sez I.

"No, I ruther think not," sez she.

We stood stock still a minit, and then I put my hankercher in my coat pocket agin, and, sez I—

"I swanny, Miss Beebe, you've got a grist of harnsome gals here to-night. I'll be darned if I aint eenamost in love with some one on 'em."

"I'm sure you ought to be," says she, a puckering up her mouth, "you don't know how much they have been a talking about you. I declare you've got to be quite a lion since you took to writing, cousin Slick."

"A what?" sez I.

"A literary lion," sez she, with one of her old Weathersfield smiles.

"Wal," sez I, "that's a queer name, but I don't care what they call me, if they don't call me late tu dinner."

Jest that minit a tall harnsome young feller cum up to us, and Miss Beebe turned tu him and spoke softly, with her eyes half shet, jest as if she was a dying off, and she asked him if he wouldn't sing.

"With that he puckered up his mouth and said he couldn't, cause he'd got such a bad cold; but anybody that had his eye teeth cut might have seen that he only wanted her tu coax him. A lot of young gals crowded round and begun tu put the soft sodder over him.

"Oh du—now pray du," sez one, and the rest on 'em took it up till the poor feller, he didn't know which eend his head was on. So he sot down and flung back his head with his eyes half shet, and he began tu sing. I swanny, it eenamost made the tears cum into my eyes tu hear him, it was rale ginuine music; but the very minit he begun, the young gals that had been a teasing him so tu sing, went on a talking and a larfin, as if he hadn't done what they wanted. I raly felt sorry for the feller; yit he didn't seem tu mind it, but sung away as if everybody was a listening.

Jest then, cousin Beebe called out my name from t'other side the room. I wish you could a seen how they all stared; it warn't more than ten minits arter that, afore eenamost every one in there was at cousin Beebe tu be introduced tu me—the fellers with the brustles and all. The purtyest gals in the room kept a flocking round me as if they'd never seen a man that wrote for the newspapers afore. Talk about soft sodder—there's nobody on arth can put it into a chap so smooth as a harnsome gal. Somehow they melt it with their smiles, till it sinks through his heart afore he knows it. I was talking with a rale peeler of a gal, with two of the brightest black eyes that I ever see, when somebody struck up a tune on the pianner-forty, and two or three couple got onto the floor as if they wanted tu dance.

"Do you dance quadrills, Mr. Slick?" sez the black eyed gal, as if she wanted me tu ask her to dance.

"Wal, I don't know," sez I, "I never tried them kind of things; out I ruther guess I can, if you'll show me how."

With that, I took the tip eend of her white glove between the fingers of my yaller one, and went with her into the middle of the room. I didn't know what they were a going tu dance, but I warn't much afeard, anyhow—for there warn't a chap in all Weathersfield could beat me at a double shuffle, or could cut so neat a pigeon-wing without music, as I could.

Wal, the music begun, and one of the fellers that had the hair on his lip, begun tu slide about with his eyes half shet and his hands a hanging down, and looking as doleful as if he'd jest come away from a funeral. Did you ever see a duck swim a mill-dam, or a hen turning up its eyes when it's a drinking? If you have you can git some idea how the lazy coot danced. I thought I should go off the handle tu see him, but the gals all stuck out their little feet, and poked about jest in the same way. Think sez I, when it comes my turn, I'll give you a little specimen of ginuine dancing. I only wish I thought tu put a little loose change in my pocket tu jingle, if it was only jest tu show how well I keep step.

A young lady, with her hair twisted all up with little white flowers, balanced up tu me, jest as you've seen a bird walk, and then it come my turn. I took two steps for'ard and then I cut a peeler of a pigeon-wing, and ended off with a little touch of the double shuffle, but my trousers was so plaguy tight that I couldn't make my legs rale limber all I could du, besides, the music warn't much more like a dancing tune than Greenbank or Old Hundred. At last I went up tu the gal that was playing, and sez I—

"Look a here—jest give us something lively—Yankee Doodle, or Money Muss, or the Irish Washerwoman, or Paddy Carey. I aint a going tu twist and pucker round in this way."

With that the young fellers with the hair lips begun tu push their cambric hankerchers into their mouths, and the young gals puckered up their mouths as if I'd done something tu poke fun at. But instid of sneaking off and letting the stuck up varmints think they'd scared me so I darsn't dance, I felt my dander a getting up, and sez I tu myself, "I guess I'll let 'em see that I warn't brought up in the woods to be scared at owls, any how;" so I jest turned tu the black eyed gal that was my partner, and sez I,

"Cum now, Miss, let us show 'em how it's done," and with that I begun tu put it down right and left like a streak of lightning. It warn't more than two minits afore I heard the guls a talking tu each other, and a saying,

"How odd—how strange—quite the eccentricity of genius—these literary lions never do anything as other people do!—I don't wonder Miss Beebe's proud of him."

The young fellers joined in and stopped larfin as quick as could be, the minit they begun to see how the wind was a blowing up in my quarter, and when I finished off and led the black eyed gal tu one of the footstools, there was no eend tu the soft sodder they all put on tu me. Sez I tu myself, nothing like keeping a stiff upper lip with these stuck up fashionables, for arter all they aint more than half sartin what's genteel and what aint.

Jest then the music begun agin, and one of them tall hairy lipped fellers got up with a purty little gal, that didn't look more than eighteen years old, and he put his white gloves on a little tighter, and then I'll be darned if he didn't begin to hug her right there afore all on us. He put one arm round her little waist jest above the hump on her back, and he took one of her hands in his'n, and then she looked up into his eyes and he looked down into hers as loving as two pussy cats, and then they begun to make cheeses on the carpet till you couldn't have told which was which.

I never felt my blood bile so in all my life; it raly didn't seem decent, and if she had been a relation of mine, I'll be darned to darnation if I wouldn't have knocked that pesky varmint into a cocked hat in less than no time. I'd a made him glad to eat himself up hair and all, greasy as it must a tasted, tu have got out of my way. Oh! but I was wrathy with the coot for a minit; and then says I to myself, "I don't know as the chap's so much to blame, arter all, it's the gal's own fault; if she likes to be hugged and whirled round so afore the folks, the feller must bo an allfired fool not to like it as much she does; but, thinks I, if the gal means to git married, her bread will be all dough agin, arter this, for no decent honest man would want to marry a gal arter he'd seen her tousled about afore fifty people, by such a shote as that chap is."

As soon as the two critters sot down, the fellers and the gals all locked arms and begun to stream out of the room. I thought I might as well see where they were a going, so I jest crooked my arm, and the black eyed gal put hers through it, and out we went into the entry way tu a room further back, where all the company was standing about round a table sot out with everything good on arth that a feller ever thought of eating.

I thought the table, when I eat dinner at cousin John's, took the shine off from everything that I'd ever seen afore in my life, but it warn't a circumstance to this. There was no eend to the silver dishes and baskets all sot out with flowers, and a running over with bunches of white grapes and oranges, and everything else good that ever grew on arth! and there were more than half a dozen little steeples, all made out of red and white sugar candy, hung over with flowers and curlecued about with little sugar images, and sich lots of cake, and presarves, and jelly, and things that I'd never seen afore in my life. Everything glittered and shone so it fairly took away my appetite. There was another little table kivered over with decanters and with a lot of them cider bottles that I've told you about, standing on it; but I kept purty clear of that, I can tell you. Cousin Beebe cum to me with one of 'em in his hand, and sez he, sort of larfin,

"Come, cousin Slick, take a glass."

Says I, "No, if you'd jest as lives, I'd a little ruther not, your York cider don't agree with me."

"Oh," sez he, "it's only sham pain, try a little."

"I'm jest as much obliged to you, but I'd a little ruther not, it warn't sham pain that I had in my head the day arter I drunk it before, I can tell you."

With that cousin Beebe larfed, and sez he, "you must be gallant, and help Miss Miles, she hasn't got no refreshments yit" looked toward the black eyed gal, and sure enough, there she stood as mute as could be, looking on, while all the rest was a eating. I went up to her again, and I made her a bow, and sez I,

"Miss Miles, what will you take? arter you is manners for me, and I begin to feel a little as if I should like a bite."

I could see that tarnal purty mouth of hern begin to tremble, as if it wanted to say something funny, but she looked in my face, and sez she,

"I'll take a little blue monge if you please."

I didn't know what she could mean, but there was some stuff in some little blue glasses, that looked as much like soap suds as anything else, and I took one of 'em out of the silver thing that it stood in, and I jest stirred it up a little with the spoon, afore I give it to her. I dont know what on arth become of the blue monge, but I hadn't more than touched it when off it went, and left the glass eenajest empty. Miss Miles larfed a little, and says she,

"Thank you, the syllabub will do jest as well. A few grapes, and a trifle of that jelly, if you please."

"But," sez I, holding the glass, and a lookin down on the carpet and over my new trousers, "where on arth can that monge have gone tu! I hope there aint none of it got on tu your silk frock, Miss Miles."

"Oh, no," sez she, "don't mind it, the grapes will do jest as well."

I took up a plate and gave her a great whopping bunch from off one of the dishes, and then I made another bow, and, sez I—

"Anything else, Miss Miles? I'd do anything on arth to oblige you."

She twisted up that plump little mouth of hern in one of the handsomest smiles I ever see, and, sez she, "I'll take that rose bud that dropped from the grape basket when you took these out."

I swan, but she looked plaguy harnsome, I couldn't but jest keep from staring right in her face all the time. I felt my heart a floundering about, like a pullet with its neck twisted, when she said this, and I took up the rose bud between the fingers of my yaller gloves, and I stepped back and made as genteel a bow as I could, considering I hadn't room to square my elbows, and, sez I—

"I hope you'll keep that ere to remember me by."

She gave me another of them tarnation bright smiles, and she stuck the rose in her bosom, and sez she, kinder larfin a little—

"What shall I give you, Mr. Slick? This myrtle sprig? it'll keep green longer than your rose."

"No thank you," sez I, a looking at her as killing as could be, "I'll take it; but I don't want anything to make me remember you."

I kinder expected that she'd have blushed a little when I said that; but somehow these city gals don't color up very easy. She smiled again, and sez she—

"Well, Mr. Slick, you must call and see how well your rose keeps with me. Mrs. Beebe, will come with you any time."

Sez I, "but I aint sartin as you'll be glad to see me, you must have a great many beaus, and I may be in the way."

She was a going to answer me, but jest then that tarnal varmint with the hair come up with a plate in his hand, and sez he—"Let me help you tu a jelly, Miss Miles."

I could have knocked the critter into the middle of next week, I was so tarnal mad; but there he stood a bowing and a smiling through his hair lip like an etarnal monkey that had got the stomach ache, and I couldn't get a word in edge ways. I couldn't eat a morsel, but I took up one of the cider bottles without a thinking what I was a doing, and I drunk two glasses right off, and arter that I felt a little better; but I'll be darned if it didn't make me grit my teeth tu see that stuck-up coot work his arm as if he warnted to go into t'other room with Miss Miles. She looked round as if to see where I was, and then I went right straight up, and, sez I tu him—

"Arter *me* is manners for *you*."

With that I took her little hand in my yaller glove, and I put it into my arm as genteel as could be, and walked straight into t'other room with her. She sot down on one of the settees, and I jest pulled one of the footstools close up to her, and there we both sot as sociable as could be till the folks all come back agin. Arter that I had to git up and give a pale-looking gal my seat; but I kept a standing up by the eend of the settee, till Cousin Beebe come up tu me, and, sez he—

"Cousin Slick, jest step this way a minit."

He went right between the silk winder curtins into the place where the bushes, and the birds, and the swarry was, and sez he—

"Cousin Jonathan, did you know that the straps to your pantaloons have slipped out from under you boots?"

"You don't say so," sez I, a looking down at hisen, tu see how he fixed them, for I didn't want him to think that I'd left 'em so on purpose; but I felt awful streaked when I see his was buttoned under the sole of his dancing pumps.

"Here, jest lift up your foot," sez he.

I histed my foot up, and he jirked the strops down quick enough; but I swan if I didn't feel as if he'd corded me up tu see how long I'd keep. I didn't wonder the chaps sidled and wriggled about so when they tried tu dance, a feller couldn't take a regular strong step tu save his life, girt up in a pair of these new-fashioned trousers.

"Look a here, cousin Beebe," sez I, jest as he was a going out, and I pinted tu the naked marble woman a standing among the bushes, with the light a coming in from t'other room onto her, till she looked like a harnsome ghost a walking among the bushes by moonlight; "if you'll take a fool's advice you'll buy a frock and petticoat for that purty swarry of yourn, afore you have another party. How should you feel if some of them young gals was tu cum in here?"

John bust out a larfin, and I raly thought the critter would never stop.

"Now what are you a haw-hawing about?" sez I, sort a wrathy, "because I cum here with my trousers slipped up a leetle. I don't s'pose anybody but you see them."

"Oh never think about it," sez he, a biting in, but the tears kept a running down his cheeks, for all that. "If they did see it, they'll set it down for the eccentricity of genius, as the young ladies say. You literary chaps can do a'most anything now-a-days."

"I begin to think we can," sez I, for jest that minit I remembered all that tarnal sweet critter, Miss Miles, had been a saying to me, and I looked down tu see if the sprig of myrtle was in my button-hole yit.

When we went into the room, there warn't scarce any of the party left. I stood by one of the doors till I saw Miss Miles cum down with her purty face half buried up in a great silk hood—so I jest went with her to the door, and there stood a carriage with a nigger a standing by the door—so I jest took hold of her hand and helped her to git in; and arter that I felt so lonesome, I bid cousin Mary good night and made tracks for my office. I ruther think I won't tell what I dreamed about—you old steady folks do love to larf at a young chap so—and as I ruther think I shall cum hum tu thanksgiving, I don't mean to let you all poke too much fun at me.

      Your loving son,
          JONATHAN SLICK.

LETTER VII.

Scenes in Broadway—Jonathan's Interview with the Count and Flirtations with Miss Miles.

DEAR PAR:

I am eenamost sartin that you was disappinted because I didn't come hum to thanksgiving, but somehow I couldn't raise pluck enough to start, all I could du. I raly don't know what seemed to be the matter with me; but arter Miss Beebe's party, I begun to git as peaked and wamblecropped as could be. I swauny, if it didn't set me all in a fluster the next morning, when I got up and found the sprig of myrtle that Miss Miles give me a lying on the floor jest where it had dropped from the button hole of my new coat.

I didn't hardly give myself time to put on my clothes, afore I went out to a crockeryware stand and bought a tumbler to put it in; and then I set it on my desk, and tried to write a little, for I didn't feel jest like eating any breakfast. But it warn't of no use trying—all I could du, every idee in my head got fixed on the myrtle, and Miss Miles, and the party. I didn't write two words together, but scrabbled all over the paper, and figgered out little heads, and meeting-houses, and hay-stacks on it, as nat'ral as could be; but if I'd been hung and choked to death, I couldn't a wrote two rale ginuine lines. I felt sort of odd all over, and I hadn't the least notion what could ail me; it warn't a very tedious feeling, though, but it seemed as if I was a dreaming yit, and all about that tarnation little Miss Miles. I kept a seeing them bright black eyes and them long curls of hern all the time, as plain as day. I'll be choked if I didn't git afeared that I was a beginning to have a kind of a sneakin notion arter her, and sez I to myself, "Mr. Jonathan Slick, this won't do no how. Arter what you've seen of woman natur in that Judy White, you must be a darned crazy shote to poke your fingers in that fire agin." But a feller may as well drink tu much lickor and ask it not to make him stagger, as to git his head chock full of the gals and then try to talk common sense to hisself. It is like giving advice to a rat when his leg is in the trap.

The long and short of it was, I couldn't set still, and I couldn't think of anything on arth but that gal, so I jumped up all tu once and sez I to myself—" Wal, one way or t'other, by hook or by crook, I'll see her agin—I will, by hokey! it's of no use to git down in the mouth about it, she can't do more than give me the mittin, any how, and it will be the first gal I ever got it from, if she does, I can tell her that."

I was so anxious that it seemed forever afore I got on my dandy coat and trousers agin. My hankercher smelt purty strong yit of the essence of peppermint, so I fixed it right in my pocket, put on my yaller gloves, and stuck the sprig of myrtle in my bosom afore I gin the last peak into the leetle looking-glass that hangs in a corner of my office. I don't think there could be much said agin my looks, as I went down Cherry street with my head flung back, sort of independent, and the tip eend of my yaller gloves stuck in my pocket. Consarn that Broadway tailor! he made the trousers so tight that I couldn't get a hull hand in no more than I could fly.

Miss Miles lives clear up to the further eend of Broadway, so I took a short cut across the Park, and went along by the Astor House. A lot of dandyfied looking chaps stood on the steps a staring at the harnsome gals as they went by, all furbelowed and finefied out like a stream of garden flowers all in full blow.

They may talk about England and France and Garmany, as well as all the other big places that a feller can pint out on the map; but, for my part, I don't believe there is a place on the arth where the wimmen dress so allfired costly as they du here in York. It raly is enough to make a feller grit his teeth to see the harnsome critters sideling and curchying along the stun walks, wrapped up in silks and satins and velvets, and all sorts of feathers, as long as them that Captain Jones wore in his training cap, as if it only wanted a fiddler to set them all a dancing, when their husbands are out a shinning and working themselves to death to keep their notes from being sued by the lawyers. It don't seem right, but yit they do look tarnal killing in their furbelows—it's of no use denying that.

But one thing did raise my dander a leetle as I went along, that's a fact. Any body that had half an eye could see that all the young gals were possessed after them foreign chaps with the brustles and whiskers. Every once in a while one of the indecent varmints would come along with his head twisted round under some party woman's bonnet, talking as soft and as mealy-mouthed as could be, like an old grey cat mewing round a bird cage, and the gals seemed all in a twitter, they were so tickled, and screwed up their mouths, and smiled to show their teeth, and looked as proud as peacocks of the etarnal impudent critters. I'll be darned if I don't believe every one of them chaps are barbers or chair-makers when they are to hum, and hearing what a chance the York gals give every kind of animals that come from foreign parts, and how they begin to turn up their noses at a rale true born American, whenever they can git a chance to make fools of themselves with them hairy lipp'd fellers, they've come over here to York to court the gals and git up a new crop of hair to begin bisness with when they git hum agin. Think sez I, it wouldn't be a bad joke sometime about six months arter this, if some of them same gals that don't think nothing of chasing arter them fellers, should buy his whiskers and all the rest on 'em that they fall in love with, stuffed into a footstool, sich as I saw at Miss Beebe's. Stranger things than that has happened afore now, I reckon.

It raly made me feel bad to see tall, harnsome-looking fellers, ginuine Americans, with revolutionary blood in their hearts, a standing on the tavern steps, and a walking all alone up and down the streets as molancholy as mice in an empty mill, while their own wimmen folks, that ought to feel ashamed of themselves, were a talking and smiling and giggling with that pack of varmints. It made my blood bile to see it, I can tell you.

You wont think it exactly like a Christian to run on as I du about them fellers, I'm afeard; but the truth of it is, I *do* hate 'em like pison. If I owned a caravan of living animals, darn me, if I wouldn't catch some on 'em for specimens, and cage 'em up for a show. They wouldn't be a strutting up Broadway and a showing themselves for nothing much longer, I can tell them that! They talk about Yankee speculations; I reckon this would be a prime one—wouldn't it? If a feller could only get a good trap made, there wouldn't be no difficulty but we could find purty gals—them that live in fine houses and hold up their heads as if they were queens too—that would be willing enough to let you use them for bate.

You wont be surprised that I am wrothy about them chaps when I tell you how I was struck up jest arter I went by the Astor House. I was thinking about one thing or another, when all to once I lifted my head and there was Miss Miles a coming toward me a looking as fresh and harnsome as a full blown butter cup, and close to her side, that Count with the crabbed name that I saw at Miss Beebe's was a twistifying himself along, with his head bent sideways till the great long white feather that she wore in her bonnet all but swept across his eyes. I eenamost felt as if I should holler out, and I raly believe I should have boo hooed right in the street if I hadn't been so allfired wrathy at the sight of him. Oh! but my Yankee grit did rise—I dug my hands down in my trousers' pocket and walked right straight up to them a grinning like a hyena, for I was determined to let them see that I didn't care a copper how much they walked together. They were so busy twisting their heads about and a looking soft sodder at each other that they didn't see me till I stood right afore them as stiff as an iron crowbar, with my head up straight, and one foot stuck out for'ard, as an independent and true born Yankee ought to do when he sees himself imposed on.

There was no mistake in Miss Miles this time any how. She gave a little scream and blushed as red as a turkey's comb, and then she looked about sort of skeery as if she was afeard somebody would see how slick I'd caught her. I was mad as all natur, but as true as you live I couldn't but jest keep from haw hawing right out to see how that hair lipp'd Count acted when he saw me a standing up afore him. He kinder stepped back and stuck out one foot a little sideways, jest as if he was a going to make a bow, and he twisted his little stuck up waist round till his head poked out like a mud turtle when he wants to see if anybody is near. Then he took a thing out of his vest pocket hitched to a gold chain that he wore round his neck, and held it up to one eye, and there he stood a staring at me and twisting his face and a brustling up his hair lip, like an eternal monkey. I didn't seem to mind him, but looked right straight at Miss Miles, and sez I—

"How do you du, Miss Miles?"

She didn't seem to know how to take me at first, so she looked at the feller and then at me, and, arter a while, sez she—

"Oh! Mr Slick, is it you?"

"Wal, I ruther guess it is," sez I, "but I s'pose my room's as good as my company, I don't want tu keep you from talking tu your beau there."

"Oh! Mr. Slick," sez she, a twisting up her mouth and a looking in my face, jest as she did the night afore, "how odd you men of genius are! The Count, I'm sure, will be happy to meet you, won't you, Count?"

She called the coot by his hull name, but how she could twist that little mouth of hern so as to git the word out, I can't tell. Arter that she turned her head a little, and said something sort of low to him. She smiled so harnsome, and her voice was so soft and coaxing, that I had eenamost forgot the chap, but her talking to him made me rile up agin—and jest as he was letting that half of a pair of spectacles down from his eye, and was a beginning to put his face ship shape agin, I walked right straight up to him, and sez I—

"Look a here you chap, I ruther guess you mean to know who I am the next time you see me."

"Sare?" sez he, a standing up straight and opening his great black eyes till they seemed chuck full of fire and brimstone.

"Wal, what on it?" sez I.

"You are impertinent," sez he.

"Wal, now I reckon that aint what I was baptized. I'll tell you what, Mr. Hair-lip, I haint a going to let you nor any body else call me names," sez I, a taking both hands out of my trousers pockets, and a pulling up my yaller gloves, as spiteful as could be, jest to show him that my mawlers were fit for use.

The feller's lips began to grow white, but he twisted them up as if he wanted to make me think he didn't care for what I said.

"Sare," sez he, "do you know whom you are speaking to?"

"Wal," sez I, larfin in his face a leetle, "I ruther guess I du, though I haint just made up my mind what kind of horned cattle you call yourself yit: they give all sich stranger-critters a name, and I s'pose you'll git one by-am-by, as well as the rest on 'em."

With that he turned as white as a tub of curd, and sez he—

"This is too much, sare; remember you are speaking to a Count." Here he out with a name as long and crooked as a sassafras root.

"You don't say so!" sez I.

"I'm a nobleman!" sez he, and he was a going on to give me another string of foreign jaw-breakers; but I jest sot down my foot, and sez I,

"Look a here, you feller—I don't care the value of a butnutshell how many names you've got; we don't own no Counts in this ere free land of liberty, but them that can count down the most hard chink, and they have to work tarnation hard afore they git the title, I can tell you. As for your noblemen, we have raised a new-fashioned sort of 'em in this land of liberty. In the Revolutionary War a hull grist on 'em sot their titles down on our glorious Declaration of Independence, and there they'll stay, as bright as the stars, to all eternity, and a day longer. We don't ask our noblemen who their fathers were, or how they got a living. *Great deeds* and—what's the same thing—*good deeds* make noblemen here. Every man has to work out his own title and when he dies, instid of leaving it to some booby of a son, writes his date out in the history of his country, and takes it back to him who gave the power to arn it. As for any other noblemen—though I believe arter all that the true ginuine lords and counts that come out here are as scarce as hen's teeth—" (here the count didn't seem to stand easy,) "we *true* Americans, rale full-blooded Yankees, don't care any more for their titles than we do for the stuns under our feet. It's only your half-blooded Americans that have been baked over in Europe, and our silly finefied gals that chase after you. An honest straight for'ard Yankee gal would take you for jest what you are worth as *men*, and when they du that, I rather guess we can pull an even yoke with any of you that come from t'other side the water."

Here I gave Miss Miles a squint that made her wilt like a broken rose in the hot sun! "Mr. Slick," sez she, eenamost crying, "I beg, I entreat, let us walk on. See how the people are remarking us."

"Wal," sez I, sort of mollified, "I aint doing nothing to be ashamed on, am I?"

"Oh, no," sez she, "I didn't mean to say that."

"Wal, there aint nothing on arth that I wont du to oblige a harnsome critter like you," sez I, a going round to the other side on her. She gave me another of her prime smiles, and that seemed to pacify me. So we all three walked along together till we got agin the Astor House once more. The Count looked as sour as a vinegar barrel—I suppose, because I was determined to hang on, but I kept a stiff upper lip, and marched down the stun walk as straight as a bean pole stuck up on eend. Miss Miles begun to smile agin, and she talked to him as sweet as could be, but I couldn't make out a word she said, for she didn't speak rale American, but every now and then, jest as I was beginning to get rily about it, she would turn her face to me, and pucker up her mouth so coaxing, that somehow I couldn't git right down wrathy if I tried ever so much.

When the Count saw that I wasn't to be scared away, he jest give me a good long stare right in the eyes, and then bending a little for'ard to Miss Miles, he lifted his hat about an inch from his head and went into the Astor House. I don't know what on arth could be the matter, but the minit he left us I begun to feel as sheepish as could be. I didn't know what in nature to talk about—so I jest took my red silk handkercher and gave it a flirt out of my pocket, and then put it back agin.

"Do you like the smell of essence of peppermint, Miss Miles?" sez I.

"I'm very fond of perfume," sez she.

"I hope you didn't like the stuff that are Count had on his handkercher," sez I. "I swanny, It eenamost made me sick; he smelt more like a musk-rat than anything else."

"You can't expect every body to have *your* taste in selecting perfumes for his toilet, Mr. Slick," sez she, a puckering up her mouth till it looked like a red clover top full of honey.

"I swow, Miss Miles, you look as harnsome as a full blown rose this morning," sez I; "it aint a mite of wonder that I couldn't sleep a bit last night."

With that I jest took a good squint at her as we went along, for I couldn't think what to say next. I don't believe the things she had on cost one cent less than fifty dollars, enough to rig out all the gals in Weathersfield with boughten finery; her cloak was the queerest thing I ever did see; it only reached jest down to her knees, and was made out of rale silk velvet. I know it was silk, for I jest slipped off my yaller glove, and felt on it to be sartin, as we walked along. It was kinder purply, like the damsons that grow in our corn lot, and was loaded down with some kind of long fur. Under that she wore another dress of black silk velvet, that shone in the sun like a crow's back. The cloak had great open sleeves, edged with fur, a hanging round her arms; and I could see the corner of a hankercher a sticking out from the eend of her little black muff jest enough to show how harnsomely it was figger'd off; a bunch of red flowers was stuck agin each side of her face under her bonnet, and her eyes looked bright, and her cheeks rosy enough to make a feller catch his breath. The more I looked at her, the more uneasy I got about that Count. I wanted to say something to her about him dreadfully, but some how I didn't know what to say first. I took out my hankercher agin, and then I wiped my nose and put it back; then I begun to examine the fingers of my yaller gloves, to see how they stood the weather. Finally, I lost step, and it took me three minits to get the right hitch agin; at last I bust right out, and, sez I—

"Now, Miss Miles, between you and I and the post, jest tell me do you raly care anything about that are Count?"

She turned her roguish black eyes to my face, and, sez she, "Why, Mr. Slick, how can you ask sich a question?"

"Now that's Yankee all over," sez I, "you aint told me yet: only asked me another question to match mine."

"What do you want to know for?" sez she, sort of softly.

"Oh, not much of anything; I should kinder like to know, that's all," sez I. With that, think sez I, I'll try and make her jealous a leetle, and sez I,—

"Do you know, Miss Miles, that they've been a printing my picter clear off in Michigan and down in Cincinnati? I guess I shall go out there one of these days and see how I like the folks out West, I begin to git eenamost tired of York." I warn't wrong; that brought her to her senses purty quick.

"You don't really intend to leave the city," sez she, a looking at me as arnest as could be.

"Wal, I don't know," sez I, "them Western editors want me to come dreadfully. One on 'em sent me word that they had a grist of harnsome gals in his State."

"Is the picter out West so very well painted?" sez she.

"Wal," sez I, "it's a purty good likeness, considering it was took in my old clothes," (and with that I took out the paper and I showed it to her. "I ruther think it will be best for me to go on there," sez I, a putting up the picter; "that are Count will think I want to cut him out, I'm afeard."

I looked straight at her as I said this, but she begun to smooth down the fur on her muff with her little hand, and when she did speak I had to bend my head down to hear what she was a saying.

Afore I could make out what she meant to say, a couple of harnsome young gals cum along and they stopped as if they were tickled to death to see her; I thought there warn't much chance for me to git another word in edgeways; so I cut for the office and left them a talking as they went along.

Think sez I, as I was a going along through the Park, arter all, human natur is purty much the same in all places. I don't see as there's much difference between our gals there in Weathersfield, that wear calico frocks and straw bonnets, and these York tippies that go out all furbelowed off in their silks and satins. They are six of one and half a dozen of t'other the world over. If it hadn't been for that are Count I should not have been much at a loss to know how to take Miss Miles. When a gal begins to talk down her throat, and fingers her muff as she did, it's a purty sure symptom that there'll be a change of weather in her heart afore long, but somehow that tarnal Count, consarn him, put me all out on my natural reckoning. But who cares? sez I to myself. I'll bet a cookey if there warn't but two men in the world, and them were that darned feller and Jonathan Slick, and she'd got to marry one or t'other, she wouldn't be long a making up her mind whether to take a chap for what he's got in his head or for the hair that grows outside on it; for a gal with half an eye might see that when a feller's brains all run to hair, he can't have much sense left.

But when these fellers are so chased after by all the gals, there is no saying what kind of a chance a plain, honest chap like me might have among 'em. But any how, I'll try my luck tomorrow, for if I don't go tu see her I shall be sick abed, that's sartin.

Your loving son,
Jonathan Slick.

LETTER VIII.

The Morning Call—A Coquette's Dressing Room.

Dear Par:

Arly the next morning, I got up and put on my new clothes agin, and sot afore the fire, thinking of eenamost every thing on arth, till the clock struck nine; then I slicked down my hair a leetle, and pulled foot up Broadway agin. I kinder expected every minit that I should meet Miss Miles, as I did yesterday;

out somehow there didn't seem tu be any body a stirring. There warn't a single one of them whiskered chaps in sight, and all the women-folks that I could see, up or down, seemed tu have on nothing but their everyday clothes. I saw tew or three rale homespun, modest-looking young critters, but they warn't dressed up, and some on 'em were a carrying band-boxes and sich things afore them. Once I got allfired wrathy, for a nigger woman stood out on the stun side-walk with a great long brush in her hand, a scrubbing the winders of a big house with it; and jest as I come along, she give the brush a flourish, and sent a hull thunder-shower of dirty water all over my new clothes.

"You etarnal black nigger, you! you'd better look out, and keep your soap-suds for them that wants washing," sez I.

But she hee-he'd out a larfin, and begun tu brush away agin jest as if I hadn't said a word tu her. Think sez I, it wouldn't be jest the thing for any body tu see me a jawing here with a nigger wench, so I may as well grin and bear it, for I don't know of anything that proves a feller a leetle soft in the garret, so much as keeping up a quarrel with a person that is so much beneath him that there aint nothing tu be gained, though you du git the upper hand. So I choked in, and took out my hankercher and wiped off my coat-sleeves, and went along; but it warn't no easy matter tu navigate so as not tu git a second ducking, for every nigger in York seemed to be out a washing winders. I come near slipping up tew or three times, the stuns were so wet afore all the housen. I can tell you what, this going tu make morning calls ain't no joke, especially if a feller happens tu be dressed up. The niggers will sponge his coat for him, if the tailor forgot tu, without charging him for the trouble.

Jest afore I got up tu the great four-story house where Miss Miles lives, I begun to feel sort of anxious agin. Think sez I, what on arth shall I say tu her when I du get there? So I kept a thinking over a capital leetle speech that I meant tu make. I'd read in story-books about lovers that always went down on their knees when they talked soft sodder to sich stuck-up gals as Miss Miles; but tu save my life, I couldn't make up my mouth to it; the gal must be something more than common flesh and blood that would ever bring Jonathan Slick on his marrow bones,

I'm thinking; so if she calculates that I'm a going to make such a mean coot of myself as that, why she may go to grass for what I care.

Besides, sez I tu myself, how on arth would I kneel down in these new-fashioned trousers, if I wanted tu ever so much; when arter putting one thing and another together, I made up my mind that kneeling down tu the gals must have gone out of fashion here in York when the chaps give up wearing them trousers puffed in at the waistbands. This kinder made my mind easy on that point; so I went on thinking over what I should say tu Miss Miles when I got tu her house.

Now it ain't no ways hard to make first-rate speeches up in a feller's head, when he's a going tu see a gal that he's a beginning tu take a shine arter; but somehow the worst on it all is, a chap al'ers forgets every word on it when he comes where the gal is.

I begun to grow awful uneasy jest afore I got to the house, and my heart sot to beating in my bosom, like the pestle in an old fashioned samp mortar. It seemed to me as if somebody was a looking arter me, and as if they knew that I was going a courting in broad daylight, which was enough to make any decent chap look sheepish that had never thought of making up to the gals only on a Sunday night arter dark, when these things seem to come nat'ral.

Wal, when I got agin the house, I took a squint up to the winders, for I thought mebby Miss Miles would be a looking out; but there warn't nobody to be seen, so I went up the wide marble steps, that looked as white as snow, with a great chunk of marble a curling down each side on 'em, and there I stood stock still, for my heart floundered about so that it eenamost choked me, and if I'd been hung I couldn't a got up pluck to pull the silver knob and make somebody come and let me in; for all tho York people keep their doors fastened in the day time, so that if a feller's in ever so much of a hurry, he's got to stand out doors till a nigger comes to let him in.

By-am-by a black gal stuck her head up from under the steps, as if she was a going tu speak; so I turned my back to the door, and stuck both hands in my pockets and began to whistle, as independent as could be, jest to let her see that I didn't feel anxious to get in. Arter that I went down the steps agin, jest giving a lectle touch of Yankee Doodle, sort of easy, as I walked up and down on the stun walk afore the house, a trying to git up courage. At last a gal come to the door with a tin basin in her hands, and begun to scour the silver knobs so; I jest went right up the steps agin like a house a fire, and sez I to the gal—

"Is Miss Miles tu hum?"

She kinder stared at me, as if she was a going to ask what I wanted, but I warn't a going to stand there a talking to her, so I jest pushed ahead, and went into the entry way. There warn't nobody there, but one of the mahogany doors that opened on one side was wide open, and I went in.

If any thing, the two great rooms was more harnsome than them at Cousin Beebe's: the footstools and the settees and the chairs were all kivered with shiny red velvet, figgered off like all natur; but they stood about over the carpet every which way. Two or three little stun tables stood out in the middle of the room; one on 'em was kivered with decanters and wine glasses, and some of the books lay all kivered with gold, a glittering and shining on the carpet. The grates were all lined with solid silver, but there warn't a spark of fire in either on 'em yit, and the ashes lay all scattered out over the stun hearths as thick as could be. A part of the great silk winder curtains were hitched up, and the rest on 'em fell clear down to the floor over the winders, till the sunshine that come a pouring through them looked as light and red as a hundred glasses full of currant wine. Thinks I, what on arth has become of all the folks? One would think that they hadn't eat breakfast yit, by the looks of things; yit that couldn't be, for by that time it was eenamost ten o'clock, and any body that has the least idee of gitting a living won't wait arter six for his breakfast.

Wal, arter wandering about the rooms a good while, I went into the entry way agin; by that time the gal that I'd seen at the door had got up on a chair, and was a hauling down a great round glass thing, which was hung by a sort of chain up to the ruff of the entry. When she see me a coming out of the two rooms, she yelled out as if she didn't know that I was there afore.

"What do you want here?" sez she, as imperdent as could be.

"Hold your tarnal yop, you critter you," sez I, "and jest tell me where Miss Miles is; I've come to make her a morning call."

The gal seemed a leetle mortified by that, and sez she to a leetle stuck up cuffy boy that cum up stairs jest then, "Here's a gentleman wants to see Miss Miles—is she up yet?"

Wal, now, think sez I, if this York aint the beatumest place that ever I did see —there aint a nigger in it but what's a poking fun at you or a throwing water or some tarnal thing or another. I wonder if these leetle coots think I'm soft enough to believe that an honest, harnsome gal like Miss Miles, lies abed till ten o'clock. They don't stuff me up that way, any how, if I did come from the country.

"What name shall I take up?" sez the teinty cuffy, a bowing.

"Oh, I haint parlic'lar," sez I; "you may take up any yor like best—but I wish you'd jest tell me where she is, for I begin to feel eenamost tuckered out, a walking and a standing round here."

The leetle cuffy looked at the gal, and then they both begun to giggle and tee-hee like any thing.

"Look a here, you damination copper colored image you," sez I to the nigger, "jest you step up this minit if you don't want to git an allfired thrashing!"

The poor leetle varmint looked scared out of a year's growth, and sez he, as humble as could be, "Who shall I say wants to see Miss Miles?"

"Never you mind that," sez I, "go ahead, and I guess she won't be long a finding out."

With that the nigger went up stairs, and I arter him full chisel; he looked round as if he wanted to say something jest as he stopped by a door in the upper entry way; but I told him to go ahead and hold his yop, for I warn't a going to wait any longer. So he rapped at the door and somebody said, "Come in." My heart riz in my throat, for I knew whose voice it was, and I begun to feel as if I'd pitched head for'ard into a mill dam. The cuffy opened the door, and sez he, "Ma'am here's a gentleman that would come up."

I heard somebody give a leetle scream, and with that I jest

pushed the nigger out of the way, and sez I, "Miss Miles, how du you du?"

I sniggers, if I didn't rAly pity the poor gal, she looked so struck up in a heap; but what on arth made her act so I couldn't tell at fust, for I felt kinder streaked as if I'd done something that wasn't exactly right, though I couldn't think what, and it was as much as a minit afore I looked right in her face. But jest as I lifted up my head, and drew up my foot, arter making one of my fust cut bows, she stood jest afore me. By the living hokey, I never was so struck up in my born days! You know what I've told you about Miss Miles, about her plump round form, her red lips, and her rosy cheeks. Well, I'll be darned if there was one of them left—I shouldn't have known her no more than nothing. if it hadn't been for her eyes and the way she spoke. Her neck and for'ard that always looked so white and harnsome, when I see her at Cousin Mary's, and in Broadway, was as yaller as a safron bag. There warn't the least mite of red in her face, and her hair was all frizzley, and done up in a leetle bunch, about as big as a hen's egg behind! She had on a great loose awk'ard-looking gown, that made her seem twice as chunked as she used to, and that looked more like a man's shirt cut long and ruffled round than any thing else. It warn't any too clean neither, and both her leetle shoes were down to the heel.

There I stood a looking at her with all the eyes in my head— my foot was drawed up tight, and my arms were a hanging straight down, jest as they swung back arter I'd made my bow. I kinder seemed tu feel that my mouth was open a leetle, and that I was a staring at her harder than was manners for me. But if you'd a given me the best farm in all Weathersfield, I couldn't have helped it, I was so struck up in a heap at seeing her in sich a fix. I guess it was as much as two minits afore either on us said a word; and, at last, Miss Miles turned to the nigger as savage as a meataxe, and, sez she,

"Why didn't you show Mr. Slick into the drawing room?"

"Oh, don't seem to mind it," sez I a walking into the room, and a setting down on a chair with my hat between my knees, I'd jest as livs set up here as any where."

She looked as if she'd burst right out a crying, but at last she sot down and tried to act as if she was glad to see me. She begun to make excuses about herself and the room, and said she wasn't very well that morning, that she took a new book, and sot down jest as she was to read it.

"Oh," sez I, "don't make no excuses; it aint the fust time that I've ketched a gal in the suds. Marm used to say that she never looked worse than common that somebody wasn't sartin to drop in."

"Will you excuse me one instant, Mr, Slick," sez she, a minit arter I'd said this, and a looking down on her awk'ard dress, as if she couldn't help but feel streaked yit.

"Sartinly," sez I; "don't make no stranger of me."

With that, she opened the door and went into a room close by. I jest got a good peak into it as she went through the door, and an allfired harnsome room it was. There was a great mahogany bedstead a standing in the middle, with a high goose feather bed on it, kivered all over with a white quilt and great square pillows all ruffled off, and the winder curtains were part white and part sort of indigo blue. I couldn't git a chance to see what else there was, she shut the door so quick. "By gracious," sez I to myself, arter she went out, "who on arth would ever have thought that Miss Miles was so old. When I saw her yesterday, I'd a took my Bible oath that she warn't more than eighteen, but now I'll be choked if she don't look as ancient as the hills. If ever she sees thirty agin she'll have to turn like a crab and walk backwards five or six years." What puzzled me most was how in creation she contrived to look so young—but it warn't a great while afore I made it out as clear as one of Deacon Sykes' exhortations. Arter she'd gone out I jest got up and took a sort of survey of the room; everything was t'other eend up, helter skelter in it; there was no eend to the finery and harnsome furniture, but it don't make much odds how extravagant one is a laying out money if things aint kept neat and snug in their places. The more things cost, the more it seems to hurt a feller's feelings to see them flung about topsy turvy, as they were in that room. I ruther think she didn't have her company up there very often—but a gal that's got a good bringing up will be jest as particular about the place she keeps for herself, and which company never sees, as if it was likely to be seen every day of her life.

I begun tu be allfired glad that I didn't ask her to have me yesterday, for if she'd been as young as she seemed tu be, and as harnsome as an angel, I wouldn't a had her arter seeing that room of her'n. A pocket hankercher, worked and sprigged, and ruffled off with lace, was a lying on the settee, but it was all grimmed over with dirt, and looked as if it would a gin any thing for a sight of the wash tub. The carpet was as soft and thick as could be, and it was all kivered over with bunches of posies as nat'ral as life; but there was a great grease spot close by the fire, where somebody had upsot a lamp, and all around the edges and in the corners it looked as if it hadn't been swept for ever so long. A chest of drawers, solid, shiny mahogany—with a great looking-glass, swung between two pieces of mahogany on the top, stood on one side of the room, and there, a hanging over the edge on 'em, as true as I live, were the long, harnsome curls that I'd seen on Miss Miles when she was tu cousin Mary's party! Wal, think sez I, if this don't take the rag off the bush! What du you think I saw next? A glass tumbler about half full of water, with three nice, leetle, white teeth a lying in the bottom on it! I couldn't help but give a leetle whistle when I saw them. Think sez I, it's jest as like as not that Miss Miles wont pucker up her mouth and smile, quite so much this morning as she did yesterday, any how.

There were two leetle china cups with the kivers a lying down by them; one was filled with white stuff, kinder like flour, only ruther more gritty, and t'other was full of something that looked as much like rose leaves ground down to powder as anything. A leetle chunk of cotton wool was stuck into it, but what on arth it was for, I couldn't make out. There were two or three silk cushions chuck full of pins, on the drawers, and there was no eend tu the leetle glass bottles all sprigged off with gold, a lying round on the mantle-shelf, as well as on the tables and the chest of drawers.

In one corner of the room there stood a great looking-glass, a swinging between two leetle posts cut out of mahogany, and right over it two silk frocks were tumbled up together. I begun to finger them a beetle, for somehow I felt curious tu know how the tarnal cunning critter contrived tu make herself look so plump and round. It didn't want much cyphering tu find her out. The tops of her frocks, both on 'em, were all stuffed full of something soft that made them stand out as nat'ral as life. I hadn't but jest time tu drop the frock and set down agin—looking as innocent as if butter wouldn't melt in my mouth—when Miss Miles come back agin. She'd put on another frock, all ruffled off, and somehow or other, had fixed up her hair so as to look ruther more ship shape; but she hadn't had time to put herself all together, though her face did look a leetle whiter than it did when I fust went in. There warnt a bit of a hump on her back, and she was nat'ral all the way round!

I felt ruther uneasy, for, think sez I, it's jest as like as not she'll expect me to talk over a leetle soft sodder with her, as I did yesterday; but I'll be darned if it don't make me sick tu think on it. I hitched about on my chair, and I looked at every thing in the room but her, then I took up my hat and begun to balance it on my two fore fingers, and at last sez I—

"Wal, Miss Miles, I s'pose I may as well be a jogging."

"Don't be in a hurry," sez she, a trying tu smile, but without opening her lips a bit, "I hope you won't make strangers of us."

I let my hat drop, and picked it up again.

"What book was that that you've been a reading?" sez I, determined tu say something.

"Oh, that's the Countess of Blessington's last work," sez she; "it's a charming book. Do you like her writings, Mr. Slick?"

"Wal, I don't know," sez I; "I never read any of her books, but it kinder strikes me that she aint no great shakes herself, anyhow."

"Oh, you shouldn't be censorious, Mr. Slick," sez she. "You know Mr. Willis visited her and was delighted."

"Wal, now," sez I, "it's my opinion that Mr. N. P. Willis couldn't be over hard to please, if a woman only had a title to her name; but I wonder how on arth he contrived tu git so thick with the quality over there in England. I ruther think I shall go over there and try my luck one of these days, in his way, they seem to be so taken up with us Yankees, but arter all if a feller has to go over England to let them lords and editors puff him, afore anybody will take notice on him, he'd better take tu some other bisness. There ain't a man in all this country that ever wrote more genuine things than that chap did when he was a leetle shaver in Yale College, and yet nobody would believe a word on't till he went off to England. Now it's my opinion that he never wrote anything arter he went off, half so much to his credit as he did afore, and when he came here to York from about our parts, jest as I've come now, if he didn't desarve tu be treated well then, why he don't now, that's sartin. But I used to know him down East, and it's my opinion that he's a first rate, hull-hearted feller, and a rale ginuine poet tu boot! But I swanny! Miss Miles, I must be a going, you hain't no idea how much I've got to du!"

With that I got up and made a bow. She made a curchy, and, sez she, "Mr. Slick, call agin, we shall always be glad to see you."

"Sartinly," sez I; so I made another bow and cut stick down stairs into the open street. But if Miss Miles ever ketches me on her premises again, she'll ketch a weasel asleep. That Count may marry her—what there is left of her—and go to grass, for what I care.

Your loving son,
JONATHAN SLICK.

LETTER IX.

A New York Parvenu.—Jonathan's Account of his Cousin Jason Slick, and how Jason was too lazy to work, and got rich on soft sodder.—The dinner of a Connecticut Coaster.—A New York Coat of Arms, lions couchant and levant.—Yankee Ancestry.—The way a Yankee speculates, and gets up States, Railroads and Banks, by soft sodder.

DEAR PAR:

It is eenamost twelve o'clock jest arter New Years, and here I be as wide awake as a night hawk, and a feeling purty considerably rily in the upper story. So I believe it'll be about the best thing I can du tu clap down and tell you all about New Year's Day here in York.

But first I want tu tell you something about all the trials and troubles that I've had tu go through since I wrote my last letter —I don't believe there ever was a human critter so chased arter as I've been. They talk about Cherry street not being fashionable, but I'll be darned if I believe there's a more genteel street in the city. It's the folks that live in a place that make it genteel or not, and if Cherry street aint at the top of the mark afore many more weeks, it'll be because I move my office out or it, for there's no eend to the great shiny carriages that come down and stop afore my door, eenamost every hour in the day. It raly does look funny enough to see great pussey fellers, as big as the side of the house, a sitting in them things all bolstered up with cushions and kivered over with skins, like a baby shut up in a go-cart afore it begins tu run alone.

T'other day there was one of these fat chaps come into my office, and sot out tu make me believe that he was a sort of a relation of mine. I didn't feel jest right, for since I begun to print my letters in the Express it beats all natur how many relations, that I never heard on afore, have been a trying tu scrape an acquaintance with me. Wal, after a good deal of beating about the bush, this chap at last made out purty tolerably clear that he was a kind of a great toe cousin of our'n, and that he was born and brought up in Weathersfield. He come his soft sodder over me mighty smooth, and had a good deal to say about how much he thought of us all, and how fond he'd been of Sam and me. I wish you could a seen how he pussed out his mouth and breathed through his nose, and what a heap of pomposity he put on when he was a talking. He acted jest like our old turkey gobler, when he goes training the young turkeys round the barnyard, with his wings feathered out and his tail spread. Wal, arter talking all kinds of rigmarole for about an hour, he begun to tell how hard it was for a young man tu start in the world, and git along without somebody tu give him a push up the hill, and that it didn't make much odds how much genius a man had, or how smart he was, if he hadn't some rich and influential friend tu back him up.

"Now," sez he, "cousin Slick," and you can't think how easy he seemed tu call me cousin; "you've done purty well since you come to York, considering that you hadn't nobody to help you along but Mr. Beebe; but you must git a peg higher yit; we must introduce you among the aristocracy."

"The what?" sez I.

"The aristocracy," sez he agin, strutting back, and poking one hand down into his trousers' pocket, as if he was a going tu take something out.

Wal, think sez I, I s'pose arter he's fumbled about long enough, he'll show me what aristocracy is, if he carries it about in his pocket like the rest on 'em; but he only took out a piece of pinted gold, and begun to poke it between his teeth; and arter he'd got through, he made out tu finish what he was a saying.

"Now," sez he, "I think I've seen Mr. Beebe at the New England dinner, and at one or two places of that sort where one meets almost every body, and for a merchant that hasn't made enough to leave off business, I dare say he's a very respectable sort of a man, but he don't exactly belong tu the—the; that is, tu the class—who—which I mean tu take you inter, Mr. Slick; a class that claim some standing from their ancestors—men of family, that can be traced back like our's, cousin."

"Yes," sez I, sort o' pleased, "I believe we never had many relations tu be ashamed on. Par always used to say that grandpa Slick could make about the harnsomest pair of cow-hide boots of any feller in Weathersfield; and as for uncle Josh, I'd be darned if ever I saw his equal at shoeing a hos. They were prime old chaps both on 'em—rale peelers, I can tell you. Now, come tu think on it, there was one lazy coot of a feller that never would work for a living; but he went off when I was a little shaver, and our folks don't know what became of him. He warn't much credit to us, that's a fact."

"I don't know what on arth made my pussey cousin get so fedgety all tu once, but he begun to hitch about in his chair, and turned as red as a winter apple; and, sez he—

"Cousin Slick, this isn't the way we gentlemen prove that we are men of family. If that was the way we did it, there aint many men in the country that would go back two generations without breaking their neck over a lap stone or an anvil. Now I have taken a good deal of pains to trace out our family line, and the only way I could du it was to skip all the mechanics and farmers, jest touch slightly on the merchants, lawyers and ministers, but to dwell purty particularly hard on them that lived high and did nothing; now a days it helps a feller along a good deal if he can count up an author or so; and it was considered something of a feather in a man's cap if any of his relations were sent to Congress a few years ago; but now, since they've got a kicking up a dust every other day in the Capitol, and to spitting fire at each other like dogs and cats, it don't help a man much to claim any of them for connexions except here and there one that has got decency enough to be ashamed of the rest. I begin to be glad that none of our family ever got into politics much; but step to the door cousin Slick, and I'll show you the coat-of-arms that I've got on my carriage."

"Wal," sez I, "I don't care if I du, though it comes kinder tough to leave the stove this cold day." With that I tipped down my chair, and took my feet off from the stove and went to the door. By gracious! but he had a smasher of a coach standing there. It glistened and shone in the sun like a house afire. A great strapping nigger sot on a kind of double chair with a low narrer back, kivered over with fine brown broadcloth, all fringed and tossled off like any thing—and a great bear skin was hauled up over his legs, all scolloped off with red cloth and stuck over with coons' tails. The horses beat all live critters I ever did see; they were as black as crows, and I couldn't say which glistened the most, their tarnal smooth coots, or the harness put over them. They were all kivered over and sot out with silver. The horses had great yaller roses stuck on the sides of their heads, like a gal when she's dressed up for a party. My pussey cousin, he opened the door, and sez he,

"Look a here, cousin, haint this purty well got up?"

I looked inside, and there was a leetle sort of a room about big enough for cousin Beebe to put his swarry in, if he wanted to carry it about with him. It was all lined off and stuck full of cushions, and tossled and fringed like a curtained bed. Tw great spotted skins lay tumbled up in the bottom, and there were leetle glass doors with steps to them on both sides; it raly was harnsome enough to make a feller's eyes feel snow-blind.

"Wal," sez I, a looking at my pussey cousin; "this does about take the shine off eenamost all the coaches that ever stopped to my office—and there's been a grist on 'em, I cap tell you, and some with tarnal handsome ladies in them too."

"Yes," sez he, sort of interrupting what I was going to say; "but you haint a looking at the coat of arms—that is what I want you to see."

"Wal," sez I, a giving the nigger a purty general survey, that sot back of the horses dressed up in sort of regimentals, all fine-fied off with buttons and yaller cloth; "The coat is well enough—I don't see much to find fault with in it, though to own the truth, Captin Wolf, of the Weathersfield Independent Company, had a training coat that beats it all tu nothing. As for the critter's arms, niggers may be different to white people in that way, but I don't see much odds—mebby you mean this other chap's, and his are long enough, that's a fact."

With that I jest took a good squint at a great tall shote of a feller, with arms like a pair of flails hung up arter threshing. He was a standing up back of the coach, and a hanging on to a couple of great tossels fastened to it, as independent as a monkey in a show. His coat and trousers were just like the nigger's, and he had a great wide band of gold stuff round his hat! my pussey cousin only shook his head when I looked at the chap. The nigger twisted his neck round, and the tall varmint stuck his'n up, and they begun to grin and tee hee at each other over the coach.

"See here, this is what I mean," sez my cousin; and his fat cheek begun to grow red with the cold or something. With that he put his finger on a picter, all sprigged out with gold that was figgered on the door, and sez he, "this is the coat and arms."

"Wal," sez I, "I've seen a good many picters, but I never heard them called by that name afore. I s'pose this is some York notion that you've picked up, aint it?"

"It's the ginuine thing," sez he, "and I paid a deal of money 'or it, I can tell you."

"Wal," sez I, a looking at the consarn purty sharp; "them two critters a lying down there cut a considerable of a dash, that's a fact; but the rooster on the top, that are beats all. It's so nat'ral, it seems to me as if I could hear it cockadoodledoo right out."

"Yes," sez my cousin. "that is well done, aint it? But I see you don't exactly comprehend the science of heraldry. Now all these things mean something."

"You don't say so!" sez I.

"These are lions couchant," sez he, a pinting tu the wild criuters.

"You don't say so!" sez I agin; "I've seen a good many lions in the shows that travel through Weathersfield, but I never saw a croushong afore. They look purty much alike, don't they though?"

With that the two varmints stuck up at each eend of the carriage begun tu tee hee agin, and my pussey cousin, sez he, "Mr. Slick, supposing we go in."

"Wal," sez I, "but if you'd jest as lives, I should kinder like tu know what the rooster means afore we go."

"Can't you guess what part of the Slick family that belongs to?" sez he, a strutting up and rubbing his hands together as proud as could be.

"Wal," sez I, "I don't know, without it belongs to Aunt Lydia—par's old maid of a sister; she sartinly did beat all natur at raising chickens. You never heard of an egg turning out rotten, or a duck gitting drowned, on her premises."

With that the two chaps giggled right out, and stuck their fists into their darn'd great tatur-traps as if they felt a cold; and my pussey cousin, sez he, "it's a gitting cold—less go in."

"Wal," sez I, "I don't care if we du; but I tell you what, it them two chaps don't jest hush up their yop, I'll give them both an allfired thrashing—I will, by gosh!"

I ruther guess the two mean critters hauled in their horns a few at this; and arter I'd gin them both a purty savage look, we went into the office agin.

"Now," sez my pussey consin, jest as soon as we'd both sot down agin, "Cousin Slick, I've found you out, and I mean to du something for you—something harnsome, you may depend on't. Jest you call up to my house next New Year's day, and git acquainted with my folks, and arter that you needn't be consarned about anything. I'm purty well known here in the city, and *my* relation can hold up his head almost anywhere, I should think! I was down tu the Astor House t'other day," sez he, a stopping to git breath and stretching both his legs out straight, while he stuck both hands in his pockets, mighty big, "and there was that foreign Count and Miss Miles's brother running on about you, and swearing that they'd skin you alive the first time they caught you in Broadway; but I went up tu them, and sez I, 'that young gentleman is a near relation of mine, and anything you say agin him, I take tu myself.' You can't think, cousin Jonathan, what an impression it made! So you needn't have the least fear of what they can du while I stand by you—they know me."

With that, my pussey cousin got up—and arter he'd shook hands with me, he went off, carriage and all. I say, par, I wish I could give you some idee of him. Did you ever see a great spotted toad a swelling under a harrer, or a turkey gobbler jest afore thanksgiving?

I say nothing; but didn't I larf arter he'd gone. The great stuck-up bear, with his family, and his hens and roosters—he go to grass.

Wal, jest as soon as my pussey cousin had cleared out, I put on my hat, and streaked it down to Peck slip, for Captin Doolittle has jest put in agin with another load of garden sarce; and think sez I, mebby he can tell me something about this chap, for he knows eenamost everybody that ever lived anywhere about Weathersfield.

The Captin had jest sot down to dinner, and was a digging away like all natur, at a hunk of cold pork and a raw onion; a mug of something hot stood on the locker afore him, and he looked like live, I can tell you.

"Wal, Jonathan," sez he, a looking kinder skewing at my new trousers, "Wont you set by and take a bite?"

"Wal," sez I, "I shoudn't mind if I did, but to-morrow is New Year's, and I've got tu go and see a hull heap of these York gals, and I'm afeard my breath will smell of the onions."

I wish you could a seen how Captin Doolittle stared, as he stuck his face close up tu mine, giving his jack-knife a grip, he struck the butt eend of it down on the locker, and sez he,

"Jonathan, they're a spiling you down here in York, they be, by hokey! Go hum, I tell you, and marry Judy White—she knows what's what, and I can tell you these York gals that turn up their noses at the smell of onions, can't have decent bringing up any how. They've sot you agin onions already, and it wont be a great while afore you'll turn agin your own relations."

"Now," sez I, "Captain Doolittle, don't say that are, it makes ne feel bad, and I don't desarve it. A feller that will let money, or a stuck up name, or the handsomest gal that ever trod shoe .eather set him agin his own father and mother, desarves tu be kicked tu death by grasshoppers."

This seemed to sort of mollify the captin, but he stripped the peel off another onion mighty wrothy, and arter a minit sez he. "Wal, Jonathan, I'm glad to hear that you've got some of your old notions left, but I always make a pint not to talk when I'm a eating, so if you won't set by, why just keep a stiff jaw while I stow away another slice of pork and this piece of onion, and then I'm the man for you."

With that he went to cutting off a chunk of pork and a chunk of onion to hand about, till it fairly made my eyes water to see him crunch them down. Arter a while he wiped his jack-knife on his cuff, shut it tew with a jerk, and put it in his trousers' pocket; then he took a pull at the mug, and arter he'd got a long nine purty well a going, he stretched out his legs, and sez he:

"Wal, Jonathan, what did you come for, if you didn't want nothing to eat?"

With that I sot down and told him all about my pussey cousin. I could see that the critter had heard on him afore by the way he twisted his mouth around about the long nine; but when I told him about the carriage and rooster and so on, he jest took and gave the long nine a fling, clapped his thumb agin the side of his nose, and winking one eye, make his fingers twinkle up and down for as much as a minit without saying a word; arter a while he asked the critter's name, and when I told him, he jump ed up, cut a pigeon wing over the locker, and stopping right afore me, winked t'other eye, and sez he—

"Look a here, Jonathan, didn't your par never tell you about Jase Slick, the great lazy coon, that got married and went off West, because he was so allfired lazy that he couldn't git a living like other folks? Jest let me cool off a leetle, and I'll tell you all about him."

With that the Captin brushed away the onion skins and we sot down together on the locker, and sez he—"Mebby your par never told you what an etarnal lazy shote Jase was, but he did beat all natur for doing nothing but swop jack-knives and pitch coppers. He was a tickler though at trapping mushrats and shooting foxes, and he use to send the skins down here to York. Now it aint common that you'll find a lazy shack of a feller very tight about money, but Jase was as close as the bark of a tree; he'd a skinned a musketoe any day for the hide and taller. I don't believe the critter ever stood treat in his hull life; I don't, by gracious.

"Wal, arter all, he warn't a bad hearted feller; but when he see that all the gals turned up their noses at him, and didn't give him invites to their quiltings and so on, he coaxed me to let him work his passage down here to York. He used to send his skins by me, and so I kinder felt for him, and kept track on him a good while arter he got here. He did purty tolerably well at first, considering who it was—he bought a hand-cart, and took people's trunks and sich things up from the steamboats and sloops that put into Peck slip; but there was too much work about that to suit him; so he got somebody to lend him a little money and sot up a rum shop close by the slip.

"Arter that," sez the Captin, a picking up his long nine and a lighting it, "arter that I kinder lost track on him, but somebody told me that he'd swopped off his stock and gone out West. Wal, two years go by purty quick, you know, Jonathan—or if you don't know, you will, when you git to be as old as I am—and I couldn't but jest believe it was so long since I'd seen the critter, when I met him smash in the face one day when I was a scooting up Wall-street, to get specie for a five dollar bill. Gracious me! how he was a strutting up the side-walk—didn't he cut a swarth—with his shiney black coat and the bunch of golden seals a hanging down from his watch fob! He didn't seem to know me at fust, but I went right straight up to him and sez I—

"'Wal, Jase, how do you do?' I never—how he did look! First he kinder held out his hand a leetle, and then he hauled it back agin, and, sez he, 'how do you du, sir?' but he seemed to be all in a twitter. I didn't seem to mind it, but I stuck my hands in my pockets jest as you do, Jonathan, there in your picters—and sez I—

"'Tough and hearty as ever. How does the world use you about these times?'

"It was as much as I could du to keep from larfin right out, to see the etarnal pussey critter skew his head round and look at the stream of men that was a going up and down on each side of the way, as if he was afraid that some on 'em would see us, the mean sneaking coot! Arter a minit he sez, sez he, 'Captin, I'm in a hurry now, but I s'pose you can be found in the old place. Good morning.'

"With that he jest put both hands under his coat tail, and tilting it up a leetle, went sailing along up the side-walk like a prize hog jest afore killing time. I snorted right out all I could du to help it. Then I bent down my knees a leetle, and stuck my hands down hard in both pockets, and I ruther guess the whistle I sent arter him made all the folks stare a few. It wasn't good manners, but I sarved him right. Jonathan, I'd been a friend to the critter when he wanted one bad enough, and any man on arth that's ashamed of his acquaintances because he's got a peg above them in the way of money is a coward and a mean shote,—there's no two ways about that.

"Wal, arter seeing Jase in the street so stuck up, I jest inquired a little about him, what he'd been a doing and so on; and arter a while, I found out what made him so mighty obstroporous. You see he'd found out it warn't so easy tu git a living in York without doing some kind of work, so he absquatelated, as they say down here—but I don't think that's a ginuine word—and went off West.

"There he mushquashed round in the woods till he got tired

of that kind of fun, and then he squat down on a section of wild land, cogitating a way tu git a living without grubbing for it. Arter a while he went round to all the places that had any people to brag on, and put up to the taverns, and told every body he met there about the spot where his land lay—what capital land it was—what good water and allfired heavy timber. He sent here tu York and got him a map all pictured out chuck full of water privileges and all sorts of things, till he raly made the people believe that he'd found the very spot where the millinium was a going tu begin; a place where every holler tree was stuck full of honey comb, where the wild cats went pouring about like so many rabbits, and the hen hawks cum down as kind as could be to tu help the hens feed their little chickens.

"Wal, it warn't long afore his soft sodder begun to work among the greenhorns like yeast in a kneading trough full of dough. Jonathan, if you ever see a flock of sheep shut up in a paster, you know something worth while about human natur. The minit one takes it into his head to clear the stun wall for another lot, the others all foller hilter skilter, as if the old Harry had kicked them on eend. Your Cousin Jase knew a thing or two about the natur of mankind—he got the first sheep to make a jump, and, hurra! it warn't no time before his section was all cut up into town lots, and grist mills whirling three stuns, wherever there was a quart of water tu make them go; and there was no eend to the corduroy roads and log bridges, and great kivered waggons, chuck full of women and children and other housen stuff, with baskets and brass kittles a hanging on behind, that travelled over them eenamost from one year tu another. When folks began tu wonder what on arth he'd du next, the critter got his territory transmogrified into a State, and then he sot railroads a twistyfying every which way all through his lands; and that made things rise in value like a toad stool in a hot night.

"By the living hokey, the critter wasn't content with this, but he got another kink into his head that did beat all. One way or t'other, I don't know how, he got all his land and railroads and so on, worked up into pieces of paper that they call scrip; he bundled them all into his great coat pocket and come down to

York again. And in less than no time he had the scrip all cut up into these red-backed bills with picters on 'em, that they offer here in York for money—then he sot up a bank on his own hook, where he keeps a making money hand over fist. He has a good chance, I tell you, for he owns all in the bank; so he's President, Cashier, and everything else, all himself, and arter all his laziness, he's worth an allfired grist of money considering how he got it."

I swanny, I couldn't hardly keep still while Captin Doolittle was a talking. I felt all over in a twitter, and my mouth would keep a sort of open with thinking so eager of what he was a saying. The minit he'd done I jumped up and hollered right out—

"Hurra," sez I, "if that aint Yankee all over. I haint the least doubt now but the critter is jest what he says he is—Slick to the back bone. Do you s'pose there is any animal on arth besides a full-blooded Connecticut Yankee that would have gone that way to get rich—all soft sodder and no work? I tell you what it is, captin, I'm raly proud tu own the critter. He's done some good in his day and generation, if he is so stuck up; for it aint in the natur of things for a feller to git rich himself without making a good many others better off. To help himself a great deal a chap *must* help others a little, that's my notion."

"Yes," sez the captin, "but it's an etarnal shame for these chaps tu curl up their noses at honest men."

"Jest so," says I.

With that I put on my hat, and was jest a going to cut stick—but Captin Doolittle, sez he—

"Look a here, Jonathan, if I was you, I'd make this chap pay over a little of his chink, or else I wouldn't ride about with him—I wouldn't, by gracious! He's tickled tu death tu get hold of a chap like you to brag on; for now that he's got rich, you haint no idee how anxious he is to make people think he knows something and always did. He talks about his aristocracy. The men of genius and talons make the real aristocracy in this country, and he's in hopes of getting among 'em by claiming relationship with you because you write for the papers. Supposing you ask him to lend you a couple of thousand dollars."

"No," sez I, "i'll be darned if I du. If I can't cut my own fodder I'll go hum agin."

"Wal," sez the Captin, "mebby you can git him tu help you print your letters in a book. Your par would be tickled tu death if you could print a book like that Sam writ."

"Wal," sez I, sort o' proud, "there needn't be no hurry about that are; but if I du print one, and it can't pay its own expenses and a leetle over, it may go tu grass!"

With that I bid Captin Doolittle good-bye, and made tracks for my office agin.

LETTER X.

New-Year's Calls—A real Yankee's New-Year's Treat of Dough-nuts and Cider—Jonathan's ideas of the real difference between a real lady's House and Furniture and the House of a stuck-up Parvenu—Jonathan's ideas of Love and Ladies.

Dear Par:

I made a leetle inquiry about how people did a New Year's Day, and found out that it was the fashion for the wimmen tu stand treat that day, to set out things, and invite everybody that come tu take a bite. So arly in the morning I put a clean white towel on the leetle table in my office. Then I went into the cubby house room, where I keep my new clothes and kindling wood, besides my tooth brush and sich things as I don't want to use every day, and I drew a quart mug of that outrageous good cider, that you sent me by Captin Doolittle. I guess I looked like live when I went out agin, with the mug brimming over in one hand, and the pillow-case stuffed full of dough-nuts, that marm sent me t'other day—besides the hunk of cheese, and the lot of baked sweet apples, tucked under t'other arm. I heaped up a pile of the dough-nuts on one corner of the table, and sot the apple-box on the other, an made room for the cheese and the cider in the middle; and it raly made me feel sort of bad because marm couldn't see how nice I'd fixed it all. Think sez I, there wont be many people in York that'll set a better treat afore their visiters than this I reckon, any how, and as marm aint here I'll stand treat to every body that comes in for her sake.

Wal, who should be the fust critter that come in but cousin John Beebe, tu see what I was a going tu du with myself all day. Arter I'd sot him a chair by the stove, I went up to the table, and sez I,

"Cousin John supposing we take a drink; it's an allfired cold day, and you look as if you couldn't stand it." My gracious, but didn't his eyes snap when he saw what I'd got. I mixed the cider up, purty hot with ginger, and then I sot it on the stove, and kept a stirring on it up with a little ivory thing that a purty gal sent me tu fold my letters with; it begun to foam and sparkle like anything; then I took a sip jest to try it, and handed the mug over to cousin John.

"Here," sez I, "take a swaller; it aint like the pesky stuff you give me when I eat dinner up to your house. Instid of kicking up a dust in your upper story, it goes tu the right spot tu once, and makes a feller feel prime all over in a giffy." I ruther seem to think that cousin John warn't much afeard of the mug anyhow; he gave a sneezer of a pull tu it, and then his eyes begun to glisten, and, sez he—

"I'm beat, Jonathan, if this aint prime; where on arth did you find it? I've sarched from one eend of York tu t'other for it a dozen times, but never made out tu get a drop yit." With that he sot into it agin like all natur. "I declare," sez he, agin, choaking off long enough tu ketch his breath, "this does taste nat'ral."

"Aint it the rale critter?" sez I, a bending for'ard and rubbing both hands together a leetle easy. "It eenamost make me humsick when I first tasted on it, it put me so in mind of Weathersfield. Par sent me a whole cag on it, by Capt. Doolittle."

"Then it *did* come from the old humstid?" sez he, a eying the mug agin—"I must drink a leetle more, for the sake of them that sent it." With that, he jest finished up the mug; and when he sot it down, he drew a long breath, and sez he agin, "that's prime, Jonathan."

"Aint it," sez I, starting off tu fill up the mug agin, for it tickled me tu see how he took tu the drink, and how much he made himself tu hum in my office. When I cum out of the leetle room agin, John he looked sort of eager at the jug, and then at the eatables laid out so tempting.

"I declare," sez he, "I begin tu feel as I use tu when we were boys, Jonathan." With that I sot the table between us, and the way we laid into the provinder was a compliment to marm. Arter cousin Beebe had eat ten of the doughnuts, and a hunk of cheese as big as your fist, he stopt short, and sez he—

"Cousin, this wont du; if we keep on eating as much as we want, we shan't find room for all the eatables and drinkables that the folks will give us to-day, when we make our calls."

"Look a here, cousin Beebe," sez I, kinder anxious, "you know I'm a sort of a greenhorn about New Year's, for we don't have no sich things over amongst us. Supposing you jest tell me how they act and so on. I don't want tu make a coot of myself; and that pussey cousin of mine is a coming tu take me round in his carriage, where I suppose he means tu stick me up like a swarry for folks tu look at; and if I don't du everything according to gunter, he'll be turning red and fussing about like an old hen that's got ducks for chickens. What on arth shall I say to the gals, and what will they expect me to du?"

Cousin Beebe he sot still a minit, kinder nibbling away at the end of a dough-nut, for he seemed mortal loth to choke off, and at last sez he—

"When you come tu a house where you want tu call, jest go into the room where the ladies will be a waiting tu see folks, and arter a while they'll ask you to take some refreshments: with that they'll go up tu a table where there's wine and so on, if they hain't teetotalists, and if they be——"

"It don't make no odds tu tell me how *they* act," sez I, "for I don't call on anybody that sets up to be wiser than our Savior; he turned water into wine, and when I set up tu be better than him, I'll turn up my nose at it, but not afore. I wish you could a heard par argufy that question with the ministers. I rather guess——"

Here cousin Beebe sot in, and sez he, "Well, jest fill up a glass for the lady about half full, not a drop more, then pour out a glass for yourself——"

"What, full?" sez I.

"Sartinly," sez he.

"Wal," sez I, "that seems kinder hoggish tu give yourself more than you du to the lady; I don't seem tu like that."

"It's the fashion," sez he.

"Oh, is it?" sez I; "wal I think as like as not they know how to help themselves arter a feller's gone. I always notice that the gals that are so mighty stuck up as if they couldn't swaller anything but air before folks, stuff like all natur back of the pantry door."

John larfed a leetle as if he agreed with me, and sez he, "Never mind that now, but when you've poured out the wine, jest step back and make a bow, and say, 'The compliments of the season,' or any other interesting thing that you like. A person of your genius should not be at a loss for pleasant sayings—and after that drink off the wine, take a leetle of anything else that is on the table, and go away agin."

"Wal now," sez I, "I can remember what to say well enough, though it does seem to me that there would be a leetle too much soft sodder in the speech, if it warn't made to a lady; but suppose you jest go over the manœuvre about the wine, so that I can git the kink on it, if you hain't no objection."

"Very well," sez he, "remember I'm you, and you are the lady."

"Jest so," sez I.

"Wal," sez he, a taking up the cider mug, "observe me." With that he made a purlite bow, and give another allfired pull at the drink. I see what the critter was at; but think sez I, I ruther think you've had your share of the cider. With that, I put out both hands a leetle easy, and took the mug from his mouth.

"See if I hain't larnt it," sez I, as sober as a deacon; and with that I made him a low bow, and while I was a drinking off the cider, I jest winked one eye over the top of the mug, tu let him see that I was up tu a thing or two. The minit I pulled up, he began tu laugh as good-natured as a kitten; and arter I'd got my breath, I sot in, and we had a good haw-haw right out in the office.

Arter we'd both got sobered down, John he gave me an invite to come up and see Mary, and then he cut stick tu go home and fix for visiting. I hadn't but jest time to run out and git a piece of Injun rubber to clean my yaller gloves with, and begin tu fix up, when my pussey cousin come up the street, hurra boys, carriage and all, arter me. The tall chap let himself down from behind the carriage, and knocked at the door.

"Come in," sez I, a poking round the office arter a pin tu stick my shirt-color together, where the etarnal washerwoman had washed the button off, consarn her!

The feller was dressed up like a Connecticut Major-General, all in yaller and blue, as fine as a fiddle; he kinder grinned a little when he see my table, and that I hadn't got my fix on yet; but when I looked in his face, he choked in, and, sez he, as humble as could be—

"Mr. Slick, my master is a waiting."

"Tell him not tu be in a pucker," sez I, "I ain't quite spruced up yet." With that he went out—I pitched on my clothes in less than no time, stuffed a baked apple and a few dough-nuts into my coat pocket, for fear of accident, and follered arter. There he stood a holding open the glass door, and a set of little steps, all carpeted off, hung down tu the ground ; and there was the fat nigger a twistifying his whip-lash round the horses' heads, as crank as a white man. I jest had time tu see that Jase had got his lions and roosters and crouchants pictered off on the curtain that hung round his seat ; and then I jumped into the carriage as spry as a cricket. The tall chap folded up the steps as quick as marm could undu a cat's cradle, and shet the door tu, and away we went like a house a-fire. I swanny! but these coaches du go over the ground as slick as grease ; it seemed jest like being bolstered up in a rocking-chair! My pussey cousin seemed tu swell up bigger and bigger every minit, when he see how surprised I was with the spring of it ; and, sez he—

"Now, cousin, I'm going tu take you tu see somebody worth knowing, and when they know that you're my relation, they'll take a good deal of notice of you ; so jest put your best foot foremost."

Think sez I, it's looky that I got cousin Beebe tu show me how it's done; but I kept a close lip and said nothing, for it was snapping cold, and a feller's words seemed as if they'd turn tu ice, before he spoke 'em.

The nigger driv like fire and smoke, and it didn't seem no time afore we stopped by a great house clear up town, and the tall shote opened the door and undid the steps again, as if he expected us tu git out.

"This is my house," sez my pussey cousin, "you go in and call on the ladies, and I'll dive round to one or two houses, and take you with me again, by and by."

I got up sort of loth, for it seemed kinder awk'ard to go in alone; but afore I had a chance to say so, the tall shote shet tu the stairs, gin the door a slam, hopped up behind agin, and away they went like a streak of lightning.

I stood a minit, a looking about. It was cold enough to nip a feller's ears off, so I jest tucked my hands into my pockets as well as I could, and begun tu stomp my foot on the stun walk. It raly was fun to see the streets chuck full of fellers running up and down, hither and yon, as if the old Nick had kicked them on eend. Every one on 'em was dressed up in his Sunday-go-to-meeting clothes, and they all had their hair slicked down exactly alike, and most on 'em looked more like gals in boys' clothes than anything else. Not the shadow of a petticoat could a feller see, from one eend of York tu the other—it seemed as if the hull city had run tu boys for one day. The streets raly looked lonesome; for, arter all, it don't seem nat'ral to go out and not see gals and women a walking about with their purty faces and fine clothes. A city without them, looks like a piece of thick woods without any sweet, green under-brush and harnsome flowers. I don't know exactly why, but when I go into a place where there's nothing but men, it seems as if all the sunshine and posies of human natur was shet out; and as I stood there afore my pussey cousin's house, it made me feel sort of melancholy not to see the least glimpse of a red shawl or a furbelow nowhere about.

I believe arter all, that when a chap is a leetle scared about doing a thing, the best way is tu pitch for'ard, hit or miss, without thinking on it. So as soon as I'd got a leetle grit raised, I up and pulled the door knob as savage as could be. It was an allfired big chunk of silver though, and the piece spread out on the door was as big as a dinner-plate, and there was "JASON SLICK" cut out on it in all sorts of flourishes and curlecues. Think sez I, my pussey cousin means to hang out a specie sign, anyhow. I wonder he didn't have his rooster and lion and crouchants pictered off in his door too.

Arter a minit a tall chap that looked like a twin tu the feller that stood behind the carriage, all dressed out jest as he was, too, like a major-gineral, stood a bowing and shuffling in the hall, as if he wanted to larn me how to dance. The way he sidled and bowed and spread out his hands as he opened the parlor door for me, was enough to make a feller bust with larfin. Wal, afore I knew which eend my head was on, there I stood in the middle of a great long room, that was enough to dazzle a feller's eyes for a month, eenajest to look at it. The settees were all bright red, and glistened with thick velvet cushions. Great, heavy, yaller curtains hitched up with spears and poles, made out of gold, or something plaguey like it, hung over all the winders—all furbelowed and tossled off with great, blue balls, mixed up with red fringe. The carpet was the brightest and softest thing I ever did see—but it was enough tu make a feller stun blind tu look at it, the figgers on it were so allfired gaudy. Everything in the room was as costly and harnsome as could be; but somehow it seemed as if every individual thing had come there on its own hook, and was so proud of itself that it wouldn't agree with its neighbors. The chairs looked dreadfully out of sorts with the settees, and the great looking-glasses made everything seem ten times more fiery and bright with their glistening. The hull room seemed more like a garden planted with poppies, sun-flowers, and marygolds, than anything I could think on. There was a table sot out at one eend, jest afore one of the looking-glasses, that made it seem as long agin as it raly was. It was all kivered over with silver baskets and knives and forks, and glasses, and everything that could be thought on tu eat and drink. At both eends were leetle meeting-houses with steeples tu them, all made out of sugar-candy, and hull loaves of cake with flowers and birds a lying down on top ot 'em; besides some had leetle sugar lambs curled up on 'em. as nat'ral as life. I never did see a table so set off in my born days; it was a sigut to look on. Cousin Beebe's warn't a touch tu it; but somehow the things were all crowded on so, and there was sich heaps of everything, that it didn't seem half so genteel as Cousin Mary's did. It must have cost an allfired swad of money, though.

I was so struck up with the room and the table, that it was more than a minit afore I found out that there were any folks in the premises; but by-am-by I discovered a fat chunked woman a sitting in a rocking chair all cushioned with red shiney velvet. She sot close by the fire, but when I stepped back and put my foot out to make a bow, she got up and made me a curchy—but sich a curchy I never did see—it was about half-way between the flutter of a hen and the swagger of a fat duck. It was as much as I could du to keep from snorting right out to see her; but I choked in, and sez I, bowing again, "You see I make myself tu hum, marm. Mr. Slick, my pussey cousin, out there, wanted me to come and make you a New Year's call."

I wish you could a seen how the critter strutted up when I said this; but all tu once she seemed to guess who I was, for she stuck her head a one side, and begun to smile and pucker up her mouth like all natur. Up she cum tu me with both hands out, and sez she—

"Cousin, I'm delighted to see you. Mr. Slick was telling me about you yesterday, and sez I, invite him by all means. It ain't often we can make free with a relation, they are so apt to presume upon it. Raly, some of Mr. Slick's family have been very annoying, they have indeed; they don't seem to understand our position; but you, cousin, you that have so much mind, can comprehend these things."

Afore I could get a chance to stick in a word edgeways, she took my hand, yaller glove and all, between both her'n, and led me along to the fire. Arter I'd sot down, she kept a fingering over one of my hands as if it belonged to her. Think sez I, what on arth can the old critter mean? I ll be darned, if she was fifteen years younger, I should think she had such a notion to the family, that she wasn't particular how many on 'em she made love tu. As soon as I could git her to give up my hand, she jest let her'n drop on my knee as affectionate as a pussy cat, and sez she, a screwing up her mouth, and sticking her face close up to mine—

"Cousin, you can't think how delighted I was to read your letters in the *Express*. I du like to see such upstarts as the Beebe's taken off; only think of the idee of her giving parties, and her husband not out of business yit! When I read that letter, sez I to Mr. Slick, 'bring the young gentleman here, where he can see something of *real* high life; it would be a pity to have him throw away his talons in describing such low affairs as Mrs. Beebe's must be.' " With that she looked round her blazing room as proud as could be, as if she wanted me to give her some soft sodder back agin; but I felt sort of wrathy at what she said about cousin, and I wouldn't take the hint; but sez I, "I beg pardon, marm, but Mr. Beebe is my friend and relation, and a chap that'll set still and hear a friend run down, don't deserve one, according to my notion; as for cousin Mary ——"

"Oh," sez Mrs. Slick, a twisting round like an eel, "she is a lovely woman, without any doubt. I sartinly should have called on her long ago; but then one has so many acquaintances of that sort to remember, that really I have never found time." Think sez I, if you wont call till Mary wants you, I don't think you'll put yourself out in a hurry; but I didn't say so, for jest that minit she seemed to remember something, and she sung out, 'Jemima, my dear."

With that the yaller curtains by one of the winders were rustled and flirted out, and a young gal, finefied off to kill, come from where she'd been standing back on 'em to look at the fellers as they went along the street. I ruther guess there was a flirting of ribbon and a glistening of gold things when she made her appearance. She came a hopping and a dancing across the room, and when she come jest afore me, she stopped short and let off a curchy that seemed more like one of her mother's run crazy, than any thing I could think on. The old woman she spread out her hands, and sez she, "Jemima, my dear, this is your cousin, Mr. Slick, the gentleman whose letters you were so delighted with."

With that the queer critter gave me another curchy and looked as if she' a been glad if she'd known enough to say something; but the old woman sot in with a stream of talk about her till any body on arth would have sot her down for an angel jest out of heaven, dressed up in pink satin and loaded off with gold, if they'd believed a word her mother said. Think sez I 'o myself, as I stood a looking at the old woman and the gal, it's enough to make a feller sick of life to see two such stuck up critters. The gal's furbelows didn't look so bad considering she was so young, yet it always seems to me as if heaps of jimcracks and finery piled on to a young critter looked kinder unnat'ral. Wimmen are a good deal like flowers to my notion, and the harnsomest posies that grow in the woods never have but one color besides their leaves. I've seen gals in the country with nothing but pink sun bonnets and calico frocks on, that looked as fresh and sweet as full blown roses—gals that could pull an even yoke with any of your York tippies in the way of beauty, and arter all if I ever get a wife I don't think I shall sarch for her among brick houses and stun side-walks.

The old woman raly had made an etarnal coot of herself in the way of fixing. She had on a lot of satin, and shiny thin stuff twistified round her head kinder like a hornet's nest; in front on it, jest over the leetle curls all rolled and frizzled round her face, a bird—a rale ginuine bird, all feathered off as bright as a rainbow—was stuck with its bill down and its tail flourished up in the air, as if it had jest lit to search for a place to build a nest in. I never see one of the kind afore, for its tail looked like a handful of corn-silk, it was so yaller and bright; but, think sez I, it must be some sort of a new-fashioned woodpecker, for it's the natur of them birds always to light on any thing holler—and if he was once to get a going on that old woman's head, I've an idee there'd be a drumming. She had a leetle short neck, all hung round with chains, and capes, and lots of things—besides, a leetle watch, all sot over with shiny stuns, was hung to her side, and her fat chunked fingers was kivered over with rings, that looked like the spots on a toad's back more than any thing else. She had a great wide ruffle round the bottom of her frock, like the one cousin Mary had on at her party; but she warn't no where nigh so tall as Mary, and it made her look like a bantum hen feathered down to the claws. Wal, think sez I, if you wouldn't make a comical figger-head for Captin Doolittle's sloop. I wonder what your husband would ask for you, jest as you stand —hump, ruffles and all? I shouldn't a taken so much notice of her, if she hadn't let off such a shower of talk on me about her darter; but when a woman begins to pester me by praising up her family, I always make a pint of thinking of something else as fast as I can. If you only bow a leetle, and throw in a "yes marm, sartingly," and so on, once in a while, you're all right. A woman will generally soft-sodder herself, if you let her alone when she once gits a going, without putting you to the trouble of doing it for her.

Arter she'd talked herself out of breath, she went along up to the table, and spreading her hands, sez she, "Take some refreshments, Mr. Slick?"

"Wal," sez I, "I haint much hungry, but I do feel a leetle dry —so I don't care if I du."

I went up to the table, and took a survey of the decanters and cider-bottles; and arter a while, I made out to find one decanter that looked as if it had something good in it, and poured about a thimble full into two of the wine glasses, and filled up one for myself. Mrs. Slick and her darter took up the glasses, and then I stepped back and made a low bow, and sez I, "The compliments of the season!—or any other interesting thing that you like. A person of your genius ——" Here I stuck fast, for somehow I forgot how cousin Beebe told me to top off in the speech. But the old woman puckered up her mouth, and curchyed away as if I'd said it all out; and the gal, she went over the same manœuvre, and laughed so silly, and put back her long curls with her white gloves—for she had gloves on though she was to hum—and sez she, "*Oh*, Mr. Slick," and then her marm chimed in, and sez she, "Now that you've mentioned genius, Mr. Slick, I do think my Jemima has a talent for poetry."

Think sez I, it raly is surprising how much genius there is buried up in these York brick houses. I hain't been to see a family since I've been down here that hadn't some darter that *could* write so beautiful, only she was so proud and diffident and modest, that she could not be coaxed to have any thing printed. Think sez I, if that leetle stuck up varmint has took to poetry, there'll be a blaze in the newspaper world afore long. She's sartin to set the North River on fire, if nobody else ever did.

I remembered what cousin Beebe told me about helping myself to eatables, so I sot down by the table and hauled a plate up to me, and begun to make myself to hum. There was no eend to the sweet things that I piled up on my plate and begun to store away with a silver knife and a spoon. Mrs. Slick, she begun to fuss about, and offered to help me to this, that and t'other, till I should raly have thought she didn't care how much I eat, if she hadn't contrived to tell me how much every thing cost all the time. Jest as I was finishing off a plate of foreign presarves, the door-bell rung, and in streaked five or six fellers, dressed up tu kill. It raly made me eenamost snicker out to see how slick and smooth every one of 'em had combed his hair down each side of his face. They all looked as much alike as if they'd been kidney beans shelled out of the same pod. When the old woman and the gal sot to wriggling their shoulders and making curchies to them, I begun to think it was time for me to get up and give them a chance. So I bolted the last spoonful of presarves, and took out my red silk hankercher to wipe my mouth. I thought it come out of my pockets purty hard, so I gave it a twitch, and hurra! out come three of the doughnuts that I'd tucked away to be ready in case of fodder's getting scarce, and they went helter-skelter every which way all over the carpet. At fust I felt sort of streaked, for the young chaps begun to giggle, and Miss Jemima Slick she bust right out. I looked at her, and then I looked at the fellers, and then, instead of sneaking off, I bust right out, jest as if I didn't know how they come there, and sez I,

"Did you ever!"

I didn't say another word, but jest made them a low bow all round, and was a going out, but Mrs. Slick got hold of my arm, and told me not tu seem to mind the doughnuts, and said, sort of low, that she'd tell the gentlemen that I was a relation of her'n, and that there warn't no danger of their poking fun at me about it. Think sez I, I see how to get out of the scrape: she'll think I'm awful mean not to offer her some of the doughnuts, when I had them in my pocket, so seeing it's new-year's day, I'll make

"So I bolted the last spoonful of preserves, and took out my red silk handkercher to wipe my mouth I thought it come out of my pocket purty hard, so I gave it a twitch, and hurra! out come three of the dough-nuts"—*Page* 110.

her think I brought 'em tu make her a present on, for relation's sake. I jest went back, aud picked up the tarnal things, and heaping them up in one hand, I made a smasher of a bow as I held 'em out tu her, and, sez I—

"I thought mebby you'd like tu see how a prime Weathersfield doughnut would taste agin; so I jest tucked a few one side, tu bring up here; take 'em, you're as welcome as can be; I've got enough more tu hum."

She looked at the gentlemen, and then she turned red, as if she didn't exactly know how tu take me.

"Don't be afeard on 'em," sez I, "they're fust rate; chuck full of lasses, and fried in hog's lard as white as snow."

With that she took them out of my hand and put them on the table, and, sez she, a puckering up her mouth, "you men of genius are so droll."

Think sez I, I've made a good hit off this time, any how, so I'll cut stick. I made another bow, and out I went, jest as the chaps were all a bowing and saying, "the compliments of the season," one arter another, like boys, in a spelling class.

I hadn't but jest got to the door, when my pussey consin driv up, so I got intu the carriage, and off we went, down Broadway, at a smashing rate, till at last we stopped afore one of the neatest-looking houses that I've seen in York: it warn't crinckled and finefied off with wood-work and iron fences, but the hull was solid stun. The steps were made of the same, with great stun sides a rolling down from the door tu the side-walk. The door was sunk clear intu the front; there warn't no chunk of silver in the middle, tu write the owner's name on; so I s'pose he thought that every body ought to know where a rale fashionable chap lives, without his hanging out a sign to tell folks. Jason was jest a going tu give the knob a twitch, but he seemed to remember, and, sez he, to the tall chap that had got down,

"Why don't you ring?"

With that the chap made a dive up the steps, and it warn't a second afore the door swung open, and a nice old feller, dressed up as neat as a new pin, but without regimentals, stood inside. Arter making a bow, he opened a mahogany door, and made a little motion with his hand, as much as to say—"walk in."

Jason he kinder seemed loth to go in fust; and arter all his money, I couldn't help but think the old feller in the hall looked as well and acted a good deal more like a rale gentleman, than he did. There's nothing like being rich to git up a man's pluck; arter fidgeting with his watch-seals a minit, Jase stuck up his head like a mud turtle in the sun, and in he went. I follered arter as close as a bur tu a chestnut; for in my hull life I never felt so scared.

The house didn't seem like Miss Miles's nor Cousin Beebe's, nor yet like my pussey cousin's. Coming from his house into that, seemed like going out of a blustering wind into a calm snow-storm. Every thing was so slick and still, that it didn't seem like anything else that I ever see. Cousin Slick went in fussing along, and a tall harnsome lady got up from a chair, where she sot by the fire, and cum towards us. Arter Jason had give her a little information about the weather—told her it was dreadful cold, and so on, he stepped back, and spreading out his hands sort of like his wife, sez he—

"Mrs. ——, this is Mr. Jonathan Slick, a young relation of mine."

I declare it made my heart beat to see how purtily she smiled —her curchy was as soft and easy as a bird—she didn't wriggle up her shoulders and stick out her feet as some of the rest of 'em did, but jest seemed to droop down a little easy, and then she asked us to sit down; and in less than no time we felt as much tu hum as if we'd known her ever since she was a nursing baby. Instead of beginning to give me a lot of soft sodder, as some of the other women did, she jest set in and began to talk about old Connecticut, and sich things as she must a seen was likely to tickle me like all natur, and her voice was so soft, and she kept a smiling so, that I never felt so contented in my life as I did a talking with her.

At last she began to ask Jason some questions about the Western country—so I had a chance to look about me a leetle. Instead of being dressed out like a thing sot up for a show, she hadn't nothing on but a harnsome silk frock, and a leetle narrow velvet ribbon tied round her harnsome black hair, that was brushed till it looked as bright as a crow's back. I never did see anything braided up so nice as it was behind. She hadn't on the leastist bit of gold nor furbelows of any kind, only jest a leetlo pin that glistened like a spark of fire, which pinned the velvet ribbon jest over her white forehead. It raly beats me to make out why I can't tell you what was in the room, jest as I du about all the other places; but somehow it aint easy to tell the difference, for there was settees, and chairs, and tables, and curtains, and so on—but yet it warn't a bit like any room I ever see afore. There warn't no glistening and shining, and gold and silver; but I couldn't get the notion out of my head that everything cost a good deal more than if there had been ever so much of it. The room seemed made exactly for the things that were in it, and there warn't a thing that didn't fit exactly into its place like wax-work. There was one consarn that looked awful harnsome, and it was rale ginuine too; but at first I thought it was some of these York make-believes. It was a slim green tree, eenamost tall enough to reach my head, all blown out and kivered over with as much as twenty of the biggest and whitest roses I ever did see. It was sot jest below the two winders, and when the sun came kinder softly through the curtains down into the white posies they seemed to sort o' blush like a beach blow; yit they raly were as white, according to natur, as the cleanest handful of snow you ever see. The tree grew out of a great marble flower-pot, and when I asked its name of the lady, she looked as bright and sweet as one of the flowers, and told me it come from Japan, away east. There was some picters hung agin the wall, that struck my eye so that I couldn't keep from looking at 'em. She see how I was took up, and sez she—

"That's a beautiful picter, Mr. Slick, don't you think so? There is something in Doughtie's picters that I love to look on; his grass and hillocks are so soft and green, he does excel every American artist most certainly in his atmosphere."

"Wal, marm," sez I, "I aint no judge of picters, but sartinly, to my notion that does outshine cousin Jason's lions and roosters, and croushongs, all to nothing. It don't glisten so much, but somehow them great trees du look so nat'ral, and them cows lying down under them so lazy; it eenamost makes me hum sick to go back to Weathersfield when I see it." Here

8

Jase trod on my toe with his consarned hard boot. Wal, think sez I, what have I said now; and I looked right in the lady's face to see if she'd been a laughing; but she looked so sweet and unconsarned as could be, and sez she, a getting up and going across the room; for Jase made a motion as if he was in a hurry, sez she—

"Let me help you to some cake and wine."

With that she went to a table that had some decanters and wine-glasses on it, besides a loaf of cake as white as drifted snow. I sniggers, but it did look as neat as a new pin. There was a heap of rale flowers and leaves, jest picked from the bush, fresh and fair, twisted round the edge of the cake, and a leetle white sugar dove snuggled down in the middle.

Cousin Jase filled the glasses and he made a leetle speech— but somehow it didn't seem to me as if I could go to talking soft sodder tu that harnsome critter—she looked so sweet yet so proud. All I did was jest to drink the wine, and then bend my head kinder softly to try and match her curchy—but if I didn't wish her a happy New Year in my heart, I'm a lying coot, that's all. When we went away, she gave us an invite to come agin, and she was mortal perlite to me. If I don't go, it'll be because I'm afeard, for I don't know when I've taken such a shine to anything that wears petticoats.

Jest as soon as I'd got clear of the door, and Jase had bowed and scraped himself out, we got into the carriage agin, and sez he—

"Wal, cousin, how do you like Mrs. ——?"

"Like her!" sez I, "if I don't there's no snakes. She's none of your stuck up, finefied, humbug critters, but a *rale ginuine lady*, and no mistake."

"It's a pity she hasn't more taste and emulation to fix up her house," sez he. "She raly don't know how to cut a dash, and yet her husband is as rich as a Jew."

"Wal, raly, I don't know what to think of that," sez I. "Somehow when I see everything in a room kinder shaded off, one color into another that's eenamost like it, till the hull seemed to be alike, jest as it is in that lady's room,—it seems to take my notion amazingly. I can't tell you why, but it made me feel as if the room had been made up into a big picter, and so it is in part, and I begin to think that——"

I was a going to say something allfired cutting about these stuck up flashy houses and people that I'd seen here in York—when the carriage driv up to another door. In we went, eat and drank, and then out agin; and then it was riding from one house to another, and eating and drinking till it got eenajest dark, and I was clear tuckered out, besides beginning tu feel wamble-cropped a leetle, with the heap of sweet things I'd been eating all day.

This New Year's day here in York is sartainly as good as a show,—such lots of gals as a feller sees, and such lots of good living; but give me a Thanksgiving dinner yit afore a York New Year's,—a gook turkey with plenty of gravy and tatur. I swanny, how I wish I'd been a eatin them things instead of this heap of tarnal cake and sugar things. I shan't feel right agin in a month, I'm sure on it.

I guess you Weathersfield tee totalists would a stared some tu see how the young chaps begun tu make fence along the stun side-walks towards night; some on 'em were purty well over the bay I can tell you. I went to see lots of women and gals, and cousin Mary amongst the rest, and arter I got back to my office I couldn't get one wink of sleep. My head was chuck full of gals all night,—such a whirring and burring as there was in my upper story you never did know on,—every time I shet my eyes the office seemed chuck full of purty gals and feathers and gold and decanters, cut glass, till it seemed as if I would go crazy a thinking over all I'd done; but the last thing that got into my brain jest afore I dropped to sleep, was the *real lady* and my pussey cousin's stuck up wife.

But I can't stop to write you on all my dreams that night. I don't think doughnuts or sugar candies set well on the stomach, and I don't think seeing so many gals sets well on my head. There is a terrible all over-ish sort of a feeling in a young feller when he's been cruising among the gals all day, and comes hum and cuddles up in bed at night. When he gits one gal stuck fast in his head and his heart, as I had Judy White, he's as quiet as a kitten, and his head's a sort a settled; but arter he's been a roving over the world as I am a doing, his natur gits ruther rily, and there's nothing that sticks in it except the dregs, the pure essence sifting out all through.

Getting in love is somewhat like getting drunk, the more a feller loves the more he wants tu,—and when the heart gits a going, *pitty pat, pitty pat,* there is such a swell, that it busts up all the strings, so that it can't hold the ginuine grit at all. When Judy White fust took hold a my arm I give the coat sleeve a rale hearty smack, where her hand had lain, and that coat I raly did love better than any other I ever had on; but I never think the better of my yaller gloves for shaking the hands of all the gals in York. I've only got Miss Miles out of my head, to git a thousand new shinin faces in. Lord knows what'll become of me, Par, if I go on to be bedivilled arter the women, as I have been this new year's day. When a feller is made any thing on by 'em he must have been brought up under good preaching in Weathersfield to stand it here in York. I feel as if I shouldn't be good for much afore long, myself, the way I am going on, but to skoot up and down Broadway like that ere Count, and to hang round gals' winders with fifes, and bassoons, and drums, and gitars at night.

I can't look full into a purty gal's face all a flashing so, without being kind a dazzled and scorched. It warms me up in this cold weather, and kindles such a touso in my heart, that the blood runs through it as hot as if it had scooted through a steam-boat pipe. And then the allfired critters have so many sly ways of coming over a feller, that I don't think much of a man who can see their purty mouths tremble, and not feel his tremble tu. If they sidle up, I can't help sidling too if I died; and when them black eyes fall flash on me, I wilt right down under 'em as cut grass in Weathersfield on a hot summer day. It is natur all this, and I can't help it no how.

But you know, Par, I was brought up under good preaching, and I go now to Dr. Spring's meeting always as straight as Sunday comes round, and twice a day. If wimmin do snarl up a feller's heart strings, though, they keep him out of other scrapes, anybody will tell you that. A man that is in love a leetle is not always a running into rum-holes, and other such places. He don't go a gambling, and isn't a sneakin round nights.

Love, according to my notion on it, is a good anchor for us on this 'ere voyage of life!—it brings us up so all a standing when we put on too much sail. It puts me in mind, now I think on it, of our cruise through Hell Gate in Captin Doolittle's sloop; for jest as the tide and the wind was a carrying us on the rocks, we dropt anchor and kept off. I look on the uses of women purty much as I look on the freshet that in the spring brings down the Connecticut the rale rich soil for the meadows in Weathersfield. They make a great deal of splutter and fuss in their spring-time, with their rustles and their ribbons, and their fooleries, I know; but when they light on a feller for good, they are the rale onion patches of his existence. Put us together, and the soil will grow anything; but keep us apart, and we are his thistles and nettles.

Your loving son,
JONATHAN SLICK.

LETTER XI.

Visit to the Park Theatre—First Impressions of the Poetry of Motion, as written on the air, in the aerial feats of Mademoiselle Celeste—First shock at the exhibition of a Ballet Costume accompanied by the "twinkles" of Celeste's feet—with her pigeon wings, double-shuffles, gallopades, and pirouettes.

DEAR PAR:

I've been a trying tu git time tu write you a letter this ever so long; but somehow I've had so many parties tu go tu, besides sleigh-rides, balls, and so on, that I haint known which eend my head is on more than half the time. Besides all that, I've felt kinder loth tu write you, for I aint jest sartin that you and marm won't be in a pucker about what I've been a doing since I writ tu you before. But I've got my pluck a stirring jest now; so I'm determined tu up and tell you all right out, jest as it is—for arter all, a feller must be a consarned coward that'll do a thing, right or wrong, and then back out from owning on it.

Wal, t'other night Mr. Beebe he cum up tu my office about sundown, and sez he, "Cousin Slick, supposing we go tu the Park Theatre to-night, and see Madame Celeste dance."

My heart riz right up into my throat as he said this, for the very idee of going tu the Theatre set me all over in a twitter. Ever since I cum down here tu York, I've had an etarnal hankering tu go and see some of their plays; but I tried all I could tu pacify myself, and thought over more than forty times all the preachings you used to make agin them—how you used tu say they were filled with sinful devices and picters of the devil's own painting, and that they warn't nothing more nor less than scraps of the infarnal regions sot up here on arth tu delude away poor mortals.

I wanted tu go awfully, but insted of giving in tu cousin John when he fust come, I jest sot too and let off one of your preachments to him; he didn't seem to mind it a mite, but, sez he, "Cousin, would you think it right if a feller was tu cum out like all blazes agin one of your letters in the *Express*, if he hadn't read 'em?"

"I should like to ketch a feller at it—I should," sez I.

"Wal," sez he, "du you think it fair tu run out agin the Theatres till you've seen something on 'em?"

"Wal," sez I, "I don't know as it is; but haint my par an old man as well as deacon of the church, and hadn't he ought tu know? What's the use of a man's experience, if his children won't profit by it, as long as he can't turn about and live his life over agin?"

"That's true," sez cousin John; "but are you sartin that your father was ever at a play in his life?"

"What, my par at the Theatre!" sez I, a holding up both hands, "Mr. Zephaniah Slick, Esquire, Justice of the Peace and Deacon of the Church, at the Theatre! Look a here, cousin John, why don't you ask if he ever plays all fours, or 'I had as many wives as the stars in the skies,'—he'd be about as likely tu du one as t'other."

"Wal," sez John, sort of parsevering, "how can he judge about them sort of things without he's seen 'em? Come, come, jest put on your fix and let's go down."

So with that he come his soft sodder so strong that I couldn't hold out no longer, so I jest giv up, and we started off; but my heart felt sort of queer all the way, for I couldn't keep from thinking how you and marm would feel when you found out where I'd been tu. I don't think there's anything very scrumptious about the outside of the Theatre anyhow. Think sez I, as I looked up tu it, if this is raly a temple of Old Nick, he haint put himself out much tu finefy it off. A good many of the meeting-houses here in York go ahead of this all tu nothing. It looks more like a town hall or a tavern than any thing else that I can think on.

When we got into the entry-way, cousin Beebe he took out a dollar bill, and went up tu a little hole cut out in the wall, and stuck in his hand, and sez he, "A ticket."

Think sez I, wal, if this don't beat all! They raly du mean tu carry on all kinds of develtry; who'd a thought of finding one of these darnation lottery offices here.

"You wont want a ticket," sez cousin John.

"No," sez I, "I guess I don't; if there's any thing on arth that makes my blood bile, it's gambling. I was a going on tu give him a piece of my mind, but jest then he pushed a door open, all kivered over with green flannel, and give his paper tu a tall man that stood there, looking as solemn as an owl in a storm; and, sez he, a pinting tu me, this gentleman belongs tu the press. The feller looked at me as sharp as a needle, and he begun tu fumble over a paper, as if he didn't know exactly what he wanted; but at last he held out his hand, and said it was custom for the press to leave cards at the door. I never was so struck up in my whole born days. Think sez I, wal, if this don't beat all natur; they think because a feller is green enough tu go tu the Theatre that he must play cards, and every thing else that's bad. I shouldn't wonder, sez I tu myself, if he wants me tu begin and cuss and swear next. I looked him right in his eyes, and put my hands down in my pockets allfired hard, and, sez I—

"Look a here, you sir, I ain't no gambler—none of your foreign chaps, that git their living by playing cards. You must be soft in the upper story if you don't see that the first giffy. You don't see no hair on my upper lip. I don't carry a cane with a bagonet in it, nor wear checkered trousers, so you needn't ask *me* to give you any cards, I haint touched one of the pesky things since marm broke the tin dipper over my head for singing out, 'high, low, Jack and the game, by gauley,' one day when I and another little shaver got hid away in the corn-house a playing all fours."

The feller opened his eyes a few when I said this, but three or four finefied young fellers, with white gloves on, and little canes in their hand, come to the door, and stood a grinning at me like so many hungry monkeys. Cousin John spoke sort of low, and sez he,—

"It is your name the man wants. If you haven't any cards, write it out on a piece of paper."

With that the man handed over a piece of paper, and cousin Beebe give me his gold pencil.

Think sez I, "If they will have my name, I'll give 'em a smasher,"—so I flourished the "J" off with an allfired long tail, and curlecued the "S" up till it looked like a black snake in the sun. I ruther seem to think the feller stared a few when he saw the name. The grinning chaps cum and looked at it, but made themselves scarce in less than no time arter they had made it out, and the tall chap, he bowed close down to the floor, and sez he—

"Walk in, Mr. Slick, Mr. Simpson put your name on the free list ever so long ago."

I was going to ask him to tell Mr. Simpson that I was very much obligated, though I hadn't the least idea what he meant by his free list, but that minit there was such a smashing of fiddles and drums and toot-horns inside that I eenamost jumped out of my skin. It seemed as if a dozen training bands had all been set a going tu once.

Cousin John he took hold of my arm, and hauled me along through a little door into a great big room built off more like a meeting-house than anything else—and yet it wasn't like that neither. It was shaped kinder like a horse shoe, the floor was chuck full of benches, kivered over with red cushions, and there was four galleries all pillared off and painted, and set off with gold and great blazing glass things that made every thing look as bright as day. In the second gallery there were five or six pens all boarded off from the rest, with lots of gold picters all round them, and hung over with silk curtains, till they looked more like the berths on board a steamboat than any thing I could think on. These places were chuck full of allfired harnsome gals and spruce looking fellers, that were dressed off to kill, and talked and laughed as chipper as could be. The ruff was an etarnal way up from the floor; it rounded up, and was crinkle-crankled off with gold and picters till it looked like the West jest afore sundown, when the red and yaller and purple lie in heaps and ridges all over the sky.

Think sez I, if that's what par means by a device of the devil, Old Nick is no slouch at putting the shine on the ruff of his house, anyhow.

We sot down on one of the red benches in the lowest gallery, and I got a leetle over the twitter that I was in at fust, and jest made up my mind to look amongst the folks to see what was going on.

It warn't a mite of wonder that the musicianers made me jump so when I was in the entry way, for clear on t'other eend of the room was a long pen chuck full and running over with fiddlers, base drums, and great brass horns, all pulling and blowing and thumping away like all natur; didn't they send out the music!—never on arth did I hear any thing like it! It made me choke and sigh and ketch my breath like a dying hen; and all I could do, my feet would keep going over the steps, and my yaller gloves seemed as if they never would git still agin, they kept so busy a beating time on the leg of my new trousers. Jest over the pen where the fiddlers sot, hung a great picter as big as the side of a house. I thought of what you said about theatres being filled with picters of the devil's own painting; but I couldn't make up my mind that that was one on 'em, for it was so green and cold, and a pale man, pictered out on a heap of stuns in the middle on it, looked as shivery as if he'd had a fit of the fever and ague—besides there was water painted out, and every body knows that Old Scratch aint tee-total enough to paint a picter chuck full of clouds and water and sich like, without one spark of fire to make him feel to hum in his own premises.

By-am-by sich sights of the people, all dressed off as if they were a going to a general training ball, kept a pouring in through the leetle doors in the galleries till the seats were all chuck full; such a glistening of harnsome eyes and feathers, and flowers, I never did see. A purty leetle gal cum and sot close down by me, and now and then I took a slanting squint at her; by hokey, she was a slick leetle critter, with the consarnedest soft eyes I ever looked into.

I wonder what on arth is the reason that I can't sit down by a harnsome gal, but my heart will begin to flounder about like a fish jest arter he's hooked. Think, sez I, if there's any dancing a going on to-night, darn me if I don't shin up to that gal for a partner. But, where on arth the folks were a going tu find a place to dance in I couldn't make out, for in the hull building there warn't room enough tu hang up a flax-seed edgeways.

I was jest a going tu ask cousin John about it, when the fiddles pulled up a minit, and all tu once that great picter give a twitch, and up it went like a streak of chalk, into the ruff, or the Lord knows where. I jumped right on eend, I was so struck with what I see.

Clear back where the curtain had been was a purty little garden, as nat'ral as one of our onion patches. It was chuck full of trees and flowers, and a snug leetle house stood on one side; clear back. jest under the edge of the sky, lay the soft water, looking as blue and still as could be. What to make on it I couldn't tell; it warn't like a picter, and yet I couldn't think how on arth there could be room enough tu have sich a place near the theatre. While I sot there a bending for'ard with one of my yaller gloves pressed down on each knee, and staring like a stuck pig with my mouth a leetle open, a lot of folks dressed off in short jackets and trousers cut off at the knees, come a dancing out of the house, and begun tu talk all at once, and chatter and laugh together as chipper as a flock of birds. They seemed as happy as clams in high water; and the fellers skipped and hung round the gals like good fellers.

But the gals were dressed out too bad. I'll be darned if some of 'em didn't make me feel streaked, their frocks were so short. They didn't seem tu make no bones of showing their legs half-way tu their knees. I swanny if I wasn't ashamed of the purty gal that sot by me. Think sez I, if she don't blush and feel all overish I'm mistaken. Arter a while, I give her a slantidicular squint, but she sot as still as a kitten, and looking as if butter wouldn't melt in her mouth, but was a staring right straight at the garden without seeming to mind the gals' legs a bit more than if they had been so many broom sticks.

It warn't a great while afore I didn't seem to mind it much either, for a little old comical looking chap come out in front of the garden, and begun to chatter and larf, and fling his arms about every which way, and to tell about some young gal that was a going to be married. Madeline, he called her.

Wal, while he was a talking, a feller, all in red regimentals, come round the house, as big as my pussey cousin, with a set of letters in his hand, and blowing a tin toot-horn, as if he wanted us all tu come tu dinner. He turned to be a sort of post-rider, with letters; he give one to the funny old chap that owned the house, but it only had another letter in it, and that was for the gal that was a going tu be married.

I begun to feel awful curious tu see that gal, arter hearing them talk about her so much; but the post-office feller cut up his shines, and ordered the folks about as obstroperous as my pussey cousin; a prime chap he was—and I took a sort of a notion to him, he acted out so slick.

By-am-by in come the purtyest looking critter that ever I did see; she walked and sidled through the garden like a bird among the green trees, and her voice sounded so funny when she spoke; she kinder cut her words off, and lisped 'em out so sweet, that every word sounded chuck full of honey. I swan it made my heart rise right up in my mouth every time she spoke. She had tarnal harnsome eyes, as bright as the biggest star in the gill-dipper, and I could almost tell what she was a saying by the cut of her face; I never did see a critter look so happy. She had the cunningest leetle white hat that I ever did see, stuck on one side of her head, with blue ribbons streaming from it over her shoulders; on t'other side her long shiny curls hung down on her shoulders, and a harnsome white rose was stuck in them back of her ear; but it didn't seem much whiter than her forehead and neck, for they were as white as the froth on a pail of new milk afore it is strained. She had on a blue silk frock, cut off a leetle too short at the bottom, for my notion, and her cunning leetle feet raly cut about in them new shoes a leetle *too* spry; I never did see anything so subtle as she was in my life.

The minit she came into the garden, all the folks in the galleries, and on the seats below, begun to stomp, and yell, and holler, till I was afeard that I made a mistake, and got into a political meeting agin. She began to curchy, and lay her hand on her bosom, and curchy agin, all the while a looking so sweet and mealy-mouthed that I wanted to eat her hull, I swow I did. Arter a while they begun to get tired of making sich etarnal coots of themselves, and then she begun to go round among the folks in the garden, and give them presents, because she was a going to git married in the morning, tu a rich gentleman that lived close by.

All tu once the comical old chap called "Madeline!" and give her the letter the post-rider had brought for her.

Arter she'd gone into the house, he begun to tell the folks all about her—how she was a poor leetle French gal that he'd undertook tu bring up and keep out of harm, when everybody in her country was afeard of their lives—and how she'd got a brother yet in France, whose life wouldn't be worth four-pence-half-penny if he should once set foot over in England; for they made believe that all this garden and things was a going on in England.

Wal, arter they'd all gone in, out come Madeline agin with the letter in her hand. I swanny, but I couldn't help but feel for the poor critter. She looked as if she'd been crying her eyes out, but she kept a kissing the letter and reading it sort of loud, and a crying all the time, so that we all found out it come from her brother, and that he was a coming tu take her away with him in the morning; and it seemed to make her feel bad because he didn't know that she was a going to be married then. When she'd read her letter through, she went into the house agin, looking as peaked and wamble-cropped as a sick lamb.

When the picter was rolled up agin, the garden was all gone, and there sot the purty leetle Madeline in a room with a chest open by her filled with wimmen's clothing, and there was a rale harnsome young feller a standing by her that she seemed so fond of, and that she called her brother.

While they were talking together, and afore she had time to tell him she was a going to be married, there was an allured noise outside of the door, and you never seo a cat jump up spryer than she did. She turned as white as a sheet, and wrung her leetle hands, and seemed more than half crazy, for she said the officers had cum arter her brother to hang him for a spy. She hugged him one minit, and then she'd wring her hands, and look round so anxious for some place to hide him in. At last she run to the chest, pulled all the clothes out on it, and made him git in there—she put them all back agin, and kivered it over with a great red shawl. She hadn't but jest sot down and took up her sewing work, when a great etarnal coot of a feller, that made my blood bile every time I looked at him, cum into the room along with another feller, and begun to sarch arter the poor young chap that she'd hid away.

We could see that the poor gal was eenamost scared out of her senses, for she turned as white as a ghost—but she cocked one foot over t'other, and went on a sewing as fast as could be. I swanny, it made me wrathy tu hear the varmint how he run on agin the poor gal. I never did see sich wicked eyes as hisen were in my life, nor sich a ragged drunken looking shark; it made my grit rise every time he looked towards that sweet gal.

The officer couldn't find nobody, and wanted to go hum, but the tall shack went up to the chest, and begun to poke about among the clothes, and asked what she'd got there. She looked as if she would go off the handle at that; but she didn't give up. Arter a minit she jumped up and took up a gown and showed it to the officer, and then she took up a shawl and told him it was her wedding shawl, and she began to run on and smile, and talk so coaxing, and spread out the shawl all the time, till the young feller in the chest crept out and got into another room, while she held the shawl afore him. They went off grumbling, and consarnedly wamble-cropped, for a reward had been offered for the purty French gal's brother, and the etarnal scamp meant tu git his revenge on her and money tu boot.

I was a looking steady into the room, when all tu once it slid away, and there was the garden agin, and the outside of the house, and it was dark as midnight among the bushes. By-am by out came the ragged scamp and stood jest under the poor French gal's winder, to see what was a going on, and while he was there, the good-hearted chap, that she was a going tu be married tu, came along tu look at her winder, as fellers will when they are over head and ears in luv.

Then the French gal cum to the winder, and the young feller that she'd been a hiding away, jumped out, and she put his cloak on and hugged him as if her heart was eenamost ready to bust. When she see her brother clear off she went back tu bed, but the squire and the ragged scamp had seen her, and sich a row as it kicked up never was heard on afore.

In a little while there was sich a hubbub in the garden; all the wimmen that she'd gin presents tu, got together, and begun to run out agin her, and saying that they always thought she was no better than she ought tu be. The squire said he wouldn't marry her, and the tarnal old man turned her out of doors.

I thought I should a boo-hooed right out, when I see her cum out of the door with a bundle in her hand, a crying as if she hadn't a friend on arth. She was a going away so slow and sorrowful, when the squire cum up and offered her some money, for he seemed tu feel sorry for her, though he thought she'd been a cheating him.

She looked at him so still, and yit so proud, as if her heart was brim full of grief, but she wouldn't take his money. A last he told her that the man she'd had was took prisoner. Oh. how she did take on then! She wrung her hands, and sobbed, and cried enough tu make one feel wamble-cropped to see her, and she said now that her character was gone and her brother taken, that she wanted to die.

The squire felt dreadfully when he found out that the man was her brother. So he made up with her, and she got on tu a horse and rode off full chisel tu get her brother's pardon.

By-am-by she got back with the pardon for her brother, and

there was such crying and kissing and shaking hands, as you never heard on. I bellered right out a crying, I was so allfired glad tu see the poor gal happy once more.

Wal, by-am-by, a bell tinkled; the picter rolled up agin and the fiddlers begun to put on elbow grease till the music came out slick enough. Instead of the garden there was a long ballroom with rows of great shiney pillars running all through it. It was as light as day, for there seemed to be candles out of sight among the pillars, besides a row of lamps that stood along the pen where the musicianers sot. I was staring with all the eyes I had in my head, when the harnsomest critter I ever sot eyes on cum flying into the middle of the room, and there she stood on one foot with her arms held out and her face turned towards us, looking as bold, and smiling as soft as if she'd never done nothing else all her life. I was so scared when she fust sprung in, that I raly didn't know which een my head was on. The darned critter was more than half naked—she was, by golley! To save my life I couldn't look at her right straight with that blue-eyed gal a setting close by me. At fust I was so struck up that I couldn't see nothing but an allfired harnsome face a smiling from under a wreath of flowers, and naked legs and arms and neck, a flying round like a live wind-mill. I thought I should go off the handle at fust—I felt sort of dizzy, and as if I was blushing all over. I don't think I ever was in such an etarnal twitter in my hull life. I partly got up tu go out, and then I sot down agin as streaked as lean pork, and kivered my face with my yaller gloves, but somehow I couldn't hold my hands still all I could du—the fingers would git apart, so that I couldn't help but look through them at that plaguey, darned harnsome, undecent critter, as she jumped and whirled and stretched her naked arms out toward us, and stood a smiling and coaxing and looking tu the fellers. It was enough to make a feller cuss his mother because she was a woman; but I'll be darned if there ever was a feller on arth that could help looking at the critter.

I've seen a bird charmed by a black snake, but it was nothing tu this—not a priming. One minute she'd kinder flutter round the room softly and still like a bird that's jest beginning tu fly, then she'd stand on one foot and twinkle t'other out and in against the ankle so swift you couldn't but jest see it. Then she'd hop for'ard and twist her arms up on her bosom, and stick one leg out behind her, and stand on one toe for ever so long, till all on us had had a fair sight on her that way. Then she'd take another hop and pint her right toe forward, and lift it higher, till by-am-by round she'd go like a top, with her leg stuck out straight and whirling round and round like the spoke of a broken waggin with a foot tu it. It raly did beat all that I ever did see. When she stood up straight, her white frock was all sprigged off with silver, and it looked like a cloud of snow, but it didn't reach half way down tu her knees, and stuck out dreadfully behind. I hadn't dared to unkiver my face yet, and was sort of trembling all over in a dreadful pucker, wondering what on arth she meant tu do next, when she give a whirl, kissed her hand, and hopped away as spry as a cricket, jest as she came in.

I swan, if I didn't think I never should breathe straight agin; I raly wouldn't a looked in that purty blue-eyed gal's face for anything; but somehow I happened tu squint that way, for I felt kinder anxious tu see how red a gal could blush, and there she sot a smiling and a looking as she raly liked the fun. She was whispering to a young feller that sot t'other side, and sez she—

"Aint it beautiful! Oh! I hope they'll call her back!"

"She will come, I dare say," sez the feller a larfin, and beginning to stomp and clap hands with the rest on 'em that were a yelling and hooting like all possessed. "Celeste treats the Americans very much as a lover does his lady."

"How so?" sez the gal, looking sort of puzzled.

"Why, she can't leave them without coming back again and again to take *farewell!*" sez he, a larfin; "but here she comes!"

True as a book, there she did cum, and begun tu sidle and whirl, and cut up her crancums all over agin. By leetle and leetle I let my hands slide down from my face, and when she give her prime whirl and stuck out her toe the last time, I sot a staring right straight at her, so astonished I couldn't set still, for as true as you live, the nice, leetle French gal that was so sweet and modest, and the bold, beautiful critter with her foot out, her arms a wavering around her head, and her mouth jest open enough tu show her teeth, was the same individual critter, and both on 'em were Madame Celeste.

I went hum. But I'll be choked if them legs and arms, and that frock with the flowers over it didn't whirl round in my head all night, and they ain't fairly out yit.

Your loving son,

JONATHAN SLICK.

LETTER XII.

Jonathan receives an Invitation to a Fancy Ball—Dilemma about the Dress—Choice of a Character, &c.

DEAR PAR:

I du think this ere trade of writing is about the darndest bisness that a feller ever took to. The minit a man begins tu git his name up here in York, the way the gals du haul him over the coals is a sin to Crocket, as they say down here. They talk about the Yankees having a nack of cheating people out of their eye teeth. By gracious! if the York folks don't know how to hold up ther end of the yoke at that trade, I'm a coot, that's all. They may take my grinders and welcome, but I'll be darn'd if I give up my Christian name, without making an all-fired rumpus about it. I can't go down Cherry-street now without somebody's stopping me to find out who writes my letters, jest as if I didn't write 'em myself. Some on 'em seem to think it's a Portland chap, an allfired smart critter, that come from down East, and that's been a writing a capital history of the war down on the territory that haint got no boundary; and people keep a coming to the Express office every once in a while, to find out if Major Jack Downing don't write 'em and sign my name. I should like to ketch him at it once! Let him or any other chap put my name to any thing that I don't write, and if I don't lick him within an inch of his life, then he may steal my name and welcome.

Now, jest to git the York people out of the etarnal twitter

that they're in to find out who writes my letters, I've made up my mind to tell 'em here, in one of my letters; and if I don't tell 'em the truth, I hope I may be hung and choked to death, so there!

In the first place, I aint intimate with Major Jack Downing, and never sot eyes on him in my life, till t'other night at "the Grand Fancy Ball," as they call it. He's a smart chap, but I'll be darned if he ever writ a word of one of my letters in his life,—and more than all that, he don't know me from Adam; no more does the Portland chap, or any of the rest on 'em,—and I du think it's allfired hard, if I can't have the credit of writing letters on my own hook, and nobody's else. Now these two chaps are prime fellers, and old hands at the bisness; but I never tried my hand at writing a letter in my hull life, till I sent the fust one to the Express—and that I put my name tu as large as life. Neither the Portland Major Jack Downing, nor the New York Major Jack Downing, nor our Sam, nor nobody else, has a finger in my dish; but all the letters that has my name and picter to 'em are writ by me.

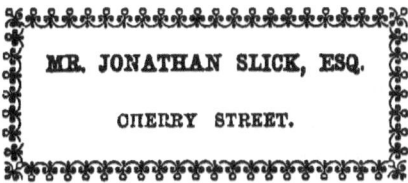

MR. JONATHAN SLICK, ESQ.

CHERRY STREET.

That's my card! as they say at the theatre,—and now I hope the Yorkers wont pester me any more, to know who I am.

Arter going to the Park Theatre t'other night, I begun to feel sort of dissatisfied with the carryings on in this place, and I eenamost made up my mind to come back to Weathersfield and stick to the old business for life. Somehow I couldn't git them naked legs and arms, and so on, of Marm-sel Celeste out of my head,—and I couldn't help feeling awful streaked when I thought of them in the day-light. Sich sights aint fit for any thing but candle-light, and then a feller must be half corned before he can see them without feeling ashamed of all womankind.

I du think, when a chap begins to have a bad opinion of the wimmin folks, it's a sign that there is something out of the way in his own heart; but it comes tough to keep a feller's heart in the right place, while sich sweet, purty, indecent critters as that Celeste, are a kicking up their heels and flinging all sorts of queer ideas into his mind. Arter seeing her flurish her white short gown, without petticoat, afore all them folks, I begun to hate the gals like pison; it seemed to me as if they warn't made for men's wives, or tu be mothers and sister's. It was a hull week afore I could make up my mind to go out of my office, and the sight of a furbelow raly made me sick. I began to rale out agin all the feminine gender like all natur.

Wal, one morning I got up, and sat down by the stove, with my legs stretched out, and my hands fingering the loose coppers in my trousers' pocket, when Cousin John come in, looking as tickled as a puppy dog.

"See here, Jonathan," sez he, "I've got an invitation, for you to go to a fancy ball to-night, clear up town, so I've come to see what you'll wear, and all about it."

"Wal," sez I, kinder melancholy, "I've got eenamost tired of sich things; it raly don't seem to agree with me frolicking so much, but I suppose I may as well go."

"Wal," sez cousin, "what do you mean to wear?"

"What du I mean tu wear?" sez I, "why, my new clothes sartinly: I ruther guess all the shine haint worn off from them yit, by a great sight."

"Yes," sez he, "but you must go in character to this ball."

"Look a here, cousin," sez I, a rilin up a leetle, "I don't know as you've ever seen me go to any place that was out of character yit, so you needn't say that."

John, he colored up and larfed a leetle, and sez he, "Don't git wrothy, Jonathan—I didn't mean nothing, but the fact is, it will be best for you to dress in something a leetle different to your common clothes. Supposing you dress like a Turk?"

"What! like one of them chaps that keep a hull caravan of wives shut up in their housen?" sez I. "I'm much obliged to you for the idee—but I'd a leetle ruther not. I'd jest as lives go to sleep and dream I was a gad fly in a black hornet's nest."

"Wal," sez he, "supposin you let me dress you up like an Injun—how would you like that? I'll dress Mary up like a squaw, and you can walk in together."

"Why," sez I, sort of puzzled to find out what he was at, "I'd ruther be an Injun any day than be one of them tarnal Turky fellers; but what will the folks think of us if we come fixed out so? I should feel as streaked as a piece of ribbongrass, I'm sartin."

"Oh, never mind that, they'll be glad to have you come like an Injun; you don't know what a sight of folks are a going. There'll be Kings and Queens, nuns, Scotch ladies, Englishmen, and women born two hundred years ago, and all sorts of people."

"Gracious gaully how you talk!" sez I, all in amaze, for he seemed as arnest as an ox team.—"Why, they haint sent invites over the water, have they?"

"You'll see," sez John, a larfin a leetle easy, and rubbing his hands. "But I want a favor,—wont you lend me them old clothes of yours to go in?"

"What, old blue, with the shiney buttons, and the pepper and salt trousers!" sez I. "Wal now, I'd jest as lives you had 'em as not? but raly if you want to slick up, hadn't you better take the new fix, it'll look a good deal more scrumptious?"

"No," sez he, "I want them that your picter was took in, they're jest the thing."

"They'll fit you to a notch," sez I. "The trousers may be a leetle too short, but I can get the gallus buttons sot on strong, and the pockets are nation handy."

"Do," sez he, "and I'll git your dress. Come up to our house, and, we'll all start together."

With that John he went away, and I sot down all in a flustration to try and make out what he wanted me to fix up like a born Injun for; but the more I tho't the more I got in a pucker about it, so l jest give it up, and stopped thinking about it as much as I could.

Your loving son,

JONATHAN SLICK.

LETTER XIII.

Jonathan Slick and the Grand Fancy Ball—Jonathan in the character of an Injun, and Cousin Beebe in the character of Jonathan—Cousin Mary as Jonathan's Squaw—Jonathan among Kings and Queens, Spaniards, Turks and Jews—Jonathan meets his pussey Cousin in the character of a Turk—Jonathan cuts his pussey Cousin.

DEAR PAR:

Wal, Thursday, jest afore dark, I bundled up old blue, and the pepper and salt trousers, and pulled foot for Cousin Beebe's as chirk as a grass-hopper. The nigger set me in and took me up stairs to a little room, where John was sittin in a great chair, with the tarnationest heap of feathers and things about him that ever you did see. He jumped up as soon as he saw me with the bundle under my arm, and sez he—

"Come, hurry now and get off your things, I want to paint you." With that he come along with a saucer of red stuff, and begun to stir it up mighty savage.

Wal, think sez I, that don't look over inviting—but I s'pose I may as well die for an old sheep as a lamb; so I took off my coat, and unbuckled my stock, and let him brush away. Didn't he snake on the paint though! Think sez I, I don't know how I shall feel—but if I don't look streaked, it wont be the fault of this ere leetle brush any how. Arter a while he begun to ri-bob-skew my hair up on the top of my head; I raly couldn't but jest wink, he drew it so tight; but I grinn'd and bore it as well as I could. By-am-by he made me put on a red shirt, and sich a heap of nigger gimcracks as would've made you larf only jest to look at. When he'd tied, and pinned, and stuck on all the feathers he could find, he told me to get up and look in the glass. Gauly-oppalus—what a darn'd lookin critter I was! I raly thought I should a bust, I larfed so; my hair was all girt on the top of my head, and a hull grist of red feathers stuck into it every which way, till my head looked like an allfired great beet, a running to seed—my face was painted a sort of a brick color, with two or three streaks of black and yaller, to make it look lively; I had on a sort of a leather nightgown, without any sleeves—all fringed off with beads, and feathers, and quills, that made a noise every time I moved, like the loose ice rattling off a tree arter a freezing rain; besides the legs of a pair of leather trousers, that only come up to my knees, but they were fringed and finefied off to kill, I can tell you. The shoes were smashers, though they sot to my feet as slick as a biscuit, and felt as soft as a silk weed pod You never saw anything worked off so—purty leetle shiney beads glistened all over with them, and they were kivered all over with flowers, and spangled off with silver, till they took the shine off eenamost anything I ever did see.

I don't know what got into me, but the minit I got the Injun toggery on, I begun to feel as subtle and slimpsey as an eel, and the way I flourished about and kicked up my heels, beat Miss Celeste all to nothing. I raly thought Cousin John would a died a larfin. "Look a here," sez he, "don't kick up a pow-wow till you get to the ball. Did you ever see a rale full-blooded Injun?"

"I ruther surmise so," sez I.

"Wal," sez he, "du you think you can act one out?"

"Can't I! Look a here—don't I du it as slick as a whistle?" sez I, and with that I looked as savage as a meat-axe, and begun to strut up and down the room like a turkey-gobbler on the sunny side of a barn-yard.

"That'll du," sez John; "now you must have some medicine."

"I'll bet a copper I don't, though," sez I; "I despise all kinds of doctor-stuff, and if you git any o' your rhubarb, o, calomel, or Brandreth's pills down me I'll lose my guess."

Here John went off the handle agin, like a broken coffee mill, and the way he did tee-hee was enough to make a feller's dander rise.

"Look a here," sez I, a walking straight up to him, "you needn't larf, nor try to come your soft soddor over me. I don't believe its the fashion to take pills here in York, afore a chap goes to a ball; and I won't do it. There now, I've sot down my foot."

It was a good while afore John could ketch his breath; but arter all he gin up—and, sez he, "Here, you haint no objections to carrying this thing, and calling it medicine, have you?"

"Not the least in natur," sez I,—and with that I took a sort of a young woodchuck skin, stuffed out till it looked nat'ral as life, and I tucked it under my arm, and went down stairs to see how Cousin Mary looked.

As sure as a gun there she sot all dressed out to kill—her hair was braided in great long tails, and all hung over with silver and gold, and leetle bunches of red feathers. A row of short red and yaller and blue feathers went round her head, and was twisted together on one side, with a gold cord that had two long tossels made out of gold and leetle shiney beads, that hung glistening over her shoulder as bright as a handful of ripe currents, when the sun strikes 'em.

I swow, but Mary did make a purty leetle squaw—her frock was made out of the whitest leather you ever did see, and was kinder like my no-sleeved coat, only a great deal harnsomer and hull all round. It didn't come clear down to her feet and that tarnal leetle foot and ankle of her'n did cut a swath in the leetle glistening shoes and them figgered silk stockings. It raly made me ketch my breath to look at her, she was so consarned harnsome. I thought I should a bust when cousin Beebe came into the room in my old blue coat and pepper and salts, with his hat stuck on the back of his head, and his hands in his pockets. It was me all over, cow-hide boots, red hankercher and all.

By-am-by the nigger come in and said that the carriage was at the door, so we all up and got into it about the quickest, and off we driv full split up town, till we come to a whopper of a house clear up to Seventeenth street. When we got eenamost there, the horses couldn't but jest git along, there was sich a grist of carriages streaking it one arter another toward the house. They put me in mind of a string of onions jest broke loose, they were so tarnal thick.

Arter a good while we driv chuck up to the stun walk that had a lot of tow sheets stretched out over it to keep folks dry, and went right straight up to the stoop, where a couple of sprucelooking chaps with red ribbons stuck in their button holes, come up and took us through a great long entry way, where the lights eenamost dazzled a feller's eyes, to a sort of a twistified pair of stairs.

I kinder wanted to stop by a stun table, sot off in the back part of the entry way, and take a swig of punch, but I hadn't time to git a hull swaller afore John and Mary were half way up stairs, so I pulled foot and went arter 'em sort of wamblecropped at having to choke off from the punch, for it was the rale critter, I can tell you.

Mary she went into a great harnsome room, chuck full, and running over with gals, for I took a sly peak through the door as she went in, jest to see what was a going on; and then Cousin Beebe and I went into another room, and walked round till she cum out agin. Down we went through the entry way till we come to a door at the further eend.

"Why don't you give Mary your arm?" sez John to me, jest as I was walking along toward the door.

"If I'm to play Injun to-night," sez I, "I'll do it according to my own notion if you'd jest as livs. I never see an Injun and squaw a hooking arms yet,—so cousin Mary may jest walk behind me, if she aint too stuck up."

With that I tucked the woodchuck under my arm, and walked right straight ahead as stiff as a crowbar. Gracious me! what a smasher of a room we went into—it was all set off with yaller and blue settees and benches, and every sich thing, eenamost as slick as my pussey cousin's room, and the darndest set of critters were a dancing and a sidling about that ever I did see. There warn't no carpet on the boards, and if they'd a been a mind tu, they might have shinned it down about right, but instead of that they went curchying and scooting about, jest like so many tom tits on the bank of a river. It raly made my grit rise to see a set of folks come from all the four quarters of the globe, to a party, that didn't know how to dance an eight reel or munny-muss as it ought to be done. They didn't seem to mind us when we went in, or else I should a felt awful streaked a standing up there like a darned Injun, with Mary by me. I felt sartin of not being known, and so I kept a purty stiff upper lip, and looked on jest to see how foreign gentry acted when they were tu hum. There was a swad of tarnal harnsome wimmen in the middle of the room curchying and twistifying and wriggling about one another, and making believe dance like all natur. But, oh forever! hcw they were dressed out! One on 'em had on a great long black silk cloak, with sleeves to it, and a sort of white bib hanging down before, for fear she'd spill the wine and sweet sarce on to her dress when she eat, I s'pose, and she looked sort a like a nice harnsome chap, and sort a like a gal, kinder half and half, like a fence politician. There was a gal close by her dressed out to kill; her shoes were tied on with red ribbons, over a leetle stuck up foot, that looked good enough to eat; and she had on three open dresses, one over t'other, made out of white silk and thin shiny stuff, bound and trimmed off with strips of gold; the sleeves hung down like a feller's shirt, but there warn't no ristband to 'em, and they hung wide open, so that her pesky white arm shone out enough to dazzle a feller's eyes. She had two allfired great breast pins, one on 'em spread out like a sun on her bosom, and another down to her waist, all sot chuck full of stuns, that kept a glistening in the light, like a handful of sparks out of a black-smith's chimney. She wore another of these glistening leetle suns on her harnsome white forehead; her long shiney curls hung down on her shoulders, and a white veil, that looked like a cloud with the sunshine a pouring into it, dropped over them. I whispered to cousin Mary, and asked who the darned likely critter could be. She said she come from Peru, and was a priestess, or something, of the sun. Before I could get a chance to ask whose son it was that she preached tu, and to say that I shouldn't grumble if sich a critter as that should preach a trifle easy to Mr Zepheniah Slick's son—up come a leetle black-eyed gal, about knee high to a toad, with a stick in her hand, and curls a hanging all over her shoulders.

"Hellow," sez I, "none of that are," as she hit my woodchuck a dab with the stick, and run off larfin, ready to bust her leetle sides. Before I knew which eend my head was on, up comes another set of leetle queer looking gals, so young that they didn't seem much more than babies, that ought to have been spanked and put to bed, instead of being there. They were dressed off in short frocks, and glistened like a hail storm; but where they come from I couldn't tell, for they all had wings on their shoulders, and I never read of such winged critters on this arth, and it didn't seem as if children would be sent from t'other world to a York ball. Before I could say Jack Robinson, they made themselves scarce, and then sich sights of men and wimmen cum a walking about, some dressed like angels jest dropped down, some in regimentals, and all sorts of ways, that ever a feller dreamed of. I swan, if I didn't begin to git dizzy with looking at 'em.

I kept by the door yit, a huggin my woodchuck, and a wonderin how on arth the man that gave the party made out to send round to all parts of the world to git his folks together, when I happened to give a squint towards cousin Beebe, and I bust right out a larfin, all I could du to help it. There he stood with his mouth sort of open, and both hands dug down into the pockets of my old pepper and salts, a staring about like a stuck pig. Arter a minit, he went up to the slick leetle gal, right from Spain, with shiney black hair, eyes as bright as a hawk's, and a great long black veil a streaming down her back, and he made a bow and asked her to dance as genteel as I could a done myself. Pokehontas! but didn't he make the old cowhides flurish about. The way he balanced up and played heel and toe back agin, was Weathersfield all over. The old blue and pepper and salts had put the grit into him about right. I don't believe he'd felt so nat'ral afore since he left Connecticut. I thought Mary would a gone off the handle, she was so tickled, and I had to go away to keep from haw-hawing right out.

I went along through a great wide door into a room all set off with blue, that had a pen full of fiddlers at the further eend, where some folks from Turkey and Amsterdam were a whirling the foreign gals round and round like so many horses a grinding cider. I couldn't look at 'em without feeling my dander rise, yet I couldn't help but be sort of glad that the great people from foreign parts made as tarnal coots of themselves as we du here to hum. There wasn't a gal dressed out like a true born

American among 'em; but the way they did flirt round with the men a hugging them, and the light a pouring down from the heaps of glass and white candles over head, was as bad as I ever see in a rale York party. It kinder made me dizzy to look on, so I jest turned my back and begun to take an observation of the consarned harnsome picters that hung agin the wall and listened to the music that come a streaming from the fiddles and horns and bass viols as slick as a streak of chalk iled at both eends. By-am-by I seemed to git tired of that, so up I went to see if I couldn't find out where the Kings and Queens had hid to; for I had a kind of a hankerin notion to see what kind of stuff they were made on.

Wal, I went along the entry-way, only jest stopping time enough to take a swig of drink from the stun table, till I got into a room where they kept the Kings and Queens. The light come down almighty powerful over the great thick red carpet, and the settees and foot-stools and chairs glistened out like a bed of tulips in a hot sun. But the Queens, it raly did make me ketch my breath to look on 'em. Sich consarned beautiful critters I never did see. They beat all horned cattle that ever I sot eyes on. One on 'em sot on a foot-stool, with her feet sort of crossed in a letter X. She had shiney trousers on, all spangled off, and a kind of a silk frock-coat puckered up awfully at the waist, with a lot of them shiney stuns round her neck, and on her arms, and among her thick hair, and all over, till she glistened as if she'd been out among a storm of firebugs. There was a leetle hump-backed critter of a man, all finefied off with satins, and feathers, and velvet, and gold; but a darn'd queer shote he was for a king! So I jest went by him, and the odd looking Queen squat on the foot-stool that he was a talking to, as chipper as could be, and sidled sort of bashful, woodchuck and all, up to a tall, harnsome, stuck-up looking Queen, that stood a talking to a chap with a great long feather in his cap, that they called a Night. She had on a great long shiney velvet dress, that streamed out behind like the tail of a comet, and round her beautiful head was a rale ginuine crown, that seemed as if it struck fire every time she moved her head; it raly made my eyes snap to look on it.

Think sez I to myself, "Wal, I never did speak to a Queen yit—but, by gaully! I'll have a try at it this time—Injun or no Injun."

I didn't exactly know how to begin, but I'd heard say that folks always got down on their marrow bones when they spoke to sich stuck up quality; and think sez I, what's manners for a white man, must be manners for an Injun. So I went whop down on my knees, and sez I—"Look a here, Marm Queen, shouldn't you like a nation well to have a look at a rale prime Yankee woodchuck? They are curious critters, I call tell you!"

With that, I held up the consarned little critter, and begun to stroke down his back as if he'd been a pussy cat.

The Queen kinder jumped and stepped back, and said, "Oh, my!" and a leetle finefied boy, dressed off to kill, that stood behind her a holding up the eend of her frock, he begun to snicker, and at last he tee-heed right out.

Arter a minit, the Queen begun to larf too, and she sartinly was about the sweetest lookin critter that I ever did see, with her purty mouth opening like a red rose-bud, and her leetle white teeth a shining inside.

"Before I take your medicine," sez she, "tell me what tribe you belong to?"

I didn't know what on arth to say, for I never could twist my jaws with one of them crooked Injun names—but, sez I to myself, I calculate that a queen aint nothing but a woman arter all, and it'll only make her think the more of me if I keep dark, so I shook my head as if there was a good deal in it, and sez I—

"Oh, marm, that's telling. You aint the first gal that has tried to find me out; but it's plaguey hard work a kneeling down here, so if you'd jest as livs I'll stand up—but I raly wish you'd let that leetle shaver of your'n tend my woodchuck awhile—I'm eenamost tuckered out a carrying it."

Here the other Queens and all the Kings and Nights come a crowding round us all in a twitter to hear what we were so chipper about. I begun to feel a sort of streaked with so many of them lofty foreign cattle a looking at me, so I put out my elbow, and sez I to the Queen— sez I,

"Will you take my arm and let's go and see if we can't find a bite of something to eat—I'm a gittin kinder hungry, aint you?"

She seemed to hang back a minit as if she was loth to go, but they all begun to giggle and said they'd go along, so she put her leetle white hand on my arm, and away we went, the eend of her frock a streaming out behind, and the leetle chap a holding on as you've seen a kitten to an old cat's tail.

"Wal," think sez I, "if marm could see me now a streaking up these ere stairs with a ginuine Queen on one arm and a stuffed woodchuck under t'other, and a hull grist of Kings and Queens coming arter us, it seemed to me that she'd allow that I'd been lifted up a notch or two above the vulgar since I left hum."

In all my born days I never saw a table that could hold a candle to the one we found all set off in one of the big rooms up stairs. There was no eend to the silver and glasses a glitterin and flashin up among the eatables and drinkables. The visiters couldn't git to but one side of the table, and on t'other side was a hull grist of waiters and niggers a bustling about like a swarm of black wasps in a tantrum.

I gin the Queen a heap of good things, and it raly did me good to see how she nibbled at 'em; the way she stowed away the jellies and presarves was as much like any of our York gals as if she hadn't been a Queen.

When she'd eat about enough I crooked my elbow, and we went down stairs jest as we cum up—Kings and Queens and Nights and Injuns and all—a rale mixed up squad. As soon as I'd found a seat for the queen I cut stick as stiff as could be. At fust I was a going to make her a bow before I went away, but I wasn't exactly sartin whether Injuns ever larn them things, so I pulled in and cut away to the big ball room tickled eenamost to death with the notice that had been taken of me.

I was a looking round arter Cousin Mary, when a leetle slim stuck up critter cum up to me with her yaller hair all a flying and her wings spread like a frightened butterfly, and afore I thought what I was at, I bust right out.

"Good gracious," sez I, "If it aint my etarnal pussey cousin's leetle finefied darter Jemima!"

The critter heard me and run up and spoke to a fat old Turk of a feller in a frock and trousers and with a red hankercher twisted round his head. He got up and whispered to a pussey sort of a woman all kivered over with yaller silk and glistening like a bank of ice with gold and stuns, and up they all three cum a fluttering like a flock of hens at seeing a handful of corn, and the woman she stuck out her fat hands and squealed out,—

"Oh, cousin Slick, is that you? I declare I'm delighted that Jemima has found you out. How very bright of her wasn't it? but then she is——"

I didn't hear any more, for the foreign quality turned round and stared with all the eyes they had in their heads. I cut and run—pulled foot like sacred sheep, till I got outside the door. For there, as sure as a gun, was my pussy cousin and his wife turned Turks. It was bad enough to have him a struttin round to show a feller off, in his black coat and trousers; but I raly believe I should a gin up if he'd a cum up in his Turk's frock and great wide silk trousers to claim relationship with me.

My heart riz up in my throat at the idee of going back tu join the stuck up varmints, and it was a good while before I could make up mind to skulk back and look up Cousin Beebe and Mary. She was a dancing with the humped-backed King, and John was a shinnin it down like all natur with a purty woman, that wore a shiney black velvet dress, all kivered over with silver stars. It raly did me good to see him take the double shuffle; but I was allfired anxious to git away, for fear of seeing them pussy Turks agin, that he choked off, and we went hum about as well tuckered out as ever you see three critters.

Arter all I don't think these ere foreigners are anything to speak on more genteel than our ginuine Americans. Mebby it's because they hain't got used tu our ways yet, but some on 'em seemed tu be rather awk'ard in their blazin fine dresses, but I s'pose it made 'em feel bad tu see how kinder easy we free born Americans felt with them.

Your loving son,

JONATHAN SLICK.

LETTER XIV.

Advice to Jonathan from the Humstead—Jonathan's criticism on his Brother Sam's book—The ennui of Jonathan in good society—Jonathan's entre into a Milliner's Establishment, and sad mistake about a Side-saddle.

DEAR PAR:
It raly makes me feel bad to have you keep a writin so much advice to me. I du want to please you; and I don't think there ever is a time in the world when a chap can know enough to turn up his nose at his father's advice; but it's my ginuine opinion, that when you let a feller go away from hum, it's best to let him cut his own fodder.

You've gin me a first rate edecation for your parts, and you've also told me to be honest and industrious, but sharp as a razor. The truth is, you've sort of cultivated me, as you du our onion patches, but arter you've dug them up and put the seed in, and kept the weeds out till the ginuine roots get stuck purty deep and the tops shoot up kinder thrifty, haint you also found it to du best to leave 'em grow accordin to natur, with nothing but the night dew and rich arth and the warm sunshine to help 'em along; and don't they git ripe and run up to seed and down to root, and bring in the hard chink jest as well as if you kept diggin about 'em and trimmin 'em up from morning till night? If you keep the weeds out when they're young, and manure the arth well in the spring, there haint so much danger that the soil will grow barren all tu once, or that the weeds can spring up so quick as to choke a good tough onion. It ain't in natur, ask our minister if it is.

Now don't you be scared about me, if I du go to the theatre once in a while, or dress up like a darned coot of an Injun jest to see what etarnal ninny-hammers kings and queens and quality can make of themselves. I ain't in no danger, I can tell you. A feller that's got his eye teeth in his head can al'ers see enough to larf at in his sleeve, and to make him pity human natur without forgitting that he's a man, and that he was born to du good, and not spend his hull life in trying to cut a dash. Don't you nor marm worry about me—I may be a leetle green at fust, but I shall come out right side up with care, yit, you may be sartin on it.

I feel sort of wamblecropped to day, par, for I've jest been a reading our Sam's new book about the Great Western. I was up to cousin Beebe's when he brought it hum, and begun to read it to Mary. He hadn't read more than twenty pages afore cousin Mary made believe a headache, as women always du when they feel oneasy about anything, and she cut and run with about the reddest face I ever did see. I felt as streaked as a winter apple, and cousin John, sez he—

"Jonathan, if the folks off in Canada hadn't made Sam a judge, I'd stick to it that he wasn't a relation of mine; his book raly ain't fit to read afore the wimmen folks."

I wanted to stick up for Sam, but I'll be darn'd if I could see how to du it, for the book's an allfired smutty thing, and that's the fact; but I thought what consarned rough words the printers sometimes put in my letters to you, when I've writ something very different,—and so, think sez I, I'll put it off onto the printers and publishers; for I'll be choked if I don't believe they've made as much of a mistake in publishing the book as Sam did in writing it. So sez I,

"Sam's fust book was a peeler, and a credit to the family; and I haint the least doubt that this one would been jest as good, if Sam hadn't strained to beat t'other, and so broke his bridle The ginuine grit aint all sifted out on 'm, I'll bet a cookey; and I haint the least doubt that the printers spiled this one. They're etarnally twistifying my words into some darn'd thing or other that would make a minister swear. Sometimes they transmogrify what I write till I shouldn't know as it was mine; but then you know, cousin John, it aint everybody that knows how tu spell out the ginuine English as we du in Weathersfield."

Cousin John he smiled, and then I kept on, and sez I,

"It raly made me grit my teeth to read sich things, and think the purty gals would believe that I writ them. I didn't blame my par," sez I, "for writing me a great long letter of admonition about sich words; but he ought to have known better than to believe I put them there. It aint in my natur to write anything that the most mealy-mouthed gal on arth mightn't read out loud afore all the chaps in creation; and if any on 'em see anything that don't come right up to the chalk, in the way of gentility, they may be sartin it aint *mine*."

My dear par, jest you keep easy about me,—and if you and marm want to jaw any body, haul our Sam over the coals and sarmonize him; you'll find fust rate picking on that goose,—but I haint but jest begun to put out my pin feathers yit.

Wal now, I may as well give you a leetle notion of my goings-on here, since I went to that smashing ball, and eat presarves with a rale queen. Somehow I've begun to git sort of tired of the big bugs and the tippies, they're all too much alike, and arter a chap's been to a few of their parties, and balls, and so on, he kinder loathes their darned soft finefied nonsense, as well as the cider and sweet sarse that they stuff a feller with.

Going among quality is like boarding at a fust rate tavern. At fust a critter don't know what to du with himself he's so tickled with the nice things on the table, but by-and-by his stomach begins to turn agin the chickens, and turkeys, and young pigs, and takes tu a hankering arter pot-luck and plain pork and beans.

This sort of feeling kinder settled on me arter the ball. I raly was eenamost sot agin the harnsome critters that sidle up and down Broadway, with leetle round things, made out of silk, about as big as a good sized toad-stool, stuck up before their faces, to keep the sun off; so I eenamost made up my mind to put on the old pepper and salts agin, see a leetle of human natur among the gals that git their own living, and work themselves to death to make them stuck up critters in Broadway look as harnsome as they du.

I'd heard say that there were lots of purty gals to work in the milliners' stores up in Division street, and in the Bowery, but somehow I didn't exactly know how to git acquainted with any on 'em. I never felt a mite bashful about scraping acquaintance with stuck up critters, like my pussey cousin's wife and Miss

10

Miles; but when I see a harnsome innocent young gal a going out arly in the morning and a coming home late at night, and working like a dog to arn a decent living, somehow my heart rises up in my throat, and insted of shinning up to' em, and talking soft sodder, as I du to the tippies, I feel sort of dashed, and as if a chap ought to take off his hat, and let them see that honest men respect them the more because they are alone, with nobody to take care of them.

I never see one of hem harnsome young critters going along hum, arter working hard all day, to arn something to live on, and mebby to feed their pars and mars with, but I git to thinkin how much a ginuine chap ought to prize them for keeping honest, and industrious, and vartuous, when they haint much to encourage them to du right, and generally have a good deal to tempt them to du wrong, insted of turning up their noses at 'em afore folks, or a tryin to tempt them into sin and wickedness behind people's backs. It has raly made my blood bile more than ever to see foreign and dandefied chaps, like that hairy lipped Count, go by them gals in the day time, with their noses up in the air, and a looking as if the purty critters warn't good enough to go along the same stun walk with them, and the stuck up quality ladies; when any body that took pains to watch the etarnal varments arter dark, might ketch them a hanging round the dark corners of the streets, and a chasing arter them same working gals like so many darn'd yaller foxes scouting round a hen coop, arter the geese and turkeys; chaps that would run a man through with a sword-cane or a bagonet if he dared to look sideways at his wife or sister, will impose on an honest gal if they can git a chance, and think it's allfired good fun tu. Darn such fellers! hangin's too good for 'em! I tell you what, par, you may talk about people's being born free and equal, and about liberty, and independence, and all that, but it's my opinion that there aint a place on arth, where the people try to stomp each other down to the dirt more than they du here in York.

Wal, I wont finish off this ere sarmon, so your minister needn't get wamblecropped, for fear I'll cut him out. But I'll jest tell you what put all these sober notions into my head.

You haint forgot that Judy White had a cousin that come here to York t* larn a trade. She was a tarnal sweet purty critter when she come away from Weathersfield, as plump as a partridge, and with cheeks as red as a rosy. Judy made me promise a good while ago that if ever I come down to York I'd go and see her cousin, but somehow it does make a feller forget old friends to be always going to parties and dinners with these big bugs, and it warn't till t'other day that I thought anything about Susan Reed.

The fust minit she come into my head I up and went straight along the Bowery, detarmined to find the place that she worked at, and see how she was getting along. I had forgot the number, but when I come to a store that was all windows in front, and that had a smasher of a bonnet hung agin every square of glass, besides beautiful caps and ribbons and posies as nat'ral as life, hung up between, I made up my mind that I'd hit the right nail on the head, and so in I went as independent as a wood-sawyer's clerk.

A leetle bit of a stuck up old maid stood back of a counter, all sot off with bonnets and feathers that looked tempting enough to make a feller's purse jump right out of his trousers' pocket. She had on a cap all bowed off with pink ribbons, that looked queer enough round her leetle wizzled up face, and a calico frock, figgered out with great bright posies, besides one of them ere sort of collars round her neck, all sprigged and ruffled off as slick as a new pin. Her waist warn't bigger round than a quart cup, and she stuck her hands down in the pockets of her dashy silk apron, as nat'ral as I could a done it myself. I was jest a going to ask if Susan Reed worked there, when a lady come in and wanted to buy a bonnet. At it they went, hand over first, a bargainin and a tryin on red and yaller and pink and blue bonnets.

The milliner she put one sort on, and then another, and went on pouring out a stream of soft sodder, while the lady peaked at herself in a looking-glass, and twistified her head about like a bird on a bramble bush, and at last said, she didn't know, she'd look a leetle further, mebby she'd call agin, if she didn't suit herself, and a heap more palavar, that made the leetle w man look as if she'd been a drinking a mug of hard cider.

While the lady was trying to edge off to the door, and the milliner was a follering her with a blue bonnet, and a great long white feather a streaming in her hand, I jest took a slantindicular squint at the glass boxes that stood about chuck full of jim-cracks and furbelows, for there was something in one of 'em that raly looked curious. It was a sort of a thing stuffed out and quilted over till it stood up in the glass box as stiff and parpendicular as a baby's go-cart.

I jest put my hands down in my pockets sort of puzzled, and stood a looking at the critter to see what I could make on it. Arter I'd took a good squint at the consarn, up one side, down t'other, and down the middle, right and left, I purty much made up my mind that it was one of them new-fashioned side-saddles, that I'd heard tell on, and I took a notion into my head that I'd buy one and send it to marm. So when the leetle old maid cum back from the door, I jest pinted at the saddle, and sez I,

"What's the charge for that are t. ing?"

"Why, that pair," sez she, a sticking her head on one side, and a burying her hands, that looked like a hawk's claws, down in the pocket of her cunning short apron, "I'll put them to you at twelve dollars; they're French-made, 'lastic shoulder straps, stitched beautifully in the front, chuck full of whalebone—and they set to the shape like the skin to a bird."

Lord a massey, how the little stuck up critter did set off the the talk! I couldn't shove in a word edgeways, till she stopped to git breath, and then sez I,

"I s'pose you throw in the martingales, sirsingle, and so on, don't you?"

"The what," says she, a stepping back, and squinting up in my face sort of cross, as if she didn't like to throw in the whole harnessing at that price.

"The martingale," sez I, "and the sirsingle; but mebby you have some other name for 'em down here in York. I mean the straps that come down in front to throw the chest out, and give the neck a harnsome bend, and the thing to girt up in the middle with. Marm wont know how to use this new-fashioned thing if I don't send all the tackle with it."

"Oh," sez the milliner, "I didn't understand; you want the

laces and the steel in front; sartinly we give them in. The steel is kivered with kid, and the laces are of the strongest silk."

"Wal," sez I, "I never heard of a steel martingale, and I should be afeard they wouldn't be over pliable."

"Oh," sez she, "you can bend 'em double, they give so."

"How you talk," says I, "it raly is curious what new inventions people du have, but somehow it sort of seems to me that a silk girt might be a leetle too slimpsey, don't you think so marm?"

"Lor, no sir," sez she, "they are strong enough, I can tell you; jest take a look at the Broadway ladies, they never use anything else, and they girt tight enough, I'm sure."

I hadn't the least idee what the critter was a diving at; she see that I looked sort of puzzled, and I s'pose she begun to think that I shouldn't buy the saddle.

"Look a here," sez she, a putting her hands on both sides of her leetle stuck up waist; "I've got 'em on myself, so you can judge how tight they can be fitted."

"Gaully offalus!" sez I, a snorting out a larfing, and a eyeing the leetle finefied old maid; but I didn't think it was very good manners to burst right out so, and I tried all I could to choke in. Gracious me! think sez I, no wonder the York gals have such humps on their backs, since they've got to wearing saddles like horses.

By-am-by, arter I'd eenamost bust myself a trying to stop larfing, it come into my head that the critter of a milliner was a trying to poke fun at me, cause I wanted to beat her down: for I couldn't believe the tippies quite so bad as to girt up and strap down like a four year old colt. Wal, think sez I, I'll be up to her anyhow; so I looked jest as mealy-mouthed as if I believed her, and sez I, as innocent as a rabbit in a box trap, sez I,

"If the wimmen folks have took to wearing saddles, I s'pose they haint forgot the bridles tu; so I dont care if I take this ere pair for some old maids we've got in our parts. If I had my way, they'd all be bitted the minit they turned the fust corner. Darn'd talking critters them old maids are, marm," sez I, a looking at her sort of slanting, jest to let her see she hadn't got hold of quite so great a greenhorn as she seemed to think.

Lord a Massey, how she did look! Her leetle wizzled up face begun to twist itself up till it looked like a red winter apple puckered up by the frost. I didn't seem to mind it, but put my hand down in my pocket sort of easy, and begun to whistle Yankee Doodle.

"You haint got no bridle's then?" sez I, after a minit; for she looked wrathy enough to spit fire, and sot up sich an opposition in the pocket line, that I was raly afeard her leetle hands would bust through the silk or break her apron strings, she dug down so.

"Bridles! no!" sez she, as spiteful as a meat-axe jest ground, "but I'll send out and git a halter for you, with all my heart."

"Gaully!" sez I, "but you're clear grit—smart as a steel trap, aint you?"

"Yes," sez she, more spiteful yet, "when it snaps at some animal like you, that don't know enough to keep out of its teeth?"

Think sez I, Mr. Jonathan Slick, Esq., it's about time for you to haul in these horns of your'n. You aint no match for a woman, anyhow; there never was a critter of the feminine gender, that couldn't talk a chap out of his seven senses in less than no time.

"Gaully," sez I, "you've about used me up—I begin to feel streaked as lean pork in the bottom of a barrel. I guess I shan't tackle in with a smart critter like you agin in a hurry! but don't git too mad; it'll spile that harnsome face of your'n. I swan! but I should think you was eenamost thirty this minit, if I hadn't seen the difference before you begun to rile up."

Didn't the puckers go out of her face when I said this! She was mollified down in a minit. I don't s'pose she ever had twenty years took off from her good fifty so slick afore in her hull life; but it aint human natur to come out all to once,—at any rate, it aint an old maid's natur, when her back once gits up. So when I see her darned thin lips begin to pucker and twist into sort of a smile, I let off a leetle more soft sodder, that wilted her down like a cabbage-leaf in the sun; and then sez I, a pinting to the glass-box—

"Come, now, s'posing we strike up a trade. I've took a sort of a sneaking notion to that ere new-fashioned side-saddle. So if you'll throw in the tackling, I'll give you ten' dollars for it, cash on the nail."

"That what?" said she, a looking fust at me and then at the saddle, with her mouth a leetle open and her eyes sticking out like peeled onions. "That what?"

"Why, that are saddle," sez I, beginning to feel my dander rise.

"That saddle," sez she, "that saddle; why, sir, did you take that pair of French corsets for a saddle?"

With that she slumped down into a chair, and kivered her face with both hands, and larfed till I raly thought the critter would a split her sides. The way she wriggled back'rd and fored, tee-heeing and haw-hawing, was enough to make a Presbyterian Missionary swear like a sea captain.

"That saddle!" sez she, a looking up from between her hands, and then letting off the fun again as bad as ever. "That saddle! *Oh, dear, I shall die.* Did you really take that pair of *French corsets* for a side-saddle, sir? Oh, dear, I shall die a larfin!"

Didn't I feel streaked though! Only think what an eternal coot I had made of myself, to take a pair of gal's corsets for a side-saddle. "Darn the things," sez I, and it was as much as I could du to keep from putting foot to the glass case, and kicking it into the street. I felt the blood bile up into my face, and when the old maid bust out agin, and I see a hull grist of purty faces come a swarming to a glass door, that they'd hauled back a curtain from, I could have skulked through a knot hole, I felt so dreadful mean. But by-am-by I begun to think they had more cause to be ashamed than I had. Who on arth would ever have thought them stiff indecent looking things were made for a delicate gal to wear? I felt dreadfully though, to think that I'd been a talking about a gal's under-riggin, to a woman so long, but after a few minits I begun to think that I needn't fret myself much about that. The woman that stuck them things out in the street for young fellers to look at, needn't go off in a fit of "the dreadful suz," because a chap asks the price of them. "So, who cares!" sez I.

The old maid jumped up, arter she'd larfed herself into a caniption fit, and out on it agin—and she run into the back room where the gals were. It warn't more than a minit before there was in there sich a pow-wow and rumpus kicked up,—the gals begun to hop about like parched corn on a hot shovel. They sot up sich a giggle and tee-heeing, that I couldn't a stood it one minit longer. But all tu once I heard somebody say,

"My gracious, it's Mr. Jonathan Slick, from our parts!"

At that they all choked in, and were as still as mice in a flour bin. I looked to the glass door, and there stood Susan Reed, a holding back the curtain with one hand and peaking through a square of glass to be sartin it was me. I tell you what, but the gal looked like a picter, and a darned purty picter tu, as she stood a holding back the heap of red cloth in her dark colored calico dress, and black silk apron that made her neck and face look as white as a lily. The rosy cheeks that she used to have in Weathersfield were all gone, and her eyes seemed as if they'd grown larger than they ever were before. I don't know when I've seen a gal that has took my notion as she did while she was a standing in that door. Arter a minit I see her fling her head back till the long shiney curls streamed in heaps over her shoulder, and I heard her say,—

"Oh, let me go out!—I'm sure it's him."

"What of that?" I heard the old maid squeak out, as sour as vinegar; "he aint no relation, is he?"

"No, no," sez Susan, a droppin the curtain, and a speaking as if her heart was brim full and a running over; "but he come from Weathersfield,—we went to school together; he come from *home*,—I must speak to him!"

With that she opened the door and come towards me, a holding out her hand and a trying to smile; but the tears were a standing in her great blue eyes, and I raly thought she was a going to bust right out a crying. I knew she was a thinking about the old humstead, and when I remembered how them darned lawyers cheated her old mother out of house and hum, I felt so bad I could a cried tu, jest as well as not.

I went right up and shook hands, and sez I—

"How do you du, Susan? I swanny! but the sight of you is good for sore eyes; it raly seems like old times, only jest to look at you."

She kinder smiled a leetle, and sez she " How are all the folks in Weathersfield ?"

" Oh, they were all so as to be crawling about when I come away," sez I. " Sally Sikes has got married, I s'pose you know."

" And how is cousin Judy ?" sez she.

" Purty well, considerin," sez I; and you can't think how all-overish I felt to hear any body speak of Judy so fur from hum. I was jest a going to say something to keep her from asking anything more about the gal, when the old maid she come out, and sez she—

" Miss Reed, I don't hire you to talk with young fellers in the front shop."

Gaully! didn't my blood bile, I could a knocked the stuck up leetle varmint into a cocked hat, but Susan she looked sort of scared, and, sez she,

" Call and see me, Mr. Slick, at my boarding-house: I shall be so glad to talk over old times." The tears bust right into her blue eyes as she spoke, and she looked so humsick I raly felt for her.

" What time shall I call ?" sez I, a follering her to the glass door.

" I haint a minit that I can call my own till arter eight o'clock at night," sez she; " but if you'll call some evening I shall be glad to see you."

" I shall sartinly come," sez I, and arter shaking hands with her agin I went out of the store and hum to my office, a feeling purty considerably humsick and with more ginuine human natur bilin up in my heart than I'd felt since I cum to York.

Your loving son,
JONATHAN SLICK

LETTER XV.

Jonathan visits the Milliner girl—Reflections about her situation.

Dear Par:

I couldn't seem to rest easy till I went to see Susan. She boarded in a sort of a gloomy house eenamost up to Dry-dock. I knocked away at the door with my knuckles ever so long afore I could make any body hear. By-am-by Susan come to the door herself, and she took me up a pair of stairs, kivered with rag carpeting, into a leetle stived up room with a stove in it. Two leetle squalling brats were a playing on the floor, and a harnsome woman, but not over nice in her fixings, sot in one corner, a sewing on a round-about. Susan she was dressed up jest as she was in the milliner's store; she looked peaked and eenamost tuckered out, but the minit I'd got seated, she took hold with the woman and begun to sew away for dear life.

"You seem to be ruther industrious," sez I.

She smiled sort of mournful, and sez she, so low I couldn't but jest ketch the words,

"I'm obliged to be or starve."

Think sez I, there's something that aint right here, and with that I begun to talk about the prices of the work, till I found out that with all her hard trying, it was more than she could du to arn a decent living. I begun to talk about hum and the time when I used to lend her my mittens when she was a leetle gal and her fingers were cold; but all I could do she wouldn't chirk up, but the other woman she got rale sociable and told me lots of stories about milliners and sewing girls, and as I was going hum I took it into my head that I'd write some on 'em out for the Express.

I mean to send one on 'em next week, but I raly think they ought to shell out more chink than they du for my letters, for I've had to study the dictionary two days a ready to sarch out long words, and I haint got half enough yit. I went to Cousin Beebe about it, and he said that mebby I'd better study some of the arly English writers before I begun to write stories, or else Washington Irving, Cooper, or some of them chaps might cut me out. I didn't jest know what he meant by arly writers, but made up my mind that it was them that begun to write when they was shavers, so I went into a bookstore and told them I wanted to buy a good book that was writ by some English youngster.

"Here's a work by Boz," say he, a handing down a big book; "he begun the youngest and writes the best of any of the folks across the water." I bought the book and went back to my office. Gaully-oppalus, but aint that Boz Dickens a smasher! if he don't beat all natur, nobody does. If I could write like him I raly should bust my dandy vest, I should be so puffed up. I kept on reading eenamost all night, and more than once I bust right out a crying afore I knew it. I swan to man that leetle Nell that he writes about is the sweetest, purtyest critter that anybody ever dreamed on. Oh! how I wish you would read the story about her, it's as good as the Pilgrim's Progress any day.

Then there's a mean, etarnal sneaking coot, a Mr. Quilp, that drunk bilin hot licker out of a skillet, and licked a poor peaked little critter—his wife—amost to death every once in a while, and when he hadn't her handy he took to cudgelling a wooden image. I swan to man, it made my blood bile to read about sich dreadful carryings on; but yit when I cum to consider and think on it all over, it kinder seems to me as if Boz Dickens had stretched his galluses a trifle, in writing out sich an allfired spiteful varmint. Human natur is bad enough, any how; but my paper is run out, and I aint but jest room to subscribe myself

Your loving son,
JONATHAN SLICK.

LETTER XVI.

MISS JOSEPHINE BURGESS—A TALE.

In which Jonathan shows up the Hardships of Sewing Girls—Describes a Tammany Hall Ball—Milliner Aristocracy and Exclusiveness—Informs the reader how Miss Josephine Burgess took a tall man with whiskers into her Establishment, who took her in in return—The desperation of a little Apothecary—His Marriage, and the Ascent of Miss Josephine Burgess from the front store to a work room a little higher up.

Miss JOSEPHINE BURGESS was as purty a gal as ever trod shoo leather; but she was awfully stuck up, and got into all kind of finefied notions, arter her par, the old shoemaker, died and left her his arnings. She was an awful smart critter though, and had a sort of a notion which side her bread was buttered on, as well as anybody you ever sot eyes on. Instid of spending the seven hundred dollars, which the stingy old coot of a shoemaker left behind him, all in hard chink, she sot up a milliner's and dress-maker's store in the Bowery; and it raly would have done the old chap's ghost good, to have seen how she contrived to turn the sixpences and half dollars that he'd been hoarding up so long in an old pepper-and-salt stocking, for fear of losing 'em. A tarnal snug bisness Miss Josephine Burgess was a doing, I can tell you. If she didn't know how to make things gibe, there wasn't a gal in the Bowery that did, you may be sartin. She raly had a talent for the bisness—a sort of genius in the bonnet way. With her own harnsome leetle fingers she cut and snipped and twisted and pinned on the shiney stuff and ribbons to all the caps and bonnets turned off by the ten peeked looking thin young girls that worked twelve hours out of every twenty-four, in a garret bed-room, in the back of the house, where Miss Josephine Burgess kept her store. Her thin peeked looking young girls might have enjoyed themselves if they only had a mind to!

There never was such a prospect as they had to look upon when they got tired. If they jest turned their bright eyes up to get a peek at the sky, there was a hull regiment of chimnies, all a sending out smoke like a company of Florida sogers; and if they looked down, there were ever so many backyards cut up into sort of pig pens, with lots of bleech boxes a pouring out the brimstone smoke, and old straw bonnets strung out to dry, that made every thing look comfortable and like live. Miss Josephine Burgess was a purty good boss considerin. She let her gals have half an hour to eat their dinners in, and if any on 'em didn't happen to get to the shop at seven o'clock in the morning she never docked off more than half their day's wages. She was rather apt to get out of temper once in a while; but then insted of blowing the gals up, as some cross grained critters will, she only blew up their work, and made them du it all over agin; which was a more easy way of spitting out spite, and putting a few coppers into her own pocket; for when it took half of a day to du the work, and another half to alter it, she only made the poor gals lose a half day's wages; and if they didn't like that she'd al'rs give them leave to get a better place; which, considering that half the sewin gals in York are always out of work, was raly very good natured and considerate in her. Besides this she had a good many ginerous leetle ways of turning a copper. When the peeked, haggard young critters came down from the work-room, at twelve o'clock Saturday night—for Miss Josephine Burgess was awful pious, it wasn't only once in a great while that she made the gals work over into the Sabberday morning—as she paid them their wages Miss Josephine always found out that some mistake had been made in the work—a piece of silk cut into, or a bit of leghorn burnt brown in the bleaching, which melted down the twenty shillings which they ought to have had apiece, to eighteen, or mebby two dollars; all of which must sartinly have been to the satisfaction and amusement of the pale troop of gals, who had two dollars to pay for board, besides clothes and washing to get along with, out of the twenty-five cents that were left; and if they didn't seem to like it, Miss Josephine wasn't agoing to fret her herself about that. She al'rs contrived to tucker them out with hard work before she settled up, so that there was no fear of their saying much agin what she took of their wages. Sometimes the tears would come into their eyes; and some on 'em that hadn't no hum to go tu, except the leetle garret bed-rooms which they were over head and ears in debt for, would burst out and sob as if they hadn't a friend on arth; but crying is a good deal like drinking—it hurts them that take to it more than it does anybody else. Miss Josephine Burgess didn't care a copper for tears and sobs; she'd got used to 'em.

Miss Josephine Burgess raly had a talent for her bisness. Nobody ever learned so many prudent ways of laying up money. She used to dress up like a queen, and her Sunday-go-to-meeting clothes were the genuine things and genteel all over. Eenamost every Sabberday she would go to meeting in a branfire new bonnet; and if some of her good natured customers that staid to hum because theirs warn't finished, had one just like it come to the door on Monday morning, the leetle gal that waited for the band-box only had to say, that she sarched and sarched on Saturday night and couldn't find the house. It doesn't hurt a dashing bonnet to wear it eenajest once. Miss Josephine never kept her customers a waiting over more than one Sunday, only when they were very busy or paid beforehand. Folks that are always a minding other people's business used to talk about Miss Josephine, and call her extravagant and stuck up; but the varmints didn't know what they were a talking about more than nothing. If she had her silks and satins made up every month, the making cost eenamost nothing. The working gals always expected to sit up till twelve o'clock Saturday nights in hurrying times; and when it wasn't hurrying time Miss Josephine had always a frock to finish off for herself or something of that sort. The frocks answered jest as well to make bonnets out on, arter she'd dashed out in 'em once or twice, and the sleeves and waist cut up scrumptiously for ruffles and furbelows.

Miss Josephine Burgess understood the soft sodder principle like a book. She had a way of bantering off the bonnets and gimcracks that was raly curious. If a customer happened to take a notion to having color and shape of a bonnet, she would insist upon it that she should try it on afore the glass; and while the lady was a gittin good natured, and a beginning to feel stuck up with the looks of herself, Miss Josephine would twist about the bows, and spread out the ribbands, and tell how very nice it all was, the face and the bonnet agreed so well. She had jest *that* face in her mind when the bonnet was under way—so delicate—so graceful—so—so—*very* handsome. Some people hadn't the least notion of harmony and grace. It raly did her heart good to make things for a lady who knew which was which. She always kept them sort of hats for her most fashionable customers. She wouldn't have them get common for anything—raly she couldn't tell how that one got out on the counter; but shop gals were the most careless critters on arth—sometimes she did feel as if she couldn't git along with 'em—but in them hard times it raly went agin her heart to turn 'em away, so she got along as well as she could.

Here Miss Josephine Burgess would break sharp off and let the customer look at herself in the glass, only just throwing in a word once in a while to help along. Then she'd pull the bonnet a leetle for'ed, tuck away the lady's curls under it, and stick her own head a one side to "take an observation;" arter that she'd kinder put up both hands and say "beautiful!" jest as if the word bust right out, all she could do to help it. By-am-by Miss Josephine Burgess would sort of fold her hands over the black apron, and step back a leetle to give her customer time to twistify afore the glass, and wonder whether the milliner meant the bonnet or her face, or both together, when she said "beautiful." The hull of it eenamost always tarminated by Miss Josephine Burgess selling the bonnet, and the lady's swimming off chuck full and brimming over with soft sodder, like a darn'd turkey-gobbler, stuffed out with Injun meal.

If a customer did *not* take a notion to the bonnet, or seemed to hanker arter something else, Miss Josephine had nothing to do but to alter her tune for another sort of a dancer.

"Folks with homely faces," sez she, "ought to be squeamish about colors;" in fact they couldn't help it, if they wanted to look decent; but some folks raly seemed to look harnsome in anything; it was the face arter all that sot off the bonnet. Some people had such clear skins that they could bear a bright orange color, and look purty as a pink arter all. Once in a while Miss

Josephine sartinly did overdo the bisness a leetle, but she almost always made out to trade somehow, without her customer turned out to be some sly coot of a sister milliner a running round to hunt up patterns, or some darned critter out a shopping on a fourpence-ha'penny capital.

Besides tending her shop, and cutting and trimming, and all that, Miss Josephine Burgess found time to do a leetle courting, over work, with a finefied sort of a pothecary feller that sold doctor stuff over the way agin her store. But she didn't let this take up much of her time, nor no sich thing—she wasn't a gal to let her heart run away with her head, any how they could fix it. While the finefied stuck up leetle 'pothecary shut up his shop over the way, and sot more'n half the time twisting up the thread and leetle bits of ribbon that Miss Josephine Burgess snipped off with a pair of sharp pinted scissors, hitched to her side by a black watch guard, and kept a puckering up his mouth and a talking darned finefied nonsense, as sweet as the jujube paste, and the peppermint drops that he brought in his trousers' pocket, she sot as independent as a cork-screw, with one foot stuck upon a bonnet block, a twisting up bows, and a sticking pins and feathers into a heap of silk and millinery stuff. Once in a while she managed to stick a peppermint drop into her leetle mouth, and to turn her eyes to the 'pothecary with *sich* a look, so soft and killing, it went right straight through his heart, like a pine skewer through a chunk of butcher's meat.

There was never anything went on so slick as these critters did, arter they took to hankering arter each other—it raly was better than a play to see how they got along. The 'pothecary chap was a sneezer at figures. He'd cyphered thro' Dayboll's Arithmetic three times, and could say off the multiplication table without stopping to catch breath. So he sometimes overhauled the milliner's books, not because he wanted to know any thing about them, but 'cause women folks are so apt to be imposed on. He writ out her leetle bills, and kept a sort of running notion of her cash accounts, for she warn't much of a judge of money, and so always sent her bank bills over to his shop to know whether they were ginuine or not. She did all these leetle trifles in a delicate genteel sort of a way, that was sartinly very gratifying and pleasant to the 'pothecary; he raly begun to fat up and grow pussy on the strength on't; it wouldn't aben human natur if he hadn't.

Miss Josephine Burgess was a setting in her back shop a thinking over the 'pothecary chap, and the dollars and cents she'd skinned out of the gals' wages that week, a making them work at half price because the *times were so bad*, when the 'pothecary came a tip-toeing through the store looking as tickled as if he'd found a sixpence. He took two ball tickets out of his vest pocket and held one on 'em out to the milliner, and stood a bowing and a grinning like a darned babboon till she read the writin' on it.

"I raly don't know what to say," sez she, "I never have been to the Tammany hall, and I—I——"

"It'll be the top of the notch, this one," sez the chap, "they're a goin to be awful partickler who they invite—nothing but the raly genteel who get tickets, I promise 'em."

Miss Josephine Burgess puckered up her mouth, and said "she didn't know: she was afeard she might meet with some of the working classes—she——"

"Don't say no—it'll break my heart, it will sartinly," sez the lovyer. "Don't drive me to takin pison on your account—oh don't."

Miss Josephine kinder started up—gave a sort of a scream—and said she wouldn't drive the 'pothecary to taking pison, and that she would go the ball. The minit she said that the leetle chap went right off into a fit of the dreadful suz: he slumped right down on his marrow bones, and begun to nibble away like all natur at the four little fingers, that stuck out of Miss Josephine Burgess's right hand mit.

"Oh, say only jest one thing more, and I shall be so happy, I shall want to jump out of my skin," sez he, all in a twitteration.

"Oh, dear me, what do you mean? I swanny, I'm all in a fluster," sez she.

"Here, down on my knees, I ask, I entreat, I conjure, most beautiful of 'wimmen folks," sez he, "that you be my partner, not only at the ball, but through this ere mortal life, that is a stretching before us like a great paster lot covered over with tan sey, wild rhubarb and sage roots all in bloom—don't blush, my angel, but speak!"

Now Miss Josephine knew as well as could be, that it was the fashion to feel dreadfully at sich times—to get up a caniption fit, or any how to give right up and set kivered all over with blushes; but the bit of cotton wool that she used always to put on her blushes with, was tucked away in the top of her stocking, and she couldn't get at it handy without being seen. So she puckered up her mouth and looked as if she had just lost her granny.

"Give me *one* word of hope, now du," sez the anxious 'pothecary, a squeezing the milliner's hand, mit and all, between both of his, and a twisting his head a one side, and a rolling up his eyes, like a hen that's jest done drinking.

"Oh dear suz, what *can* I answer?" sez Miss Josephine Burgess, a wriggling her shoulders and kivering up her face with one hand, "I never felt so in all my life—dear me."

"Don't spurn me away from these ere leetle feet—nobody will ever love you so agin," sez the anxious chap, and with that he struck his hand sort of fierce agin his heart, that was floundering away under his yaller vest like a duck in a mud-puddle.

"Git up—oh du," sez Miss Josephine, catching a sly peek at the 'pothecary, through her fingers.

"One word of hope," sez the chap, a giving his bosom another tarnal dig; "say that you will be mine."

"I'll think about it," sez Miss Josephine Burgess, a sighing through her fingers.

"Say that you will be mine, or I will die on this ere very spot, and be sent down to posterity a living monument of winmen's hard-heartedness," sez the 'pothecary, a running his fingers through his hair, till it stuck up sort of wild every which way over his head. "Do you want to make this ere body a morter, and pound my loving heart to pieces with the pestle of delay? If not, speak and say that my love is returned."

"It is," said Miss Josephine Burgess, kinder faint from behind her hand.

"Angelic critter," sez the lovyer.

"Now leave me," sez Miss Josephine Burgess.

"Harnsomest of created winmen! I will," sez the 'pothecary.

"Oh how my heart beats," sez Miss Josephine Burgess.

"And mine," sez the 'pothecary, a getting up and a spreading his hand out on his yaller vest.

"Leave me now," sez Miss Josephine Burgess.

"My dear critter, I will," sez the 'pothecary.

With that he made tracks across the street, opened his empty money drawer with a sort of a chuckle, as much as to say, " if you're starved out in this way much longer I lose my guess," and then he drank off a glass of cold water, with a leetle brandy in it.

Miss Josephine Burgess sat still as a mouse, till the 'pothecary chap made himself scarce, then she let down her hands and took a squint in the glass to see how her face stood it. Arter that she went to a big drawer, where she kept her slickest dry goods, and cut off a lot of shiney red velvet, which she took up stairs, and told the gal that had charge of the work-room, to have it made up into a ball dress before the gals went home. The ten poor tired young critters were jest a beginning to think about going hum to supper, but they sot down agin and looked in each other's faces, as melancholy as could be, but said nothing. The young gal that had charge of the work-room, happened to say that in the course of a week they would have a prime lot of red velvet bonnets to sell. At this Miss Josephine Burgess looked as cross as if she'd swallowed a paper of darning needles, and told the young gal to hold her tongue, and mind her own business. At this the young gal drew up, and was a going to give the millner her change back agin, but jest that minit she happened to think that taking sarce from a stuck up critter was bad enough, but that starving was a good deal worse; and so she choked in and went to work at the dress, with her heart a swelling in her harnsome bosom, like a bird when it's first caught.

"Don't let them gals go to sleep over their work," sez Miss Josephine Burgess, as she was a going down stairs.

The young gal who had charge of the work-room, said something sort of loud about people's having no feeling.

"What's that you say?" sez Miss Josephine Burgess, a coming back as spiteful as could be.

"Nothing," sez the young gal who had charge of the workroom.

"It's well you didn't," sez the milliner, and with that she went down stairs, and the poor tuckered out young critters didn't get hum to supper till ten o'clock at night, because they had to stay and finish off Miss Josephine Burgess's ball finery.

Miss Josephine Burgess was a sitting in the leetle room up over her store, ready dressed for the ball, when the little apprentice gal cum up and told her, that the gentleman from over the way was a waiting down stairs. The milliner jumped up and began to wriggle about afore the looking glass to be sartin that the red velvet frock, the golden chain, and the heap of posies that she'd twistified in her hair, were all according to gunter. Arter she'd took a purty gineral survey, she went down stairs about the darndest stuck up critter that you ever sot eyes on.

The 'pothecary stood afore the looking glass a trying to coax his hair to curl a leetle, and a pulling up fust one side of his white satin stock and then t'other, to make it set up parpendicular. He'd got a leetle speck of dirt on his silk stockings and his shiney dancing pumps, a coming across the street, so he took his white hankercher out of his pocket and began to dust them off; but the minit Miss Josephine Burgess cum in he stopped short, stepped back agin the wall, and held up both hands as if he raly didn't know what to du with himself, and sez he—

"I never did! Talk about the Venus de Medici, or the New York beauty! Did ever anything come up to that are?"

Arter this bust of feeling, he gin a spring fore'd and ketching her hand, eenamost eat it up, he kissed so consarned eager. It didn't seem as if there was any contenting the darn'd love-sick soot. But when he hung on too hard, the milliner's vartuous indignation begun to bile up, and so he choked off and begged her pardon; but said he couldn't help it, as true as the world he couldn't, his heart was brim full and a running over.

I ruther guess the people stared a few when the leetle 'pothecary walked along the Tammany ball-room with Miss Josephine

Burgess, in her red velvet and golden chains, a hanging on his arm. Sich dashers didn't show themselves at every ball by a great sight. There was a ginuine touch of the aristocracy in the way the leetle 'pothecary turned up his nose, and flourished his white gloves; and when they stood up to dance, Miss Josephine held out her red velvet, and stuck out her foot, and curcheyed away as slick as any of the Broadway gals could a done it. But jest as she was a going to dance, who should stand afore her in the same reel but the very young gal that took charge of her work-room. The milliner had jest took a fold of the red velvet between her thumb and finger, and was flourishing out her foot to balance up as genteel as could be, but the minit she ketched sight of the working gal, she gin her head a toss and reaching out her hand to the 'pothecary, walked off to a seat in a fit of outraged dignity that was raly beautiful to look at. Arter this Miss Josephine Burgess said she wouldn't try to dance among sich low critters; and so she and the 'pothecary sidled about, eat peppermint drops and talked soft sodder to one another—alers taking care to turn up their noses when the harnsome working gal cum within gun-shot of 'em.

"Who *can* that gentleman be, that's a eyeing me through his glass," sez Miss Josephine Burgess to the 'pothecary, "what harnsome whiskers he's got, did you ever?"

"I don't see anything over genteel in him, any how," sez the 'pothecary a looking sort of oneasy. "I really can't see how you ladies can take a fancy to so much hair."

"But how nicely he's dressed," sez she.

"I aint over fond of shaggy vests and checkered trousers," says the 'pothecary.

"Dear me he's coming this way," sez the milliner all in a twitter,—"I hope he wont think of speaking."

"I hope so too," sez the 'pothecary, a looking as if he'd jest eat a sour lemon, without any sweetening.

The chap come along sort of easy and independent, and stood close by 'em.

"Shan't we go t'other end of the room?" sez the 'pothecary to the milliner, kinder half whispering, and a eyeing the strange chap as savage as a meat-ax. "Not yet," sez the milliner, giving a slantindicular sort of a look at the strange chap. He wasn't a feller to be sneezed at in the way of good looks any how, nor a man that was likely to lose anything by his bashfulness; for it warn't more than three minutes afore he asked the milliner to dance, and walked her out as crank as could be, right afore the 'pothecary's face. Didn't the poor leetle chap look wamble-cropped when he see that. There he stood all alone in a corner, feeling as sick as if he'd swallowed a dose of his own doctor's stuff, and there he had to stand; for arter the tall chap and Miss Josephine Burgess had got through danc'ng, they sot down together by a winder and begun to look soft sodder at one another, and talk away as chipper as two birds on an apple tree limb in spring time. It didn't do no good for the 'pothecary to rile up and make motions to her—she didn't seem to mind him a bit; so he stood still and grit his teeth, for it seemed to him as if the milliner and the red velvet, besides the account books, the stock in trade, and the hard chink too, was a sliding out of his grip like a wet eel.

"Darn the feller to darnation," sez he, arter he'd bore it as long as he could—and with that he went up to Miss Josephine Burgess, sort of humble, and asked her if it wasn't about time to be a going hum?

The milliner said she wasn't in any hurry about it, and went to talking with the tall chap agin. It was as much as the poor lovyer could do to keep from busting out a crying, or a swearing, he warn't partic'lar which; he felt all struck up of a heap, and went off to his corner agin as lonesome as a goose without a mate.

By-am-by the milliner she come up and told him she was about ready to go hum; the tall chap he went down stairs with them, and stood a kissing his hand to her till she got into the street. The 'pothecary raly felt as if he should bust, and he gin her a purty decent blowing up as they went along Chatham-street. She didn't give him much of an answer though, for her head was chuck ful! of the tall chap's soft sodder, and she didn't know more than half of what he was a jawing about.

The leetle 'pothecary went hum and hurried up to bed, but all he could du he couldn't get a wink of sleep. He got up ariy in the morning, but he hadn't no appetite for his breakfast, and kinder hung about his shop door a keeping a good look out to see if anybody went to the milliner's, and a wondering if it was best for him to go over and see how she seemed to be arter what he'd said to her the night afore. So he brushed up his hair and was just taking his hat to go over and try his luck, when a harnsome green buggy waggon hauled up jest agin the milliner's, and out jumped the tall chap with the whiskers.

The 'pothecary he turned as white as a sheet and begun to cuss and swear like all natur. He had plenty of time to let his wrathy feelings bile over, for it was more than three hours afore the green buggy waggon driv away agin. The minit it was out of sight, the 'pothecary snatched up his hat and scooted across the street like a crazy critter. Miss Burgess was a sitting in her leetle back room dressed out like anything. This made him more wrathy than he was afore, for she never dressed out when he was a coming, so he went straight up to her, and sez he, sort of wrathy,

"Miss Josephine Burgess, what am I to think of this ere treatment?"

The milliner looked up as innocent as a kitten, as if she hadn't the least idee what he meant.

"What treatment?" sez she, as mealy-mouthed as could be.

The 'pothecary felt as if he should choke; he griped his hand, and the words came out of his mouth like hot bullets.

"Oh you perfidious critter, you," sez he, "how can you look in my face arter you've been a sitting three hull hours with that darn'd nasty tall coot that you danced with all the time last night."

"I'm sure I don't know what you mean more than nothing. I danced with a gentleman last night, and he has been here this morning, but I raly don't see why *you* should trouble yourself about it," sez Miss Josephine, a taking up her work, and a beginning to sew as easy as she ever did in her life.

The 'pothecary was so mad, he couldn't but jest speak out loud. "Look a here, Miss Burgess," sez he, a speaking sort of hoarse, "aint we as good as married? didn't you engage yourself to me?

and wasn't the day eenajest sot afore that consarned etarnal ball ?"

"Not that I ever knew on," says Miss Burgess, a pinning a pink bow on to a bonnet she was to work on, and a holding it out to see how it looked, " I raly don't know what you mean."

The 'pothecary begun to tremble all over, he was so tarnal mad to see her setting there as cool as a cucumber.

"You don't know what I mean, do you?" sez he. "Look a here, marm, haint I been to see you off and on for more than a year? Haint I footed up your books and made out bills and done all your out-door business, this ever so long? Haint I give you ounces on ounces of jujube paste, emptied a hull jar of lemon drops, and more than half kept you in pearl powder and cold cream ?"

"Wal, you needn't talk so loud and tell everybody of it," sez the milliner a going on with her work all the time, but the leetle chap had got his grit up, and there was no "who" to him. On he went like a house afire.

"Wasn't it me that stopped you from taking them are darn'd Brandreth's pills. Didn't I tell you they warn't no better than rank pisin, and that no rale lady would ever think of stuffing herself with such humbug trash? I'll be choked if I don't wish I'd let you swaller fifty boxes ot 'em—I wish I had—I do by gracious!"

"Don't make such a noise," sez the milliner, "it wont do no good, I can tell you."

"Wont it though? wont it? I rather guess you'll find out in the end. I'll sue you for a breach of promise—if I don't jest tell me on't, that's all."

The 'pothecary was a going on to say a good deal more, but jest as he begun to let off steam agin some customers come into the front shop. Miss Josephine Burgess put down her work and went out as if nothing on arth had happened. The 'pothecary waited a few minits a biling over with spite, and then he kicked a bonnet block across the room, upset a chair, and cut off through the store like all possessed. The milliner was a bargaining away with her customers for dear life—she looked up and larfed a little easy, as the poor feller sneaked through the store, and that was all she cared about it.

The poor coot of an apothecary went over to his shop and slammed the door tu hard enough to shake the house down. Then he went back of the counter, took down a jar full of corrosive supplement and poured some on it out in a tumbler, but somehow there was something in the thought of dying all of a sudden, that didn't exactly come up to his idee of comfort; so he poured back the pison and took a mint julep instead—that sort of cooled him down a trifle—so he made up his mind to put off drinking the pison till by-am-by.

Every day for three weeks that green buggy waggon, and the tall man with the whiskers, stopped before Miss Josephine Burgess' door. The 'pothecary grit his teeth and eyed the pisin with a awful desperate look every time the buggy came in sight; and when he heard that Miss Josephine Burgess was a gitting her redding frock made, and was raly a going to be married to a oreign chap as rich as a Jew, that had fallen in love with her at the Tammany ball, he filled the tumbler agin brimming full, and then chucked the pison in the grate, and said he'd be darned if he made sich an etarnal fool of himself any longer; the critter wasn't worth taking a dose of salts for, much less a tumbler brim full of pison. Arter this he bore up like a man; and one day when he saw the green buggy come a trifle arlier than ever it did afore, and see the tall chap jump out all dressed off tu kill, with white gloves on, and a white hankercher a streaming out of his coat pocket, he jest put his teeth together and looked on till he saw Miss Josephine Burgess come out with a white silk bonnet on, and a great long white veil streaming over it, and see her take a seat in the buggy waggon with the tall man in whiskers. It wasn't no news to him when he heard that Miss Josephine Burgess was married, and had sold out her shop; but when he heard that the young gal that took charge of the work-room had got some relation to buy out the stock for her, the apothecary brightened up like anything; and he was heard to say that arter all the young gal that took charge of the work-room wasn't to be grinned at in a fog; for his part, he thought her full as harnsome as Miss Josephine Burgess.

There was no two ways about it,—Miss Josephine Burgess was raly married to the tall man in whiskers, and she had sold out to the young gal that had taken charge of the work-room. About three days arter the wedding, the tall man with whiskers sot in the room over what had been Miss Josephine Burgess's store, and leetle she that had been Miss Josephine Burgess herself, sot in the tall man's lap, with one arm round his neck. Her purty slim fingers had been a playing with his shiny black curls so long that some of the black color came off and made them leetle fingers look sort of nutty. Once in a while the bride would pat the tall man's cheek and call him a naughty critter, and ask him how many ladies he'd been in love with afore he see her; and the tall man would say—" not one upon my honor!" at which she would pat his cheek agin and say she didn't believe a word on it. Then the tall man in whiskers would begin to look as if he raly had been a killing critter with the women folks, and would say that he wouldn't deny it—he had now and then his leetle flirtations, like all men of rale fashion—but he'd never in his whole life took *sich* a notion to a critter as he had to her. With that Miss Josephine Burgess (that was) would fling both of her arms round the tall man's neck, and declare that there was not so proud and happy a critter on the hull arth as she was.

Wal, arter this, the tall man in wiskers took hold of the chain that his bride had round her neck, and sez he, " My dear love, I raly can't bear to see you rigged out in these ere old fashioned things. When you was only a milliner they did well enough, but now you musn't wear no jewelry that aint at the top of the notch; jest pack all on 'em up, that are watch of your'n and all, and I'll go and swap 'em off for a set of jewelry that's worth while. When I take you hum among all my folks, they'd larf at these awk'ard things."

With that the bride begun to looked streaked enough, so she sot to work and lugged out all the gold things she had; her watch and great heavy chain, and ear-rings, and ever so many gim-cracks. So the tall man put them all in his pocket and took up his hat, and sez he, " I'll soon get rid of these ere things, and bring you something that is something."

Miss Josephine Burgess that was, said there never was so kind a critter, and jest to let her see that she wasn't much out in saying that are, he cum back from the door, and sez he, "Seeing as I'm a going out, I may as well take that are little sum of money and put in some bank for you; of course I don't want anything of it, but it raly don't seem jest safe here, among all these sewing gals." Miss Josephine Burgess that was went to her chest of drawers and took out a heap of bank bills and gave them to him. The tall man in whiskers put the bills in his trousers' pocket, buttoned it up tight, then give the pocket a leetle slap and was a going out agin. But Miss Josephine Burgess that was she follered arter and sticking her head through the door she sung out sort of easy, sez she,

"My dear darling, you've forgot something!"

"You don't say so," sez the tall man in whiskers, and he stood up straight as a loon's leg, "what is it—any more jewelry, my pet?"

"Can't you guess?" said Miss Josephine Burgess that was, sort of sly, a twisting her head a one side, and pussing out her mouth awful tempting.

"Oh," sez the man in whiskers, and then there was a litt'e noise as if a bottle of Newark cider had been uncorked kinder easy.

"You'll come right straight back, dear?" sez Miss Josephine Burgess that was, a running to the door agin—"you will, won't you?"

"Sartinly, my sweet love," sez the tall man in whiskers, a stopping on the stairs and kissing her hand over the railing.

"By-by," sez Miss Josephine Burgess that was.

"By-by," sez the tall man in whiskers.

Miss Josephine Burgess that was sot by the window and looked arter the tall man till he got eenamost down to Chatham square. She waited a hull hour and he didn't come back; then she waited two hours; then all night; and the next week and the next, till she'd been a waiting three hull months,—and arter all the tall man in whiskers didn't seem to hurry himself a bit.

About a year arter the Tammany ball, the leetle 'pothecary was sitting in the back room of what once was Miss Josephine

Burgess's milliner store—his wife that used to take charge of the work-room, stood close by; and the 'pothecary was a looking over his wife's day book. Jest as he was a adding up a tarnal long row of figures, one of the hands come down stairs and was a going out.

"Look a here, Miss Josephine Burgess, or Miss what's your name." sez the 'pothecary, "if you're determined to go home the minit your hour is up, these hurrying times, it's my idee that you'd better look out for some other shop to work in."

The color riz up in the poor woman's face, but it was her turn to be snubbed and drove about, without daring to say her soul was her own. So instead of riling up, she spoke as meek as could be, and sez she, "I aint very well, I've got a dreadful headache."

"Cant help that," sez the 'pothecary, "we pay you twenty shillings a week, fust rate wages, to *work*, so you may jest step back to the work-room with your headache, or I'll dock off fifty cents when it comes Saturday night if you don't. Go troop—I'll have you to know you aint mistress in this shop, or master neither."

Miss Josephine Burgess had a temper of her own, but she owed for her board, and so choked in and went up stairs as mad as all natur.

The apothecary's wife was a good hearted critter, and it raly made her feel bad to see her old boss used so.

"Don't speak so to her," sez she to the 'pothecary, "she raly looks tired and sick, don't hurt her feelings."

"Humbug," sez the 'pothecary, stretching himself up, and a buttoning his trousers' pocket as pompously as could be, "humbug, what bisness have sewing girls with feelings."

"I was a sewing gal once," sez the 'pothecary's wife.

"Yes—and how did that darned stuck up critter use you, tell me that?" sez he.

The 'pothecary's wife didn't answer; but the minit her husband had gone out she went into the kitchen and took a bowl of ginuine hot tea up to the work room. Miss Josephine Burgess that was, sot on a stool looking as mad as a march hare; she began to sew as soon as the 'pothecary's wife come in, as grouty as could be; but when the kind critter gin her the bowl of tea, and told her it would be good for her head-ache, the poor sewing girl boo-hooed right out a crying.

JONATHAN SLICK.

LETTER XVII.

Jonathan gets Ill and Homesick—Resists all entreaties to go to Washington, and resolves on going back to "the Humstead" with Captain Doolittle.

DEAR PAR:

Wal, arter writing that story about the Bowery Milliner, I begun to think York was a going to be rather too hot to hold me. All the boss milliners in York got into a tantrum and kicked up sich a darned rumpus that I raly begun to be afear'd that they'd cum down to my office in Cherry-street, and get up a fourth of July oration, or a she caucus, and girt me to death in a pair of them darned French corsets. But the peaked little working gals, they were cenamost tickled to death with that story, and there warn't no eend to the harnsome sweet critters that cum to my office a crying and yet half a smiling, to thank me for taking up on their side. One thing though made me feel bad enough. That etarnal leetle stuck up old maid got so allfired wrothy that she turned Susan Read out of her place, and cheated her out of some of her wages too. Darn her it makes me gritty only jest to think on it. But she'd better look out, I can tell her; for if I take her up agin, consarn me if I don't use her up till she aint bigger than the tip eend of a pine stick whittled down to nothing.

Wal, as the spring come on I began to git peaked, and every morning felt sort of wamblecropped in my stomach when I woke up. I s'pose it was cause I cou.dn't git pork and dandelines and prime fresh young onions right out of the arth, as I used tu to hum. The editors of the *Express*, they wanted me to take an emetic, but I told 'em I couldn't think of sich a thing, it was agin natur. I looked sort of solemn, jest as I always do when they use any of them French words that I don't understand, and made up my mind to look in Boyer's Dictionary, and find out the meaning of emetic the fust thing arter I got hum.

"Wal," sez they, "if you don't like that, Mr. Slick, s'posing you take a trip to the Seat of Gineral Government, and see how them Loco Foco chaps are a carrying on there, it 'll answer all the same."

"Wal," sez I, arter thinking it all over in arnest, "it seems to me as if I was kinder hankering arter the green trees and the grass and cows, and the wind that comes straight down from heaven, where you can breathe it out on your own hook, and not take it second hand, as we do in York. I raly think I should feel like a new critter if I could only go hum a spell and weed the young onions." With that I begun to think about the humsted, and how it was gitting towards planting time; and think sez I, par 'll miss me about these times, and marm too, for she wont have any body to do her milking when it rains, nor to bring water and du up all the leetle chores that I al'rs did for her. Then I seemed to see our orchard all a leaving out thick and kivered over with apple blows; and it seemed tu me as if I was a setting on the stun wall, jest as I used to when I was a leetle shaver, a looking how fast the grass grew and a wondering how long it would be afore green apple time. There was the well-crotch and the pole, and the bucket a hanging to it, as plain as day, and the peach tree that grows by it chuck full of pink blows. There was you a gitting out the oxen to go to ploughing, and there was marm out in the meadow at the back door, a picking plantin leaves for greens, with her old sun bonnet on, and a tin pail to put the greens in.

Oh dear, how humsick I did feel! I could a boo-hooed right out, if it would a done any good, when I sort of come tu, and found out that I was setting in the *Express* office, with nothing but picters of that old critter, Gineral Harrison, and a heap of newspapers scattered every which way over the floor, to look at

"Wal," sez the Editor, sez he, "Mr. Slick, what do you think about it? you raly ought to go to Washington, to see the President and the lions."

I put one leg over t'other, and winked my eyelids for fear he'd see how near I come to crying; and arter a leetle while, sez I—

"I haint no kind of doubt that that are Washington is a smasher of a city; but somehow, if you'd jest as livs, I'd a leetle ruther go hum."

"Yes," sez he, "I haint the least doubt on it; but then, if you git out of the city, it don't make much difference which way you go."

I see that he'd made up his mind to have his own way; but think sez I, you don't git it without another tough pull, anyhow; so sez I—

"I raly feel as if I must doctor a leetle; and when a feller feels tuckered out, or down-hearted, there is no place like hum, if it's ever so homely,—and nobody can take care of a feller like his own marm. Now I know jest how it'll be—the minit I git hum, the old woman will go to making root-beer; she'll sarch all over the woods for saxafax-buds to make tea on, and there'll be no eend to the snake root and fennel seed bitters that she'll make me drink. I raly feel as if I must go; so don't you say any more about it," sez I; "I shall come back agin as bright as a new dollar."

If there is anything on arth that holds on hard, it's a York Editor; a lamper-eel is nothing to one on 'em. They'd have their own way, if the Old Nick himself stood afore them as big as the side of a house.

By-am-by the hull truth come out; sez the Editor, sez ne, a speaking as soft and mealy-mouthed as could be, sez he—

"But, Mr. Slick, you can't write any letters for *us* in Weathersfield; so jest make up your mind to start right off. You can go hum any time."

"But I want to doctor," sez I.

"Oh, take a box of Sherman's cough lozengers," sez he, a smiling; "they cured you last winter, you know." With that, he let off a stream of soft sodder, sez he, "a man of your talents oughtn't to bury himself in the country. The members of Congress are all a-tip-toe to see you, and so are the gals in Washington—the Russian Elbassador's wife and all on 'em."

It warn't in human natur to stand agin this; so I sort of relented.

"Oh, you're a joking," sez I, a hitching on my chair; "I don't raly s'pose the Washington gals ever heard of me in their hull lives."

"Hain't they, though," sez he.

"Wal," sez I, "I should kinder like tu go, jest to see what Congress people look like. I've a sort of a notion that mebby I shall run for Congressman myself one of these days. I don't believe there's a feller in all York better qualified. When I come away from Weathersfield, I could lick any feller there, big or leetle; and I've a sort of a sort of a notion that I can dress out any of them varmints in the Capitol, if they do practice a leetle more than I du."

The Editor of the Express, he larfed a leetle easy, and sez he, "Well, Mr. Slick, it's all settled then—and the sooner you start the better."

"I'll think about it," sez I.

Wal, I went back tu the office and sot down, kinder loth tu go so far from hum as Washington City, and yet anxious to oblige the Editor of the Express; but all I could du, thoughts of the humsted kept a crowding intu my mind till I couldn't stand it no longer, but kivered up my face with both of my hands and took tu crying like a sick baby. Jest then—while I was a feeling dreadfully—somebody opened the door of my office, and in walked Captain Doolittle, with his hand out, and a grinning from ear tu ear as if he was eenajest tickled tu death to see me agin.

I jumped right up and shook hands with him, while I turned my face away and wiped my eyes with the cuff of my coat, for I felt ashamed to let him ketch me a crying.

But there is no cheating that old coot, he's wide awake as a night hawk.

"Jonathan," sez he, "What's the matter—you look as thin as a shad in summer—consarn me if I don't believe you have been ooo-hooing."

"You've lost your guess this time," sez I, a trying to put on a stiff upper lip.

The old feller, he looked in my face, and then agin on the cuff of my coat—then he folded his arms and stepped back and eyed me all over, and sez he at last,

"Jonathan, one thing is sartin, either you've been a crying, or you've told a whopper to your old friend, or—"

"Or what?" sez I, wiping the cuff of my coat on my trousors' leg—"or what?"

"Or your deginerated—deginerated!" sez he, "deginerated from the Weathersfield stock!"

"Wal, I don't seem to understand how you'll make that out,' sez I.

"Jonathan," sez he, as arnest as could be, "there was tears in your eyes jest as I come in, and you was ashamed on 'em. Now, sich tears as a smart, honest young man may feel in his eyes naturally, are nothing to be ashamed on; when he gets to thinking of hum or old friends, or perhaps them that are dead and gone,—the drops that come up unawares to moisten his eyes are wholesome to his natur. I've seen the time, Jonathan, when minister's prayer didn't seem half so easing to the heart. An honest chap might as well feel streaked about saying the Lord's Prayer; for the tears that thinking of them that we love sets a going, have eenamost as much religion in 'em as singing and praying and going to meeting altogether. Prayer, Jonathan, prayer falls upon the natur like the warm sun on a patch of young onions—and tears, ginuine tears that come from tender thoughts, Jonathan, darn me if they ain't the rain that keeps the young shoots green. You wouldn't have been scared about my seeing sich tears, Jonathan, and I know you've got tu much grit for any other—you aint the chap to snuffle and cry because things go crooked with you—I'm sartin of that."

"I reckon you may be," sez I.

"Wal, Jonathan," says the captin, a folding his arms close up to the red shirt that kivered his bosom, "there aint but one way of accounting for it. I never would a believed it, but you've deginerated. These Yorkers have larned you to be ashamed of eating onions—it's jest arter dinner time—I see through it all—

you've been a thinking of hum, and tried a raw onion for once--your eyes aint used to it now, and that's what makes 'em so red and misty. I have seen the time, Jonathan Slick, when you could cut up a hull peck without winking; I've seen you cronch one like a meller apple; and now, arter living in York, this is the eend on't."

"Come, captin," sez I, a holding out my hand, "don't make a coot of yourself, I can eat a raw onion without winking as well as ever I could. Seeing as you can peak so consarned far into a mill-stun, I may as well own up and settle the hash to once. I've been kinder peaked and hum-sick ever since spring opened. I sot down here all alone, got a thinking of old times and things to hum, and that sort of made me cry afore I knew it; that's the hull truth, and I'd jest as livs you knew it as not."

Captin Doolittle, he gin my hand a grip, and sez he, "That's right, Jonathan, own up like a man, I see intu it now—hum-sick as git out—just what I wanted. The old sloop is ready to sail right off—pack up your saddle-bags, jump aboard, and we'll be in Weathersfield in less than no time. Your par and mar, and Judy White, and all the folks tu hum will be tickled eenamost tu death to see you."

I felt my heart jump right intu my mouth, but it sunk agin like a chunk of lead when I thought that I'd eenajest agreed to go tu Washington. "Captin," sez I, "I'm afeared I can't go—I've nigh about promised to go tu Washington City."

"Washington City be darned," sez he, a going intu my back room and a lugging out my saddle-bags; "Washington City can't hold a candle tu Weathersfield this time of the year. You can't think how fresh and green everything looks; the square before the meeting-house is as green as grass can be—the laylock trees in front of the humstead are all in full blow—we've had young lettuce and pepper-grass there these three weeks—think of that! with good sharp vinegar, plenty of pepper and salt, and a sprinkle of young onion-tops mixed in jest as they come from the patch by the eend of the barn,—Gosh, but don't it make your mouth water only to think on it, Jonathan."

"I swow, captin, there's no standing it, I must go."

"Sartinly you must—the old woman would go off the handle

if I should come back without you and Judy White. That Judy is a nation harnsome gal, Jonathan. She told me tu jest mention that the orchard over agin the house was in full blow and every tree chuck full of robins' nests. You can smell that orchard half-a-mile off, Jonathan, but Judy says it kinder makes her molencholy tu see the trees a budding out so agin, and the birds a singin from mornin to night among 'em, and nobody tu enjoy it but her."

"I'll go, by gauly offalus—I'll go," sez I, "but what will the editors of the Express say," sez I, feelin all over in spots about goin off so.

"The Express go tu grass," sez Captin Doolittle, a crowding my pepper and salt trousers intu the saddle-bags.

"Jest so," sez I, a helping him strap up the bags; "I'll write a letter hum tu say I'm jest a startin, and send it through the Express, and that will let the editors know what I've detarmined on."

"Jest so," sez Captin Doolittle, "and I guess I'll go down to the sloop with the saddle-bags. I only jest got in last night, took out the ladin this morning, and we shall be a cuttin down the East river afore sunset; quick work, I reckon, don't you think so, Jonathan?"

"I should ruther think it was," sez I.

"Wal," sez he, a shoulderin the saddle-bags, "write off the letter and come right down. You mustn't let the grass grow under your feet, now I tell you. Your marm will be about the tickledest critter that you ever sot eyes on when you git back agin—she's got a hull lot of winter apples saved up yit agin you cum. I wish you could a seen the old critter a knittin away all the long winter evenings tu git you a hull grist of socks made up; she seamed every darned one on 'em clear through, jest because it was for you, Jonathan."

"You don't say so!" sez I, kinder half cryin agin; "now du git out, will you? I want tu write my letter."

With that, the Captin he went off saddle-bags and all. I sot down and wrote off this letter about the quickest, I can tell you. I shall send it up tu the Express office, and if we have good luck, it won't be long arter you git it afore you will shake hands with us.

Your loving son,

JONATHAN SLICK.

LETTER XVIII.

JONATHAN SLICK RETURNED.

Jonathan's Arrival in New York from the onion beds at Weathersfield—Jonathan puts up at the Astor House—His notion of that great heap of stones—Jonathan's Ideas of a New York Cab, and the usual quarrel of a Stranger with Cabmen—A Sensation is created at the Astor.

Dear Par:

Here I am down in York agin, as large as life and as springy as a steel trap. Hurra! but don't it make a feller feel as suple as a green walnut gad to have these stun side walks under his shoe leather once more! I raly felt as if I could a'most have jumped over the housen, eend foremost, I was so glad to git ashore at Peck Slip. Captin Doolittle, he kept his gab a going, a hull hour, a trying to make out it warn't worthy a ginuine Yankee to hanker alter the York big bugs so. Now my opinion is, Captin Doolittle ain't no bad judge of onions and other garden sarse, and he did run the old sloop down here as slick as grease, but when he sets himself up to talk about genteel society, he raly is green.

Look a here, par, did I ever tell you what a looking place that Astor House is? If I didn't, jest you suppose that all the stun walls in old Connecticut had been hewed down as smooth as glass, and heaped together, one a-top of t'other, over two acres of clearing, up and up, half away to the sky and a leetle over; suppose then the hull etarnal great heap cut up into winders and doors, with almighty great slabs of stun piled up for steps and pillars standing on eend, on the top, to hold them down—bigger than the highest oak tree you ever sot eyes on, and then you have some idee what a whopping consarn that Astor House is.

At fust I felt a leetle skeery at going to board there, for think sez I, if they charge according to the size of the house, I guess it 'll make my puss strings ache; but, think sez I agin, the best taverns, according to my experience, all'rs charge the leastest prices, I will give 'em a try any how.

I gin a cuffy on the wharf two cents to go and get a carriage for me, for I meant to du the thing up in genteel style, and cut the hull figger when I once begun. Besides, the cabin was so stived up with onion barrels and heaps of red cabbages, besides the turnips and winter squashes, that I hadn't no room to fix up in till I got a hum somewhere else, and my dandy clothes have got a leetle the wus for wear, and don't cut quite so much of a dash as they used tu. I hadn't but jest time to rub them down a trifle with a handful of oat straw that I took from one of the winter apple barrels, and to slick down my hair a few, with both my hands, when the nigger cum back and said he couldn't find a carriage, but he'd got a fust rate cab.

Sartinly that cab was one of the darndest queer animals that ever run arter a hoss. It looked like a set of stairs on wheels, with a great overgrown leather trunk sot on eend half way up, with the lid turned over one side. The horse was hitched to the lowermost step, and on the top step of all, clear back, sot a feller histed up in the air with a great long whip, and lines that reached clear over the hull consarn to the horse's head, and this chap was the driver; but he looked as if he'd been sot there wrong eend foremost, and felt awfully streaked and top-heavy about it. It raly was curious to watch the chap as he laid his lines on the top of the box and crept down stairs to stow away my saddle-bags and the hair trunk that marm gin me. When he'd got through, I jest lifted one foot from the ground, and there I sot in a little cushioned pen, like a rooster in a strange coop, or a rat in an empty meal bin. The feller slam'd tu the door and went up the steps behind agin, then I ketched sight of the lines a dangling over head, like a couple of ribbon snakes a twisting about in the sunshine; and away we went trundling along like a great oversized wheelbarrow, with a horse before, a driver behind, and a poor unfortunate critter like me cooped in the middle, with a trunk and pair of saddle-bags for company.

Well, on we went hitch-a-te-hitch, jerk-a-ty-jerk through the carts and horses till we got out of the slip, and then we kept on a leetle more regular till by-and-by the horse he stopped all of himself jest afore the Astor House.

"Wal," sez I to the driver, a feeling in my trousers' pocket for a ninepence—for the nigger told me that them new fangled cabs had sot up a sort of cheap opposition to the hacks—so sez I,

"Wal, what's the damage?"

"Only a dollar," sez he, a giving my saddle-bags and trunk a jerk onto the steps, and eying my old dandy clothes sort of supercilious, as if he thought it would be a tough job for me to hand over the chink. I begun to rile up a leetle, but arter a minit I happened to think that no ginuine gentleman ever gits mad with sich a ruff scuff, so I jest looked in his face, and sez I,

"How you talk!"

With that I gin him a quarter of a dollar, for I didn't want to be mean; but the varmint begun to bluster up as if he wanted to kick up a tantrum. I didn't seem to mind it, but the critter hung on yit for a whole dollar, like a dog to a sassafras root, and when some waiters cum down and took away my things, he followed, and ketching hold of the saddle-bags, said the things shouldn't go till he'd got his pay. With that I went up to him agin, and sez I,

"Make yourself scarce, you etarnal mean coot, or I'll give you the purtyest specimen of Weathersfield sole leather that you ever sot eyes on—one that'll send you up them wheelbarrow steps of yourn swifter than you cum down, a darned sight. You needn't look at me—I'm in arnest, and I'll du it, or my name aint Jonathan Slick."

Oh human natur', how the varmint wilted down when I said this; he took off his hat, and sez he—as mean as a frozen potater—says he,

"I didn't know as it was you."

"I rather guess you didn't," says I.

The feller seemed to feel so sheepish that it sort of mollified me, and so I up and gave him another four-pence-ha'penny. With that I went up the steps, up and up till I cum to a great long stun hall that reached tu all creation, with a kind of a bar-room at one end. It was a sort of a stun side-walk a shut up in a house; for lots of men were talking and walking about as easy as if they'd been in the street. I went up to the bar-room, where a chap sot with sour looks, as if he felt to hum all over, and says I—

"Do you take in boarders here?"

The chap looked at me from the top of my head to the sole of my foot, as if he'd never seen a full sized Yankee in his life; and after fidgeting about, says he—

"Yes, we du sometimes, but mebby you've mistook the place."

"I reckon not," says I. "How much du you charge a week? I paid two dollars and fifty cents down in Cherry-street, but I s'pose you go as high as four dollars, or say four fifty."

The feller looked sort of flustered; so thinks says I, I haint got up the notch yet, so I'll give one more hist.

"Wal, sir, it goes agin the grain; but seeing as it's the Astor House, per'aps I might give as high as five dollars, if you'd throw in the washing. I aint hard on clothes, say a shirt and three dickeys, with a pair of yarn socks a week, and a silk hankercher once a fortnight. I shall have to be a trifle extravagant in that line."

The feller grew red in the face, and looked as if he was tickled tu death at gitting such an offer. Think sez I, I hope to gracious I haint made a coot of myself, and bid up too high. I got so consarned before the chap spoke, that I sort of wanted to git off edgeways. There was a great day-book a lying by him, and sez I—

"I see you trust out board by your books; but I'm ready to hand over every Saturday night; so per'haps you'll take less for cash."

The feller sort of choked in a larf, and sez he—

"That aint a day-book, only one we keep for folks that come here to write down their names in."

Think sez I, I guess I'll write my name, and then he'll see that he's got hold of a cute hand for a bargain, and may dock off a trifle on that are five dollars.

"O," sez I, "that's it; well, give us hold here, and I'll write my name right off for you."

The feller handed over the pen. I stretched out my right arm, turned the cuff of my coat over, flourished off a long-tailed J, till the ink spattered all over the book; then I streaked along to the S, curled it up harnsomely, and finished off with a K that would have made Mr. Goldsmith, the writing-master, in Broadway, feel awk'ard if he'd seen it.

I wish you could have seen that Astor House chap, when he read the name; he looked as if he didn't know what to du, but at last he stepped back, and he made a bow, and sez he,—

"Mr. Slick, we are glad to see you at the Astor House, and we hope you'll stay with us as long as you remain in the city!"

I made him a snubbed sort of a bow, for I didn't want him to think I was over anxious to stay till we'd clinched the bargain about the board, and sez I,—

"Wal, now about the price of your fodder; I s'pose you'll dock a leetle on that offer of mine. It's an allfired hard price, now ain't it?"

"O," sez he, "never mind the board, Mr. Slick, we shan't be hard with you on that score. The man will show you a room, and I hope you'll feel yourself quite to hum with us."

With that a feller cum up to look at the big book, and then he whispered to another, and it wasn't two minits afore a hul squad of fellers cum around, as if I'd been a bear set up for a show, at a copper a head.

One of the chaps he cut up stairs like all possessed, as if he was a going tu bring up somebody else, so I begun to think it about time for me to cut stick; so I hollered arter a waiter, and told him to take me up where he'd put my trunk. The chap went ahead, and I follered arter.

I tell you what, it wants a steady head to navigate through all them long entry ways, and up them stairs, around and across every which way, as I did, till I came to a room door up at the tip top of the house. My head went around like a fly-trap. When the door was shut I was so dizzy, I opened the winder, and looked out tu see if the cold air wouldn't du me good. O gracious me! didn't it make me ketch my breath tu see how high up they'd stuck me. The clouds seemed to be purty close neighbors. I looked right straight over the biggest trees in the park, as if they'd been black alder bushes, and my nose cum jest about on a line with the City Hall clock. It sartinly did make me feel a leetle skittish to look down into Broadway. The men went streaking along like a crowd of good-sized rats a going out a visiting, and the gals that went sidling along under their parasols, were the darndest harnsome little finefied things I ever dreamed of. It seemed as if all the wax dolls had broke loose from the store winders, and was a walkin out to take the air with each on 'em a toad-stool to keep the sun of. Taking the hul together, men and gals, conches, cabs, trees, and horses, it was about the funniest sight I ever sot eyes on.

It was worth while to look down on the front of the housen too, only one felt all the time as if he was a goin to topple down head fust. The winder to my room wasn't none of the largest, and a round vine, all cut out of the solid stun, was twistified round it on the outside; and a heap of the same sort stretched along the right and left side like a string of purty picters hung out for show. Think sez I, if any body would look up and see me a standing here, they might see the true profile of Jonathan Slick cut off at the shoulders and hung in a frame, a live picter, without paint or whitewash. I wish to gracious some of them York artists would paint me jest so, for I raly must a looked like a picter while I stood in that winder, but it made me worse insted of better, so I hauled in my head.

Arter I'd gin myself a good sudsing in the wash-hand basin, I unbuckled my saddle-bags, and thought I'd fix up a leetle, for somehow my clothes seemed to smell sort of oniony arter sleeping so long in the sloop cabin. Since I've been hum my hair has grown about right, only it's a leetle sun-burnt; but that don't show much when I've combed it out slick with a fine tooth comb, and rubbed it down with a ball of pomatum, scented with wintergreen. I parted it straight down the middle, like some of the gals afore class meeting; and I slicked it down with both hands, till it glistened like a black cat in the dark.

Arter I'd purty near satisfied myself with that, I sot tu and put on the red and blue checkered trousers that marm cut and made arter my dandy clothes made in York. They are a ginuine fit, except that they strain rather severe on the galluses, and pucker jest the leastest mite about the knee jints; but they aint so coarse for all tow, nor the cam-colored coat neither. The cotton dicky that you and Judy fixed up for me, curled up around my chin and under the ears about the neatest; they looked as good as linen, every mite; and when I twisted that checkered silk scarf, that Judy gave me for a keep-sake arter she got mollified about my going to York, around my neck, and let the long ends, fringe and all, hang down sort of careless over my green vest, criscrossed with red streaks, I ruther guess you haint seen a chap of my size dressed up so in a long time.

You know that great harnsome broach that I bartered away the apple sarse for in Hartford last fall. Wal, I was jest a sticking that into my shirt bosom, and a thinking what a consarned harnsome feller was a peaking at me out of the looking glass, when somebody knocked at the door. I stopped to twistify my dicky down a trifle, and to shake a leetle speck of essence of wintérgreen on my hankercher, and then I went to the door.

One of the chaps that I'd seen down stairs was there; he didn't say nothing, but made a bow and gin me a piece of stiff paper about as big as the ace of spades, with "Fanny Elssler" printed right in the middle on it.

Wal, think sez I, "what on arth *does* this mean? I haint seen a door yard fence nor a post since I come to York, but this ere etarnal name was stuck up on it, and now I'll be choked if it haint chased me up here into the tip top of the Astor House." As I was a thinking of this, I kinder turned the paper in my hand, and there on t'other side was a heap of the purtyest leetle finefied writing that I ever did see. It was as plain as print, and as fine as a spider's web, but I couldn't make out a word of it to save my life.

I never was so flustrated in my born days, but arter thinking on it a jiffy, I seemed to understand it, and was sartin that somebody had writ a new fangled sort of a letter to Fanny Ellsler, and had sent it to my room instead of her'n.

I run out into the entry way and hollered "hellow" to the chap like all natur, but he'd made himself scarce, and so I went back agin. I swanny, if I knew how to fix it. I didn't want the pesky critter's letter, and then agin, I didn't much want to go and carry it to her, for fear she'd take me for one of them long-haired, lantern-jawed coots that hanker round sich foreign she critters, like lean dogs a huntin around a bone. But then agin I raly had a sort of a sneaking notion to see her, if I could as well as not. So I up and went to the looking glass and gin my hair a slick or two, and took, a sort of gineral survey, to be sartin that I was according to gunter.

There wasn't no mistake in that chap, I can tell you. Everything was smooth as amber-grease, and my hair was so shiney and slick that a fly would a slipped up if he'd ventured to settle on it. I ony jest pulled the corner of my new handkercher out of my coat pocket a trifle, then I put my hat on with a genteel tip upwards, and down I went, chomping a handful of peppermint drops as I went along in case my breath hadn't quite got over the smell of fried onions that Captin Doolittle gin me for breakfast aboard the sloop.

"Look a here," sez I to a chap that I cum across in one of the entryways as I was a trying to circumnavigate down stairs, "you don't know where abouts Miss Elssler lives, now du you?"

"Yes," sez he, a stopping short, "she has the large parlor in front, jest over the great entrance on the second floor."

"What! she don't live here in the Astor House, does she?" sez I,

"Sartinly," sez he.

"You don't say so," sez I.

"Yes I *do* say so," sez he, a larfin.

"Wal, now I cum to think on it I guess you du," sez I; "but I say now, you hadn't jest as livs as not go and show me the door, had you?"

"Oh, I haint no particular objections," sez he, and with that he begun twistifying down stairs and around and across, and I arter him like the tail to a kite, till by-am-by he hauled up close to a room door, and arter saying, "this is the room," and giving a bow, cut off before I'd time to ask him how his marm was.

Your affectionate son,
JONATHAN SLICK.

LETTER XIX.

JONATHAN SLICK AND FANNY ELSSLER.

A live Yankee and the Parisian Danseuse!—Fanny sends her Card and Jonathan makes a call—Down East Yankee and French-English rather hard to be understood—Jonathan quite killed off by Fanny's Curchies and Dimples—A little sort of a Flirtation—An Invitation to see Fanny in Nathalie, which is accepted.

Dear Par:

I swow, I thought I should a choked, my heart riz so when I see that I'd got to go in alone, and when I took hold of the chunk of brass that opens the door, I felt the blood a biling up into my face like hot sap in a sugar kettle. I kinder half opened the door, and then I kinder shut it agin; arter ketching a good long breath I give the door a rap, and begun to pull up my dicky sort of careless to let 'em know I wasn't scared nor nothing, and then I rapped agin.

Gracious! before I took my fist away, the door opened softly as if it slid on ile, and there stood a woman sort of harnsome and sort a not, with a leetle cap chuck full of posies stuck on the back of her head, a looking me right in the face as cosey as if she'd been acquainted with me when I was a nussing baby. I put my foot out to give her my primest bow, but think sez I, mebby it aint Miss Elssler arter all; she looks too much like an old maid for that; so I gin my foot a jerk in and my hand a genteel flurish towards her, and sez I—

"How do you du marm?"

She looked at me sort of funny, and her mouth begun to pucker itself up, but sez she, "How do you du?" a biting off the words as short as pie crust.

"Purty well, I'm obliged to you," sez I, "Miss Elssler aint to hum, is she?"

The critter looked at me as sober as a clam in high water, but yet she seemed to be kinder tickled inside of her, and turning her head round she let out a stream of stuff to somebody inside. It wasn't talking, nor singing, nor scolding, nor yet was it crying, but some sort of sounds kept a running off from her tongue as soft as a brook over a bed of white pebble stuns, and about as fast tu. She kept her hand a running up and down as if she'd half a notion to beat time to her own new fashioned singing, till all tu once, up cum a critter from t'other eend of the room, all dressed in white, as if she'd jest cum out of a band-box, with allfired harnsome black hair sleeked down each side of her face, with a hull swad of it twisted up behind, with a golden pin stuck through the heap, like one of marm's spindles spiked through a hunk of flax. The head of the pin was as big as a shag-bark walnut, and some sort of stun was sot in it that was like a gal's mind, no two minits alike—now it was red, now yaller, now green, and again all these colors seemed jumbled together and a flashing inside of it till you couldn't tell which was which. I swanny, if it didn't glisten so that I eenamost forgot that it was stuck in a woman's head, and that she was a looking into my face as mealy-mouthed and soft as could be.

"Has the gentleman mistook the room," sez she—

The words were sort of snipped off, but oh gracious, warn't they sweet! lasses candy and maple sugar was in every syllable. It seemed as if the critter had been fed forever on nothing but mellow peaches and slippery elm bark, she spoke so soft. She kinder smiled tu, but it was nat'ral as could be. Think sez I mebby the coot has led me into the wrong goose pen, but there aint no help for it now. So I jest walked a step for'ard, and sez I—

"How do you du marm?"

"I kinder guess there aint no mistake worth a mentioning. If Miss Elssler aint to hum I'll make tracks and cum agin, it aint no trouble, I'd just as livs as not, but I guess I'll leave this ere letter for fear she may want it. Some etarnal coot brought it up to my room, but I suppose the critter didn't know no better—some of these York chaps are green as young potatoes, don't you think so, marm?"

I didn't wait for no answer, but handed over the new fangled letter, and was a going right off agin, but she looked at the letter sort of astonished, and then at me, till I didn't know what to make of it. Arter a minit, sez she—

"Why dis is the card for Mr. Slick, one of de Editors of de *Express* who has just arrived; certainly he could not be so rude as to send it back again."

Oh gracious! think sez I, "Jonathan Slick, if you haint broke your onion string now!"

"Was the gentleman out?" sez she, looking at the paper, and then at me agin.

Think sez I—"You'd better ask his marm," for I'll be darned if he can tell that, or anything else. I aint quite sartin if he knows jest this minit which eend his head's on. But there's nothing like keeping a stiff upper lip in sich places as York. In less than half a jiffy I reached out my hand sort of easy, and took the paper out of her hand, and then I giu her a smile, as much as to say, aint I a careless shote? and, sez I,

"Now I swanny, did you ever! Well now who'd a thought it,"—and with that I began to feel in my vest, and dug my hands down in my trousers' pockets, as if I'd give the wrong paper, and had lost something else, and wouldn't give up till I'd found it. I didn't seem content till I'd pulled out my yaller hankercher and shook it, and then I stopped still, and sez I,

"Now if this don't beat all, aint I the beatermost feller for losing things? Howsomever, it's well it aint no worse. I can write another almost any time. Jest tell Miss Elssler that Mr. Slick has called in to thank her for her harnsome little keepsake, and that he's felt awfully wamblecropped when he found out she wasn't to hum."

The woman that come to the door fust, she looked at the other and begun gabbling away, and then the black haired one, sez she,

"Oh, Mister Sleeke, pardon! pardon! I am so sorry to keep you so long standing. I did not know! walk in, walk in. I am most happy to see gentlemen of de press—most happy of any to see Mister Sleeke." With that she stepped back and made the purtyest leetle curchy that ever I see; it was like a speckled trout diving into a brook jest enough to give a curve to the water and no more.

"Oh dear!" think sez I, "Jonathan Slick, if you havn't been a weeding in the wrong bed agin. That critter is Fanny Elssler as true as all creation; no woman on arth could make sich a curchy but her." I guess my face blazed up a few, but I seen that there was no backing out, so not to be behind hand in good manners I stepped back, put out my foot with a flourish that made the seams to my new trousers give; then I drew my right heel into the hollow of my left foot, and kept a bending for'ard all the time with a sort of deliberate gentility, till my eyes had to roll up the leastest mite to keep sight of her'n. Then I drew up agin easy, like a jack-knife with a tough spring, and finished off with a flurish of my hand up to my hat and back agin; that last touch left me standing parpendic'lar right before her, as a free born citizen of America ought tu.

"Miss Elssler," sez I, how do you du? You haint no idea how tickled I am to see you."

That and the bow of mine did the bisness for her. I never did see a critter act so tickled—the dimples kept a coming and going round that sweet mouth of her'n like the bubbles on a glass of prime cider. Her eyes were brimful of funny looks, and she grew harnsomer every minit. Her face realy was like a picture book; every time I took a peak it seemed as if she'd turned over a new leaf with a brighter pictur painted on it.

She went along towards a bench all cushioned off, that looked as if it was tu good to be sot on, and there she stood a waving that white hand, as much as to say, set down here Mr. Slick, and don't be particlar about gitting too fur off from them square pillars for I shall set agin them myself.

I made her a kind of a half bow, and then arter giving my hand a wave to match her'n,—sez I—

"Arter you is manners for me."

The critter understands what good manners is; her black eyes begun to sparkle and the smile came around her little mouth thicker and faster, like lady bugs around a full blown rose. I begun to feel to hum with her right off, so when she sot down and looked into my face with them sarcy mischievous eyes of her'n, and hitched up to the square cushion sort of inviting, I jest divided my coat tail with both hands and sot down tu

But when I got down I'll be darned if I knew what on arth to talk about; I stretched one of my new boots out on the carpet, and then crossed t'other over it and then I did it all over agin, but still I kept growing more and more streaked, till by-am-by I jest sidled towards her kind of insinivating, and sez I—

"Wal, Miss Elssler, what's the news?"

"E—a de what," sez she, a looking puzzled half to death.

"Oh nothing partic'lar," sez I. "I swow, Miss Elssler, you've got a tarnal purty foot—git out you critter you!" and with that I gave my yaller hankercher a flirt and upset a fly that had lit on the tip eend of her finefied silk shoe. Arter I'd finished his bisness, I folded up my hankercher and wiped my nose, and then put it in my pocket agin. Then I begun to think it was best to take a new start, and sez I—

"Its rather pleasant weather for the season, don't you think so—beautiful day yesterday, wasn't it?"

She gave me one of her sweet smiles, and sez she—

"Yes it was, indeed. I was on board one French vessel in the harbor yesterday, and was so delighted."

"What sort of a consarn was it?" sez I, "a sloop mebby"—

"Oh no," sez she, "it was a *La Belle Poule*."

"Oh," sez I, "they don't call them sloops in France, I s'pose; but I say, Miss Elssler, have you ever been aboard a regular Yankee craft, say a Connecticut river sloop or a two mast schooner from down East? them's the ginuine sea birds for you! Now my Par's got one a lying down to Peck Slip that'll take the shine off from any of your Bell pulls or Bell ropes either, I'll bet a cookey. I should raly like to show you the critter, I'm sartin Captin Doolittle would go off the handle, he'd be so tickled. Supposing you and I go down some day and git a peep at her, and take a glass of cider and a cold bite in the cabin. Now what do you say?"

"Oh, I shall be very happy;" sez she, yet I thought she looked kinder puzzled, and so to make her feel easy about it sez I—

"Don't be oneasy about the trouble, it won't be no put out to Captin Doolittle, he's al'rs on hand for a spree. Supposing we set day after to-morrow, it's best to give the old chap time to slick up a leetle," sez I.

"Any time that pleases Mr. Sleeke," sez she, a bowing her head.

I wish to gracious Par, you could hear how the critter talks. She nips off some words and strings out others, like a baby jest larning. The way she draws out Mr. Slick is funny enough, you'd think she'd been greasing her tongue to do it fust rate.

Wal, arter we'd settled about the sloop, there come another dead calm and I begun to feel awk'ard agin, so I got up and went to a table that was a'most kivered over with tumblers and chiny cups, stuffed full of posies, and taking one of 'em up, I stuck my nose into the middle on it and giv a good snuff. By the time I got through, Miss Elssler she cum and stood close by me, alooking so tempting that I bust rite out and sez I—

"I swan, Miss Elssler, its eenamost as sweet as your face."

She looked at me again, sort of wild, as if she wasn't used to have folks praise her, so I choked in, and sez I—

"Are you fond of posies?"

She chewed up some soft words that I couldn't make out, and then sez I agin—

"You've got a swad of 'em here, any how. Some of your beaus sent them to you, now, I'll bet something."

"Oh," sez she, a larfing, "dey were all flung on de stage last night, de new York gentlemen dey are *so* gallant."

I said nothing but kept a darned of a thinking. There wasn't a ginuine prime posey among 'em, nothing but leetle finefied roses, and buds and leaves, and white posies tied up in bunches, jest sich leetle things as a feller might give to a young critter of a gal that he took a notion tu, but no more fit for sich a smasher as Miss Elssler than a missionary psalm book. She begun to un tie one of the bunches, and stuck a few into her bosom, and then she twisted the ribbon round a harnsome red rose and a heap of green leaves, and puckering up that sweet mouth of her'n, she gin it to me with a half curchy. Gaury! didn't my heart flounder, and didn't the fire flash up into my eyes. I pinned the ose into my shirt bosom with my new broach, and then I looked at the posies that lay on her bosom so tantalizing, and sez I—

"Oh dear! how I wish I was a honey bee—I guess I know what bunch of posies I'd settle in."

13

She didn't seem to know how to take this, and I was eenamost scared into a caniption fit to think what I'd been a saying. Think sez I, now Jonathan, if you hain't done it! I ruther guess you'd better cut dirt, and not try agin; so I took out my watch, and sez I—

"Goodness gracious! its time for me to be a going. Don't forgit, our bargin is clinched about the sloop, will you now, Miss Elssler?"

With that I edged towards the door, and arter making another prime bow, I went out, feeling sort of all-overish, I can't tell how. I kinder think she wasn't very wrothy arter all, for she curchied and smiled so, I guess there wasn't much harm done.

The minit I got to my room I was all in a twitter to find out what was on the paper Miss Elssler had sent to me, for I hadn't found out yet. Every word that I could make out was, Madame ma Selle Elssler, and something that looked like compliments spelt wrong: you can't think how I was puzzled. I turned the paper upside down, and up, and every which way, but if the rest wasn't writ in some sort of hog Latin, I hadn't no idee what it was, for I couldn't make out another word, so at last I chucked the paper onto the mantel-shelf, for I wouldn't hold in no longer, and sez I, all alone to myself, as wrathy as could be, sez I,

"Madam ma Selle Elssler, and be darned, for what I care; I wish to gracious she knew how to write coarser."

By-am-by I took up the thing agin, for it made me feel sheepish to think I couldn't make out to read so much Latin as a gal could write, arter going to grammar school so long, but it wasn't of no use, so think sez I, I'll jest go down to the bar-room and see where the critter is to be sold, and what madam it is that's going to knock her off. So down I went, and sez I to the man sort of easy, sez I,

"So you're a going to have an auction here, aint you?"

The chap looked up, and at fust he didn't seem to know me agin in my fix up, but arter a minit he smiled, and sez he,

"Dear me, Mr. Slick, is it you agin? An auction! no, not as I know on."

"Oh!" sez I, and with that I begun to twistify the square paper

about in my fingers, and at last I seemed to be a reading it as
arnest as could be, all the while a leaning sort of easy towards
him as if I'd forgot he was there. He kept a eyeing it kinder
slautindicular, till at last, sez he—

"That's purty writing, Mr. Slick—a lady's, I should think?"

"Mebby you've seen it afore," sez I, a trying to look careless,
and as if I'd read every word on't a dozen times. "Ruther
scrumptous leetle curlecues them are, don't you think so?"

With that I handed over the pesky thing kind of nat'ral, as
if I didn't really think what I was a doing, and he seemed to
read it off as easy as water.

"Oh yes," sez he, "this is her *own* handwriting; a great compliment, Mr. Slick. I know of many a fine feller that would
give his ears to get sich a card from 'the Elssler.'"

"Oh," sez I, "if she has a notion for ears, she'd better bargain for them Baltimore chaps that we've heard on. She'll get
prime ones there, as long as beet leaves, but I'm afeared she'll
find 'em ruther scarce here in York; the sile ain't rich enough
for 'em."

Here the chap bust out a larfing, and haw-hawed till it seemed
as if he'd go right off the handle. He tried to choke in, but
that only made him top off short with a touch of the hooping-
cough. Arter a while he wiped his eyes, and sez he—

"Very good, Mr. Slick! very good indeed! But of course
you accept the Elssler's invitation to the theatre to-night!"

"To the theatre," sez I, "so she goes off there, does she;
well, a feller may see the fun without bidding, so mebby I'll
go."

"Jest inquire for the Astor House box, and it'll be all right,"
sez the chap, and with that he took up the thick paper, and,
sez he,

"How neatly they do turn off these compliments in French,
don't they?"

"In what?" sez I.

"In French," sez he.

"Oh!" sez I, and more and more I was anxious to find out
what the French gal had writ to me.

"How beautifully she's turned this sentence about your talents," soz he.

"Yes," sez I, all of a twitter inside, but cool as a cucumber for what he knew. "Yes, purty well, considering, but look a here now, I'll bet a cookey you can't turn that into fust rate English as soon as I can, and I'll give you the fust chance tu."

The chap larfed agin, and sez he, "If you'd a said fust rate Yankee I should a gin right up tu once, but I ruther think I can cum up to you in English."

"The proof of the pudding is in eating the bag," sez I.

"Wal," sez he, "I can but try;" so he looked at the paper, and read it off jest as easy as git out.

"Miss Elssler's compliments to Mr. Jonathan Slick, and hopes that he will do her the honor to accept a seat in a private box at the theatre this evening, where she performs in Nathalie and the Cachuka." Then he went on with a grist of the softest sodder that ever you heard on, about my talents and genius, and the cute way I had of writing about the gals, that put me all in a twitteration; but he read so fast that I couldn't ketch only now and then a word sartin enough to write it down, and if I could it would make me feel awful sheepish to think Judy White would ever see it, so the least said, the soonest mended.

"Wal," sez I, sort of condescending, when the chap had got through, "I give up beat—you've done it as cute as a razor. I raly could a parsed the words as you went along. Mebby you might have tucked in a few more long words, but all things considered, it aint best to be critical, so I guess I may as well agree to owe you the cookey." With that I went to my room agin.

Your affectionate son,

JONATHAN SLICK.

LETTER XX.

Jonathan goes to the Express Office—His Opinion of Zeke Jones and the "Brother Jonathan" Newspaper—Explains his Absence, and enters into a new Agreement with the Editors.

Dear Par:

Arter I'd made a visit to Miss Elssler, I went up to my room, as I was a telling you, and begun to think over what we'd been a talking about, and it made me feel sort of streaked to think she took me for one of the Editors of the *Express*, when I was eenamost scared to death for fear they wouldn't print my letters agin, arter I give them the mitten so slick, and went off to Weathersfield. I didn't suppose the critters ever knew what it was to be humsick, as I was in this tarnal place, and was afeard they might rise right up agin having anything to do with me. But think sez I, there's nothing like keeping a stiff upper lip, and putting on airs of independence, and talking right up to these news paper chaps; so I on with my hat, and cut along towards the *Express* Office, detarmined to do up my chores in that quarter, without chawing over the matter any longer.

Wal, I streaked it along about the quickest, like a string of onions broke loose at the leetle eend. I begun to feel awful anxious jest as I got in sight of the office, and the feeling made me slack foot and ketch breath, I can tell you. As I went by the corner in a sort of a half canter, with my hands in both pockets —for I felt kinder ashamed of the streaked mittens marm knit for me when my yaller gloves wore out, they didn't exactly gibe with my other fix up—the people stopped and stared like all possessed.

"If that aint Mr. Slick!" sez one;—"Sure enough," sez another, "so it is." "Didn't I tell you he wasn't dead," sez another.

With that I chirked up a leetle, and sez I to myself, sez I—

Who cares if the Editors of the *Express* be mad, cause I cut stick when they wanted to send me off to Washington, when it was as hot as all natur, and jest planting time. If my letters were good for any thing, they'll be glad on 'em agin, and if they aint, why I'll let 'em see that I'm a true born ginuine American, died in the wool, and that I can up stakes and go hum agin in the old sloop as independent as a cork screw.

Arter I'd hung about the corner of the office a leetle while, I got up pluck, and walked right straight ahead into the office. I begun to feel to hum the minit I opened the door—every thing looked so nat'ral. There was the counter, jest like old times, and the pigeon holes stuck full of newspapers, and a pile of white printer's paper a lying up in one corner, and there sot the clark, a rale ginuine cute leetle Yankee; he was a writing on leetle scraps of brown paper, and a looking as if all creation would stop if he didn't go ahead.

I jest give a peak in for a minit and streaked it up stairs, to see if I couldn't find somebody there. I wish you could have seen how the work hands stared and looked at one another when I went in, but I didn't stop to say nothing to nobody, but up I went, through a room chuck full and brimming over with work hands, and there in a leetle room, about as big as an undersized calf pen, sot the critter hisself, eenamost buried up in a pile of newspapers. It raly did my heart good to look at him, he'd grown so chirk and hearty, it seemed to me as if he must a fatted up two inches on the ribs since I'd seen him.

"Gracious me," sez I to myself, "I kinder wish I'd stuck to and tried to tucker it out last year, and mebby I should a had something to fat up about. Now I wonder what he's a reading that tickles him so."

Jest as I was a thinking this, the Editor of the *Express* he looked up, and see me a standing there, as if I'd been a growing on that identical spot ever since last summer. Gauly offilus! but didn't the newspapers fly, when he was sartin who it was. I see that he was eenamost tickled to death to see me agin.

"I hain't lost my chance here yet," sez I to myself, and so I walked right straight up to him, and held out my fist, mitten and all, and sez I—

"How do you do?"—jest so.

"Why Mr. Slick," sez he, "where did you come from?"

"Right straight from hum," sez I; "but how du you git along about these times—every thing going along about straight, I s'pose."

By this time he seemed to think that there was something that he ought to git mad about. You'd a thought he'd swollered a basket of cowcumbers all of a sudden, he looked so frosty.

"Now for it," sez I to myself.

"Mr. Slick," sez he, a looking as parpendicular as if he'd eat tenpenny nails for breakfast, and topped off with a young crowbar, "Mr. Slick, I'm happy to see you in York agin, but what on arth was the reason that you left us in the lurch about them letters from Washington?"

"Did you ever have a touch of humsickness?" sez I, a straightening up and putting my hands in my pockets, till the tip eend of my nose eenamost come on a level with his'n.

"I rather think I have," sez he, a hitching up his shoulders.

"And the ager, too?" sez I.

"Don't mention it," sez he, jest a shaking the leastest mite all over with thinking about it.

"Awful sort of a chilly animal, that ager, ain't it?" sez I.

"Dreadful," sez he.

"Didn't it seem as if you'd have to take up all your bones for salt and battery on one another, afore they'd keep still?" sez I.

"A most," sez he, a larfing.

"Wal," sez I, "I didn't ketch the fever and ager."

"What did you ketch, then?" sez he, sort of impatient.

"Oh, I felt kinder as if I should git it if I didn't go hum and doctor," sez I.

"But that wasn't quite reason enough for your goin off so," sez he.

"Wasn't it?" sez I, "but that wasn't all; I got a letter from par, and he wrote that marm was ailing, and that he was getting down in the mouth, and didn't feel very smart himself, and there wasn't nobody to weed the onions—only Judy White—and she seemed sort of molancholy, and so"——

"Oh, I understand," sez he, a cutting me off short in what I was going to say. I guess he took notice how the blood biled up in my face, for he went right to talking about something else as nat'ral as could be.

So arter confabulating a spell about things in general, the Editor of the Express he begun to poke around among the newspapers agin, and to hitch around as if he'd jest as lief I wasn't there. I pulled out my mittens, for it was cold enough to snap a feller's ears off, early as it was. So I put 'em on sort of deliberate, and begun to smooth up the red and blue fringe on the top, jest as if I wanted to go, and yet didn't feel in much of a hurry.

"By-am-by I got up, and sez I, "Wal, good-day—I s'pose it's about time for me to be a jogging."

"Don't be in a hurry, Mr. Slick," sez he, a fumbling over the newspapers all the time.

Think sez I, "If you have any notion to print my letters, it's about time to come up to the scratch tu once;" but he kept on a reading, and sez I, a sliding back'ards towards the door,—

"I shouldn't be in such a pucker to go, but I want to stop at the office of the Brother Jonathan to see Zeke Jones, from our parts. He's a prime feller, Zeke is; one of them sort of chaps that make one proud of human natur. We used to be as thick as three in a bed afore either of us took to literature. I haint seen him since, but his stories are the clear grain and no chaff, ginuine all over, and enough to bring the tears into a feller's eyes once in a while, I can tell you. The critter 'll go right off the handle when he sees me, he'll be so tickled," sez I, "and I haint no doubt but he can get the editors of that creation large paper to print some of my letters for me."

"There," think sez I, "if that don't bring him up to the trough, fodder or no fodder, I don't know what will."

Sure enough, I hadn't but jest got the words out of my mouth, when the chap he spoke up like a man.

"Mr. Slick," sez he, "don't think of sich a thing as writing for any paper but the New York Express. I can't bear the idee of it a minit. You raly can't think how bad we felt for fear you was dead when we didn't git no more letters from you arter you went to Weathersfield. Now what do you say to staying in New York and going ahead agin? Supposing you pull off your mittens and take hold now?"

I seem'd to sort of deliberate a spell, for I didn't want him to think I come to York a purpose to stay; so arter a while sez I,—

"Wal, I'll think about it. Par is a getting old, but I guess he'd about as lief do the foddering an help marm about the chores as not this winter, and mebby Captain Doolittle will board there and help about when he hives up for the winter. But I don't jest know how to manage it. I hain't no go-to-meeting clothes, that are quite up to the notch. The knees of my dandy trousers bust out the fust time I got down to weed onions in 'em, and I feel rather unsartin how this new fix of mine would take the gals' eyes in Broadway."

"Oh! don't stand on trifles Mr. Slick," sez he, "Editors never do,"—and with that he took a squint at my trousers, as if he was mightily tickled with the fit of 'em and wanted to get a pattern. This sot me in conceit of 'em a leetle.

"A feller might see that with half an eye, any how," sez I. "But now I come to think of it, this ere suit of go-to-meeting clothes that I've got on aint to be sneezed at, now, are they? Marm spun and made them for me afore I cum away from hum. She cut 'em by my dandy coat and trousers, and got a purty scrumptious fit. So mebby they'll be jest the thing. Every body in Weathersfield took to cuttin their clothes arter mine," sez I, sort of bragging,—because, you know, with some folks it's best to put the best foot for'ard, and pass for all you're worth, and sometimes for a leetle more, tu.

It's all a mistake for a man to think tu well of himself; but the experience I've had here in York tells me, that a man, to make others think well of him, must make the most of himself and of all his imperfections. "A good outside for the world, and a good heart within," was one of the best lessons you larned me, par, when I left Weathersfield for York. So sez I to the editor, standing as straight as a broomstick, and striking my hand upon my hat, and then putting both in my pockets, to appear sort of independent,—

"If you think they'll du, why I don'" care if I hitch tackle with you agin; but if the notion takes me to cut stick for Washington or Weathersfield some of these days, I ain't sartin but you'll find me among the missing, but howsomever, I'll give you a try at a few letters; but I've got my hand out, I can tell you. Stringing onions and writing letters on genteel society, ain't the same thing by no sort of means. So now that's all settled, I'm off like shot off a shovel."

With that I shook hands with the Editor of the Express, and made tracks for the sloop about the tickledest feller that ever you did see.

Your loving son,
JONATHAN SLICK.

LETTER XXI.

Jonathan Visits Mr. Hogg's Garden and gets a Bouquet—Puzzled about the propriety of Paying for it—Purchases a Ribbon and starts for the Theatre.

DEAR PAR:

The minit I got to the sloop I took off my coat, for I didn't seem to hum enough in the Astor House to write there. I sot down in the cabin, and stretching out my legs on a butter-tub, I turned up my ristbands and wrote off the letter that I sent you t'other day on the top of an onion barrel, without stopping once, I was so tarnationed anxious to let you know how I was a getting along.

I had to bite off short, for a chap come aboard the sloop with Captin Doolittle to bargain for the cargo of cider and garden sarse. I was afeared that they would want to overhaul my writing desk, and so made myself scarce, and went up to the Express with the letter stuck loose inside the crown of my hat, editor fashion.

I left the hull letter with the clark, and axed him where on arth a chap could git a smashing bunch of posies, if he took a notion to want sich a thing. He told me to go right straight up to Mr. Hogg's, clear up town along the East River, and said that I'd better git aboard a Harlem car, and it would carry me right chock agin the spot for a ninepence.

"Wal," sez I, "the expense aint nothing to kill, so I guess I'll ride."

With that, I got into one of them allfired awk'ard things that look like a young school-house sot on wheels, and running away with the scollars stowed inside; and arter shelling out my ninepence, we sot out up Centre-street, through the Bowery, and all along shore, till we stopped short nigh agin the Astoria ferry, clear up town. Arter searching around a little, I found Mr. Hogg's gardin, and went in. A great, tall, good-natured looking chap cum up to me as I was a peaking about—a feller that made me feel hum-sick in a minit, he looked so much like our folks.

"How do you du?" sez I, "I'm tickled to see you; they told me that you keep posies about these ere premises, but I don't see no signs of 'em."

"Oh," sez he, as good as pie, "come this way, and I guess we can find as many as you want."

"Wal," that'll be a good many, for I'm a hard critter on marygolds and holly-hocks," sez I, "and I want a smashing heap on 'em."

With that, Mr. Hogg, instead of taking me into a garden, jest opened the door of a great long, low house, with an allfired great winder covering the hull roof, and sez he—

"Walk in."

I guess I did walk in, for the house was chuck full of the harnsomest trees and bushes that I ever sot eyes on, all kivered over with posies, and smelling so sweet, that a bed of seed onions, jest as it busts out in a snow-storm of white flowers, aint nothing compared to it. Didn't I give good long snuffs as I went in! This idea, to my notion, of posies amongst big trees and bushes, are like wimmen folks and young ones in the world of human natur. If they arnt good for something else they are plaguey harnsome to look at, and the world would be awful dark and scraggy without them. Some wimmen may be bad enough and hateful as henbane, but consarn me if I wouldn't rather love thorn bushes than none at all.

There was one tree that took my eye the minit I went in; it

hung chuck full of great big oranges, and tell me I he right out, if there wasn't a swad of white posies a busting out through the great green leeves in hull handfuls, all around on the same limbs where the oranges were a growing. Think sez I, this raly is a ginuine scripture lesson, spring and fall a gitting in love with each other and hugging together on the same bush; oh, gracious! how the parfume did pour out from the middle of that tree! I felt it a steaming up my nose and creeping through my hair, till I begun to feel as sweet as if I'd been ducked all over in a kettle full of biled rose leaves.

Mr. Hogg he went along among the great high rows of bushes sot in a heap, one on top of t'other almost to the glass ruff, with a good sized jack-knife in his hand, and then he cut and slashed among the green leaves and red roses, and piled up a bunch of posies about the quickest! Yet I wasn't satisfied, he didnt seem to pick out the rale critters, but tucked in the leetle finefied buds jest as if he couldn't guess what I wanted 'em for.

"Oh, now you git out," sez I, when he handed over a hull swad of posies done up in a grist of leaves; "you don't mean to put me off with that ere! why, it aint a flee-bite to what I want. Come now, hunt up a few hollyhocks, and marygolds, and poppies, and if you've got a good smashing hidaranger, purple on one side and yaller on tother, tuck it in the middle."

Mr. Hogg he stood a looking right in my eyes with his mouth a little open, as if he didn't know what to make of it.

"The season is over for those things," sez he, "and I haint got one in the hot-house."

"Wal," sez I, "du the best you can, all things considering, only tuck in the big posies and enough on 'em, for I'm going to give 'em to a sneezer of a harnsome gal—so don't be too sparing."

With that M. Hogg sarched out some great red and yaller posies, with some streaming long blue ones a sticking through them, and arter a while he handed over something worth while— a great smashing bunch of posies as big as a bell-squash choked in at the neck.

Arter I'd examined the concarn to be sartin that all was shipshape, I made Mr. Hogg a bow, and, sez I,

"I'm much obliged to you—if ever you come to Weathersfield in the summer time, marm will give you jest as many and be tickled with the chance. She beats all natur at raising these sort of things."

He looked at me sort of arnest, but yet he didn't seem to be jest satisfied, and after snapping his thumb across the blade of his jack-knife a minit, he spoke out, but seemed kinder loth.

"We generally sell our bokays," sez he, arter haming and hawing a leetle while.

"Wal," sez I, "mebby I shall want one some of these days, and then I'll give you a call—but any how I'm obliged to y a for the posies all the same."

I wanted to offer him a fourpence for the trouble of picki .g the posies, but he looked so much like a gentleman and a Weathersfield Deacon, I was scared for fear he'd think I want d to impose on him if I offered money. So I made him anoth r bow, and went off, while he stood a looking arter me as if I d been stealin a sheep. I have wished since that I'd offered him the fourpence, for he kinder seemed to calculate on something like it. I stopped into a store, and bought a yard of wide yaller ribbon, and arter tying it round my bunch of posies in a double bow not, with great long eends a streaming down, I took the critter in my hand, and cut dirt for the theatre, for it was a gitting nigh on to dark.

Your loving son,
JONATHAN SLICK.

LETTER XXII.

Jonathan gives a Description of the Theatre, Private Boxes, Drop-Scene, &c.—His Ideas of *Miss* Elssler's Dancing, and Dancing Girls in general—Jonathan mistakes Williams in his Comic Song of "Old Maids and Old Batchelors to Sell," for an Auctioneer who is knocking off, "La Belle Fanny," to the Highest Bidder—Jonathan is indignant that she is not his, after so much hard bidding, by winks, &c.—He flings his Bouquet at Fanny's Feet—Jonathan's Visit Behind the Scenes, and his Idea of Things seen there—Gallants Fanny home to the Astor House.

Dear Par:

The man who keeps the door at the Park Theatre didn't seem 'o know me at fust, but the minit I writ out my name the hull length, and handed it over, curlecucs and all, and told him I wanted the Astor House box, he was as perlite as a basket of chips. He handed me over to another chap, who took me up stairs and along a dark entry way, till he ended in a harnsome leetle pen, all curtained off with red silk, with purty mahogany frames that slid up and down over a sort of red pulpit cushion that run round the front side.

The feller he shut me up, and I sot down on one of the chairs in the box, and took a gineral survey of the theatre. From where I sot, it looked as if somebody had laid down an allfired big horse-shoe for a pattern, and then built after it one tier of seats above another till they got tired of the fun, and topped off with a young sky all covered over with golden picters and curlecued work.

There was a consarned great curtain hung down afore the stage, with a sort of an Injun mound in the middle, and a house built on top of it. A lot of painted fellers hung about the front of the curtain, niggers and Injuns, some a setting down and some a standing up, and looking like human meat-axes gone to sleep. One feller that was squat down with his back leaned agin a post, had something that looked like a bunch of prime onions with the tops on, stuffed inter his bosom, and he held a kind of a short handled frying-pan in his hand as if he meant to cook some and have a smart fry, as soon as he could git tu a fire.

I hadn't sot long when the men begun to stream into the theatre like all possessed, with a small sprinkling of the feminine gender, jest enough to take the cuss off and no more.

In less than no time the house was jammed chuck full and running over, till I raly felt as if it was wicked to keep so much room all to myself, when the rest was stowed and jammed up so close that you couldn't a hung up a flax seed edgeways between 'em, but think sez I, every one for himself—I know when I'm well off, and that's enough. So I leaned over the cushion, and let one hand hang a leetle over the edge, as independent as if the whole theatre was mine.

By-am-by the curtain begun to roll up, and I'd like to have larfed right out to see them painted chaps du themselves up and curl over the roller—fust their feet doubled up, then their legs and hips and shoulders—then the roller took a slice off from the bottom of the mound, and turights, the hull was twisted up into a beam, and hitched to the ruff—goodness gracious knows how I don't!

Wal, when the curtain was all rolled up snug, there raly was a picter worth looking on behind it. There was a great high mountain with rail fences cutting across it, and bridges and trees, that made a feller feel oneasy to git into the shade, and oxen and cows and folks a driving 'em, going along the road, that run around slantindicular to the top, and there, jest at the foot of the hill, was a purty leetle house half kivered over with grape vines and morning glories that made me think of hum till I could a bust out crying as well as not.

All to once there was a toot horn sounded up among the rocks, and then—oh creation! what a grist of harnsome gals cum a dancing and larfing and hopping down the mountain, all with curls a flying and posies twisted among 'em, and white frocks on, and ribbons a streaming out every which way, and *sich* feet, I swanny it made me ketch my breath to see 'em a cutting about under their white petticoats.

When they got down onto the flat before the house, the way they cut it down heel and toe, right and left, down outside and up the middle, was enough to make the York tippes, the darned lazy coots, ashamed of themselves. It was Down East all over! —they put it down about right, with the ginuine Yankee grit. I felt all in a twitter to git down and shake a toe with them. It would be worth while to cut a double shuffle among so many harnsome gals, with a hull pen chuck full of fiddles a reeling off the music for you. I'll be darned, Par, if I don't believe it would make the blood streak it through your old veins about the quickest, if you be a Justice of the Peace and a Deacon of the Church.

Arter a while a feller cum up that looked just like a tin pedler out of work—a sneaking critter with a face like a jack-knife, and a white hat on turned clear up on the sides till the flo.* an back was pinted like a butter scoop. He begun stepping abo and making motions with his arms, till the gals cut up the hill to work agin, like a coop full of chickens scattered by a hen hawk.

The chap was a strutting about as crank as a woodchuck, when in come Miss Elssler a hundred times handsomer than she was to hum, wheeling a wheel-barrow with a churn in it.

Gauly oppalus! but wasn't she a sneezer! The rest wasn't no more to compare with her than a dandalion is to a cabbage rose. On she cum a teetering along as genteel as a bobalink in a wheat lot. She had on a straw hat curled up at the sides that made her handsome face look so cunning; besides this she wore a sort of a new fashioned jacket with short sleeves, that showed a pair of the roundest fattest arms all sort of tapering off to the hand— a purty leetle finefied hand as white as curd, and that looked eenamost as soft too. With the hat on and the jacket you might have took her for an allfired harnsome boy, but there was no mistake about the rest. Mary Beebe couldn't raise a bigger bump than she had on. Arter all, the boys' and gals' clothing pulled about an even yoke on her. She had on a short petticoat that showed a purty considerable chunk of understandings, that tapered off into a pair of feet, that looked as if they couldn't be hired to keep still on no account. Take her for all, I can't but allow, that she was a smasher in the way of beauty, and her manners were sartinly very genteel.

The minit she cum on, the folks in the theatre begun to stomp, and yell, and kick up a darned of a fuss; with that she dropped her wheel-barrow as if it had been a hot potater, and begun to curchy, and smile, and put that consarned hand agin her heart, till I begun to ketch breath like a pair of bellerses.

It took nigh upon three minits afore the consarned fellers would stop their yop; but when they did choke in a leetle, she ketched up the wheel-barrow and scooted up the mountain with it, a teetering and sidling along like a young colt when they are a breaking him to the bit.

The tin pedler chap, he poked on arter, and gin the wheel-barrow a boost once in a while as chipper as could be. It made my dander rise to see the chap a hankering arter her so. If she wanted to take a shine to a Yankee why couldn't she a found a feller worth a looking at? But sometimes it does seem as if these gals couldn't tell bran when the bag's open—the brightest on 'em. I say nothing, but it seems to me that she might a gin one peak up to the Astor House box. I guess it would have made that chap sing small if she had.

Wal, arter all, the critters both came back agin. The gal had a red ribbon in her hand and she'd lost her straw hat somewhere in the bushes. It raly did beat all how she tanteralized that he coot with the ribbon; fust she made as if she'd give it to him, and jest as he gripped it, away it slipped through his fingers and she flourished it now on one side his head, and now on t'other, as if it had been a streak of lightning she was a playing with. It tickled me eenamost to death to see how darned sheepish the critter looked when she sort of hovered about him with the ribbon, now a sticking that tarnal sweet coaxing face into his'n so pert, and then darnsing off as easy as git out, with the red ribbon a streaming from her fingers so sarsy.

Oh gracious! I'd a gin something to have been in that feller's shoes, I swan if I wouldn't a give her a buss right before 'em all—I couldn't a help'd it if all creation had been at the door, and I swan, Par, I believe you'd a up and give her a smack tu if you'd been by, old as you be The sight of her tarnal sweet winning

14

ways was enough to rile up the blood in a feller's heart, if he was as old and frosty as Mathusaler's.

I don't wonder that the fellers stomped and clapped their paws,—I'm afear'd I let out a young arthquake myself in that way. I tried to hold in, but it wasn't the leastest might of use. That gal is like a sky-rocket, she busts right on a feller and takes away his senses with the blaze. I settled right down like a cabbage sprout in a hot sun.

Arter a while the gals all come down from the mountain agin, and begun to cut up their tantrums; then a harnsome man with a cap and feathers on, and clothes all kivered with silver and gold and precious stones, come tipping along leading a great strapping woman as tall as all out-doors, and dressed off in green like a bull-frog. They went into a leetle sort of a cubby house with glass winders, and sot down to see the rest dance.

Didn't they cut the dashes though! helter skelter, hurra boys; they went at it like a flock of sheep at salting time. By-am-by they all give out, and my gal, Fanny, she stood up with the leetle Yankee as if she was a going to dance a jig. She'd put on another petticoat streaked yaller and blue, but insted of running up and down, the streaks were a foot wide, and run round and round like the hoops of a barrel. She'd lost her hat, and a swad of the shineyest black hair that ever I saw on a gal's head was kinder slicked down on the sides, and twistified up in a knot behind her harnsome shaped head, and then topped off with a bunch of red roses and a pink ribbon that hung streaming down her back about as long as marm ties your cue, Par, when you go to meeting.

Wal, the leetle chap he begun to dance fust, and I thought I should a haw-hawed right out to see him strain and exart himself, while she stood by with her tarnal cunning head stuck a one side, so tickled, that the tee-hee fairly bust through, and made her larf sort of easy all over, but he didn't seem to know that she was a poking fun at him.

When the chap got through, Miss Elssler she jest sidled up as softly as a snow storm—gin her foot a twirl, and took a sort of genteel dive as if she was a going to swim in the air. Oh dear, didn't she swim, too! It was like a bird on an apple tree limb

In spring time, or a boy's kite a sailing and ducking to a south wind. She didn't kick about, and shuffle, and all that, as I've seen 'em do; nor did she pucker and twist and sidle like the darned lazy varmints that I've seen among the fashionable big bugs; but she was as chirk as a bird, as quick as a grasshopper, and as soft as a mealy potatoe with the skin off.

By-am-by she broke off short, and spread out her hands, and curchied to the chap sort of sarsy, as if to say, "Beat that if you can."

Then the feller he tried agin, and then she, turn about, till at last she let herself off like a fire cracker on the fourth of July. One foot flew up into the air like a bird's wing, and whiz—off she went like a she comet kicked on eend. Then she sort of let her foot down by degrees, as a hawk folds its wing, and sloped off easy, a spreading her hands to the feller, and curchying so sarsy, as much as to say,

"Try and beat that, now du! all over agin if you can."

The critter sneaked off as if he couldn't help it, then the show went on, all of 'em talking in signs like deaf and dumb folks. But it would take a week of Sundays to tell you all. To give you the butt eend, she was married to the harnsome chap that run off with her; and out she cum all in white, with diamonds in her hair and on her neck, and her frock shone with 'em like a snowball bush kivered with dew in the arly summer. Goodness gracious! wasn't she a beauty without paint or whitewash, and didn't she dance! The folks stomped and yelled like a pack of Injuns, when the chap gave her a grip round the waist, and she stood on one toe with t'other leg stuck out, and her head twisted toward his bosom, a twittering like a white swan that would a flown clear off, if the feller hadn't held on like all natur. It raly seemed as if you could a seen the white feathers a ruffling up she was so eager to fly away.

Consarn that chap—darn him to darnation, I say! It made me riley to see him a holding on her as if there warn't nobody in creation but himself. I'll be hanged and choked to death if it wouldn't a done me good to have licked him on the spot. The mean finefied varmint! It was lucky the curtain went down ca-smash as it did. It give me time to kinder think what I was a doing, or he'd a ketched it.

I'd eenamost forgot about the auction, for arter the Astor House chap read the card, I begun to think there was some mistake; but by-am-by out come a queer looking chap, as chirk as a catydid, and he begun to sing off a lot of men and women folks to auction.

Think sez I, goodness gracious! if any body but me bids off that harnsome critter, I shall go off the handle; I sartinly shall. He'd knocked off an old maid and a widder, and an Irishman, and was jest a crying up an old bachelor, when I made up my mind to bid on her any way, if I had to sell the old sloop, garden sarse and all, to toe the mark.

I knew the sloop and cargo wasn't mine, but that gal had got into my head, and I didn't seem to know right from wrong. I forgot Judy White and all the gals on arth for the time being. The feller kept a singing out and a knocking on 'em off, but I didn't hear nobody bid, so I s'posed they did it by winking. They tell me that's the fashion at the big York vendues. At the very tip eend of the batch, he up and said he'd got the best one yet for the young men to bid on, a gal jest eighteen, and then he run on with a lot of soft sodder about her, but I can't write what he said, I was in such a twitteration. Think sez I, it's Fanny Elssler as sure as a gun, and I'll be darn'd if any of them chaps out-wink me, so I got up and bent for'ard clear over the cushion, and the way I snapped my eyewinkers at the auctioneer was awful savage I can tell you.

"No more bids," sez he, a histing his fist, "no more bids,—going!" Here I winked like all natur. "Going." I snapped my eyes till they a'most struck fire, and I stuck out my fist to arms length and my breath seemed to stop short, I was so dreadful eager. "Gone!" sez the chap, a stepping back and a lifting his hand as if he didn't care if I shook to death, and then he made a bow to the folks in ginral, and sez he,

'Yours with one eye out."

I sallied back and clapped my hand to my eye, for at first I thought mebby it was out, I'd winked so etarnal arnest but there it was, safe and sound, and some etarnal wall-eyed coot had got that harnsome critter away from me. At first I was mad enough to bite a tenpenny nail in tu without chawing; then I began to feel dreadful wamblecropped, and eenamost boohooed out a crying. In the eend I made up my mind that it was a mean cheat, and that I'd have the gal in spite of all the one-eyed fellers in all creation; "for," sez I, "it aint the natur of things that a critter could wink with one eye as fast as I could with both winkers under full steam, so I jest made up my mind to look out the auctioneer, and stick up for my rights.

There was another play, but I felt so down in the mouth that I up and went right straight off in sarch of that auctioneer, but nobody seemed to understand who I wanted, till, arter wandering around like a cat in a strange garret ever so long, I asked the man at the door; and he said the chap had gone hum, but that he'd be there agin to-morrow night.

"Wal," sez I, "I'll come and see him agin, and he'll find out I aint to be imposed upon if I am from the country."

With that I went back to the Astor House box, jest in time to see Fanny Elssler, the critter I'd been bidding off, out on the stage agin.

There she was, all dressed out in yaller silk, with heaps on heaps of the black shiney lace a streaming over it, a hopping about and twistifying round like a love-sick yaller-hammer hankering arter a mate. She had a rattle-box on each hand, and she gin a rattle at every new twist, and sometimes it was rattle, rattle, rattle, as swift as lightning, and then twist, twist, twist; now her head eenamost bumped agin the floor, and the hump on her back stuck up higher than ever; then her arms went curlecueing over her head, and the rattle-boxes gin out a whole hail-storm of noises, and then she'd stick her arms out at full length and sidle off, dragging her feet along kind of easy, till I raly didn't know what she was a doing, till I looked on the piece of paper the man gin me, and saw that she was a doing up a Cachuca; but if it wasn't dancing, it sartinly was fust cousin to it, or I aint a judge of cat-fish. But then who knows but Cachuca is French for dancing? I don't! any how, she sartinly cachukied it off like all natur, and no mistake.

By-am-by she give her foot a flirt out and her arms a flourish upwards, and off she was a going like a trout with a fish-hook in his mouth; but the folks begun to holler and yell, and take on so, that she had to cum back whether or no.

She cum back sort of modest, a curchying and a smiling, and looking so consarned harnsome and mealy-mouthed, that I thought the men would bust the ruff right off from the theatre, they stomped and yelled, and made such darned coots of themselves. All to once, down cum a hull baking of posies, all around her, as thick as hops. But there wasn't none of them a priming to the one I had stuffed, stem downwards, in the crown of my hat.

I jumped up, and gripped the consarn with both hands, and when the rest had got through, I drew back both hands with a jerk, and it whizzed downwards with the yaller ribbons a streaming out, right over the row of lamps, and the pen full of fiddlers, till it fell ca-swash right down to Miss Elssler's feet.

Gauly offilus! didn't she give a jump! and didn't the folks in the theatre set up another pow-wow, that a'most lifted the ruff off the theatre! The chaps seemed to have a notion what a bunch of posies ought to be when mine cum down amongst the mean leetle bunches that they'd been a throwing, and sent them a streaming every which way.

Miss Elssler, arter the fust jump, looked tickled a'most to death to see such a whopper a lying there, so tempting and sweet; and I ruther guess she took a squint, and sent one of her tarnal killing smiles towards a good looking sort of a chap, about my size, that sot with a checkered vest on a leaning over the Astor House box. I say nothing, but Jonathan Slick haint been to husking balls and apple cuts ever since he was knee high to a toad, without knowing the cut of a gal's looks when she's taken a shine to you, or wants you to see her hum.

I gin her a sort of a knowing squint and a half bow, jest to let her see that she needn't feel uneasy for fear that I shouldn't toe the mark; and then I sot still, but awful impatient, till a chap cum in and picked up a hull armful of the posies He had to git down on one of his marrow bones and boost hard at the whopper that I flung; and when Miss Elssler took 'em all in her arms, and curchied over and over agin, that bunch of mine lay right agin her bosom, and spread out so as a'most to kiver her harnsome white neck. Jest as she was a going off on one side, she gin another of her tarnal sweet squints up to where I sot, and then stuck that harnsome face of her'n down into my posey so tantalizing, I swan, I couldn't stand it no longer, but up I got, and in less than no time I coaxed the door-keeper to show me the way back of the theatre, where the critter was.

The chap took me along that entry way, up stairs by the Astor House box, and through a leetle narrow door, and there he left me on the top of a lot of stairs that looked as if they'd take me down into sumbody's cellar. Sich a tarnal, dark, pokerish set of things I never did see, that's a fact. But I'd got the steam up, and there aint no whoa to me at sich times,—so down I went, hickle-te-picklety, head fust among the paint-pots and boards, and slabs, and smoky lamps, and arter wandering around like the babes in the woods, I cum ca-smash right into a room chuck full of the darncing gals that I'd been half in love with all the evening.

Oh gracious! it made me sick to think what a tarnal coot I'd been a making of myself. Some of the critters that I'd thought so darned harnsome were as old as the hills, and as homely as a sassafras root, close tu. The paint and white-wash was an inch thick on some of their faces, and most on 'em were a cutting about the room as awk'ard as a flock of sheep jest arter shearing time —and these were the light purty critters that had a'most drove me off the handle, they looked so harnsome and taking a leetle way off. I swow, but it a'most sot me agin all the feminine gender to think I'd made such a shote of myself as to take such a shine to them as I had.

The room was chock full of folks. There were old men and young ones, and all sorts of critters dressed off jest as I'd seen 'em in the play; but they didn't look no more like the same critters, close to 'em, than chalk's like a new milk's cheese. That darn'd leetle Yankee chap was there, and while I was considering whether it was best to scrape acquaintance or not, the identical auctioneer that had knocked off the old maids and widders, and Fanny Elssler into the bargain, stood right agin me. I felt my dander rise the minit I sot eyes on him, so I went up to the Yankee chap, and sez I—

"You can't tell me who that chap is, can you?"

The Yankee looked round, and sez he—

"Oh, yes, that's Billy Williams, a good hearted comical chap as ever lived. Don't you know him sir? I thought every body knew Billy Williams."

"I don't know jest yet, but I guess I shall afore long," sez I, a looking pitchforks and hatchel teeth at the auctioneer, and with that I walked right straight up to him, with my hands dug down into my trousers' pockets, as savage as could be, and sez I—

"How do you du sir? I'll jest speak a few words to you, if you haint no objection."

"Sartinly," sez he, as easy as all natur, and with that he got up and walked out of the room, and I arter him, till we cum out onto a sort of an etarnal big barn floor that was shut out from the rest of the Theatre, by that whopping curtain that I'd seen the t'other side on it. There was a hull regiment of empty hay lofts—or what looked jest like 'em, great naked rafters and posts, with rows of smoky lamps stuck on 'em, and what looked like pieces of board fence daubed over with all sorts of paint, and the wind come a whistling and croaking among them all, till my teeth a'most begun to chatter in my head.

I was so busy a wondering what on arth those awful dismal premises could be used for, that I forgot the auctioneer, till he turned round as good natured as a sucking pig, and asked what I wanted of him.

"Look a here," sez I, as wrothy as could be for the cold, "I want the gal that I bid off in the Theatre to-night, so you jest hand over and save trouble, that's all."

The feller he stared at me like a stuck pig, and then he bust right out a larfing in my face as if he meant to make fun of it all, but he'd got hold of the wrong chicken for that sort of corn, and I give him to understand as much afore he'd done with me.

"Now," sez I, "look a here. It aint of no use for you to try to bamboozle me with your haw-hawing. I want the gal that I bid off—I don't care how much the charge is. I'll hand over the chink the minit you'll go to one of them pesky lawyers and git the deed drawn out. I'm sartin that I outwinked every chap in the theatre, and darn me if I give up to any of em."

He stared at fust like a calf's head jest dressed, and then he bust out a larfin, till I was mad enough to kick him on eend till he flew up into one of the empty hay lofts.

"Come," sez I, "do you mean to toe the mark or not? I'm getting awful tingley about the fingers eends, I can tell you."

"Now," sez he, a sobering down a leetle, "did you take me for an auctioneer, in rale arnest?"

I began to feel sort of unsartin what to say, and instead of speaking right out, I circumnavigated a leetle, for a sort of a notion cum over me, that mebby, arter all, it wasn't nothing but make-believe, and that I was jest on the point of making a consarned coot of myself.

"Wal, now, you did it up as cute as a razor, didn't you?" sez I. "It was eenamost enough to make a feller think that you was in arnest, wasn't it? but then I aint quite sich a green horn as some chaps that come from the country, and know what's what. I haint seen anything that tickled me so much as that—that——"

"Comic song," sez he.

"Oh," sez I, as quick as wink, "you needn't take a feller up afore he's down. I was jest a going to say that you raly are a sneezer at saying over them comic songs, and sartinly you do look as nat'ral as life. In course I knew there warn't no wail-eyed critter a bidding, and thought I'd jest see if you was as cute a looking critter close to. More than that, I've got a notion to take a peak at the fixins back of the curtain close tu—so s'posing you and I jest walk among them hills, and housen, and trees, that looked so plaguey cool and shady."

I kept on a talking so that he needn't see how tarnal sheepish I felt, arter making sich a coot of myself as to believe he'd sold Miss Elssler in rale arnest.

"Why," sez he, as good natured as could be, "here you are, right in the midst of all the trees and hills and houses that you saw in front."

"Oh, now, you git out!" sez I, "I aint green enough to swaller that, any how."

He looked round at a pile of old wooden partitions, daubed over with paint, and a standing edgeways, and sort of slantindicular, under the naked rafters and hay lofts, and sez he—

"I'm in arnest now—this is all the scenery that you saw from the front. You stand on the stage, jest back of where I sung my comic song, and that is the curtain."

"What, that old sloop sail?" sez I. "How you du talk! I sniggers, but I can't believe it."

"Jest go to the curtain and look through the edge there," sez he.

And with that he went with me, and pulled back the edge of the curtain, and I gin a sudden peak through. Sure enough, the theatre was right before me, chuck full of folks, jest as I'd left it; and the pen full of fiddlers, was a streaming out the music right under my nose, till I couldn't hear myself think. When I turned round agin, and see how awful dark and chilly every thing looked, and found myself wandering with Mr. Williams among a hull univarse of posts, and boards, and lamps, and painted cloth, I felt chilled through and through, as if I'd got ketched in a rain storm, and had found kiver in a saw mill. Nothing but a rickety old barn, or a lot full of white pine stumps, could look half so dismal.

"Wal," sez I, if this is the theatre, I pity the poor critters that's got to get a living in it, any how."

"It's bad enuf," sez Mr. Williams, a twistifying up his face sort of comical, and yit looking as if he'd bust out a crying if you said two words more, "its bad enuf, but then we put the best side out."

"I should think you did," sez I, a looking round; but jest that minit I got a squint at a gal, a streaking it through the posts and boards, all kivered over with a cloak, but there warn't no cheating me in the critter. I knew in the dark who it was—nobody on arth but Miss Elssler could walk so teaterish. My heart riz in my mouth, and without stopping to say goodnight, I cut away from Mr. Williams and pulled foot after her like all possessed. She was jest a going out of a dark entryway that led out doors, when I ketched up with her.

"How do you du, Miss Elssler?" sez I, all in a twitter; "shall I have the pleasure to see you hum?"

With that I crooked my right elbow and looked right straight down into the darndest consarned, harnsomest pair of eyes, as arnest as could be, for I was awfully afeard of gitting the mitten; but she looked up and see who it was a standing there, with the blood a biling up into his face, and a trembling all over, he was so arnest; and then she up and give me one of them tantalizing smiles of her'n, and sez she, as nat'ral as life, sez she—

"Oh, Mr. Slick, I am so pleased to see you again," and with that she laid them purty white fingers of her'n on my coat sleeve jest as if I had been her twin brother. Gracious goodness! how the blood did tingle and cut about up my arm, and all around the vicinity of my life engine, the minit that etarnal purty leetle hand touched my arm; but when I helped her down them dark steps, and had to put my arm kinder round her waist to keep her from slipping up, I never did feel so all overish in my hull life. It seemed as if I could a danced on one toe with her to all eternity, and never felt a hungry nor a dry. There was a coach stood close to the steps right by the back door of the theatre, and a feller stood by it a holding the door open. Miss Elssler kinder staggered a trifle as I went to help her in, so I lent her the leetlest mite of a genteel boost and got in arter her, jest as if I was tu hum. The inside of the carriage was chuck full of posies, and there I sot right in the middle on 'em, with that consarned harnsome critter a smiling and a talking her soft sodder right in my face till I got to the Astor House. Gaully offilus! wasn't I as happy as a bee on a red clover top! You don't know nothing about it, Par.

Your loving son,
JONATHAN SLICK.

LETTER XXIII.

Jonathan gets out of love with Fanny Elssler—Doctors the Ague in her Face and Leaves her—Receives an Invitation from his Pussy Cousin to a Thanksgiving Dinner, with a three cornered Note for Lord Morpeth—Jonathan's Opinion of the Travelling Lords and Democratic Hospitality.

Dear Par:
When I'd seen Miss Elssler hum arter the Theatre, I couldn't shut my eyes all night a thinking about her. She seems to get into a critter's head like a glass of Cousin Beebe's cider, and dances about there till everything else is kicked out. Her harnsome face seemed to be a bending over mine and smiling into my eyes through the dark all night, and if it was to save my life, I couldn't get a wink of sleep. Sometimes it seemed as if she was a whirling round and round with one toe on the bed post, a spreading out her hands so tempting, and flying about jest at my feet. Then again it seemed to me as if she was a standing in a corner of the room and holding her finger up jest to tantalize me, larfing in her sweet, cunning way, and a cutting up all sorts of tantrims, jest to keep me awake all night. I got up arly in the morning, but it wasn't of the leastest mite of use my trying to do anything but think of that consarned critter; so arter trying to write a letter without making out anything for two hull hours, I slicked up and went down to Miss Elssler's room determined to give up to once, and not try any more, but jest stay with her till it was time to go to the sloop, and take a cold cut as we'd agreed on.

I felt in a tarnation twitter, for all she'd asked me to cum; but I knocked at the door and walked straight in as if I'd been tu hum. Miss Elssler was a half lying on that settee that I wrote to you about; her head was boosted up with pillows and cushions with tossels to the arms, and them consarned leetle feet of hern jest peaked out from under a great red shawl that she'd flung over 'em. She ris up sort of quick as I cum in, and kinder tried to smile, but oh! gracious, how her face looked! I cut right off short with a jerk in the bow I was a making, and stared at her with all the eyes I'd got in my head. She'd got the ager, and that harnsome face of hern was puckered and twistified up till it looked as if she'd been fed on crab-apples for a whole month.

Her cheeks were swelled a trifle and as red as a piney, and her eyes kinder sunk in till you couldn't but jest see 'em twinkle, and when she started herself to larf, her mouth tipped up at one corner and down at t'other, till it cut across her face slantindic'lar, and made her look all one side every time she squinched her face. I swow, but it made me feel wamblecropped to see her; I begun to think there wasn't much chance for a cold bite aboard the sloop that day, but think sez I, there's no harm in doctoring any how. So I thought over all the cures marm has for the ager, and arter calling a waiter, I told him to bring up about a peck of hops biling hot with vinegar.

When the chap cum back, I tied a hull swad of 'em in a pink silk long shawl that I found a lying on a chair, and crossed them over the critter's face, and tied the shawl in a double bow knot on the top of her head; but the hops were rather hot I reckon, and she squalled out like all natur till I took 'em off, and sent the waiter off for a ginger plaster and a bag of hot ashes. Arter she'd tried them a few minits, they seemed to mollify the ager quite considerable; but as the pain went off, her face begun to swell and puff up, like a baking of bread wet up with turnpike emptins, and I see that there warn't no chance left of her going to Captin Doolittle's cold bite, nor nowhere else for a long spell.

By-am-by that old maid, that I'd seen before, she cum in, and begun too look pitchforks and darning-needles at me, as if she thought my room was as good as my company, so I up and went off, jest stopping to make a leetle chunk of a bow at the door, to let the old maid see I hadn't forgot my manners if she had.

I cut for my room, feeling a leetle streaked to think how I'd been a follering round arter Miss Elssler. I'd been a hankering arter that critter for nothing on arth but her harnsome face and finefied manners, when a trifle of cold could transmogrify it so tarnally. It made me feel cheap, and I couldn't help it.

Marm al'rs said that harb tea was a cure all, but raly I never should a thought of taking it to get rid of a lovesick fit, and arter all I'm afeared that Miss Elssler's face will git cured up afore I git over the tantrum it's sot me into.

Wal, when I'd got to my room agin, there was a letter on the mantle shelf, sealed with a great whopping bunch of wax, and stomped down with a round "O," as big as a cent, with a rooster stuck right in the middle of it. I broke the consarn open, and found out it was an invite to Thanksgiving Dinner to Cousin Jason Slick's. Arter writing a hull page of soft sodder, the pussy coot let the cat out of the bag. There's an English lord a putting up here, and he wanted me to ask him up to his house to dinner, and said Lord Morpeth would sartinly come if I asked him, because we were both kinder of literary together.

Now, if there's anything on arth that I despise, it's a genuine true born Yankee a hankering arter the big-bug lords that come over here, on'y jest because they've got a long tail to their names. For my part, I haint no idee of demeaning myself in that way anyhow. If a lord behaves himself like folks, he's as good as a Yankee any day; and he ought to be treated jest as well, and I don't think the most ginuine republican amongst us ought to be ashamed to ask him to take pot luck or a glass of drink, if he likes it.

As long as they treat us according to gunter, when we go to see them on t'other side of the water, it is no more than the fair thing if we take turn about, and do the genteel by them a trifle. We ought to feel streaked with all our lands and barns full of grain, if we can't give a foreign chap something to eat and drink without grudging on it, and then agin, without being tickled to death because they don't feel too much pomposity to eat it.

Jason had sent a leetle finefied letter inside of mine, doubled over and twisted up at the corners like an old fashioned cocked hat, and smelling as sweet as a garden pink root in full blow. It was directed in leetle finefied writing to His Highness the Right Honorable Lord Morpeth—Howard Member of Parliament, &c.,

&c. Think sez I, this English chap needn't be consarned that his kite wont sail high among the Yankees for want of a long tail to it, if they all tuck the etceteras onto his name so strong as cousin Jase does.

But I hadn't no idee of being waiter to my pussy cousin, any how. If Jase has a mind to send his invite to a lord, done up like a cocked hat, let him be his own nigger, or else send it by the post-office—I wasn't a going to do it for him nor touch it. No lord that is any great shakes will think the better of an honest Republican for acting as if he was scared to ask him to eat dinner, or tickled to death if he didn't feel tu much stuck up to come with plain Yankee asking.

I made up my mind, that if Lord Morpeth took a notion to eat Thanksgiving with Jase, he'd be jest as likely to get his paper cocked hat from the Post Office, as anywhere. So, as I was a going through the Park, I took the consarn between my thumb and finger, for fear of siling it, and tucked it through a slit in the post office, made a purpose for city letters; and off I went, a tickling myself eenamost to death, with thinking how the post office clarks would giggle and stare, and snuff up their noses to see such a pinted critter directed to a Lord, and a smelling so sweet, with a long tail of names curled up in all the corners,—and Lord Morpeth, tu, wouldn't he set our Jase down for a shaller pated coot? I've a kind of a sneaking notion that it's as like as not he would, but that's none of my bisness. In this country, a feller aint to blame for his relations, that's one comfort.

Your loving son,
JONATHAN SLICK.

LETTER XXIV.

Description of Cousin Jason's Equipage—Figure cut by Mrs. Jason Slick and her Daughter—Manners of a Noble Lord—The Dinner.—Jason boasts of his Birth, Heraldry, and Coat of Arms—Jonathan creates great Consternation by proclaiming the Head of the Family as a Shoemaker—Makes a Speech.

Dear Par:

Wal, next day was Thanksgiving, and down come another letter to say that Lord Morpeth was a coming, and that Jase was a going to send down his span fired new carriage to the Astor House, arter Lord Morpeth and I, afore dinner time; and he gin me to understand, that if I could keep the carriage a spell afore the Astor House steps, where folks could get a chance to see the new fixings and horses, there wouldn't be no harm done to nobody,—the darned mean pussy coot! When a feller tries to make me do a mean thing I'm awful ugly, my Yankee grit is up in a jiffy, and I'm jest like a skeery horse that al'rs backs up hill when you want to lead him down.

Afore this I'd been on a cyphering voyage through my purse to see if I couldn't afford to go down to Lynde & Jennings' and bye a new narrow collar'd coat and some other dandy consarns, seeing I was a going to dine with a Lord; but when this letter cum I determined to go in the old fix up, jest to let this Lord and my pussy cousin see a ginuine Yankee that wasn't ashamed of hisself in a homespun coat and trousers.

Howsomever I gin myself a purty good sudsing, and shaved as close as a Wall street broker; besides I did some extra fixing to my collar and hair, and paired off my finger-nails harnsomely, and scrubbed the yaller from off my teeth with the corner of a brown towel that I found in my saddle-bags; for there aint no reason that I know on, why a true born American shouldn't wash up and keep a clean face and a stiff upper lip, if he does weed his own onions and wear a homespun coat. A chap may live in a land of Liberty and let these lords know it tu, without swellin like a toad to outshine the British, or going slouching about as if we put a tax on soap and water, jest as they do on winder glass.

For my part, I didn't mean to let Lord Morpeth think that we give so much soft soap here in York without keeping enough to wash our own faces on thanksgiving day.

When I was fixed up about tu the right noch, down stairs I went, with the eend of my checkered silk neck-hankercher a tucked under my streaked vest, my hair slicked down on both sides, my face a shining like a new pin, and my boots blacked up till they glistened like a gal's eye.

I tucked up my yaller silk hankercher clear into my coat pocket, for I didn't feel like showing all out to once, and I put my new mittens on sort a careless, and streaked the blue and red fringe up as I went down the Astor House steps through a double row of dandies that had swarmed out of the stun hall above to see my pussey cousin's carriage and horses that stood a glistening jest afore the house.

There the carriage stood right in Broadway, about the dashingest consarn that ever I sot eyes on. The wheels were a good ways apart and black as a minister's coat, and a great harnsome box swung over 'em, shut up tight, and a glistening in the sun till it a'most blinded a feller's eye-sight to look on it. There was a door on each side as big as them in the pulpit of our meeting house, with a whopping square of glass in the top and bottom all figgered off with gold, and then crouchonts, and lions, and roosters all pictered out in gold tu, and looking as nat'ral as life, for all they were so yaller and jammed down in a heap till it seemed as if the lions would roar right out, and the rooster give a coo-co-doo-dle-do if any body went tu tuch them.

Behind the hull consarn, was a great wide flat stair, with two pussy fellers a standing on it,—each on 'em holding to a yaller tossel fixed tight to the coach and dressed out like folks in the theatre, with great high boots, and topped off with a wide rim of white, wide white cuffs to their coats, and white ribbons and beaus twisted round their hats.

Right in front was a seat with a great square cushion on it, and all hung off with the finest kind of boughten cloth and piles

15

of heavy yaller fringe, with the golden lions, and crouchants, and roosters pictered out and a glistening among the folds, till it a'most outshined the sun—and that was purty bright for November.

A tall feller dressed out like the chaps behind, sot on this heap of gimcracks with a great long whip stuck up by his elbow, and a holding in two tremendous harnsome black horses that stood hitched to the carriage, under a hull net of black shiney leather, golden buckles, and deers' heads cut out in chunks of gold, and sot on to the blinder, and saddle-trees, and every place an inch square that they could be poked in.

If there is a critter on arth that I take tu, it's a good horse, and I couldn't help but be proud of them smashing arnimals as they shook their heads up so sarsy, as if the sun hadn't no business in their great eyes that had fire enough in 'em without its help, and pawed on the ground with their fore-feet—the mettlesome varmints!—like a couple of harnsome women, chuck full of music and crazy to dance it off.

When the chaps saw me a coming down the Astor House steps, one of 'em jumped down and opened the door and let out a hull grist of steps down to the ground, all kivered over with the brightest kind of carpet, till it looked as if somebody had been a flinging hull baskets full of posies all over 'em for me to stomp down with my shiney boots, if I wanted tu.

Jest as I was a thinking whether it was best for Lord Morpeth to come before I got in myself—for I didn't want to du nothing that wasn't according to gunter, if he was a lord—a feller come down the Astor House steps dressed off to the nines, with a harnsome cloak slung across his shoulder, and one side of his hat tipped up jest enough to show a hull swad of curly hair a frizzling round his ears.

He had a leetle dab of hair a curling jest under his nose, and another leetle peaked consarn up in a pint from his chin.

When this chap come down the steps, the other varmint that stood behind the carriage in his white topped stompers give a dive to the arth, and stood a one side the door which t'other one held open. Think sez I, this is Lord Morpeth as sure as a gun; so I haul'd back my foot from the fust step, for I was jest a going to get in, and I stepped back as the chap come up, and arter making him a half bow--for I never give off the extra touches in a bow only to the harnsome gals—sez I,

"Walk in, Lord Morpeth, and I'll foller arter."

The feller looked at me sort of supercillious, and I could see the dab of hair on his lip curl the leastest mite scornful as if he smelt something that didn't agree with him. He didn't make a bow, but stepped back as if he didn't jest know what to du.

I give my mitten a short flourish towards my hat, and arter stepping back agin, sez I—

"Arter you is manners for me. Make yourself to hum, Lord Morpeth."

The chap looked at me agin, and then he went close to the feller that held the door, and said that Lord Morpeth couldn't go jest yit, but that we'd better go on and he'd come by-am-by; and with that he went up the steps agin without as much as saying, git out, to me.

Gawrie, but wasn't I wrothy to see that crowd of York dandies see me slighted so by a lord. There they stood a puckering up their faces like monkeys in a show, and there I stood feeling as mean as the meanest among 'em; but arter a minit my dander ris right up.

"Darn the critter," sez I, "a'most out loud, and a pulling my mitten up so wrothy that a whole swad of frieze gin away in my hand. Does the stuck up varmint feel above riding with an honest Yankee, because he haint got no title? I'll be licked if a lord ever gets a speck of good manners from me agin, consarn the hull biling on 'em."

With that I gin an allfired jump, and settled down in the carriage, as savage as a young arthquake, and sot down on one of the harnsome cushions kivered over with silks and figgered off with blue and white roses, that kivered the two seats and sort of sprangled up over the sides and ruff of the carriage. A narrow finefied border squirmed all around the cushions, around the doors, and into all the corners, and the hull consarn made a chap feel as if he was shut up in a band-box, lined with silk and with a chunk of the sky, white clouds and all, shut over him for a lid.

I was so allfired wrothy, that, without thinking on it, I histed my boots agin one of the cushions, jest as it's nat'ral tu, when a feller's so mad he can't help it, and left a purty considerable smooch of blacking amongst the blue and white posies, that sot them off ruther more than cousin Jase would like, I calculate.

Them carriages do cut dirt so soft and easy like a streak of greased lightning, that there is no knowing how fast a feller gets along. It didn't seem more than a half a jiffy when we drew up co-wallop right afore Jase's house. Down got the two varmints in white topped stompers, open went the door, and out I jumped.

I didn't have to ring at the silver knob, but the door swung open of itself, or seemed tu, and in I poked, as independent as a clam in high water, but not afore I'd ketched a squint at that shaller little Jemima, a peaking out from behind the winder curtains to see who was coming with me.

A chap took my hat and things in the entry way, and asked me what my name was, sort of low, as if it was something I ought to be ashamed of; and the minnit I told him, he went to the door of the keeping-room and bawled out,

"Mr. Jonathan Slick."

I went in and there sot our Jase, in a great armed chair, as red and pussy as a turkey-gobbler, jest afore Christmas. He got up and come for'ard, but looked nation wamblecropped when he see that there wasn't nobody with me. That wife of his'n cum up with her fat hands stuck out, and asked how I was, and why Lord Morpeth didn't cum, and Jemima, she stood a giggling worse than ever, and a tossing them yaller curls of her'n about on her shoulders and cousined me off to kill.

I told Jase how Lord Morpeth had sarved me, but he didn't seem to mind that, arter he found out that he was a coming by-am-by, so we sot down. I took a sort of a survey of the premises. Now if there is anything that makes me mad, it's to see a chap a selling off his harnsome things when they git a little siled or out of fashion. I couldn't no more sell a cheer or a table that any of my friends had eat off from, or sot on, than I would strike my granny. Jest think how you'd feel to see grand par Slick's arm'd chair sold at Vandue, or the chest o' drawers that marm kept her "leetle things" in when I was a baby bought in by the neighbors. It makes me feel wamblecropped only jest to think of it, and yet there wasn't a single thing in the two great rooms that I went into at Cousin Jase's, that had a place where it was the last time I was there. Everything looked spick-span new, and I haint no doubt that the hull house had been transmogrified and titivated up jest cause a Lord was coming to eat dinner there. The carpets were a'most all red, with a vine of pink and yaller a running crinkle-crankle all over 'em as if somebody had been a scattering a hat full of butter-cups and meadow pinks all over it, the whole consarn giving under your feet like a flat meadow lot thick with a fall arter growth.

Great smashing looking-glasses were set into the wall from top to bottom between the winders, and a hull dry-goods store of red silk curtains sot off with yaller bordering, fell in great heavy winrows from over a couple of long spikes, feathered off at the eend, and a glistening with gold, kivered both ends of the room all but the looking-glasses and winders. A whopping great picter of Jase a setting in his easy chair, and reading a book, kivered with velvet and gold, was hung over one mantle-tree shelf, and over t'other sot his wife, all feathers and flowers, and silks and satins, with her red pussy face a shining among the whole, and all pen'd up in a gold frame, as wide as a slab, and a glist'ning like all natur.

Cousin Jase had gone into the fine arts to kill, arter he got hopes of a Lord. There was Jemima's shaller head cut out in marble, a kind of half swarry, with stun curls a hanging like icicles down her back, and a stun post to stand on, a rolling up its eyes to a corner of the room; and there were two funny sort of women, with wings that looked as if they'd been made of gold at fust, and then touched off with a thin coat of blacking, that made a sort of amalgamation critters, black and gold, stood each side of the looking-glasses, a holding back the silk curtains that would have fell ca-swash over the whole eend of the room if it hadn't been for them; then out on the carpet was tables made out of black shiny stuff, and the whole round tops kivered over with picters that seemed as if they were polished down clear into the black wood, and all around was benches and foot-stools of the same black wood, sprigged off with gold, and cushioned off with red silk, besides the settees that had high backs and high arms at one eend, but curlecued down at the back, tapered off to a square bench on t'other, and sot out like the stools with thick red cushions.

Right over the pictered tables was a sort of a golden tree, chained to the ruff, and kivered over and over with chunks of glass, that shone like tears in a gal's eye, when she gits the grit up.

Besides all these, was tu great round silk cushions, as thick as mother's cheese tub, a sitting right squat on the carpet, and tassled off to kill, with a mess of other things that I hadn't a chance to look at afore the door was pushed open by the help that stood in the hall; and there stood a tall man, with a blue coat on, and gilt buttons, each on 'em pictered off like our ten cent pieces, ou'y instead of the Eagle, there was a Lion, and some kind of a one-horned animal, a pawing up hill arter a sort of a cap with pints to it.

Afore I saw these pictered buttons, I kinder thought the chap must be Lord Morpeth himself, for he come in sort of softly, and yit independent, like a feller that felt himself to hum any where, but yit didn't want to walk over other folks, as them big bug foreigners al'rs du; but on a second peak I see that it wasn't the chap that I had seen at the Astor House, and beside that he was shaved clean, and hadn't a speck of hair, only on his head and eye-brows, and that was a little mite gray; so, think sez I to myself, that other chap was the Lord, and this is his waiter, cum to tell Jase that the big bug has gin up cumin. For no Lord that can git dye stuff or buy a wig, would ever come a visiting with gray hairs in his head. You wouldn't ketch one of our York tippies at that, let alone a ginuine Lord.

I never saw Jase so wrothy as he was when he ketched sight of the feller, for he got a peak at the buttons the fust thing, and sez he,—

"By gracious! if his lordship haint sent word to say he can't come!"

With that he went to the door, and sez he to the man, sez he,—

"Wal, Sir, did you bring a note for me, or what?"

And then he strutted right in the door-way, as pussy and pompous as a prize pig jest afore killing time, and there stood the tall chap, jest afore him, a looking right into his red face, with a pair of eyes as black and keen as a weazle's, yit sort of easy and good natured, as if he couldn't think what the matter was. He took off his hat sort of easy, and kinder bent his head a leetle, and sez he,—

"Is it Mr. Slick?"

He spoke so soft and humble that it seemed to mollify Jase; he stepped for'ard and waved his hand about as big as cuffy, and sez he, as condescending as could be, sez he,—

"Put on your hat, my good fellow, I've been a poor man myself. What word did his lordship send? don't be afeard to speak!"

The chap looked at Jase, and I could see his mouth pucker up the leastest mite in the world, and his eyes begun to twinkle as if he'd choked back a smile from his lips that was detarmined to break through somewhere. He bowed his head a little, and then he handed over a piece of square pasteboard jest like that Miss Elssler gave to me.

Didn't my pussy cousin look as if he'd fell through a thin place in the ice! He wilted right down, and looked as sneaking as a a turkey gobbler ketch'd out in a rainy storm; but when he see that Lord Morpeth didn't seem to know that he'd mistook him for a waiter, he walked into the room a spreading his hands and a sending out a storm of excuses, and welcomes, and friendships, like a junk bottle of cider letting off steam.

Lord Morpeth, he walked along into the room jest as if he'd been to hum, and then Jase he spread himself agin, and made him acquainted with his wife.

Lord Morpeth made a little slow bow, and Mrs. Jase Slick she gin her turban a toss, spread out the skirts of her velvet frock that was jest the color of a wild cherry, and then, after sticking out her fat foot, she began to fold up her jints, till she threatened to settle down on the carpet all in a heap, before she'd a let out all her kinks agin. Jemima she come up and begun to flourish out her foot, and show her curls, and her teeth, and twitter about, while Lord Morpeth was a bowing to her. I swow, it made me grit my teeth to see what tarnal coots the whole consarn were a making of themselves! Then cum my turn. I stood a leaning agin the mantle-shelf, detarmined to show this Lord that all the Slicks on arth warn't darned etarnal chuckleheads if some of them was. I'd a seen him in Guinea and further yet, afore he'd a got one speck of a bow more than he give me.

Well, Lord Morpeth, he bowed his head rather sparing of his neck, and I stood right straight up, and gin him as good as he sent, and no more on it, by hokey; yet there was something about this critter that took my notion amazingly; he didn't seem stuck up a bit, nor yet as if he wanted to poke fun at us, but sot down on one of the curlecued settees, and begun to talk about the weather, and things in general, jest like our folks. Miss Slick, she sot down by him, and purty soon let him into the state of things here in York. She went into a fit of the dreadful suz, to think Lord Morpeth didn't ride up in the carriage—it was a dreadful thing to walk in the streets among the common people—her daughter Jemima had once brushed the skirt of her tunic agin a mechanic, as she went down Broadway, and they felt it their bounden duty to keep her from walking over since,—Jemima was so delicate, so very literary, so—here Jemima, who sot on a bench close by the settee, turned up them eyes of her'n and gin a sigh that made the pucker come to Lord Morpeth's mouth agin, and when Miss Slick got up and handed over some varses that she said Jemima had writ the minit she heard that Lord Morpeth had come to this country, the tickle burst into his eyes, and he went to the winder with the paper in his hand, jest as if he wanted to read it over agin. Miss Slick she stretched up and looked at Jase, and Jemima, and me, and nodded her head, as much as to say—

"That's clenched the business. If Lord Morpeth don't take a shine to my darter arter reading that, I want to know, that's all!"

Jase he twirled his great gold watch key, and peaked at Lord Morpeth from under his eye-brows, and Jemima, she struck her head a one side and tried to look as if she couldn't help it, till Lord Morpeth he come back agin from the winder, a looking as meek as a gray cat with a dab of cream on her whiskers, jest as if he hadn't been tickling himself to death behind the curtains there; and I, consarn me, if I didn't feel as mean as a frozen potater, to think my name was Slick.

Miss Slick she spread herself out on the settee agin beside Lord Morpeth, and give him another dose of soft sodder, till I raly felt sorry for the poor critter. She held up her two chunked hands, and rolled up her eyes like all natur, when he told her which side f Broadway he come up; but Lord Morpeth said the west side was the most crowded, and so he took t'other.

"On'y jest to think, Jemima," sez Miss Slick, "Lord Morpeth come up on the east side of Broadway, dear me!"

Jemima she lifted up her head, and looked a whole biling of lasses candy at Lord Morpeth, and said she shouldn't wonder if it would be all the fashion to walk that side after that.

Lord Morpeth bowed agin, and looked as meek as new milk, and kinder acted as if he'd jest as lives talk about something else, but my pussy cousin stuck to him like a dog to a briar.

"Now my Lord," sez she, a laying her hand on to his'n, rings and all, "now, arter reading my darter's poetry, jest give me your opinion; we shouldn't think of ever letting her print anything, on'y we've heard that it's getting to be the fashion for English Lords and ladies to be sort of literary, and Jemima is so full of poetry and writes so sweet and soft—don't you think so, my Lord?"

"Very soft," says Lord Morpeth, as sober as a deacon, but yet giving a sort of a sly squint at Jemima, where she sot a puckering up her mouth and half shutting her eyes, and a shaking for'ard her yaller curls, till they eenamost touched her lap, and a trying to look like a love-sick robin on an apple-tree limb.

"Oh, you can't form no idee, you can't, indeed," sez Miss Slick, "without you hear Jemima read them herself, but she's so modest, so sensitive—but mebby she'll be persuaded by your lordship."

Lord Morpeth give another squint at the stuck up little varmint, and sed, "he was afeared to urge the young lady agin her feelings."

"Oh, but she'll do it to oblige you, I'm sartin she will," sez Miss Slick agin; "and here's our literary cousin, he will persuade her, I am sure;" and with that she cum across the room and put her hand on my coat sleeve, and sez she, "Now do, cousin."

"Oh, you go to grass," sez I; "If Jemima there is a mind to

make a coot of herself, she can do it without my boosting her along." Lord Morpeth kinder give a start, and looked at me like all natur, but yet he didn't look mad.

"Why, Cousin Slick!" sez my pussey she cousin, a dropping her hand as if it had gripped a hot potatoe.

"Oh dear!" sez Jemima.

Jase he let his watch-key drop, and turned as red as a tomato "What on arth do you mean by that, Mr. Jonathan Slick?" sez he.

"Wal, I reckon I mean just what I say," sez I, a dropping my hands into my trousers pockets; and a crossing one boot over t'other, as I leaned sort of slantindicular, with my shoulder agin the mantle-tree. "If there's anything on arth that makes a man sick of all the feminine gender, it's the etarnal hankering which some on 'em get to show off and trot themselves out afore the men folks, jest to show that their stockings have been in a dye-tub, and that what they are lacking in brains, is made up by impudence. I wouldn't marry a gal that could get up afore a stranger, before a hull room full on 'em, and shake her curls about, roll up her eyes like a pious hen, and squinch her face over a lot of poetry, whether it's her's or anybody else's. I swow, I wouldn't marry her if her heart was a solid lump of gold, and every hair of her head strung with diamonds. That's my opinion, and Cousin Jemima is welcome to it such as it is."

I wish you could a seen Jase and his wimmen folks when I burst out with that speech. Didn't they turn red and white in streaks? I ruther guess so! And Lord Morpeth! I never seed a feller's face brighten up as his did. Jase put his arm through mine, and asked me to slip into the hall a minit.

"Look a here, cousin, this is ruther too bad," sez Jase, een-amost crying; "you ought to make apology to his lordship for speaking so afore him—what'll he think of American manners?"

"What'll he think," sez I, "darn me if I care what he thinks; if he's a ginuine nobleman—one that's got good English common sense—he wont think the better of us for trying to make believe we're a notch above what we raly be, and he'll like my human natur better than your soft sodder by a jug full. If he expects the hull nation of America to pucker and twist itself out of all nat'ral shape jest to gibe with his notions, he *ought* to be disappointed and that's the long and the short of it; and if he believes that we want to see our wimmen folks to be spitting out poetry and varses afore strangers, or that the ginuine wimmen of America want to du sich things, he'd better stay to hum and read Mrs. Trollope's books. Now, jest hold your gab, Jase," sez I, as he was a going to speak again, "I'm in the right on't—if we want to give these English Lords a true idea of us, act out human natur, and give me a warm, honest welcome, but less soft soap."

As I'd spoke out, jest so, the bell rung, and a hull grist of big bugs got out of some carriages at the door and come in. There was three or four harnsome wimmen and gals dressed off in silks and satins, with the dresses all fringed off round the bottom and a hugging tight up to them white necks as close as the skin to an eel, and a showing off the wide shoulders and leetle tapering waists about the best of any dresses I ever sot eyes on. The men folks had on span white gloves, and looked as if they'd jest come out of a band-box. While Jase was a blustering about from one to t'other, I jest cut stick for the other room, detarmined not to have any more jaw with the critter if I could help it. Miss Slick and Jemima, looked sour enough to turn new milk; but Lord Morpeth he cum right up to me and begun to talk as if I'd been his twin brother. He asked me about every thing on arth, and more too; all aboūt the way we raise onions and garden sarce, how much hay our Weathersfield meadows give to an acre, and all about our district schools, meeting houses, and the old blue laws of Connecticut. When I told him that a man was fined five dollars for bussing his wife on the sabberday arter he'd been away to sea four years, Lord Morpeth he larfed right out as nat'ral as could be. Then I took turn about and asked him a few pozers about Old England, and he answered right up like a man that understood things, for all he was a Lord. I raly took a shine to the critter, though I'd made up my mind agin it, tooth and nail, and while he was a talking I took a good squint at his head and face.

He aint so over harnsome, not quite so good looking as a sartin chap I could tell you on if I wasn't so mealy-mouthed, but then he's got an allfired big head, high up over the ears, and one that looks chuck full of brains as an egg is full of meat. His eyes aint great black starers like some folk's, but as bright as diamonds, and as sharp as a hull paper of cambrick needles, and they know how to look right straight through a feller without flinching the first glance.

Purty soon, the gals and them chaps I'd seen in the hall cum a pouring in, and then there was no more talk with Lord Morpeth; he had to be led around like a race-horse by Miss Slick and Jemima, and I cum in for my share of the fun, for arter he and I got so thick together, they begun to think what I'd said was according to gunter, and sot it all down for eccentricity of genius instead of ginuine common sense; howsomever, I did not care so long as all was ship-shape agin with 'em, for I hate to get a woman a pouting with me, for if I'm ever so right it makes me feel kinder ugly.

THE DINNER SCENE.

We hadn't but just got settled down when the great wide looking-glass that I've told you of, seemed to slide back of the curtains to the lower eend of the room, and by gauly! there was another room further on, with a table sot in it all kivered over with silver plates, and soup dishes, and Chiny ware, with one of them trees of gold and glass all lighted up, and swung to the wall, a glittering, and flashing, and pouring down the shine over the heap of silver things, till it made a feller ketch his breath on'y jest to peak in.

Lord Morpeth he gin his arm to my pussy she cousin—Jase gin his to a harnsome gal that stood close to him, and I crooked my elbow up to Jemima, for I kinder wanted to make up for what I'd sed about her reading—poor critter! she aint to blame if she is a little shaller. The rest on 'em followed on two and two, and arter a little we all sot down round the table with six great strapping fellers, with blue and white regimentals on, and gloves on all their twelve hands, a standing up behind our chairs. I can't give you no idea of what we had to eat, for they called every thing by some darn'd jaw-breaker of a name, and kept a carrying things on and off and giving a feller clean plates all of solid silver, till it a'most made me dizzy with seeing them a flashing about so in the critters' hands. They had all sorts of mince meat with hard names tucked to it, and fish kivered with gravy, and butter, and every thing else, and sich a darn'd heap of things that I can't begin to tell you all. I tried to take a bite of everything, but it wasn't of no use—I was purty well filled up afore the puddings, and pies, and custards cum on, and arter they were carried off I thought we'd all made a purty good Thanksgiving dinner, considering it wasn't to hum, and I can't tell when I've felt so big and pussy; but jest as I was thinking we'd got about through, the fellers went to work and swept the hull table clean as could be, and by-am-by on they cum agin with silver baskets full of grapes, and oranges, and prunes, with a grist of fust rate apples, and hull bunches of raisins that made a feller feel wrothy because he'd eat enough, they looked so tempting a hanging over the sides of them silver baskets, and a looking so meller in the light that cum a shining down from the consarn overhead.

When the wimmen folks had jest eat a few grapes, and mebby a chunk of orange or so, Miss Slick she got up and off they went into t'other room, but yet a looking back sort of longing, jest as Eve did when the angels made her quit the garden of Eden, poor critter!

The minit the wimmen folks had made themselves scarce the servants begun to cut about like all possessed, and a hull regiment of decanters and cider bottles with sheet-lead caps to 'em. marched onto the table, and arter them cum another regiment of glasses, some of 'em round and bulky with short stems and kinder dark green, some white as ice, and then agin some that was short and slender, cut on in squares, and red as a gal's lip, besides the long necked cider glasses that stood poking up among the rest, like a Down East gineral, and his officers ready to lead on the red and green militia agin the hull squad of bottles and decanters, till one side gin up beat. The help gin the first shot, for each on 'em took a bottle, and pop, pop, pop, went the corks—then the red, and green, and white glasses marched up, and cum off chuck full and a brimming over with plunder. As for me, I sent up a long necked feller and took a swig at the cider, and Lord Morpeth he went dead into the green glasses, but they put me in mind of an old maid's goggles, and I couldn't take a notion to 'em till arter I'd drunk two hull glasses of the cider, and then I didn't seem to care what I drank out on. By-am-by some one called out and wanted a toast. I never heard of topping off a Thanksgiving dinner with toast afore, but it made me think of hum, and so I thought I'd have one tu.

"Look a here," sez I to the chap that stood back of my chair, "you may make me a toast tu, but none of your dry stuff now, but make it as marm used to, you remember Jase," sez I, "half a pint of hot milk with a chunk of butter about as big as a piece of chalk melted in, and then the hull soaked up with slices of toasted bread—hum made is best—one slice laid on top of t'other. Now you git out, and make some right off," sez I to the chap, sez I.

"Look a here, Jonce, what are you about?" sez Jase, a poking his elbow sort of sly into my ribs. "It aint that we mean, we're a going to drink a toast."

"Wal," sez I, "I haint no arthly objection, but if the feller makes it according to rule it'll be ruther tough to swaller without some chawing."

"I tell you," sez Jase agin, "we are a going to drink a toast to Lord Morpeth in wine."

"Wal," sez I agin, "I haint no objection, if Lord Morpeth likes toast and wine, it's his idee of what's good, and I can't help it; but as for me, hand over a bowl of ginuine toast and cider with the bread crumbled in, Weathersfield fashion, ruther hot, and sweetened well with lasses, that's my notion. Lord a massey, how marm does mix them critters up, it's enough to make a feller's nose tingle to think on it, aint it, cousin Jase."

It warn't of no use a speaking to him, there he stood a strutting over back with a glass in his hand and a singing out, "Our noble guest, Lord Morpeth," like all possessed. Every critter at the table, excepting Lord Morpeth and I, jumped up with glasses in our hands, and begun to drink like a patch of seed onions after a six weeks' dry spell; but Lord Morpeth and I sot still and looked as if we didn't know what possessed the critters; but the minit they sot down up he jumped like a house a fire, and the way he cracked jokes and said smart things, made the fire fly from every body's eyes round the table. I swanny, if he didn't take me a'most off the handle with his consarned sweet voice and harnsome manners. It raly was eenamost as good as a play, to hear him reel out the common sense and soft sodder about this land of liberty and old England. When he sot down, it was as much as I could du to keep from going right up and giving him a hug, if he was a lord. Arter this we mixed in the talk altogether, like lemon, and sugar, and brandy in a punch bowl, as sociable as so many chickens in a coop, till by-am-by, Jase he begun to swell up and talk to Lord Morpeth about the Slicks, and the crouchants, and lions, that belonged to the family coat of arms as he called it; he gin us all to understand that the Slick's warn't a family to be sneezed at by any of the English Lords, and gin out some purty broad hints about a barron-night, and a lord, that gin a start to the name ever so long back in England; then the consarned shote branched out into a sarmon about ancient birth, and pure blood, a running from one generation to another, without being siled by anything low since the Slick's cum to this country, jest arter the Pilgrims, and a hull lot of the darndest stuff that ever a transmogrified hand-cartman thought on. I'd topped off my cider with two or three glasses of hock, the feller called it, and it made me feel dreadful smart, and I felt jest like tackling Jase in his own camp.

"Look a here, cousin Jase," sez I, "what on arth do you want to make out that we Slick's are anything but jest what we be, for aint it a darned sight more to our credit, Yankees as we are, and Republicans as we ought to be, to own it at once, that we had to hoe our own row up, and found it a purty tough one?" Now you know well enough, for all your crouchongs, and lions, and roosters,—that you've picked up, lord-a-massey knows where —that you begun life, or any how begun to save up chink, fust by a horse cart on Peck Slip, and that wife of your'n went out a nussing other folk's children till arter you married her, and that aint no disgrace to her nor you neither, so long as you don't try to make out that you're something more than you raly be. It is too bad you're trying to make out that you're a English big bug, when you can prove yourself as good a nobleman as ever lived, by going back to our grand-par, the brave old shoemaker, that swung his lap-stone over his shoulder when the Revolution broke out, and jined the patriots when their struggle was dark as the grave. The old man never gave way once, but fought like a lion when fighting was to be done. He clung to his companions in good and bad luck, and though he fought, and marched, and suffered with the toughest of 'em, never once gin out or got discouraged, but arter a long day's march would unsling his lap-stone, take out his rusty tools, and hammer and stitch away half the night long, to make up shoes for his tired and sore footed feller soldiers, whenever he could find a scrap of sole leather or a piece of cow skin to make up!"

I was a going on, but Lord Morpeth he got up, and sez he, "Let us drink to the memory of Mr. Slick's ancestor, the 'brave Shoemaker.'"

Jase looked sort of ugly about what I'd said—but I couldn't help that, and when Lord Morpeth jined in, the hull biling on us got up, and another squad of wine glasses was put into action. When the rest had sot down, I felt as if I couldn't break off so, but I thought it wouldn't do no harm to give 'em a short specimen of Weathersfied chin music, seeing as there was a lord to hear me.

"Now," sez I, "it's of no use denying that we Yankees do think a good deal of noble birth and pure blood, and all of them ere things that the English have boosted up their throne with so many hundred years; for my part, I du feel a kind of love and reverence for a family of any kind, whose blood has run pure from one generation to another, through brave men and good women, till it beats full of warm ginerous human natur in the heart of a true nobleman, whether he has a title or not. It gives a man something to be proud of, something to guard and keep himself good and honorable for. A man must be mean as pusley, and meaner yet, who could do a small action while he knew that his blood had been kept, pure as spring water, by a hull line of good men, all a sleeping in their graves."

"But, arter all," sez I, "what is the nobility of Old England more than that which we Yankees have a right to?"

"Was William the Conqueror, that they brag so much about, any thing to be compared to our Washington? Was his conquest of Old England, half so great, or so tough a job as the tussle we had to get New England into our own native land? Now, the whole truth is, blood is like wine, the older it is, the stronger and clearer it grows. If it warn't for that, we Yankees, that had forefathers in the Revolutionary war, have as good a right to brag about our pure blood, as the greatest and oldest line of proud England." Here I stopped jest long enough to make a bow to Lord Morpeth, and on I went agin. "I say," sez I, a stretching out my arm, "there aint a true born American on arth, if he owns the truth, that haint English grit and pride enough about him to feel a kind of respect for an English nobleman, if he behaves himself like folks: but if he don't," sez I, "we've got a right to dispise him more than we do one another when we act mean; for he not only disgraces hisself, but all the forefathers that he ought to be proud on, and a man that can do that must be mean as git out and meaner tu, a darned sight. Now," sez I, a looking at Lord Morpeth, "we Yankees and the English are purty much alike, for all. If they've got their lords, and dukes, and princes, haint we no military captins, and generals, and deacons, and squires,—rather small potatoes compared to the English, but yet it shows a sort of native notion we've got arter sich things, and don't du no sort of harm one way nor t'other. Now," sez I, "in a few hundred years from this, we Americans, shall have a sort of republican nobility of our own. I aint sartin about the titles, but by-am-by, when the 'tea party,' and the battle of Bunker Hill lies clear back in our history, as William the Conquerer's does among the British, Cousin Jase there, wouldn't have to make up a story about his British ancestors; for the pure blood of this ere country will be that which goes right back to the Revolutionary war. All Yankee noblemen will have to sarch for their titles on the pension list of this ere very generation; and the old man that now draws his twenty dollars a month, will be the founder of a line, jest as noble as any that ever sprung up in the heart of old England! That's my gintine opinion. Now," sez I, "if we Slicks wanted to make out that we are any great shakes, it aint no very hard job to du it. It aint by no means sartin that we, any on us, ever had any forefathers afore the old Shoemaker, that we've jest been a telling on; but he was a hull team and horse to boot. When the ammunition gin out at Bunker Hill, he flung away his gun, and went to storming a hull regiment, tooth and nail, on his own hook, till in the eend he was shot down dead with a piece of the old lap stun in his hand, that he gripped like an Injun arter his teeth was sot, and his fingers stiff and stun cold. Old England, I must own, has got a grist of noble families and great men, that are an honor and eternal glory to it, but the blood that biled up in that old man's heart, was as red, as brave, yes, and as noble tu, as ever poured itself out on the sile of old England, in the time of William, or any other Conqueror; and if I ever set up for a big bug, and put picters on my carriage door, I kinder think that I shan't be much ashamed to have Jonathan Slick's coat of arms, a 'hand gripped hard on a lap-stun;' for consarn me, if we, any on us, ever get to be much, it will be through the old Shoemaker, and I aint ashamed to own it."

With that I took another swig at the hock, and was a going on agin, but all tu once my head began to whirl round like a top. The table began to spread itself into half a dozen, and it seemed as if the glass consarn over head had got a hull family of leetle ones around it, dancing jigs and pouring out the shine all over the room—and then the wine bottles, and the decanters, and the grapes, and apples, and raisins, seemed to get onsteady, and more on 'em kept a starting up. Then the waiters in regimentals grew taller and taller, and I'm consarned if Lord Morpeth hadn't half a dozen chaps a looking like so many twin brothers a dodging up and down all around him, awful onsteady though, for Lords. Then, arter all, the floor begun to rise and pitch up and down till I was obliged to give up, and so I sot down, and held onto my chair with both hands, and called out 'Whoa' like a house afire, for it seemed as if everything was a getting upsot; and between you and I and the post, Par, my ginuine opinion is, that all the chaps in the room had got about half seas over, except me. I was as steddy as a judge, and sot up parpendicular and independent, jest as a true born Republican ought tu, determined to set that English Lord and the rest on 'em a good example. It wasn't no wonder, though, that they got a leetle how come-you-so, for they all drank wine, but I only took that sparkling white cider and hock, for I was detarmined not to make a shote of myself. Yet it made me feel so bad to see how they went on, that I got a'most sick thinking about it.

Arter a while we all went back into the keeping-room, and there the wimmen folks sot on them red benches, all in pimlico order, drinking coffee out of some leetle finefied cups, but I'm afeared they didn't set up so straight as young ladies ought tu in company—their heads did seem to set rather unsartin on their shoulders every time I looked at 'em.

I drunk off a cup of coffee jest to oblige Jase, and then I begun to be kinder sociable with a young gal that sot by Jemima, while Jase took Lord Morpeth round to look at his marble head, and the two whopping picters of himself and wife.

Arter he had gone the rounds—as we Editors say of a prime article—Lord Morpeth made his bow and went out, I begun to feel kinder as if I'd like to take a snooze, and so I jest gin one smashing bow at the door for all, and arter getting my hat, I follered Lord Morpeth out. It was tarnal cold, and I begun to chirk up a leetle, when I see that Jase's carriage stood there. Lord Morpeth stepped back when he see me close to him, and moved his hand as much as to say—Git in; but I stepped back, and sez I, "I guess I've been taught better manners than to help myself fust,"—so with that he got in, and I arter.

We had a good deal of talk in the carriage; and when we both got out, Lord Morpeth shook hands with me as if I'd been his twin brother, and asked me to come and see him to his room, for he wanted to talk with me about picters and the fine arts, and things in general.

I gin his hand an allfired grip, and sez I, "Lord Morpeth, you can depend on this chap, for he'll tell you the truth and no soft sodder. I didn't take much of a notion to you at fust, for I aint a chap to run arter you because you're a lord, but I like you in *spite* of that, for you're a darned good hearted, smart critter, and lord or no lord, that's enough."

With that I shook hands agin, and went up stairs to bed.

Fanny Elssler didn't keep me awake that night I reckon. That hock is tarnal sleepy stuff, Par.

Your loving son,

JONATHAN SLICK.

LETTER XXV.

Jonathan rides to Mill—The Millerite Excitement—His Marm waits for the World to come to an End--Letter from New York—The old White Horse.—

To the Editors of the New York Express, a darned great Newspaper down in York.

DEAR GENTLEMEN SIRS:

I s'pose your letter came down from York like a streak of chalk, but I've got kinder out of the literary world since I cum back hum here, and I didn't hear a word about it till the 22d of April, jest as all Weathersfield had got their robes made and their caps sot for t'other world.

I'd been out to work all day in the onion patch, and toward night I thought it wouldn't do no harm to take a ride and git the kinks out of my back. So I jest went to the barn, and arter saddling the old horse, and measuring out some rye from the bin I went into the house for some bags, and concluded I'd go to mill, and take the way back by old White's, jest to see how Judy got along arter the last singing school.

Wal, I took a short cut through the orchard, and it made me feel kinder chirk to hear the robins a singing in the apple trees, and to see the young buds busting out all over my head, and the grass a sprouting under my feet, all on it a looking fresh as a gal's lip, and greener than a hull meetin-house full of Millerites. The peach trees in the back yard had jest begun to blow out; they warn't in full blow yet, but seemed to be kinder blushing all over at their own back'ardness; and that are old pear tree by the well, looked as if natur had shook a flour bag all over it, and yit, the old critter wasn't in full blow more than the rest on 'em. I wasn't dry, but the air smelt so tarnal sweet, and the water in the bucket, that was a leetle leaky, kept a falling drop, drop, drop, down the well, so kinder tempting, that I couldn't help ketching hold of the well-pole as I went by, and after tilting the bucket on the curb, I tipt it down and took a drink that raly did me good.

Wal, I went through the yard, and opened the back kitchen door to ask marm for the bags, and there she sot, close by the table, with her linsey woolsey apron on yit, jest as she'd washed the morning dishes. Her old gray hair was sort a rumpled up under her cap, and her steel spectacles had slid half way down her nose, she was bending so arnest over the big Bible, and reading the Prophecies of Daniel. Poor old marm, she looked dreadfully wamblecropped, as if she'd jest made the discovery of a new mare's egg in the Bible, and was waiting to see what sort of a critter it would hatch out.

"Marm," sez I, "if you'll give me the bags I'll go to the mill, the last grist must be purty nearly out by this time."

Marm sot still, looking at the Bible, and didn't seem to know as I was talking. She shook her head kinder awful, till the specs rattled on her nose, and then she groaned out something consarning fire and brimstone and the eend of all things; and she wiped her eyes with her apron, as if she felt dreadfully and couldn't help it.

"Marm," sez I, "what on arth ails you? you'll make me boohoo right out, if you look so melancholy and take on so."

Marm give a jump, and looked up sort a skeery, and sez she, "Oh, dreadful suz! Jonathan, is it only you?"

"Wal, I reckon so," sez I; "where's the bags?"

"Oh, Jonathan!" sez she, "are you ready for the eend?"

"Yes," sez I, "I guess I be; I ruther calculate these two strings are tough enough to tie up the eend of any bag on these ere premises."

Marm shook her head agin, and her face was as solemncholy as a gal that's got the mitten, and sez she, "Jonathan," sez she, "have you ever calculated on the beast with the horns?"

"Wal," sez I, a putting my hands in my pockets, "I can't say that I ever calculated much on them critters; if you and par want me to take 'em, I don't object to the old oxen, but I'd a leetle ruther have the black steers, if you'd jest as lives."

Marm shook her head worse than ever.

"Wal," sez I, "the old oxen will do, so chirk up and tell me where the bags are."

With that I went up the back stairs and found the things myself, and was a going out when she called arter me, and, sez she, "Jonathan, Jonathan, don't go on so—oh dear me, poor unregenerate critter, what do we want of another grist; have you forgot Miller and his promise?"

"Goodness gracious, no," sez I, a swinging my bags over the old horse, "how could I forget him—he's as clever a critter as ever lived, and he promised to give this grist a tarnation bolting: I told him how mad you was about t'other."

With that I got out the horse, hitched up the bags to make 'em lie even under me, give the bridle a shake and jogged on, wondering what on arth had sot marm up so. Jest as I was a turning down the lane toward Squire White's, I looked back and there she was a standing by the winder, with both hands up, and her cap knocked a one side like a crazy critter. Jest then par come across the corn lot, where he and old uncle White had been a ploughing, and I told him what a tantrum marm was in about the oxen and the grist.

Par shook his head, and sez he, "Consarn that Miller! she's been a brooding over the varmint's nonsense this ever so long, till she couln't sleep a nights, and now as it's jest coming on to the 23d of April, I s'pose she's broke out in a new spot."

"Darn the old scamp to darnation!" sez I, "it's jest got through my head what ails marm; the sneaking old varmint, he ought to be sung to death by screech owls, and knocked into the middle of next week by crippled grasshoppers!" With that I rode along, and par went hum, a looking jest as if he was ready to bust out a crying or a swearing, he didn't care which.

Wal, I was purty much womblecropped all the way to the mill, for somehow it made me feel sort of all-overish to think how near the time had come. I wasn't raly a skeered, but every thing looked pokerish all around. The mill was shet up, so I stum up my grist at the door, and got on to the old horse agin, detarmined to ride into town and see if I could find any thing to chirk me up. Jest as I got agin the post office, a chap hollered out that they'd got a letter for me from York, post paid and all. I turned up and laid the bridle on the old horse's neck, while I broke open the letter and read it. By gauley! didn't it make my heart jump right up into my mouth! But yet I felt a leetle uneasy about it. I wanted to come like all natur, but par hain't been willing to hear a word about York never since I took sich a shine to Miss Elssler, at the Astor House, and I was afeard that he'd say no to it. Then there was marm and Judy White both on 'em sot agin York, and hating Miss Elssler like rank pison; howsomever, I'm purty good grit when I sot out in arnest, and I rode along thinking the matter over till I got to old Mr. White's. Judy come out with her calico sun bonnet on, looking good enough to eat.

"Come, Judy," sez I, "jump on behind, and go hum with me; marm has got a fit of the dreadful suz, about that tarnal old Miller's bisness, and I want you to chirk her up a leetle, if you can."

Judy run up to the fence, so I made the old horse side up while she took off her check apron and spread it on behind. "Come up," sez I agin to the old critter; he got so close to the fence that he a'most smashed my leg agin the boards, and then shied agin; but Judy White is clear grit and no mistake—she give a jump and cum down square right on the crooper with one arm round me. The horse shied agin; Judy kinder slipped a leetle, and she hung on to me closer yit, and larfed till you couldn't tell which made the sweetest noise, she or the robins in old White's orchard. When I turned to ketch her, them pesky red lips of her'n were poked right agin my face; the harnsome varmint hung on to me with both arms like all natur, and every time she larfed out, that tempting breath of her'n come right over my mouth. Consarn the critter, I eenamost gin her a buss afore I knew it, and when the tee-hee bust out through them lips agin, I had to stop her mouth for fear she'd scare the horse.

"Now you git out, Jonathan!" sez she, a righting herself agin in no time; "aint you ashamed?"

That stubborn old varmint begun another double shuffle, right there in the street, and it was all I could du to hold him in, so I hadn't no time to mollify Judy with another buss. The critter wouldn't speak a word all the way hum, but there she sot, with one arm round me kinder loose, as if she'd a kept herself on some other way if she could, and a holding on her sun bonnet with t'other hand, till one couldn't git the leastest peep at her face. It was purty near dark when we got hum. The cows stood by the gate a lowing to be milked. The old hens, setting ones and all, come round us hilter-skilter, as if they were eenamost starved to death, and when we got into the kitchen, there stood the table jest as it was left arter breakfast, covered with dirty dishes; the strainer lay in a leetle wad in one of the sarsers, and the cat was a licking off the cream from a pan of milk that stood on a chair by the cheese-room door. Marm had gone off and shut herself up in the out room, with the Bible and a hull heap of the "Midnight Cry" newspapers.

I swanny, it eenamost made me boo-hoo right out to see how the things lay about the house. There never was a neater critter on arth than marm; but the hull premises raly looked more like a hog pen than any thing else. Judy and I went to work like good fellers—she forgot to be mad and tackled to, washing dishes and gitting supper, while I went out to milk. Marm wouldn't come to supper, and par eenamost choked with every mouthful he eat, and yit he looked more than half wrathy, as if he'd about as much trouble to keep his dander down as to hold up the tears that every once in a while kept a dropping from under his eyes down the side of his nose.

I guess you never sot eyes on so melancholy a set of critters as sot round our kitchen till midnight, for marm wouldn't go to bed, and we were afeard to leave her up alone in the out room with that pictur of the horned beast a staring her right in the eyes. When the old clock struck twelve, we heard the out door room shut to, and by-am-by marm come where we sot in the kitchen, dressed out in a great long consarn like an overgrown night-gown, with white shoes on her old feet, and that gray hair of her'n a hanging down her back; I swow, it made me ketch my breath to see her!

I haint got the heart to write all the shines marm cut up that night and all day the Sunday arter—it seems like pokin fun at one's own marm—as she went from one room to t'other, a ringing her hands and a crying her eyes out, because we wouldn't put on the robes she'd made for us, and go right up to heaven without making a fuss about it. I thought it wouldn't do no harm to try and rile her up to thinking of something besides the horned beast.

"Marm," sez I, all tu once, "I can't think of fixing up for t'other world yit, no how. I've jest got a letter from York, and if you're so detarmined on going to heaven, I ruther guess York's the place for me."

Marm jumped right up from her knees, and sez she, "Jonathan what *du* you mean?"

My heart riz; it was the only sign of gumption she had made for a hull day. Par looked up, and his chin kinder quivered, for he thought I was poking fun at the old woman, and Judy White, she sidled up to me, and sez she, all in a twitter, "Jonathan you aint in arnest now?"

"If I was, would you give up and let me go?" sez I.

Darn the harnsome critter, how mad she looked! "No I won't nor touch tu!" sez she, and afore I knew it, she bust right out a crying and went out of the room.

I didn't foller her, for marm had got down on her knees agin, and was a looking through her specs at a tarnal big thunder cloud that cum a rolling its blackness in knolls and furrows all over the sky, as if the world had raly cum to an eend, and all the niggers in creation was a going up fust.

Marm's face was as white as a taller candle, she was enough to scare anybody out of a week's growth, a kneeling there in that white gown, and her old hands a wrenching away at each other, like a crazy critter. Thinks I, I'll try and rile her up agin, but it wasn't of the leastest use, she wouldn't git up from the winder, but knelt there stock still—with her head flung back'ards, and the lightning a blazing over her steel specs, and the grizzley hair that hung away down her back. I swan to man, it made my hair stand on eend to look at her. By-am-by the thunder come a rolling and tumbling through the clouds, as if somebody was a blasting rocks up above; and the lightning come a streaming out agin in great blazes of fire, till it seemed as if all natur was turned wrong eend up, and all the brick kilns, coal mines, and founderies on arth were a playing away in the clouds, and a groaning and hissing through the rain that came down in pails-full, and a scaring folks to death.

"There!—look a there!" sez marm all tu once, a jumping up, and a stretching her arm through the winder. "I'm ready—I'm a coming!—Look a there, Deacon Zephaniah Slick—look there, my unregenerated son—look!"

Sure as a gun, there was something all dressed out in white a standing in the orchard, right agin the winder. Par and Judy White—for the critter ran back from the out room when she see that I wasn't a going to foller her—riz right up, and they wur about the streakedest looking critters that ever you sot eyes on. Jest then cum a loud noise—snort, snort, snort—from the orchard. "Oh gracious me!" sez marm—"the trumpet! the trumpet!"—and down she slumped on her knees agin.

"By gracious," think sez I, "I'll see what the matter is, any how;" so I gin a dive to the winder, and I hollered out, "shew—stuboy—git out!" but I kinder think I didn't yell over loud, the words stuck like wax-eends in my throat, and afore I could git 'em untangled, out cum the noise agin, louder, and twice as sarcy as it was before.

Think sez I, "Gracious knows, I'm afeard we're gone suckers, but I'll try agin anyhow; so sez I, a clapping my hands, "git away, you varmint, tramp—scoot—stuboy—y—y—"

I guess I yelled it out like a training gun that time. The white spirit seemed to feel it tu, for it flung its arms in the dark, and gin us another blast of his consarned old trumpet. Jest then the lightning came cutting down agin, and—oh, git out!—it was only the old white horse, a snorting and a kicking up his heels, in the orchard. I sot down, and haw-hawed right out, till it was all I could dr to catch my breath agin; then I bust out agin, till par a'd Judy jined chorus, and we made the old house ring as if there had been a quilting frolic in it: just then the clock struck twelve.

"Hurra!" I sung out, "marm, the 23d of April has cum and gone; come, marm, git up, the storm is blowing over, and the moon haint turned to blood yit. Hurra!"

I was jest a going to give poor old marm a buss, but par had got her in his arms a kissing her white face, and a boo-hooing, the old coot, like a spring colt. So as the buss was all made up, and too heavy for my mouth, I gin it to Judy. And she handed over a cuff for pay, the tanterlizing little snapping turtle.

Judy was all sot to rights agin, afore the old horse had got over his double shuffle.

"Oh dear, only to think that I should a cut up such a heap of factory cloth, and all for nothing!" sez marm arter a while.

We didn't say much to marm that night, but when par and she got up to go to bed, she took a slantindicular look at her robe, and then gin a sneaking squint at us. I couldn't hardly keep from busting right out agin, but choked in. And par says,—he never seems to mind it—"you can use it for a night-gown." When the old folks had gone, Judy and I went into the out room, and seeing as it was Sunday night, and nobody to interfere, we sot down, and hitching our chairs close together, didn't get sleepy till nigh about morning, but kept on talking, as chipper as two birds. I didn't say anything to Judy about coming to York; she is a sneezer when her dander is once up, and I kinder think it best to come off, and then write a letter to her arter it is all done. She's allfired jealous of the York gals, and dreads them that dance like Miss El-sler as a cat hates hot soap.

I guess I shall cum any how, but not jest yit. I must git in all the onions fust, and help about the grain some; arter that, you'll see me at the office as large as life, and twice as nat'ral. Par wont hear a word on it yit, I'm sartin, he got so allfired uneasy about me and Miss Elssler, that he sent for me right hum, when I was at the Express office; he thinks politics and dancing gals about the meanest things that a feller can hanker arter. But I'll set Captin Doolittle to arguing the matter with him, and as for marm, I guess she'll feel rather tu streaked to make much of a fuss about any thing jest now. I meant to cum the soft sodder over her a leetle any how; so this morning I went out to my onion bed back of the barn, where the sun comes all day from morning till night, and I pulled up a harnful of young onions that would make your mouth water; they had the tenderest green tops you ever see, and when I held 'em up and shook the dirt off, they looked more like a harnful of snow drops a blowing out at the wrong eend, than anything else. I gin these to marm, jest as she was a setting down to breakfast. She was eenamost tickled to death with them, and I reckon that is one long step towards York.

Mebby I shall be in York afore you git another letter from these parts and mebby not, there's no knowing when I can git away.

Yours tu command,
JONATHAN SLICK.

LETTER XXVI.

Jonathan arrives in New York—Travels on the Deacon's Mare—Has Trouble with the Colt—Embarks from Peck Slip, on Capt. Doolittle's Sloop, to meet the President—His Introduction—Jonathan's Idea of the Cold Collation—The Reception—Landing at Castle Garden—Review of the Troops—The Procession, &c.

DEAR PAR:

Here I am, safe and sound, but about the tiredest critter that you ever sot eyes on. Afore I got to Bridgeport, I begun to be kinder sorry that I didn't stand my chance and come on with Captin Doolittle in the sloop, for the fust thing that I see arter I got tu cousin Smith's in Bridgeport, was the old sloop a scooting down the Sound like a forr horse team, with all sails sot, and loaded down to the water with garden sarce. It seemed tu me that I could a'most see Captin Doolittle hisself, a standing on the deck and a poking fun at me for coming down on the old mare. The poor colt tu was eenamost tuckered out, and I begun tu feel sort o' wamblecropped for fear something would happen tu one of the poor critters afore I got tu York; but my keeping didn't cost nothing, and I got cousin Smith to put a good feed in one eend of my saddle-bags, and gin the colt a warm drink of milk afore we started in the morning, so we all three on us jogged on towards Stamford, in purty good condition, considerin' Our cousin at Stamford warn't tu hum, so I had to put the old mare and colt up to a tavern, and arter letting into a few of marm's doughnuts, that lightened one eend of my saddle-bags quite a considerable, I turned in till morning. The barkeeper made me pay three York shillings for the horse keeping. My grit riz at it, for the old mare looked as lank as a shad; but I didn't want to git into a scrape, so I shelled out, and rode along darning all the cousins to darnation. What are the varmints good for, if they can't be tu hum when a feller travels their way?

It was purty well into the morning when I got down to York; the old mare was eenamost tired out, and I begun to think she wouldn't cut much of a dash; but jest as we were turning down the Bowery, she got a sight of one of them consarned great rail--road cars, and seemed to take it for a stable trying to run off; for she gin a snort, stuck her tail right straight out and her ears right up, and away she streaked it arter the cars, like a house a fire and no engines to be had. The colt, it come a whinnering arter, and if we didn't cut a figger, you never saw one in the multiplication table. My coat tail was a streaming out behind, and I held on to my bell-crowned hat with one hand while I shook my bridle with t'other, and stuboyed the old critter along; for I didn't want the people to think that I was afeard to go as fast as any thing in creation took a notion to, if it was a steam engine loaded with fire and brimstun, instead of a harnsome bay mare with a nussing colt.

Jest as we got away down the Bowery, the cars stopped stock still, and the mare cum up and saw that it was only a box full of folks, she kicked up her heels till I was eenamost spilt in the street. The colt it come up and flurished its leetle spindle shanks agin the car, jest as its mother had afore, and away we went, cutting dirt down Chatham street like a streak of iled lightning, till I drew the mare up with a snort and a kick that tapered off into a double shuffle right agin the Express office.

I jumped off and streaked it into the office, and right up stairs, three steps at a time.

I walked right into the editor's room, with my hand out, and sez I, "How do you du?"

Afore he could answer, a clock in the City Hall steeple struck. The editor, he jumped up, and sez he,

"We're tu late, the boat is off. There's your ticket, Mr. Slick, but it's of no use now."

I took the paper that he gin me,—it was an invite to meet the President, and the boat was off.

"Darn me, f I don't ketch up with him!" sez I, and out I went, right ahead down stairs, with out another word.

"Look a here," sez I to the boy that held the mare, "when the President comes in, you jest lead my horse down to the landing, and I'll give you a four-pence-ha'penny, clear silver."

"I'll du it," sez the little chap.

"You'll be a man before your marm," sez I, a turning the corner, to go the shortest cut to Peck Slip.

Captin Doolittle, was jest a hauling in, but I gin the old bell crown a swing, and sez I, "Hold on, you consarned old coot, hold on, and hist sail arter the President."

With that I jumped aboard a boat, and afore I reached the sloop she had worked about and was ready for a chase. The wind was coming right up the East River—and the minit I jumped aboard, Captin Doolittle, he and the black boy gin a hurra, and the way we cut water was a caution to small craft. We ploughed right ahead, full chisel, down the harbor, till by-am-by we saw two steamboats a coming towards us, brim full, and a running over with people—with banners a flying, and colors a streaming—toot horns a blowing, and fifes a letting off Yankee Doodle—drums a rattling out "Hail Columbia," and the big paddles a playing the water up, till it seemed tu kinder ketch fire in the hot sun, and drop into the waves to get cool agin.

"Captin," sez I, "hist another flag."

The captin, he put his chaw of terbacco into t'other cheek, and sez he, "I haint got none."

"I guess I have," sez the leetle nigger, a running down into the cabin.

In a minit he cum back with one of the captin's red woollen shirts fastened to the eend of a bean pole, and he stuck it up on the stern of the sloop, jest as we cum bearing right down on the two steamboats.

A tall chap with a sort of good natered face, but the darndest fish-hawk nose that you ever sot eyes on, stood with a lot of fellers on the deck of the boat that had the most music in it—an old codger, with a blue coat lined and faced all over with yaller, and a cocked hat right on his head, with one eend curling up, jest over his nose, like a hen-hawk ready to pick his eyes out, and with his two legs swallered up in a pair of black and yaller boots, stood close by the man with the nose.

"Captin Doolittle," sez I, "get out the gun, there's the President."

"What, that old chap with the yaller legs and breast," sez he, "that looks like an overgrown grasshopper a skipping out of the last century into this?"

"Jest so," sez I, "that's the President of the United States, I haint no doubt—so three cheers, and then blaze away!"

The nigger, he went down and brought up the old gun—Captin Doolittle, he loaded her down purty tight, pushed the charge hum with his ramrod, shook down the powder in the pan, and arter trying it tu his shoulder, sez he,

"Jonathan, go ahead."

"I took a squint at the leetle nigger tu see if all was ready, and then I off with my old bell-crown," and sez I, "now"—with that I gin it a flurrish—"Hurra!!!" I yelled out like the bust of a cannon—"Hurra!!" sung out Captin Doolittle on the taper eend of my yell—"Hurra!" squeaked the leetle nigger. With that the old gun banged away, and the tall man with the nose, he bowed and flurrished his hand at us, and with that I saw Alderman Purdy, a chap that used to come to the Express office when I was there afore, and the minit he saw that it was me, the boat stopped all tu once, and begun tu snort and roll on the water like a sick porpoise, and some one sung out, "Cum aboard."

Captin Doolittle and the nigger, they let down the boat, and afore I knew it there I was, standing in the steamboat. The minit I stepped aboard, the swad of fellers on deck with toot-horns and fifes and drums, let out a hull thunder storm of music. Captin Doolittle, he banged off the old gun agin; the leetle nigger, he got up an extra shirt and gin another leetle hurra; and Mr. Purdy, sez he,

"Mr. Slick, the President wants to see you."

"Wal," sez I, "I haint no objection, only give me time to slick up a mite."

With that I took out my hankercher and kinder dusted off my new coat and trousers, and slicked down my hair a leetle, and I follered Mr. Purdy, right up tu where the President was a standing, in his yaller clothes and his cocked hat.

"Mr. Tyler, how do you du?" sez I, a taking one hand from my trousers' pocket, and a holding it out.

The yaller chap, he stepped back a leetle, and the tall coon, with the nose, he gin my hand a tarnal grip, and sez he,

"Mr. Slick, I'm glad tu see you."

"You're kinder got the advantage of me, I reckon," sez I, but that minit Alderman Purdy whispered to me,

"Why, it's the President," sez he.

"Gauly oppilus," sez I, "you don't say so!"

"Mr. President, how do you du, and how are all the folks tu hum, about these times, all purty smart I s'pose?" With that I worked away at the old chap's hand, with both mine, as if I'd made up my mind tu pump an office out of him, afore I let go.

"Wal," sez I, "Captin, I hope you mean to stay in York a spell, now you've got here; some harnsome gals about these diggings jest now, rale sneezers in the way of beauty—you haint no idee of that sort, nor nothing have you?" sez I, a giving him a slantindicular squint from one eye, and a leetle punch in the ribs with the tip eend of my finger, "no you haint now."

The captin he larfed, and sez he, "Oh no, I'm only making a little unpremeditated tour a—"

"Jest so," sez I, "an *accidental* visit."

The captin gin me a squint across his nose, and then I made him a low bow, and sez I, "Jest so, but the folks seem tu be ruther tickled with sich accidents, don't they?"

This seemed to kinder mollify the captin, and jest as I was a spreading myself for a new speech, a feller cum up with a great red and green and white rosy, pinned on to his coat, and he whispered tu the President, and the President looked round tu me, and sez he,

"Mr. Slick, they tell me that the collation is ready—will you go with me into the ladies' cabin, and lead down one of my fair friends?"

I made him a prime bow—a rale darnsing school smasher—and, sez I,

"Wal now, I don't know what kind of horned cattle a collation is, but seeing as it's you, I'll tackle in, if it's only tu git acquainted with a downright ginuine fair friend of your'n, captin, for folks say that your friends are purty darned *unfair* in a gineral way."

"Folks don't du me justice," sez he, a turning red in the gills; "No man ever had better or devoted friends on arth."

"What there is on 'em," sez I.

The captin didn't seem tu hear me, but he took out his chaw of terbacco and pitched it over the side of the boat. I dug both hands into my trousers' pockets, and sez I tu the man with the silk rosy, sez I—

"Come, now, I s'pose it's about time for you and I and the President to be a movin. Where du you keep that critter of your'n?"

"What critter?" sez he.

"Why, the collation?" sez I.

"Down in the cabin," sez he.

"Wal," sez I, "I hope the varmint is considerable tame; but come on, whose afeard!"

With that, Captin Tyler and I and the old yaller chap, with a hull swad of fellers, some on 'em in training clothes, and some on 'em with cocked hats on, went into a leetle room fenced off from the deck, and there, jest as sartin as you live, were five or six wimmen folks, right in amongst all them men, like one clover top tu a hull hive of honey bees, a lookin as contented as git out. "Wal," think sez I, "If they ain't scared, I ain't." The President seemed to know 'em, for he put his arm right under mine so arnest, that he eenamost lifted my right hand out of my pocket; and, sez he,—

"Ladies, Mr. Slick, of the New York Press."

With that, I took off old bell-crown with one hand, and I put out my right foot and gin a draw kinder softly into the holler of t'other, and I bent down like a jack-knife; my eyes had tu kinder roll up a leetle, to look into the gals', and sez I,—

"Ladies, I hope you're purty well?"

One on 'em kinder got up half way, she was a proper purty woman, and looked as good natered and kind as a robin red breast in the spring time, and reached out that harnsome white hand, and smiled sort of softly, and sez she—

"Mr. Slick, we're happy tu see you."

Another harnsome critter in a checkered frock, a rale ginuine beauty, without paint or whitewash, she gin her leetle foot a twirl, and was a beginning tu reel off a curchy, so I jest stuck out my left stomper, and sot the hinge of my back a going for her; but jest as I was gittin head's up agin and my arms a swinging back tu their place, I ketched her a looking at t'other one, and a puckering up them lips of her'n, till they looked like two red rosberries jest a going to drop off from their bushes. I settled both hands back in my pockets agin, and stood right up parpendicular, as a true born American ought tu.

"Marm," sez I, "what do you think of the weather?" and with that, I jest curled my upper lip and gin her a ginuine grin from one ear tu t'other, and sez I, "Look a here, marm, if you want tu do this kinder business up harnsome, take a lesson from me; I ile the jints of my under jaw every morning. Them screw larfs ain't good for the mouth, you may be sartin of that."

The critter, she colored all over, till she looked as sweet as a pina, then a lot of fun bust right into them blue eyes of her'n, and her pesky leetle mouth begun tu tremble and work itself about, like a red rosy a trying tu fold itself up into a bud agin; and then she bust right out into a leetle finefied haw-haw; and two leetle teenty gals, dressed out in black, they begun to titter like two pigeons on a gutter—pesky sweet leetle varmints—and a smasher of a woman, that was older than any of 'em, she jined in and larfed sort of easy and nat'ral, as if she'd fed on nothing but ripe muskmellons for a hull fortnight; and then the President he jined in, and we had a fust rate haw-haw, right there in the cabin.

Jest then, a leetle chap, with an allfired swad of yaller hair a sticking out all round his head, cum in, and the good natered lady in the gray dress, she hitched on to the President, and a great tall chuckle-headed feller, dressed out in frock and trousers like a boy, with gold buttons a glittering all over his bosom, and a streak of gold a running across his shoulder, he made a dive at the harnsome gal in the checkered frock, the consarned overgrown coot! but I jest then sidled right up with my elbow ready crooked, and sez I, a looking as perlite as all natur, sez I—

"Arter me is manners for you."

The feller looked mad enough tu eat me hull, without vinegar or sarse—but I didn't seem to mind it. The harnsome gal had clenched her white fingers over my coat sleeve, as loving as a young grape vine round a black elder bush; and when I git hitched on to a fust rate gal, all the fellers in creation may go to old Nick, for what I care. The old Sogers, they mixed in with us and the fellers with silk rosies, and out we went, on deck and down stairs. The music, it bust out agin, and one of the fellers with a silk rose, he yelled out, "Make room for the President!" so the free-born Americans on deck, they crowded back and made a lane for us.

"Make room for the President and his sweet," the feller sung out agin.

Think sez I, "That aint fair now; the gal with the President is a nice critter as ever lived; but darn me if mine aint sweeter than his'n, a pesky sight,"—so I sung out, and sez I—

"Make room for Jonathan Slick and *his* sweet;" with that I took a marching step and went down stairs heads up, and with the gal hanging on my arm, as independent as a cork-screw. Gaury, but wasn't there a feed, considering it was nothing but a cold cut—sich hunks of beef, and ham, and pork, and piles of bread, and bottles of "the critter," you never sot eyes on, without it was day arter thanksgiving. We all sot down at one eend of the table, and afore we'd got a single bite, the doors banged open, and down cum the free-born citizens from on deck, helter skelter, higgle-te-pigglety, black coats, red coats, blue, green, every color on arth, and sogers, spartans, tailors, shoemakers— every sort of two-legged animals under 'em, eating away for dear life, and a drinking like so many house gutters, right afore the face and eyes of the President and me, with all the harnsome leetle sweets a setting round us,—I swan tu man, it eenamost sot me agin my victuals: and the harnsome gal by my side, she looked kinder scared, as if she hadn't ought tu be there.

"Try and take a bite, du now!" sez I, a piling some cold pork on her plate, "it aint a mite rusty, and makes me feel a'most to hum, it tastes so nat'ral."

She put the leastest mite between them temptin lips, but didn't seem to eat with a relish yet. "I swan," sez I, a bending down to take a squint at her face, "I only wish I could git aboard the sloop, and bring you a prime bunch of young onions. Wait a minit and I'll try?"

"Oh, no, no," sez the sweet critter, "I'd ruther not—don't leave me, Mr. Slick."

"Darn me, if I du—onions or no onions," sez I, but I felt kinder disappointed though, for a bunch of white onions, tops and all, would a ben prime with the cold pork—howsomever, I gin in as a feller ought tu, when a gal is in the case; but I didn't feel a bit satisfied about the stomach. When the President got up tu go on deck agin, I looked into the gal's eyes, and tried not tu feel a hungry.

Oh, par, I wish you'd a ben standing on the deck, with us, when we went up. It was a tarnation harnsome sight; the water was a blazing with the sun, and a shining around us, all checkered over with boats, and sloops, and shipping of all sorts. then right ahead was the hull city of York, steeples, housen, and wharves, piled together and heaped up with people a swarming down tu the shore, a hanging over the water, and a climbing up the masts all along the East and North rivers, like bees in hiving time. Two allfired big ships sot on the water, right agin the Battery, with a hull regiment of men, all dressed out in white, a standing up in the rigging, tu see the President and us cum in. The hills all round Brooklyn, was kivered thick with folks a hurraing and a flinging their hats up—and a leetle island that lies close up tu York, was chuck full and a running over with human live stock.

When we got agin the big ships, the men in the riggin flurrished their hats, and gin us a thundering loud hurra. The President he took his hat off, and I and the old yaller chap boosted him up onto a chair, that everybody might have a good squint at him. Mr. Curtis wanted tu hold on tu his coat tail, and make believe boost, but the old yaller chap and I—we shoved him off about the quickest.

"Git out," sez I, "git out! if a President of the United States, can't stand without the help of a pack of office-holders, he'd better fall tu once. Here's this old revolutionary soger, and I—the army, and the people—if we can't keep him up, he'll have tu go tu grass that's all!"

But while we was talking, the two ships blazed away with every darn'd gun in their sides, and the sailors hurraed agin, and afore we knew it, a hull thunder cloud of hot smoke cum a pouring over us all—ca-smash went the chair, and the President he pitched head for'ard, right amongst the office holders. The old yaller chap and I shook our heads, and begun to feel a trifle streaked.

"I'm afeard he's a gone shote," sez I, as the old feller put his cocked hat on agin.

"A *unfortunate accident*," says a feller close by.

"Not so unfortunate as you think for," sez Captin Tyler, a jumping up and a nussing his nose with one hand, "I've had worse falls than this, and riz agin arter all. Give us another boost, feller citizens—I stand ready for a second boost."

The office-holders made believe help him, but Lord a massy! they hadn't grit enough tu hist a grasshopper out of a bog of swamp grass; but I and the yaller gineral, though, we sot him up as good as new, afore half the smoke cleared off.

Jest as all was put tu rights agin, the brass cannon at the eend of our boat, let off a blast of young thunder. We gin the ship a fust rate hurra, and the minit we were a done, Captin Doolittle and the nigger, they got up a small chance of a cheer, and let off the old gun agin right under our starn. Arter that, we made a curlecue round both the ships with our music a rolling out and our flags a flying, and Captin Doolittle he chased right arter with the red shirts a cutting capers from the bean-poles; and the leetle nigger, he stood on the bows a rolling his eyes and a blowing away at Yankee Doodle on a crooked fife like all natur. I swan tu man, it was enough tu set a feller's patriotism to working like a beer barrel. We gin the ship another hurra and cut for the Battery, with Captin Doolittle and the sloop a streaking it right arter; the guns on the little island they bellowed away at us as we cut by, and the folks on the Battery, they flung up their hats and hollered eenamost as loud as the guns that kept a roaring every minit, till by-am-by in we went ca-smash, right amongst the trees and a hull gineral training of sogers. The President and us we walked ashore and went right into Castle Garden. It was chuck full of feller citizens and sogers, and the mayor was a waitin for us to cum up; he measured off a hull bilin of soft soap to the captin, and then the captin he stuck out his right arm and gin the mayor back as good as he sent, with a pint cup full over. Then we went out amongst the trees, the captin he got on tu a horse all finefied off with gold and shiny leather, and then the leetle boys that hung on the trees as thick as acorns in the fall, they gin us a cheer, and jest that minit I see the newsboy a leading my mare right towards me. I forked over a fourpence-ha'penny and got on tu the critter, tickled eenamost tu death tu git a chance tu sit down agin.

That mare is clear grit, par, and no mistake; the music, and the guns, and the shoutin, had sot her blood a bilin, and she danced about like a two year old colt jest off grass.

I rode through the trainers full chisel arter the President, and the colt, he cum a kickin up his heels amongst the wimmen and children as crazy as a bed bug. I pushed in close up tu the captin, and he and I and the rest on 'em rode along afore the sogers as crank as you please. But the mare, she didn't seem tu like the way they pinted them guns at her, and once in a while she'd kick up and grow a leetle sarcy, and snort right in their faces like a tin toot-horn about dinner time. When we'd got about half way through the sogers—and it seemed as if all creation had got intu regimentals jest then—the mare she got anxious about the colt, and sot up a whinner that a'most shook me off from her back. I tried tu make her git along, but she only bust out in a new spot, dug her hoofs close tu the ground and backed into the crowd till I got wrathy as all natur with her; but the more I paid the gad on, the worse she got, till by-am-by she stood stock still, a shakin her head, a stompin with her fore foot, and a yellin arter the colt like a lovesick gal.

The President he was a gitting ahead, and the darn'd coots all around, begun to larf and poke fun at us, when the colt he cum a scampering through the trees, and a scattering hull squads of wimmen, and boys, and babies, every jump, till he ended off in a crazy caper, all around the mare and me. This pacified the critter, and arter whinnering over the colt a leetle, she jogged on as meek as a cosset lamb, and the colt he follered close tu, till I came up with the captin agin, and then he'd stop every once in a while, and face about, look right into the sogers' eyes, so arnest, that they couldn't help but bust out a larfin, if the President and I was a lookin at 'em.

It was about the greatest show that I ever sot eyes on. The Battery is one of the harnsomest spots on arth, all kivered with grass, and chuck full of trees, and a hull army of sogers, some in brown regimentals, some in green, with yaller feathers, and some in red, yaller, blue, and all sorts of colors, a wheelin round under the trees, was enough to make a feller proud of his country.

When we got to the gate, which opens at the eend of Broadway, Captin Tyler he got into a carriage, and wanted me to git in tu, but I was afeard to leave the mare, and so Robert Tyler, the chap with the yaller hair, we agreed to hitch tackle, and ride along with one another. A hull army of sogers with their drums a beating, and colors a flying, went ahead; Robert Tyler and I, and the colt, and a hull squad of other great men cum next, and then come on the President with his hat off, and a bowin to all the winders and stoops as he went along. Wasn't them winders and ruffs and stoops a sight tu behold! Every square of glass, and every railing that a critter could hold on to was kivered with folks. In my hull life, I never see so many harnsome gals. It seemed as if every man in York, had hung out a sample of his family, for the fellers to pick and choose from. I swan tu man, if it didn't seem to me as if all the gals in creation was a swarming round the President and I, like yaller butterflies round a mud hole, all on 'em anxious for a smile at one or t'other on us. It made the blood kinder tingle all over me to feel that hull battery of bright eyes a pouring fire down on us. I raly don't see how the President stood it! He couldn't, if the crowds of free born citizens that swarmed every step of the way, layer on layer, hadn't kept him a shakin hands out of the carriage a'most every step, till he was clear tuckered out, and a'most wilted down in the carriage, long afore we got up the *Express* office. When the news boys see me and the colt, they sot up a hurra that outdid anything I'd heard since we come away from the Battery, all the purty gals waved their hankerchers about, and every winder was jammed full, and all on 'em a lookin straight at me and Bob Tyler and the colt. So I lifted my right hand kinder slow, and took off the old bell-crown—I drew in the bridle so as to make the mare caper about right, and made six bows one arter t'other, till my forred near about touched the old mare's neck.

They gin me three more cheers of the tallest kind, as they say in York, but when I looked round, there was Bob Tyler with his hat off, and a shakin that swad of yaller hair about, jest as if *our* news boys would cheer him, or any body else, when *I* was a goin by!

"That's right, Mr. Slick," sez he, when he see my bell-crown off.

"*Par the President* must be a'most tired to death, a bowin and a shakin hands so much, it's quite proper that you and I should do a little on it for him."

"Wal," think sez I, "if you aint a self-conceited critter, I don't know who is," but the feller looked as innocent as a lamb, and I was afeard he'd feel about as sheepish as if I let out on him —so I put my bell-crown on agin, with a leetle knock at the top, for I had to settle the grit somehow, and sez I,

"Wal, Mr. Tyler—to git on a new subject—how'll you swap horses?—say my mare and colt agin that harnsome critter of your'n, saddle and bridle thrown in?"

The feller kinder smiled, but didn't answer right off, so I jest turned about, and leaned one hand on the old mare's cropper, while I whistled the colt up tu us, and pinted out his harnsome head, and chist, and the clean notion that he has got of flingin out his legs.

"He's a smart critter, I can tell you," sez I; "and as for the old mare here, she's worth her weight in silver dollars. Haint got but one fault on arth."

"And what's that?" sez Mr. Robert Tyler, sez he.

"Why, she's troubled with the *botts* a leetle, once in a while, but it aint nothin worth mentionin."

Mr. Robert Tyler he give a start, and he turned as white as skim milk in the face. Sez he, all in a twitter, sez he, "Don't mention it, Mr. Slick. My par, the President, wouldn't let a horse go into his stable that had ever gin symptoms of the botts. It's an awful disease. Don't mention it to him, for he'd never git over it if you did!"

"Wal, then, I s'pose we can't trade," sez I. "Think on it agin. Mebby you'll change your mind to-morrow."

"Hello!" sez I agin. "What's that. Captin Tyler's druv his carriage right out of the ranks, and is gone fair split down Broome street."

Mr. Robert Tyler he turned his horse, and he and I and the colt took arter the President full chisel. We cum up with him jest as he was a gittin out before the Howard Hotel. He was so beat out and tuckered down that I raly felt sorry for him; for arter all that folks say, I believe that he's a good hearted old chap, and wants to du the thing that's about right, if he could only be sartin what it was. He couldn't but jest hold up his head, and had tu go to the Theatre yit. As I was a looking at him, a notion cum intu my head, and, sez I—

"Captin, jest put on your hat a minit, and drive down to the sloop—I've got somethin there that'll make your nose tingle, and chirk you right up, till you'll be as chipper as a squirrel in the fall time."

Captain Tyler he got right up, and sez he—"I'll do anything on arth that'll make me feel better." "Mr. Robert," sez I, "tell the gals that we'll come back right off"—so down we went, I helped the President into the carriage, and in less than no time we got out and went aboard the sloop.

"Captain Doolittle had gone ashore, and there wasn't nobody aboard but the leetle nigger. I sent him to the wharf for a pitcher of cold Croton water, and then I asked the President down into the cabin. It was cleared out, and swept as neat as a new pin. The table that stood in the middle of the cabin was scoured off as white as milk, and Captain Doolittle he'd hung up the checkered curtins that marm made for him, right over the highest berth, till it looked as temptin as our spare bed. I gin the Captin a chair, and he sot his hat down on the table, close by old bell-crown, while I opened a locker and took out a hull dishfull of doughnuts that marm biled up for me afore I cum away. Just as I'd sot them on the table, the nigger cum with the cold water. I took it up tu the locker, and filled in with vinegar and lasses enough to make it prime switchel, such as marm mixes up for the workin hands since you took the pledge, par. When I stirred it up well, and took a swig, to see if it was the rale critter, I got a tumbler, and arter filling one for the President, I sot down, and sez I—

"Now, Captin, make yourself to hum, and take hold."

He didn't need much urgin, for the switchel was ginuine stuff, sweety and yet sort of tart, and cool as a cowcumber, and the doughnuts beat all natur.

The President hadn't eat more than half a dozen, and had his tumbler filled about as often, afore he begun to chirk up, and look as good as new agin.

"Mr. Slick," sez he, "this is what I call livin," but my mouth was half full of a middling-sized doughnut, and I had to wash it down afore I could answer.

"Help yourself, Captin; don't be afeard—there's enough more where these cum from," sez I, a swollering the last mouthful.

"Wal, I think I've done purty well," sez he, a stretching hisself up and putting his hands in his pockets, "I raly begin to feel like myself agin; that's excellent drink of yourn, aint it, Mr. Slick?"

"Coolin," sez I, "and ruther toothsome; shall I mix another pitcher, captin?"

"No, not now," sez he, "but I wish you'd write me out a receipt."

"I'll do it," sez I, "and glad of the chance, for darn me if I haint took a sort of a notion to you; my opinion is that you're a rale ginuine feller, if them consarned politicians would only let you be; all you want is a downright honest chap that'll tell you the truth right out, and that you can trust, he'd be worth a hull bilin of Whigs, or Loco-focos either."

"But where is he to be found?" sez the President, sort of melancholy.

"Look a here!" sez I, a flingin one arm over the chair and a leaning t'other elbow on the table; "look a here!"

The President he sot with both hands in his pockets a looking right in my face for ever so long, and sez he at last, sez he—

"Mr. Slick, will you go back with me to the hotel, and sleep with me to-night? I want to have some talk with you: of course you'll go with us to the Park Theatre?"

"With all the pleasure in natur," sez I, "and we'd better be a-goin; take another swig of the pitcher, captin, and stow away some of the doughnuts in your pockets, they'll be prime at the Theatre."

The President said he'd eat enough, so as I was a follering up my own advice, he got up and was a puttin on his gloves, when he see his own pictur a hanging by Captin Doolittle's berth, and I could see that he was kinder tickled with it.

"Captin Doolittle aint much of a politician," sez I, "but he bought that picter because he parsists that it proves you to be the most consistent President that ever lived, when you veto so many bills."

"How does my face prove that," sez he, looking sort of puzzled.

"Why," sez I, "he sez that a man that runs so ginerally to *nose* can't be expected to say yes when he don't want to."

The President he bust right out a larfin, and with that I took old bell-crown, and arter sending the nigger to put up the mare and colt I follered on to the hotel; but it's gittin late and I can't write any more till next week; but mebby you'll hear from me then, for the President and I went to the Theatre, and slept together, and are as thick as three in a bed jest now, and if he haint no objections I shall write all about it, but 'twill be jest as it takes my notion whether I send it right on or print it.

I send you my pictur and the captin's tu, but it was engraved in a hurry, and aint nigh on so harnsome as either on us; by-umby I'll set for another, and then you'll see a chap worth while a figgering in the Express agin.   Your dutiful son,

JONATHAN SLICK.

LETTER XXVII.

JONATHAN SLICK IN NEW YORK.

Jonathan attends the President at the Howard House—Visits the Park Theatre with the President and his Handsome Girl—Goes with Mr. Robert Tyler to have his Hair Cut at Clairhugh's—Takes Refreshments with the Ladies at the Howard House—Bed-chamber Scene with the President—Serenade, &c.

DEAR PAR:

I begin tu feel a leetle sort of better, but nothing to brag on yit. I raly believe that I'd a been a gone sucker, if it hadn't been for the mustard plasters and the onions that Captin Doolittle kept a filling into me, outside and in, till I can a'most feel myself sprouting out greener than ever, and twice as strong. My gracious! when this ere influenza does git hold of a feller, it aint a critter that you can scare off in a hurry. It's the worst kind of a Down East cold, double and twisted strong; and if you don't humor it like a cosset lamb, jest as like as not it ups and goes off, stuboy, into a galloping consumption; and the worst on it is, it carries you off with it, whether you will or no.

Let me see; I was a telling you about the President, and how he seemed tu enjoy the doughnuts and switchel aboard the sloop. The old chap took tu it like a nussin baby, and if he wasn't clear grit, and no mistake, arter it, I don't know the symptoms of prime living.

Wal, we went back to the Howard Hotel, and the President he jumped out of the carriage as spry as a kitten, and both on us run up the steps that open out of Maiden Lane, to git rid of a hull swad of office-holders that was a hurraing at the front door in Broadway.

The President he took off his hat, and slicked down his hair a leetle in the entry-way, and I pulled up my dickey a trifle, and hauled out a corner of my yaller hankercher, and sez I—

"Captin, go ahead, I'm all ready."

We went right intu the harnsomest room that I ever sot eyes on in my hull life. Nothing that I ever see at the Astor House was a primin to it. The carpeting was all finefied off, and curlecued with posies, and green leaves, and morning-glory vines went a twistifying all over it as nat'ral as life, and all on 'em seemed kinder tangled up and trying to unsnarl all over the floor, till it raly seemed like treading on a patch of wild posies, with the moonshine a streamin over it; you would a'most smell the roses when a feller sot his foot on a bunch on 'em, they were pictered out so nat'ral and temptin.

The President, he sidled off to one of the cushioned benches, and sot down right in a swad of the harnsomest of the gals that sot in the room. They squeezed together tu make room for him, and larfed so good natered, and looked all in a twitter they was so tickled tu git him among 'em; and there I was, eenamost alone, a standin up parpindicular, and a feelin as streaked as a pair of old cotton trousers in washing time. That pesky harnsome critter that wore the checkered frock aboard the boat, she got nigh agin the door, so when she see me a standin there, she pinted with that leetle white hand of her'n, and sez she—

"Why don't you take a seat, Mr. Slick?"

"Wal," sez I, a bowin, "I don't care if I du, jest to oblige you;" so down I sot, but the cushion give so, that I sprung right up on eend agin, and when I see it rise up as shiney and smooth as ever, I looked at her, and sez I—

"Did you ever!"

"It's elastic," sez she, a puckering up her mouth.

"I don't know the name on it," sez I, "but it gives like an old friend, so I'll try it agin."

"These cushions are very beautiful and pleasant," sez she.

"Yes," sez I, a spreadin my hankercher over the cushion and a settin down, "they're as soft and blue as them tarnal sweet eyes of your'n, but not half so bright."

She k'nder larfed a leetle cozy, and begun tu play with a tossel that hung to a corner of her seat, and then she went to talkin with the fat woman that sot t'other side, like all possessed—the darned tanterlizin varmint.

The President he was as chipper as a blackbird, with the gals around him a smilin and a twitterin as tickled as so many trout round a bait. It raly made my dander rise tu see it, and me a settin there as lonesome as git-out. There, jest afore me on the wall, was a great smashin pictur,—a ralo frame of gold, with a man and a woman a huggin and kissin, and a lookin into each other's eyes, right in the middle on it,—as if there wasn't enough rale live temptin critters to rile a feller up without tanterlizin him with pictures tu.

I say, par, did you ever see a checkered adder a charmin a bird, with his head stuck up in the sun, and kinder slanted a one side,—his mouth wide open, and that are leetle forked tongue a tremblin in the middle on it, as if it was sot to dancin by that lazy hum, hum, hum, that comes etarnally a billin up from the pison critter's throat? Haint you never observed the purty bird, half scared tu death, and yit a flutterin closer and closer to the varmint, till by-am-by, she lights right in his jaw, and lies a twitterin there while he's a swallerin it hull? Wal, par, jest take away the pison, and you've some idea how I and old bell-crown come the soft sodder round that gal; but I didn't want to git her to hankering arter me tu much, for nothin on arth is so likely to cure a chap of a love-sick fit, as to see the gal a gittin tu strong a notion arter him; so I gin my fingers another snap, to change the tune, and tapered of into Old Hundred with a touch of Greenbank, and that froze her down, eyes, feet and all, in less than no time.

The Theatre was chuck full of folks, and the minit we went in, the hull bilin on 'em got up and begun to fling their hats about and yell agin like all possessed. I tell you what, par, these ere Yorkers are nigh about tickled tu death to think that I've cum back agin The President and I, we both got up and laid our hands aginst our vest pockets on the left side, and then we begun tu grin like two 'whipporwills in a black alder bush, and sot tu bowin and rollin up our eyes, till they went at it a consarned sight more fearce than ever. Arter they begun to cool down a trifle, the President and I, we sot down on one of the front benches; so I jest gin the harnsome gal a wink to set down close tu t'other side, and then the hull on 'em begun tu pile in, till we cut about as harnsome a dash as a'most anybody need tu see.

The mayor, he was a goin tu set down by the President, but when he see me, of course he gin away, and sot on t'other seat.

Jest then the curtain cum down ca-chunk, and the folks all riz and gin me three cheers that made the blood bile in my heart like maple sap in a sugar kittle. Then a leetle, lank, office-seekin chap sticks hisself up in the back seats, and yelled out, " Three cheers for the President."

But lord a marcy, cheers aint to be hauled out of a crowd of free-born citizens like fish from a mill pond. Two or three mean looking shotes like him squealed out " Hurra!" but that bait wasn't temptin enough for known fish. I didn't want to make the President feel bad, nor jealous, nor nothin, so I jest gin old bell-crown a whirl, and hollered out, "Three cheers for *my* friend, the captin."

Gaury, didn't they let into it then! the ruff with all its picturs and curlecues seemed a liftin right up from the walls, hats and hankerchers streamed out; and sich a blast of human thunder aint heerd every night at the Park Theatre.

"That'll du," sez I, a sinkin old bell-crown, and letting myself off in a bow like an iled jack-knife. "That'll du. Now, captin, I guess we'd better go hum."

"But I've got to go to the Chatham Theatre yit," sez the President, a takin up his hat. "The Democracy, the Democracy, you know, Mr. Slick, that must be our fust consideration."

"You aint a goin, Mr. Slick?" sez the harnsome gal, a lookin with them two eyes right into mine, and a clinchin them ere white fingers over the edge of old bell crown.

"I ruther guess not," sez I, a droppin my yaller hankercher over that pesky white hand, for it looked so temptin that I was afeard the President would want to git hold on it, and somehow a President al'ers does purty much as he's a mind to with the gals, except now and then one that's got a right idee of her place.

"Wal," sez I, "captin, if you're detarmined to tackle in with that arnimal that you jest mentioned, make up your mind to cut your own fodder. I go for human natur in gineral—the best part of natur I take to be the wimmen folks—so, if you'd jest as lives, I'll stay and go hum with the gals."

With that, Captin Tyler and the mayor, and the chaps with the silk rosies went off; but Robert Tyler and I jest hitched ontu the wimmen critters, and took them hum to the Howard Hotel. The landlord, he sent us some drink that was enough to make your eyes water, besides a great dish of pine-apples sliced up, sugared off and with wine poured all over 'em, that he sot right under the glass dish full of fire, where they lay yaller and shiny enough to tempt a tee-totaler to break his pledge. The wimmen they all drawed up round the table, and while they were laying into the eatables and drinkables, I jest sidled round to the harnsome gal and took one of marm's doughnuts out of my pocket, and I slid it into her hand. I gin her a wink, and, sez I,

"Keep dark, I don't want tu be mean, nor nothin; I haint got enough to go all round."

She was so tickled that she turned red all over, and eenamost larfed out; but she took the hint and rolled the doughnut up in her hankercher, not to make the rest jealous.

Jest then, I slipped out and run down tu the sloop, for I felt a dry agin, and them pine-apples made me feel sort of womble-cropped about the stomach. Your dutiful son,

JONATHAN SLICK.

LETTER XXVIII.

JONATHAN SLICK IN NEW YORK.

Jonathan goes to see Mr. Macready—Description of the Theatre—Introduces himself to a Handsome Girl at the Theatre—Enters into a Flirtation—Promises to Visit her—Jonathan takes a Novel Method of providing himself with a Fashionable Dress—Quarrels with Captain Doolittle—Is reconciled, and starts off to make a Morning Call on the Handsome Girl.

DEAR PAR:

Here I am agin, safe and sound, large as life, and chipper as a grasshopper on a high rock in a sunshiny day. I tell you what, a few ginuine huskings to hum, with purty gals to put the music in a feller's elbows, as he strips the husks off from the corn, is jest the sort of occasions to put the grit into a feller from top to toe—jest top them off with an apple cut or so, sich as we had to our house when you and marm cut about amongst the gals and the young chaps, like two spring colts jest let out to grass; and taper the hull off with a week sich as I had a ropin onions with Judy White, with her pesky red pouters a one side, and two or three prim Weathersfield gals on t'other a turning their good natured eyes at a feller every string, till his heart is a cuttin pigeon wings agin his ribs to the music of their larf—jest let a chap get used to that sort o'pastur, and consarn me, if it don't do more towards making a ginuine man of him than a hull etarnity of York life, where every other man and gal you meet have got their hearts so tarnally used up, that they have to lean agin their back bones to rest more than half the time, and likely as not get sound to sleep at that.

The old sloop jest hit the nail on the head, and hauled into Peck Slip the night arter Mr. Macready, a smashin actor from the old country, got to the Park Theatre, where he's been a acting out things that'd make your hair stand right up an eend eenajest to see it. I tell you what, he's a hull team and a horse to let—no mistake in that.

Did you ever see a race horse up on eend for a run, with his neck curled over like an ox bow, and his skin shinen like a junk bottle? Did you ever look into the critter's eyes, and see the fire dancing through the black?—arninal lightning, every darned spark on it. If you've seen that are, then you've got some idee of the allfired smashin critter that my arm was eenamost girting afore I took a squint at her face.

Wal, she squinched a trifle and gin a leetle start, and then gin me a look with them etarnal long big eyes that made me a'most jump on eend, and yit I sot like a great gawk a staring right intu her face, jest as if I hadn't no marners. Quill wheels and cheese presses! wasn't that critter something worth while! sich lips—red as a blood beet, and shiny as a harnful of wintergreen berries! Consarn it, if ther'd been a honey bee in the theatre, he couldn't a kept from lighting right between 'em; and if he

18

didn't find the breath as sweet agin as all the honey he ever stole from a clover top, I must a been darndly cheated by the looks on 'em—that's jest it. Her neck, and that great broad for-red of her'n, looked sort brown and slick, alike a hazlenut jest afore it rattles from the shuck; and I never see a crow a flying in the hot sun so black and shiny, as the thick swad of hair that hung braided and twistified up with gold chains, rale ginui e gold, al' round that harnsome head of her'n. I swan tu man, she was the fust gal that ever made Jonathan Slick feel as if he wasn't tu hum in good company. Our black colt, with his taperin limbs, that soft shiny mane, and them eyes that seemed to ketch fire when the sun strikes 'em—is about as much like a common cider mill horse, as she is like the generality of wimmin folks. She was eenajest as tall as I be, and big enough every way to match —a rale downright sneezer of a gal, that a'most took away my breath every time my eye ketched her'n: and cousarn me, if that wasn't every two seconds while I sot there.

Wal, there we sot and sot, till the curtin right afore us came down ca-chunk agin the floor, and all the folks riz up as if it was time tu be a goin. The gal got up, took the bottle and hankercher in one hand, and seemed tu be kinder lookin around for something. I was jest a crookin my elbow, and had eenamost said, "Shall I have the pleasure to see you hum marm?" as we do at singin school, when a feller that had been settin right behind us riz up and stuck out his hand as nat'ral as git out.

The gal kinder gin a turn, and while she made bleeve pin her shawl, chucked a piece o' paper into my hand, and put the consarned little hand that I'd been a nussing in mine, right through that tall chap's arm, and went off as if nothing was the matter. I turned round like a great gawk, and took arter em. I jest ketched one squint at them tarnal black eyes and at a swad o' hair that stuck out on his upper lip, like a gray cat's whiskers, and then I found myself standing, like any other darned coot, all alone under a street lamp, a tryin to cypher out the leetle finefied words writ out on that piece o' paper. Arter a good deal of extra spellin I found out the meanin, and that was an invite to come and see that gal in the morning, at a house in——.

Wal, I did the paper up, put both hands in my trousers pockets, and arter lookin at myself from top to toe, sez I—

"Jonathan Slick, you must be a consarned sight harnsomer chap than ever I took you to be, that's sartin."

Wal, I couldn't ketch a wink of sleep all night, but kept up a tarnal thinkin about that gal; and there lay Captin Doolittle a snorin away in the berth right above me, like a tin peddler's toothorn run crazy. I swan, it was as much as I could du to keep from gettin up and chokin the varmint. Turights the daylight cum a sneakin intu the cabin as lazy as ever you see daybreak come on; and jest arter the sun got up, Captin Doolittle begun to stir his stumps about breakfast. He and I and the little nigger sot down, but I felt kinder peaked and couldn't hoe my row a bit; so the Captin and the nigger did extra duty, and stowed away for me.

Your loving son,
JONATHAN SLICK.

LETTER XXIX.

Jonathan Visits the Handsome Girl—Describes a Gambling-House in the Morning before it is put to rights—Visits the Lady's Boudoir—Describes the Furniture, the Lady, her Dress, and Conversation—Is Interrupted by the Gentleman of the House—And leaves with a promise to return and escort Miss Sneers to Mad. Castellan's Concert.

DEAR PAR:

Wal, as I was sayin, I pulled foot down one of them streets that run off kinder catecorned by the Park, till I cum right agin the house pinted out in the paper which that harnsome gal had gin me. I kinder cut across the street and stood over agin the house, detarmined tu take a sort o' observation afore I sot my foot inside the doorway. It was an allfired harnsome consarn, with one story piled atop of t'other, till you could count four rows of winders, besides a row of young ones, stuck right in tu the edge of the ruff. A lot of stone steps run up tu the front door, and an iron fence twistified and curlecued round the edges run along each eend. The winders all on 'em had green slats shut over 'em, the door follered the fashion, and the hull consarn seemed tu be shut up agin winter.

Wal, I cut across the street and went straight up the steps. There was a great chunk o' silver sot intu a kind of a silver sarser nailed agin the door post, and with a name writ round the edge on it. Arter giving the chunk a sneakin pull, to be sartin it would give and meant somethin, I gin it an allfired jerk—and turights there was a tinklin and ringin inside, as if an old wether with a fust rate bell on, had took tu scootin over the house.

I hadn't more'n got my hand off the chunk, when the green slats swung open jest as easy, and a yaller nigger stood inside a eyeing me from top tu toe, as if he had a sort of hankerin arter some human arnimal, but didn't think me jest good enough tu eat hull without considerable sarse.

"How do you du," sez I, as mealy as a pink eyed potater jest out o' the pot—"How are all the folks this mornin?—purty smart I reckon."

The coot stared and kinder shook the two great swads o' curly hair that stuck out over each side of his head; and arter lookin back intu the house, then up the street, and then agin at me, sez he, "What du you want?" sez he.

"Wal," sez I, a divin both hands down to where my pockets ought to a'been, but eenamost keelin head over heels with the dive I gin without finding bottom—"I seem tu surmise that I want tu see some body a trifle more like folks than you seem tu be—so I guess I'll walk in."

With that I gin the chap a shove with one of my mudgrapplers, and walked right intu the long entry-way, as crank as a militia trainer with his regimentals on.

"What's your name and who do you want?" sez the yaller nigger kinder wrothy, and a shakin that swad o' curly hair at me like a darned great sun flower in a foggy storm.

"Wal," sez I, "you ought tu go Down East and learn to ask questions. If your tongue was only half as greasy as your face now, you could a done it as slick agin. I aint got no name tu speak on, and all I want o' you is jest tu tell the harnsome critter that lives here, that I'm on hand, a waitin down here as spry as a cricket, and about as arnest tu see her agin as ever a chap was."

The chap he kinder eyed me askew. Fust he took a squint at my puffy trousers, then at old bell crown, and then at me all over.

"You can't be the gentleman that she told me to let in," sez he; "does Miss Sneers expect you?"

"Wal, I kinder reckon she does," sez I.

"Wal," sez the feller, lookin sort o' unsartain, "jest step intu this room and I'll go and see."

"That's a leetle more like folks," sez I, a followin the chap intu a room at one eend of the entry-way, where I sot down with old bell crown over my knees, and took a squint round. It was kinder dark, for them between slats shut out the light; but I could see that the room hadn't been fixed up since over night. Two of the chairs lay keeled up on the carpet—the kiver was a slidin off from the table a'most tu the carpet, and slopped over with wine that wasn't dry yit—a decanter with a trifle o' wine, or per'aps brandy, stood on the table where the cloth had left it bare, and an alltired purty wine glass lay on the harnsome carpet broke to smash; and round under the table and close around my chair was a hull squad of playin cards, a'most new, as if somebody had got beat a playin high-low-jack and the game, and flung the hull bilin down in a huff. I'd jest picked up two or three of the cards, when the yaller nigger turned back and sez he—

"It aint of no use—I can't tell my mistress who wants tu see her, if you wont give me your name, or a card."

"Wal," sez I, "if you must have one or t'other, there's a card —now git out, and don't let me see that consarned yaller face agin till it's wanted."

With that I handed over the jack-o'-spades; he turned his great sarser eyes, fust on the leetle feller that sot stuck up on the card, and then agin at me, as if he didn't know what tu make on't. There was no satisfy in him, I could see that, but I'd begun to get tired o' waitin, and sez I,

"Wal, there's the card, and a harnsome one tu—my name is Jonathan Slick of Weathersfield—my father is a Squire and a Deacon of the Church—my mother was Jerusha Pettebone—my ——but darn me, if you aint satisfied now, you consarned pryin shote, you may go tu grass, and the harnsome gal with you."

The feller cut stick afore I'd half done, and cum back a bowin and a scrapin, as if he'd got a set of new jints while he was a goin up stairs.

"My mistress wants tu know if you're the gentleman that she saw at the theatre last night."

"Jest so," sez I, a flingin down the ten spot o' clubs and the ace o' diamonds, for somehow I jest didn't like the touch of the varmints—"jest so!"

"Walk up stairs," sez he, a bowin eenamost tu the ground.

"Wal, I don't care if I du," sez I, follerin the chap.

I took off old bell crown and riled up my curls with a leetle flourish o' fingers amongst the thickest on 'em, as I went up stairs—then I kinder shook up the pletes of my trousers, and pulled out the eend of my yaller hankercher, as I went along behind the buff colored nigger.

I swan tu man, Par, it was like walkin through a footpath kivered over with meadow grass and wild posies, as I went up the stairs, all carpeted off and a shinin with bars of gold. Jest at the top stood a black figger, a'most as large as life and all but naked, a holdin one finger tu his lips and with a lamp in t'other hand, that seemed as if it had burnt itself out, for there wasn't any ile in it, and the wick was sooty as a nigger's eye lashes.

Wal, I follered on intu another entry-way, where another figger stood, as white as if it had been cut out of a fust rate cheese curd. It had one foot up, as if it was a darncin, one arm was flung over its own head, and both its pesky leetle hands was chuck full of posies, that looked as if they'd been planted in a snow bank and watered with new milk, afore that harnsome half dressed, indecent figger had found 'em. She looked like a ginuine purty gal froze tu death for the want of kiverin.

"Wal, while I was a lookin at the poor critter, that yaller nigger he opened the door and stood a flurishin his hand about, jest as our minister does when he dismisses meetin, and is tu allfired lazy tu use both hands tu once.

I went by the varmint and there I stood stock still in the door way a starin about like a stock calf. I swan, Par, I never sot eyes on any thing that could shake a stick at that are room in my born days. The floor was all spread off with a carpet, like a meadow that slants tu the fust spring sun when the grass is a springin up, and sot off thick with dandelions, buttercups and clovertops; and I swan tu man, there was something in the room that smelt just about as sweet.

The room wasn't over large, and a whoppin winder eenamost took up one eend on't. Yet it was kinder dark for all that, for a hull harvest of shiny silk, as thin as a locust's wing, and sort a rosy colored, like a gal's cheek jest arter a chap has kissed it —was kinder tumblin down the winder in winrows turned lengthwise, one arter t'other, till the hull was grabbed up in one alfired swad, and ketched back in a great hook all of solid gold, that glistened like a lookin-glass frame when the fire light ketches it fair.

There wasn't but two chairs in the room, and they seemed tu be made out o' solid gold tu, stuffed down with shining silk figered off with posies redder than the winder silk, and yet kinder like it. There was a bench agin the winder, standin on chunks o' gold cut out like a lion's paw, and that tu was all cushioned off with shiny silk like the chairs, and on the back on it, right agin the wall, two pillars were stuck up, all kivered over with posies that looked good enough tu smell on. Right agin the door was the harnsomest consarn that I ever sot eyes on. It was a kind of a round table cut in tew in the middle, dressed up in white and ruffled off with harnsome lace, like a gal when she means tu cut a dash. A lookin glass stood on it sot in a gold frame work, curlecued off like a great vine, with the golden grapes a bustin out all over it, and sort a droppin down over the glass. I snum, if it wasn't a sight tu behold! There was a fine fied gold watch about as big as a ninepence, a lyin on the table, and some leetle red morocco boxes, with a newfangled pitcher pictured off tu kill, chuck full of ginuine roses and green leaves, that looked as if they'd that minit cum off from the bushes.

There was one thing more a standin up in the corner that beat all I ever did see. It was an allfired overgrown candlestick a standin on legs, and ecnamost as tall as I be. That tu, seemed to be of solid gold, curlecued off with little picters. On the top was a great golden sarser, and what chawed me u was a stream o' smoke that ris from the sarser, and kinder spread all over the room, jest enough to let a chap know that there was a fire somewhere about. Jest behind the whoppin candlestick was the figger of a critter, sort o' half bird and t'other half baby, the cunninest varmint that I ever did see. The wings grew out of his chubby shoulders, and the pesky little scamp seemed tu be a larfin at me through the smoke all the while that he made believe that he was a droppin somethin down intu the gold sarser. The critter was as white as a tomb stun; but if it hadn't kept still, I should eenamost thought it was alive. There I stood bendin for'ard, with my mouth kinder opened and old bell crown between both hands, a lookin at that little varmint, and there he was a'most winken at me, when somebody said,—

"Walk in Mr. Slick,—pray walk in!"

I gin a jump and dropped old bell crown, for it seemed tu me as if the flyin baby had spoke; but in stoopin tu pick up old bell crown agin, I kinder turned round; and there, on a bench cushioned off with silk, like the one I've told you on, sot the gal I'd seen at the theatre last night; but oh, get out! more than as harnsome agin. She was all dressed out in a white gown, that hung kinder slimsy from that purty neck, till it eenajest kivered the pesky leetle feet that lay on a footstool like two black squirrels asleep together. The cloth that her dress was made on, was so thin that I could a seen her arms through clean tu the wrist, if the sleeves hadn't been made so full, that every time she moved the hull arm got more than half unkivered. I swan, it made me ketch my breath, when she kinder half ris and reached out that are soft hand, a smilin all the time as if she was tickled eenajest tu death tu see me.

I gin her hand a leetle mechin shake, and turned round tu set down in one of the chairs, for I couldn't help but feel a trifle streaked amongst all that heap o' silk and gold. But before I was quite sot down she settled back aginst the pillar, and whilst she let one foot drop from the stool, she fixed t'other pillar agin the wall; and while she was a pattin the posies on it with her hand, she lifted them tarnal black eyes and gin me a smile that had more than the sweetness of a hull bilin of sugar in it; and there she sot with that hand kin ler stuck intu the pillar yet.

Now, Par, you don't think I was shote enough tu set down in the big chair arter that, do you? I guess I wheeled round, about the quickest, and sot down so close by that harnsome critter, that I could feel her breath on my hair; and yit, I sot as fur off as I could, and close on the edge of the bench, but it was orful short, and I had tu set close any how; but oh gauly, didn't my fingers tingle. There was that leetle hand, as soft and white as a snowball, a lyin among the posies worked on that pillar right behind me, and I hadn't but jest tu lean back, and that are arm would a been a'most round me. But there I sot, close on the edge, all in a flusterfication, fust a lookin at that are hand, then at her smilin face, and then agin at old bell crown, and so over agin. Arter I'd sot about a minit, I hitched back a trifle, and gin a kind o'skeery squint at her—she was eenajest larfin. With that, I gin another hitch, and looked right straight at old bell crown, as if I wanted tu eat it. The harnsome critter didn't seem tu rile up any, so I jest dropped bell crown, dived tu pick it up agin, and riz right up parpendicler agin the pillar. I could feel the leetle hand a movin on the pillar agin my back, like a chip squirrel in its nest; but think says I, you'r ketched this time, any how, and I guess you may as well lie still. With that, I turned my head sort of a slow, and larfed a leetle, jest enough tu show my teeth round the edges, and sez I,

"How do you du marm?"

Did you ever see a spring begin tu gurgle and shine up all tu once, when you've parted the peppermint that grows over it, and let in the broad daylight on the water? If you have, per'aps you have some idea how consarned harnsome the smile was that cum bustin all over that gal's face, a dimpling up them pesky red lips, and a dancin through them great black eyes. I could see the tantelizen critter a bitin them plump lips of hern, to keep from snickerin out in my face; so I put on a leetle extra grin myself, for I'm a bull team at larfin, and a hoss tu let, when I once begin. By-am-by, sez she, as well as she could git it out, sez she—

"I hope you enjoy yourself in town, Mr. Slick."

"I reckon I du jest now," sez I, "quite a considerable deal, and upwards."

With that she sort a smiled agin, and somehow that other leetle hand in her lap kinder crept along under the loose slimsey sleeve, as if it wanted tu get better acquainted with mine. My mudgrappler didn't object tu be introduced.

"It's orful pleasant weather, for time o'year," sez I, and my hand kinder crept along towards hern a mite.

"Very," sez she, a looking at the tall candlestick as soft as summer butter; "very."

"I also kinder like tu go intu the woods in the fall, and see the trees a turnin all sorts o' colors, red and blue and yaller; and see the chesnuts, jest ripe enough tu drop from there prickly shucks, and hear the but'nuts a ratlin down tu the dry leaves. Oh, gauly! I wish you and I was there now, if it was ony jest tu watch the chip-munks and gray squirrels a carrying off the nuts in their mouths and fore paws. Did you ever see a harnsome black squirrel, with a shagbark between his whiskers, a hoppin among the trees, arter they're stript more'rn half naked by the frost?"

Then my fingers begun to travel agin like anything.

"Yes," sez she, "I love a pet squirrel dearly."

By this time my hand had got tu the eend of its journey and put up.

"Harnsome critters, aint they," sez I, a'most out o'breath, I was so skeared. "Captin Doolittle has got a rale sneezer down at the vessel, as black as git out, his tail curls up over his side like the feather in a gal's bonnet, and he's got an eye as bright and sharp as if it had been cut out o' yourn. I'll hook it from the old coot, cage and all, and bring it up tu you, if you've a notion tu it, consarn me if I don't."

"You're very kind," sez she.

"Oh, you git out!" sez I; "that aint a primin tu what I mean tu du, if you and I can only agree tu draw in the same tacklin. aint mean as some chaps that I know on—nobody ever ketched me a halving a long nine, or askin a gal tu pay her own shot when she went a slayin with me—ask Captin Doolittle, if you don't believe *me*."

The critter looked up and kinder smiled agin so darned winnin, that I histed her hand tu my lips, and gin it a cibble afore I know what I was about. She seemed tu try tu pull it away, and turned her head so that I couldn't see her face.

"You aint mad nor nothin?" sez I, a lettin go her hand. "I swan tu man, you looked so darned sweet I couldn't help it."

She got up and went tu the table that was dressed off so, and smelt of the posies on it, and then she cum back agin and sot down as good natured as a pussey cat; but she'd put me in such a tantrum, for fear I'd made her mad, that I didn't know what tu say next; so there I sot, a feelin streakeder and streakeder every minit; but arter a while I bust out agin—

"Speakin of the woods," sez I, "aint the maple trees harnsome? Did you ever see the leaves when they're jest a turnin red, a kinder tremblin on the limbs, as if every one on 'em was kinder afraid of fallin off? I've seen 'em over night as green as some of these country chaps when they fust come tu York; and then agin in the mornin, as red as your lips; and a'most as bright when the sun shines on 'em."

I could see them lips begin to pucker up agin, as if they wanted to give me a chance of judgin. So I kept on—

"I swan," sez I, "sometimes it seems to me as if the sugar had stuck up through the leaves and turned 'em red, they look so pesky sweet. Speakin o' that, du you love maple sugar?"

"Very much," sez she.

"Wal," sez I, "next time I cum I'll bring you an allfired hunk, see if I don't."

Jest then, the chap that I'd seen at the theatre with her the night afore, opened the door and cum straight in. I eenamost jumped on eend and dropped her hand, that some how or other had got intu mine agin, as if it had been a hot chesnut.

But the chap only looked around, and made a sort of a slidin bow, and shet the door agin.

"Wal," sez I, all in a twitter, for my heart had riz right up intu my mouth; "I guess I'll be goin."

"So soon?" sez she, a liftin them eyes sort o' mournful.

I wilted right down agin, like a cabbage plant in the sun.

"And who may that chap be," sez I, for I begun tu feel ugly about the heart.

"Oh, he's only my brother," sez she, "never mind him. Are you fond of music, Mr. Slick?"

"I guess I be," sez I. "When the chorister is gone, I al'ers lead the singin at meetin tu hum."

"Have you ever heard Castellan?" sez she.

"No," sez I, "I don't know as ever I've heard that instrument, but I'm great on the bas-viol, and could beat all natur on the toot horn when I was a leetle shaver, not more than knee high to a toad."

Consarn the critter, I couldn't speak but what that pesky mouth of hern would brighten and pucker up.

"Would you like to go with me and hear her this evening?" sez she. "We shall hear some fine music."

"If you'll only talk tu me there can't be a doubt on it," sez I, a bowin.

"Then you will go?" sez she.

"I reckon I will," sez I, "twice over if you want me tu, and tickled to death with the chance."

"Wal," sez she, "I'll be ready at half past seven."

"You'll find me on hand," sez I; "and now I guess I must be a goin."

With that I took up old bell crown, and arter makin a prime bow, was a goin out; but I happened tu think what a coot I'd been, and turned back.

"I swan," sez I, "I'd a'most forgot tu ask what you wanted tu see me for."

I suum, it seemed as if the maple leaves I'd been a talking of had been flung, a hull swad on 'em into her face, she turned so red; but afore she could speak I heard that chap a comin agin; so I made her a low bow, but sudden, like a jack-knife opened and shet in a hurry, and I cut for the sloop agin.

Your dutiful son,
JONATHAN SLICK.

LETTER XXX.

The Gambling House—Jonathan is taken in with Cards.

DEAR PAR:
I've tried to write tu you agin and agin since my t'other letter, but I felt so dreadful bad, there was no makin it out, all I could du. I've been dreadful sick, and about the darndest melancholy critter that ever sot up an eend in bed.

I own it eenamost kills me to begin, but the truth will out some time or other; and a feller that aint ashamed to du wrong, must be a snakin shote if he can't pick up courage tu own up tu the truth, like a man. It's a tough job, though, to own that you've been made a darn'd coot, and a leetle wus than that—but all I've got to du is to grin and bear it. I was a tellin you that Miss Sneers gin me an invite to supper. I slicked up and went, nigh about dark, a feelin sort a streaked, I couldn't tell why, and a thinkin of Judy White all the way; that pesky harnsome critter had riled up my feelins so desperately that I raly hadn't known which eend my head was on—but, somehow, as I went along, Judy seemed close by me, with her hand on my arm, kinder holdin me back; and once I was eenamost tempted tu turn back, and never think o' this York gal agin on arth. I swow, I raly believe the tears stood in my eyes when I went up the steps —for I couldn't keep from thinkin of hum all I could du, and it seemed jest as if you and marm were a holdin family prayers, and all for my sake, jest then. I do believe, Par, that the spirits of live folks that love you are as likely agin to haunt a feller when he's in danger as them of dead people. Wal, I rung the door-bell kinder loth, for I hadn't felt very chipper all day, and, somehow, thinkin of hum and sich things gin me a kind of timersome feelin. The buff nigger was on hand in no time. He swung open the door, and stood a bowin and a shakin that etarnal swad of hair till I got clear into the entry-way. I was a goin right up stairs, but the nigger he opened a side door, and says he, "walk in."

"Jest so," sez I, and I went through the door inter a room that was sot off tu kill with all sorts o' notions and foreign fixins. The winders were shut up close, and kivered from top tu bottom with a hull Niagara of red silk. The benches and settees and chairs shone and glistened all around, and overhead was one of them concerns of fire and chink glass, a blazin and flashing round us till it seemed as if the ruff overhead was made of solid gold. The wall were kivered all over with picters—them golden frames was all cirlicued off, and shone out dreadful harnsome, I can tell you. Right under that heap of swinging glass, and jest where the fire felt strongest, there was a table about as large round as marm's cheese tub, and kivered over with a red cloth, all figured off that fell clear to the carpet, and looked sort o' rich, like a pile of winter apples heaped afore a cider mill.

Two or three chaps sot afore the table, larfin and a talkin together, while they kinder tilted back the chairs they sot in, and seemed to make themselves tu hum all over.

I looked around for Miss Sneers, but she wasn't there yit, and the chaps by the table didn't seem tu know that I was standin there, and a lettin off my prime bows all for nothin. But jest as I was a goin to back out, a feller that lay on one of these new-fangled settees that have an arm chair at each eend, and a bench in the middle all cushioned off with red silk, he kinder riz up, and I see it was the chap that waited on Miss Sneers at the theatre the first time I ever saw her. He cum for'ard on seein me, and a lookin eenamost tickled tu death tu think I'd cum. He told the chaps by the table who I was, and they got up tu, and was in a mighty takin about my bein there. I sot down on a chair, and histed one leg top of t'other, and begun tu teeter my right foot sort of independent, and looked about for Miss Sneers. She wasn't there jest then, and I begun to feel rather awkward. But the man that I'd seen with her at the theatre, he sot down close by me, and begin to talk as chipper as if he'd known me a hundred years. I hadn't had a good chance tu look at the feller before in arnest, but now as he sot agin me, I gin him considerable observation. He was a tall, harnsome chap, with hair as thick and black as midnight. His eyes were black tu, and as sharb as darningneedles, but you never could ketch them a lookin at you more'n a minute at a time—they al'ers shied when a feller looked right straight into them. His voice was as soft as a mealy potater, and he kinder slid up to you across the room like a gray cat, and seemed tu be jest about as innocent. He begun tu talk about farming, and the price of produce in York, jest as cozey as git out, and seemed tu be right tu hum on any subject that cum up. The other chaps they jined in' and laid on a considerable soft sodder about my letters in the Express—but they did it slick, I can tell you, smoothed it down nice and ily, till you couldn't jest tell exactly whether it was soft sodder or not.

Arter a few minutes, Miss Sneers she cum in—I felt my heart jump intu my mouth, and the blood bile up over my face, like hot flip when the iron is put in. It seemed tu me, as if she never did look so harnsome afore—her frock was all blue shiny velvet, as bright as a damson plum—that ere round neck so pesky white, hadn't no kiverin on, but a leetle finefied gold chain, and another gold chain was tangled up with the great swad of hair that was twistified up on the nap of her neck. She kinder slid intu the room sort of easy, jest like a trout sailin along the bottom of a brook—her cheeks looked as fresh as a full blown rosy, and her mouth, the darned provokin thing, looked jest like a bunch of ripe strawberries, ready tu drop from the stems.

She kinder bowed tu the chaps that sot by the table, and then cum right up tu where I stood with both her hands out tu once, as if she was tickled all over tu see me agin.

Both them little white hands wasn't more than one handful for me, and I wasn't in no very great hurry tu let go, when I once got a good grip at 'em—she didn't seem tu mind my havin 'em, but sot down right between me and her brother, and there she sot a smilin right intu my eyes and a askin so arnest arter my helth that I couldn't but jest speak, my heart riz so. The critter really seemed tu have took a notion tu you, and marm. She was dreadful arnest tu know if I'd hearn from you, and how you stood the cold weather, and then consarn me! if she didn't ask how Captin Doolittle did, jest as if the old coot had a ben her own Par. By-am-by she bent over, and kinder whispered tu me, and sez she—

"I must go and speak tu the gentlemen there—you make me forget everything but yourself."

With that she gin my fingers a leetle grip and went up tu the table.

"You seem dull," sez she, "supposin you take a game at cards till supper is ready."

"If Mr. Slick hain't no objection" sez her brother, a lookin at me kinder anxious. "His father's a deacon you know."

They all turned on their chairs, and looked at me, as if a man that didn't like cards must a have been brought up in the woods. It made me feel kinder streaked—so sez I, "oh never seem tu mind me, I aint a skeered at a pack of cards, if my Par is."

"Du you ever play," se. Miss Sneers, a smilin on me like a June sun.

"Wal," sez I, speakin up crank, "I haint done much at it, since I was a little shaver, and used tu play high-low-jack and the game, with one of our workmen in Par's barn tu hum, but I was a considerable of a sneezer at it in them days, I recon."

Miss Sneers's brother, sez he, "Wal then, supposin you take a hand here."

I felt kinder bad at the idea of touching cards arter promisin you not tu, Par, when you ketched me at it and gin me that all-fired lickin in the barn—but Miss Sneers stood right afore me, shuffling a bran new pack o' cards in them little white hands and a lookin at me so cunnin that I couldn't stand it—yet I felt sort o' loth and held back.

"I'm afeared I've eenajest forgot how," sez I; a loungin back.

"Oh never mind," sez one of the chaps in a red and green vest, and with checkered trousers on, "Miss Sneers will show you how."

"Certainly," says the harnsome critter—a smilin right in my face again; "Shall I be your teacher, Mr. Slick?"

"Jest so," sez I—"I'd jump down my own throat, if you on'y told me tu."

With that I sot down by the table—crossed one leg a top of

t'other and wiped my nose. Miss Sneers, she leaned her arm on my chair and the rest sot down.

"Wal, what shall we play?" sez the chap in checkered trousers.

"Oh, high-low-jack and the game—Mr. Slick understands that"—sez the rest, sort a larfin. I begun to rile a trifle—"I guess Mr. Slick knows a thing or two besides that," sez I; "he wasn't born in the woods tu be skared at owls!" sez I.

They all choked in at that—one feller shuffled the cards, I cut, and the checkered trousers took the deal. I got an allfired good hand the first dive—ace, jack and the two spot of trumps, besides a ten. Miss Sneers she bent over until I could feel her breath agin my cheek, as warm and sweat as the steam from an applesarse cag when the sarse is sot off to cool. I swow, it made me feel so kinder unsettled, that the cards danced afore my eyes. like picters run crazy. We begun to play. Miss Sneers kept a pokin that pesky little finger of hern amongst my cards every minute, puttin out them that I ought to play, one by one—and afore I knew it myself, I'd beat the hull biling on 'em three games without stoppin. Miss Sneers she seemed to be eenamost tickled to death to think I'd done 'em up so slick, and the men they looked streaked enough. I tell you—that one in the checkered trousers above all. Jest as we was cuttin in for a new deal, the doors right afore me slid back inter the wall, and there was another room spread out afore us like a picter. It was as light as day from one eend of the room tu t'other—and it was enough to dazzle one's eyes to see the shiney silk tumblin down from the golden poles over the winders—the great whoppin lookin glasses a blazin all over that eend of the room—the carpet kivered over and trod down with posies—the picters agin the walls and leetle marble babies a standing round, with the candle light a pourin down over 'em. Oh, Gosh! it was enough to take a feller loose his breath, and never ketch it agin. There, right in the midst of the room, was a table a shinin and a glistenin, like a heap of ice-chunks and new half dollars piled up together in the hot. sun. The plates and the knives and forks spoons and all, was solid silver—everything else was silver but the glasses, and they were all pinted and pictered off, and cut

19

down in lines, till there was nothing but flash, flash, flash wherever the light fell, and that was strong enough; for right overhead was another of them great gold spangles branching out every which way, and runnin over with fire.

Miss Sneers she put her hand on my arm, jest so as tu let the tip eend of her leetle finger lie agin my wrist. I snore it made the blood tingle up my arm. We went intu the room with the rest a follerin arter, Indian file. A great strappin nigger stood at each side of the door-place, when we went, with white gloves on, and towels in their hands—they bowed a'most tu the carpet as we went by, and when we sot down, then they stood right up on eend behind our chairs, like militia trainers jist tryin tu drill. They lifted up the kivers from a lot of dishes, and up riz the steam among the glasses and silver, till it seemed as if they hung in a cloud. Oh gracious, I can't begin to tell you all that them dishes had in 'em. There was leetle teinty tonty birds cooked hull, claws and all—partridges with their stomachs stuffed till they looked as pussey as cousin Jasin—squirrels a lyin there like human babies jest baked over a trifle, and all sorts of wild varmints that a feller ever thought of killin.

The niggers they dodged about, fillin plates and a handin 'em round like lightnin. They gin Miss Sneers and I each on us a leetle bird—darn me if I know what it was, without it was a woodpecker stewed hull. It raly seemed tu be a shame tu stick a fork intu the teinty varmint. I kinder diddled my knife and fork about, till Miss Sneers got purty intimate with her bird, for I wanted tu see if it was the fashion tu swaller 'em down in'ards and all. She'd used her little chap purty well up, when I sot my jaws a workin in arnest. The bird went down my throat the quickest. It was awful sweet tastin; and the leg bones scratched a trifle as they went down, but nothin tu speak on.

Wal, we laid into the squirrels and other wild critters rather hard, till I begun tu feel a dry. There was a leetle bottle of water stood agin each plate. I poured some out of mine, and was a goin tu drink, but Miss Sneers, she laid her hand on the glass, and sez she—

"Mr. Slick, let me help you tu wine?"

"Not as you know on," sez I, a bowin, and a takin the tumbler from under her hand—"I'm a teetotaler, marm, tu the back bone!"

"Oh, I'd forgot," sez she, a lookin at her brother. He took up a bottle with leetle chunks of sheet lead a stickin tu the neck, and sez he—

"You will not refuse a glass of this cider, Mr. Slick—there's no alcohol in this, I can tell you."

I was jest a goin tu say no, but Miss Sneers, she held out her glass, and all the time that cider was a gurglin out of the bottle and a sendin up sparkles in her glass, she kept them smilin eyes a pourin their brightness right intu mine. When the glass was full, she touched it tu her mouth, and gin a leetle sip, jest enough tu make them pesky lips look a trifle damp, and redder than ever, and sez she, a reachin the glass towards me—

"You must drink this, Mr. Slick."

I felt the blood bile intur my face agin. I kinder part reached out my hand—then I pulled it back, and sez I—

"I've signed the pledge."

"Not agin this harmless cider," sez they altogether.

"Not when a lady kisses the glass," says Miss Sneers—a holdin out the tumbler yit, and a lookin kinder anxious, as if she'd cry right out if I didn't give up.

"Take it for my sake," sez she, a bendin close tu me, and a holdin the glass right up tu my lips. They were all a lookin at me, and kinder larfin, as if they thought I darsent take it.

"You see Mr. Slick will not give up the point, even tu you Miss Sneers," sez the man with checkered trousers. "Allow me to drain the glass your sweet lips have kissed."

"You be darned," sez I, a takin the cider and drinkin it down a'most at three swallers.

"Bravo!" they all sung out tu once. "Here's to the ladies!" Miss Sneers, she held out my glass agin. Her brother lifted the bottle, and this time the cider splashed over that leetle white hand, and come drippin over the table all the way tu my mouth. I felt streaked about makin any more touse about a leetle cider, and poured the glass down without squinchin. By the time I found the bottom of that glass, I didn't feel askeared of the next one the leastest might in the world. But, somehow, the more I drank, the plates seemed to grow brighter and more unsteady. The birds that lay yet in one of the silver dishes seemed to grow smaller, but more on em, like young robins in a nest, when they jest begin tu feather out. The wine decanters blazed out redder and redder, and the cider-bottles popped and foamed like ginger-beer in the summer time. The folks, tu, sot orful oneasy, and somehow, the feller that sot agin me looked jest as if he'd found a twin with checkered trousers, and a red-and-green vest, as much like his'n as two peas in a pod.

I kinder seemed tu remember that Miss Sneers kept a kissin the glasses for me, till by-am-by I sot out to do it myself, and kissed her instead. With that, she went intu tother room. We followed arter, and the two niggers arter us with the cider and wine decanters in their hands.

"Now," sez Miss Sneers' brother sez he, "less have another game; I'll bet Mr. Slick wont beat three times runnin agin."

"I'll bet he will," sez Miss Sneers, a pintin tu a seat by the table, and a lookin good enough tu eat.

I sot down, and the chap in checkered trousers he begun to shuffle away, like a house a fire.

Miss Sneers she bent over me agin, and her brother he sot down and cut cards. I beat agin, right straight ahead; the hull swad on em begun to grow kinder wamblecropped at that, and Miss Sneers she larfed so good-natured, and bent forward so much that her cheek a'most lay agin mine all the next game.

By gauly, I beat agin; and by that time, they all begun tu look a trifle rily. The checkered trousers he took the cards and gin em a snap along the eends that might a ben heard in the street. With that, he slapped em down on the table, and sez he, a nodden his head at me, sez he, "I'll bet fifty dollars you don't beat this time." With that, he larfed till the hair on his upper lip curled up and showed his teeth, like a dog when he snarls.

"Nonsense," sez Miss Sneers, "we can beat twenty such felers—you and I, Mr. Slick, can't we?"

"I ruther thinks so," sez I.

"I'll bet fifty dollars," sez checkered trousers, "that we beat you all hollow."

"I'll bet you don't," sez I, a rilin up.

"Plank the money," sez he, a slappin the cards agin, "plank the chink."

I took your old wallet from the leetle pocket in my under vest, and unrolled the bills that I'd put there arter sellin out the sloop load—"I spose you think I haint got it," sez I, a shakin the harnful of bills that was left. "Hurra for old Connecticut!" The other chaps they shell'd out, and a hull heap of bills lay on the table. Miss Sneers she went away a minute, and then bent over me agin, with another glass of that white cider in her hand—she held the glass to my lips, and wouldn't take it away till I'd drunk the hull.

That was prime cider, and I was a beginnin to fee. dry agin, so I drunk another glass; and at it we went, shovel and tongs. As true as you live, they raly did beat that game; and when they saw how wrothy I was, they offered tu bet a hundred dollars on my luck the next time. I don't know who beat arter that; for somehow I seemed tu be sort o' dreamin; the candles seemed tu be a darncin round us, and it seemed as if the cards were leetle teenty folks, all alive and a grinnin at us as we handled em. I took out the old wallet every few minutes—I du seem to remember that—and arter it was empty, Miss Sneer's brother, sez he, "Never mind, my boy, we'll take your autograph."

"I don't keep any such new-fangled varmints," sez I.

"Oh, on'y jest write your name here," sez he, a handin over a strip of paper.

"Jest so," sez I, a takin the pen he held out; "jest so, but good gauly, du hold the paper still. I can't ketch up with it if it moves about the table this way."

"It's your hand," sez he.

"My hand!" sez I—"you git out!"

I gin a dive at the paper and held it kinder still, while I did up a long tailed J. I had tu begin agin at the S, but arter a dive or tu, I curlecued it up about right, and then we went tu playin cards agin. They seemed tu take a great shine tu my name that night, and kept a askin me for it every few minutes, till I went away. I don't jest know when Miss Sneers went away, or exactly how I got away myself; but the next morning I woke up in my bunk with the darndest head ache that I ever dreamed on Captin Doolittle he sot in the cabin a lookin at me, and a cryin like a great baby.

"What's the matter, Captin?" sez I, a turnin over.

"Jonathan," sez he, "a risin from the locker, and diggin both hands in his old trousers pocket, "Jonathan, its time for us tu haul up stakes and go hum."

The tears run down the old chap's face, as he said this, and he turned his face away that I shouldn't see them.

I tried tu think of what had turned up tu make the captin take on so. My head beat like a drum—I partly remembered the cider, the cards and Miss Sneers. I looked at Captin Doolittle; he had the poor old empty wallet in his hands, and I could see the tears drop into it.

I lay down agin, kivered my face with the piller, and burst out a cryin.

I guess I lay still a cryin like a baby as much as ten minutes and there sot Captin Doolittle a holdin the empty wallet all the time. At last I sot up an eend and looked at the captin as well as I dare, and sez I,

"Captin what shall I du?"

The Captin he looked up, and sez he,

"Jonathan you'd better fust tell me jest what you have done a'ready." I sot to as well as I could and told him the hull story about Miss Sneers, the theatre, playing cards, the bird supper, and the cider. When I'd got through he shook his head sort of mournful, and sez he—

"Jonathan, this is a bad business; you've made a shote of yourself and gambled all your father's money away; it's eenamost as bad as stealen."

"Oh don't say that are," sez I, a kiverin my face with both hands. "I feel bad enough without bein twitted of what I've done, gracious knows?"

"Wal, I know it aint generous tu strike a feller when he's down," sez the captin, "but what is to be done? That's the question."

"Wal," sez the Captin, "supposin you put on your things and

we'll go up tu that consarned gamblin hole and see if any thing can be done to git the money back. I hain't no doubt but that Miss Sneers will be tickled tu death tu see you agin."

I got up and dressed myself as well as I could for my head ached as if it would crack open. The Captin he was as good as any thing; he poured a hull pitcher full of cold water over my hair, and arter making me drink a strong cup of tea, I felt kinder better about the head, but oh Lord a massy, how my heart ached!

I felt so down in the mouth that I couldn't talk, so we both started off towards that consarned house agin.

"Now Jonathan," sez the Captin, as we got agin the steps. "it goes agin the grain tu say so, but you jest make believe that I am a police officer, and keep a stiff upper lip, ring the bell and walk right in; I'll come arter and we'll du their bisness for em in less than no time."

I rung the bell.

"Is Miss Sneers tu hum?" sez I.

"No," sez he, as quick as "she went into the country this morning."

I was a going tu say that I'd seen her, when Captin Doolittle pushed right by and giving the nigger a shove on one side, sez he,

"Walk in, Jonathan, walk in and make yourself tu hum." With that he dove into the hall and I arter him—he opened the side door into the room we were in the night before, and gin a peak round.

"Nobody there," sez he, "go up stairs, I'll settle the nigger if he gets obstropulous, and then follow arter."

I went right up stairs, and was jest a knocking at the door of Miss Sneers' room, when I see that it was open a trifle; and as I gin a peak through, there was the chap that she called her brother shying out through the eend door—I jest gin a knock that sent the door a flyin open, and went in. Miss Sneers was settin on that silken bench, dressed out in a ruffled white frock, and with her hair twisted back in a hurry, and kinder tousled up with a gold chain in it, as if she hadn't touched it since the night afore. She jumped half up when she see me, and then settled down agin with her lips shet tight together, and a lookin hard in my eyes as if uncertain who it was.

I walked right up to her and held out my hand, "How do you du this morning, Miss Sneers," sez I.

She kinder leaned back, and lookin right straight in my eyes, sez she,

"You must have mistook the room, sir, I do not usually receive company here."

I swow, it seemed as if the critter had swallered a chunk of ice, she spoke so stiff and cold. I looked around the room a minit, and then I turned tu her agin, and sez I,

"Look a here marm, you don't seem tu be over tickled tu see me this morning, so I'll make myself scarce the minit you'll give me a chance tu see that brother of yourn."

"You are laborin under another mistake," sez she, as frosty as ever. "My brother is not in the house."

"Perhaps you'll tell me by-am-by that I mustn't believe my own eyes," sez I a getting wrothy. "Jest ask that mean shote to come out of the other room there—I saw him sneak off with my own eyes not three minutes ago."

She turned a trifle red when I talked up to her so, and arter chokin a second, sez she, as cool as a cowcumber, sez she,

"Not my brother, you did not see my brother, he is my husband, sir."

I felt the blood bile in my veins and my face seemed afire. "Your husband marm?" sez I, a getting up a laugh that eended off in a savage grin, "and so you're, you're,"—

"His wife sir," sez she, with a cold tarntalisin smile, "and now, as I am particularly engaged, perhaps you will leave the house."

"Not jest yet," sez Captin Doolittle, a bolting intu the room. "We've got some business with that husband of your'n, marm."

"And who are you sir?" sez the woman a turnin white as curd and sittin down half scared tu death.

"I don't know as that is any consarn of your'n," sez he, a hauling a piece of paper folded up square from his pocket. "I want that swindlin scamp that you call husband, and its **my** pinion that he and I get better acquainted afore I leave these ere premises."

I never see a poor critter wilt down as she did, her face was as white as snow, so was her mouth, and I could see it begin tu tremble all she could du to help it.

"Surely, surely, you havn't brought a police officer here?" sez she, a lookin at me, and them soft eyes of her'n were a swimmin in tears. I begun to relent.

"Jonathan, don't make a coot of yourself," sez the Captin, a givin me a sly poke in the ribs; then he went right up tu her, and sez he,

"I don't wonder you're surprised marm, it aint often that you get a decent chap like me in this nest of varmints, but when one on us du come we generally make purty clean work of it, I can tell you that! Perhaps your husband won't be the only one that will get hauled over the coals. I've seen purtyer women than you are afore the police magistrates afore now."

The critter began tu tremble and looked at me as pitiful as a rabbit in a trap.

"It ain't of no use," sez Captin Doolittle a pushin me back, "salt won't save you if that scamp of your'n don't shell out. Mr. Slick here haint nothin to du with the bisness now that he's gin it up tu the law. You haint got sich a mealy hearted chap as him to deal with, I can tell you."

"But what du you want?" sez she, a shakin as if she was a cold.

"I want the money you swindled out of this young feller las night," sez he. "The money and the notes you made him give and by the living hokey if it aint handed over in less than ten minutes, I'll have every darned varmint in the house marched off tu the tombs."

The poor critter grew wuss and wuss; after a minute she turned to me and sez she, a sobbin like all natur,

"So you've indicted the house, have you?"

I didn't just know what she meant, and the Captin seemed as bad off, but he gin me a poke to keep still, and sez he, "You'll find out I reckon, but as that are husband of yourn seems loth tu come out I'll jest give him a little invite." With that he went into t'other room and arter a little noise of scuffling cum out agin a leadin the woman's brother or husband by the ear. He had taken an orful hard grip, and the critter's souse looked as red as if it had just been scalded.

"Are you a goin to shell out or not?" sez the Captin. The feller gin a pull, and the Captin follered suit, which stretched his ear rather more than he seemed to relish.

"Come, we're in something of a hurry," sez the Captin, "we'd jist as leave have you as the money."

The feller gin his head a jerk, but the Captin's fingers made a fust rate vice, and the old feller put on the screws tight enough.

"Jake, Jake!" the feller yelled out.

"If your nigger's name is Jake I'm afeared he won't hear," sez the Captin a puttin a chaw of tobaccer intur his mouth with one hand, while he gin the ear an extra pinch with the other. "I locked him up in a pantry down stairs, plenty of wine bottles there, he's comfortable enough, don't disturb the poor nigger now, don't."

The feller gin the Captin's side a dig with his fist; with that the Captin jest gin him a jerk towards the door, and sez he, a turning tu me as cool as get out, sez he, "call the rest on em up Mr. Slick, I can du this feller's business; but the lady there may want two beaus agin—call 'em up."

I really felt sorry for the poor woman, she jumped up and flung her arms around the chap, and sez she,

"Du give it up, du, I cannot bear this, they will do it, you see they will."

"Tell him to let go my ear," sez the feller a turning his tarnal white face tu mine, "and I'll give you the money, provided you don't molest us agin."

"Jest so," sez the Captin, undoing his grip, "shell out, shell out."

The feller put his hand in his pocket and hauled out a swad of bills and five slips of paper with my name on em, all rumpled up together.

"Jest see tu him," sez the Captin, a nodden his head towards the chap, "while I see if it's all right." So he sot down on the silk settee close by that poor woman, and 'iisting one leg over tother, spit on his fingers and counted over the money. It was all fair, so he rolled it up in a swad, put it intu the old wallet and handed it over to me.

"There," sez he, "Mr. Slick, I spose we may as well be a joggin."

With that he told the chap that he'd find the key in the closet door and the nigger safe, and we went down.

"There Jonathan," sez the Captin, "I rather guess we've done it! But what makes you look so womblecroped?"

"I don't know," sez I, a brushin my hands across my eyes, "but it seems tu me that I've lost something more than all that money's worth."

"And what is that?" sez he.

"It's the fust time on earth that I could believe that women could raly be so deceitful and bad. I feel as though I never should think so well of them agin—as if a part of my own heart had dried up all tu once. Captin, Captin, I'd rather work night and day for the money than feel so lonesome about the heart as I do now; I'd as lives stay in a world without sun, as to have no sartinty in the truth of women folks."

I remain your humble, but loving son,

JONATHAN SLICK.

THE END.

T. B. PETERSON AND BROTHERS' PUBLICATIONS.

NEW BOOKS ISSUED EVERY WEEK.

Comprising the most entertaining and absorbing Works published, suitable for the Parlor, Library, Sitting Room, Railroad or Steamboat Reading, by the best writers in the world.

☞ Orders solicited from Booksellers, Librarians, Canvassers, News Agents, and all others in want of good and fast selling books, which will be supplied at very Low Prices. ☜

MRS. ANN S. STEPHENS' WORKS.

Complete in eighteen large duodecimo volumes, bound in cloth, gilt back, price $1.75 *each; or* $31.50 *a set, each set is put up in a neat box.*

The Reigning Belle,	$1 75	The Soldiers' Orphans,	$1 75
A Noble Woman,	1 75	Silent Struggles,	1 75
Palaces and Prisons,	1 75	The Rejected Wife,	1 75
Married in Haste,	1 75	The Wife's Secret,	1 75
Wives and Widows,	1 75	Mary Derwent,	1 75
Ruby Gray's Strategy,	1 75	Fashion and Famine,	1 75
The Curse of Gold,	1 75	The Old Homestead,	1 75
Mabel's Mistake,	1 75	The Heiress,	1 75
Doubly False,	1 75	The Gold Brick,	1 75

Above are each in cloth, or each one is in paper cover, at $1.50 each.

MRS. EMMA D. E. N. SOUTHWORTH'S WORKS.

Complete in thirty-five large duodecimo volumes, bound in cloth, gilt back, price $1.75 *each; or* $61.25 *a set, each set is put up in a neat box.*

The Artist's Love,	$1 75	The Deserted Wife,	$1 75
A Noble Lord,	1 75	The Bridal Eve,	1 75
Lost Heir of Linlithgow,	1 75	The Lost Heiress,	1 75
Tried for her Life,	1 75	The Two Sisters,	1 75
Cruel as the Grave,	1 75	Lady of the Isle,	1 75
The Maiden Widow,	1 75	The Three Beauties,	1 75
The Family Doom,	1 75	Vivia; or the Secret of Power,	1 75
Prince of Darkness,	1 75	The Missing Bride,	1 75
The Bride's Fate,	1 75	Love's Labor Won,	1 75
The Changed Brides,	1 75	The Gipsy's Prophecy,	1 75
How He Won Her,	1 75	Haunted Homestead,	1 75
Fair Play,	1 75	Wife's Victory,	1 75
Fallen Pride,	1 75	Allworth Abbey,	1 75
The Christmas Guest,	1 75	The Mother-in-Law,	1 75
The Widow's Son,	1 75	Retribution,	1 75
The Bride of Llewellyn,	1 75	India; Pearl of Pearl River,	1 75
The Fortune Seeker,	1 75	Curse of Clifton,	1 75
The Fatal Marriage,	1 75	Discarded Daughter,	1 75

Above are each in cloth, or each one is in paper cover, at $1.50 each.

RIDDELL'S MODEL ARCHITECT.

Riddell's Model Architect. With 22 large full page colored illustrations, and 44 plates of ground plans, with plans, specifications, costs of building, etc. One large quarto volume, bound, ...$15 00

☞ Above Books will be sent, postage paid, on receipt of Retail Price, by T. B. Peterson & Brothers, Philadelphia, Pa.   (1)

2 T B. PETERSON & BROTHERS' PUBLICATIONS.

MRS. CAROLINE LEE HENTZ'S WORKS.

Green and Gold Edition. Complete in twelve volumes, in green morocco cloth, price $1.75 each; or $21.00 a set, each set is put up in a neat box.

Ernest Linwood,	$1 75	Love after Marriage,	$1 75
The Planter's Northern Bride,..	1 75	Eoline; or Magnolia Vale,.....	1 75
Courtship and Marriage,	1 75	The Lost Daughter,	1 75
Rena; or, the Snow Bird,	1 75	The Banished Son,	1 75
Marcus Warland,	1 75	Helen and Arthur,	1 75
Linda; or, the Young Pilot of the Belle Creole,			1 75
Robert Graham; the Sequel to "Linda; or Pilot of Belle Creole,"...			1 75

Above are each in cloth, or each one is in paper cover, at $1.50 each.

BEST COOK BOOKS PUBLISHED.

Every housekeeper should possess at least one of the following Cook Books, as they would save the price of it in a week's cooking.

The Young Wife's Cook Book,	Cloth,	$1 75
Miss Leslie's New Cookery Book,	Cloth,	1 75
Mrs. Hale's New Cook Book,	Cloth,	1 75
Mrs. Goodfellow's Cookery as it Should Be,	Cloth,	1 75
Petersons' New Cook Book,	Cloth,	1 75
Widdifield's New Cook Book,	Cloth,	1 75
The National Cook Book. By a Practical Housewife,	Cloth,	1 75
Miss Leslie's New Receipts for Cooking,	Cloth,	1 75
Mrs. Hale's Receipts for the Million,	Cloth,	1 75
The Family Save-All. By author of "National Cook Book,"	Cloth,	1 75

Francatelli's Modern Cook. With the most approved methods of French, English, German, and Italian Cookery. With Sixty-two Illustrations. One volume of 600 pages, bound in morocco cloth, 5 00

JAMES A. MAITLAND'S WORKS.

Complete in seven large duodecimo volumes, bound in cloth, gilt back, price $1.75 each; or $12.25 a set, each set is put up in a neat box.

The Watchman,	$1 75	Diary of an Old Doctor,	$1 75
The Wanderer,	1 75	Sartaroe,	1 75
The Lawyer's Story,	1 75	The Three Cousins,	1 75
The Old Patroon; or the Great Van Broek Property,			1 75

Above are each in cloth, or each one is in paper cover, at $1.50 each.

T. A. TROLLOPE'S WORKS.

Complete in seven large duodecimo volumes, bound in cloth, gilt back, price $1.75 each; or $12.25 a set, each set is put up in a neat box.

The Sealed Packet,	$1 75	Dream Numbers,	$1 75
Garstang Grange,	1 75	Marietta,	1 75
Gemma,	1 75	Beppo, the Conscript,	1 75
Leonora Casaloni,	1 75		

Above are each in cloth, or each one is in paper cover, at $1.50 each.

FREDRIKA BREMER'S WORKS.

Complete in six large duodecimo volumes, bound in cloth, gilt back, price $1.75 each; or $10.50 a set, each set is put up in a neat box.

Father and Daughter,	$1 75	The Neighbors,	$1 75
The Four Sisters,	1 75	The Home,	1 75

Above are each in cloth, or each one is in paper cover, at $1.50 each.

Life in the Old World. In two volumes, cloth, price, ... 3 50

☞ Above Books will be sent, postage paid, on receipt of Retail Price, by T. B. Peterson & Brothers, Philadelphia, Pa.

MISS ELIZA A. DUPUY'S WORKS.

Complete in six large duodecimo volumes, bound in cloth, gilt back, price $1.75 each; or $10.50 a set, each set is put up in a neat box.

The Cancelled Will,..............$1 75		How He Did It, ...$1 75
Who Shall be Victor,.............. 1 75		The Planter's Daughter,......... 1 75
Why Did He Marry Her?...... 1 75		Michael Rudolph,.................. 1 75

Above are each in cloth, or each one is in paper cover, at $1.50 each.

EMERSON BENNETT'S WORKS.

Complete in seven large duodecimo volumes, bound in cloth, gilt back, price $1.75 each; or $12.25 a set, each set is put up in a neat box.

The Border Rover,..............$1 75	Bride of the Wilderness,........$1 75
Clara Moreland,.............. 1 75	Ellen Norbury,...................... 1 75
The Forged Will,.............. 1 75	Kate Clarendon,.................. 1 75
Viola; or Adventures in the Far South-West,...................................... 1 75	

Above are each in cloth, or each one is in paper cover, at $1.50 each.

Heiress of Bellefonte, and Walde-Warren,.................. 75	Pioneer's Daughter and the Unknown Countess,........... 75

DOESTICKS' WORKS.

Complete in four large duodecimo volumes, bound in cloth, gilt back, price $1.75 each; or $7.00 a set, each set is put up in a neat box.

Doesticks' Letters,..............$1 75	The Elephant Club,..............$1 75
Plu-Ri-Bus-Tah, ... 1 75	Witches of New York,......... 1 75

Above are each in cloth, or each one is in paper cover, at $1.50 each.

GREEN'S WORKS ON GAMBLING.

Complete in four large duodecimo volumes, bound in cloth, gilt back, price $1.75 each; or $7.00 a set, each set is put up in a neat box.

Gambling Exposed,..............$1 75	Reformed Gambler,..............$1 75
The Gambler's Life,.............. 1 75	Secret Band of Brothers,........ 1 75

Above are each in cloth, or each one is in paper cover, at $1.50 each.

DOW'S PATENT SERMONS.

Complete in four large duodecimo volumes, bound in cloth, gilt back, price $1.50 each; or $6.00 a set, each set is put up in a neat box.

Dow's Patent Sermons, 1st Series, cloth,.....................$1 50	Dow's Patent Sermons, 3d Series, cloth, ...$1 50
Dow's Patent Sermons, 2d Series, cloth,..................... 1 50	Dow's Patent Sermons, 4th Series, cloth,...................... 1 50

Above are each in cloth, or each one is in paper cover, at $1.00 each.

WILKIE COLLINS' BEST WORKS.

The Crossed Path; or Basil,...$1 75 | The Dead Secret. 12mo........$1 75

Above are each in 12mo. cloth, or in paper cover, at $1.50 each.

The Dead Secret, 8vo.............. 50	Mad Monkton,........................ 50
Basil; or, the Crossed Path,...... 75	Sights a-Foot,........................ 50
Hide and Seek,......................... 75	The Stolen Mask,.................. 25
After Dark,............................... 75	The Yellow Mask,.................. 25
The Queen's Revenge, ... 75	Sister Rose,............................ 25

The above books are each issued in paper cover, in octavo form.

FRANK FORRESTER'S SPORTING BOOK.

Frank Forrester's Sporting Scenes and Characters. By Henry William Herbert. With Illustrations by Darley. Two vols., cloth,...$4 00

☞ Above Books will be sent, postage paid, on receipt of Retail Price, by T. B. Peterson & Brothers, Philadelphia, Pa.

4 T. B. PETERSON & BROTHERS' PUBLICATIONS.

BOOKS FOR SCHOOLS AND PRIVATE STUDY.

The Lawrence Speaker. A Selection of Literary Gems in Poetry and Prose, designed for the use of Colleges, Schools, Seminaries, Literary Societies, and especially adapted for all persons desirous to excel in declamation and public speaking. By Philip Lawrence, Professor of Elocution. One volume of over 600 pages, half morocco,.........$2 00

Comstock's Elocution and Model Speaker. Intended for the use of Schools, Colleges, and for private Study, for the Promotion of Health, Cure of Stammering, and Defective Articulation. By Andrew Comstock and Philip Lawrence. With 236 Illustrations. Complete in one large volume of 600 pages, half morocco,.......... 2 00

The French, German, Spanish, Latin and Italian Languages Without a Master. Whereby any one of these Languages can easily be learned by any person without a Teacher, with the aid of this book. By A. H. Monteith. One volume, cloth,................... 2 00

Comstock's Colored Chart. Being a perfect Alphabet of the English Language, Graphic and Typic, with exercises in Pitch, Force and Gesture, and Sixty-Eight colored figures, representing the various postures and different attitudes to be used in declamation. On a large Roller. Every School should have a copy of it,.......... 5 00

Liebig's Complete Works on Chemistry. By Baron Justus Liebig... 2 00

WORKS BY THE VERY BEST AUTHORS.

The following books are each issued in one large duodecimo volume, bound in cloth, at $1.75 each, or each one is in paper cover, at $1.50 each.

A Lonely Life. By the author of "Wise as a Serpent," etc.............$1 75
Rome and the Papacy. A History of the Men, Manners and Temporal Government of Rome in the Nineteenth Century, as administered by the Priests. With a Life of Pope Pius IX.,............... 1 75
The Initials. A Love Story. By Baroness Tautphœus,................ 1 75
The Macdermots of Ballycloran. By Anthony Trollope,.............. 1 75
Lost Sir Massingberd. By the author of "Carlyon's Year,"............ 1 75
The Forsaken Daughter. A Companion to "Linda," 1 75
Love and Liberty. A Revolutionary Story. By Alexander Dumas, 1 75
Family Pride. By author of "Pique," "Family Secrets," etc......... 1 75
Self-Sacrifice. By author of "Margaret Maitland," etc............... 1 75
The Woman in Black. A Companion to the "Woman in White," ... 1 75
A Woman's Thoughts about Women. By Miss Mulock,.............. 1 75
Flirtations in Fashionable Life. By Catharine Sinclair,.............. 1 75
Rose Douglas. A Companion to "Family Pride," and "Self Sacrifice," 1 75
False Pride; or, Two Ways to Matrimony. A Charming Book,...... 1 75
Family Secrets. A Companion to "Family Pride," and "Pique,"... 1 75
The Morrisons. By Mrs. Margaret Hosmer,........................... 1 75
My Son's Wife. By author of "Caste," "Mr. Arle," etc............... 1 75
The Rich Husband. By author of "George Geith," 1 75
Harem Life in Egypt and Constantinople. By Emmeline Lott,...... 1 75
The Rector's Wife; or, the Valley of a Hundred Fires,................ 1 75
Woodburn Grange. A Novel. By William Howitt, ... 1 75
Country Quarters. By the Countess of Blessington,.................. 1 75
Out of the Depths. The Story of a "Woman's Life,"................. 1 75
The Coquette; or, the Life and Letters of Eliza Wharton,............ 1 75
The Pride of Life. A Story of the Heart. By Lady Jane Scott,..... 1 75
The Lost Beauty. By a Noted Lady of the Spanish Court,............ 1 75

Above books are each in cloth, or each one is in paper cover, at $1.50 each.

☞ Above Books will be sent, postage paid, on Receipt of Retail Price, by T. B. Peterson & Brothers, Philadelphia, Pa.

WORKS BY THE VERY BEST AUTHORS.

The following books are each issued in one large duodecimo volume, bound in cloth, at $1.75 each, or each one is in paper cover at $1.50 each.

My Hero. By Mrs. Forrester. A Charming Love Story,..............$1 75
The Count of Monte-Cristo. By Alexander Dumas. Illustrated,... 1 75
The Countess of Monte-Cristo. Paper cover, price $1.00; or cloth,.. 1 75
Camille; or, the Fate of a Coquette. By Alexander Dumas,......... 1 75
The Quaker Soldier. A Revolutionary Romance. By Judge Jones,.... 1 75
The Man of the World. An Autobiography. By William North,... 1 75
The Queen's Favorite; or, The Price of a Crown. A Love Story,... 1 75
Self Love; or, The Afternoon of Single and Married Life,......... 1 75
The Dead Secret. By Wilkie Collins, author "The Crossed Path,"... 1 75
Memoirs of Vidocq, the French Detective. His Life and Adventures, 1 75
The Clyffards of Clyffe, by author of "Lost Sir Massingberd,"...... 1 75
Camors. "The Man of the Second Empire." By Octave Feuillet,.. 1 75
Life, Speeches and Martyrdom of Abraham Lincoln. Illustrated,... 1 75
The Crossed Path; or Basil. By Wilkie Collins,................... 1 75
Indiana. A Love Story. By George Sand, author of "Consuelo," 1 75
The Belle of Washington. With her Portrait. By Mrs. N. P. Lasselle, 1 75
Cora Belmont; or, The Sincere Lover. A True Story of the Heart,. 1 75
The Lover's Trials; or Days before 1776. By Mrs. Mary A. Denison, 1 75
High Life in Washington. A Life Picture. By Mrs. N. P. Lasselle, 1 75
The Beautiful Widow; or, Lodore. By Mrs. Percy B. Shelley,...... 1 75
Love and Money. By J. B. Jones, author of the "Rival Belles,"... 1 75
The Matchmaker. A Story of High Life. By Beatrice Reynolds,.. 1 75
The Brother's Secret; or, the Count De Mara. By William Godwin, 1 75
The Lost Love. By Mrs. Oliphant, author of "Margaret Maitland," 1 75
The Roman Traitor. By Henry William Herbert. A Roman Story, 1 75
The Bohemians of London. By Edward M. Whitty,................. 1 75
The Rival Belles; or, Life in Washington. By J. B. Jones,......... 1 75
The Devoted Bride. A Story of the Heart. By St. George Tucker, 1 75
Love and Duty. By Mrs. Hubback, author of "May and December," 1 75
Wild Sports and Adventures in Africa. By Major W. C. Harris, 1 75
Courtship and Matrimony. By Robert Morris. With a Portrait,... 1 75
The Jealous Husband. By Annette Marie Maillard,................ 1 75
The Refugee. By Herman Melville, author of "Omoo," "Typee," 1 75
The Life, Writings, and Lectures of the late "Fanny Fern,"........ 1 75
The Life and Lectures of Lola Montez, with her portrait,......... 1 75
Wild Southern Scenes. By author of "Wild Western Scenes,"...... 1 75
Currer Lyle; or, the Autobiography of an Actress. By Louise Reeder. 1 75
Coal, Coal Oil, and all other Minerals in the Earth. By Eli Bowen, 1 75
The Cabin and Parlor. By J. Thornton Randolph. Illustrated,.... 1 75
Jealousy; or, Teverino. By George Sand, author of "Consuelo," etc. 1 75
The Little Beauty. A Love Story. By Mrs. Grey,................ 1 75
Secession, Coercion, and Civil War. By J. B. Jones,.............. 1 75
Six Nights with the Washingtonians. By T. S. Arthur,........... 1 75
Lizzie Glenn; or, the Trials of a Seamstress. By T. S. Arthur...... 1 75
Lady Maud; or, the Wonder of Kingswood Chase. By Pierce Egan, 1 75
Wilfred Montressor; or, High Life in New York. Illustrated,...... 1 75
The Old Stone Mansion. By C. J. Peterson, author "Kate Aylesford," 1 75
Kate Aylesford. By Chas. J. Peterson, author "Old Stone Mansion,". 1 75
Lorrimer Littlegood, by author "Harry Coverdale's Courtship,"..... 1 75
The Earl's Secret. A Love Story. By Miss Pardoe,.............. 1 75
The Adopted Heir. By Miss Pardoe, author of "The Earl's Secret," 1 75

Above books are each in cloth, or each one is in paper cover, at $1.50 each.

☞ **Above Books will be sent, postage paid, on Receipt of Retail Price, by T. B. Peterson & Brothers, Philadelphia, Pa.**

6 T. B. PETERSON & BROTHERS' PUBLICATIONS.

WORKS BY THE VERY BEST AUTHORS.

The following books are each issued in one large duodecimo volume, bound in cloth, at $1.75 each, or each one is in paper cover, at $1.50 each.

Cousin Harry. By Mrs. Grey, author of "The Gambler's Wife," etc.	$1 75
The Conscript. A Tale of War. By Alexander Dumas,	1 75
Saratoga. An Indian Tale of Frontier Life. A true Story of 1787,	1 75
Married at Last. A Love Story. By Annie Thomas,	1 75
The Tower of London. By W. Harrison Ainsworth. Illustrated,	1 75
Shoulder Straps. By Henry Morford, author of "Days of Shoddy,"	1 75
Days of Shoddy. By Henry Morford, author of "Shoulder Straps,"	1 75
The Coward. By Henry Morford, author of "Shoulder Straps,".	1 75
The Cavalier. By G. P. R. James, author of "Lord Montagu's Page,"	1 75
Rose Foster. By George W. M. Reynolds, Esq.,	1 75
Lord Montagu's Page. By G. P. R. James, author of "Cavalier,".	1 75
Mrs. Ann S. Stephens' Celebrated Novels. Eighteen volumes in all,	31 50
Mrs. Emma D. E. N. Southworth's Popular Novels. 35 vols. in all,	61 25
Mrs. Caroline Lee Hentz's Novels. Twelve volumes in all,	21 00
Frederika Bremer's Novels. Six volumes in all,	10 50
T. A. Trollope's Works. Seven volumes in all,	12 25
James A. Maitland's Novels. Seven volumes in all,	12 25
Q. K. Philander Doestick's Novels. Four volumes in all,	7 00
Cook Books. The best in the world. Ten volumes in all,	17 50
Henry Morford's Novels. Three volumes in all,	5 25
Mrs. Henry Wood's Novels. Sixteen volumes in all,	28 00
Emerson Bennett's Novels. Seven volumes in all,	12 25
Green's Works on Gambling. Four volumes in all,	7 00
Miss Eliza A. Dupuy's Works. Six volumes in all,	10 50

Above books are each in cloth, or each one is in paper cover, at $1.50 each.

The following books are each issued in one large octavo volume, bound in cloth, at $2.00 each, or each one is done up in paper cover, at $1.50 each.

The Wandering Jew. By Eugene Sue. Full of Illustrations,	$2 00
Mysteries of Paris; and its Sequel, Gerolstein. By Eugene Sue,	2 00
Martin, the Foundling. By Eugene Sue. Full of Illustrations,	2 00
Ten Thousand a Year. By Samuel Warren. With Illustrations,	2 00
Washington and His Generals. By George Lippard.	2 00
The Quaker City; or, the Monks of Monk Hall. By George Lippard,	2 00
Blanche of Brandywine. By George Lippard,	2 00
Paul Ardenheim; the Monk of Wissahickon. By George Lippard,	2 00

Above books are each in cloth, or each one is in paper cover, at $1.50 each.

The following are each issued in one large octavo volume, bound in cloth, price $2.00 each, or a cheap edition is issued in paper cover, at 75 cents each.

Charles O'Malley, the Irish Dragoon. By Charles Lever, ...Cloth,	$2 00
Harry Lorrequer. With his Confessions. By Charles Lever,...Cloth,	2 00
Jack Hinton, the Guardsman. By Charles Lever,............Cloth,	2 00
Davenport Dunn. A Man of Our Day. By Charles Lever,...Cloth,	2 00
Tom Burke of Ours. By Charles Lever,.....................Cloth,	2 00
The Knight of Gwynne. By Charles Lever,.................Cloth,	2 00
Arthur O'Leary. By Charles Lever,........................Cloth,	2 00
Con Cregan. By Charles Lever,............................Cloth,	2 00
Horace Templeton. By Charles Lever,.....................Cloth,	2 00
Kate O'Donoghue. By Charles Lever,......................Cloth,	2 00
Valentine Vox, the Ventriloquist. By Harry Cockton,......Cloth,	2 00

Above are each in cloth, or each one is in paper cover, at 75 cents each.

☞ **Above Books will be sent, postage paid, on receipt of Retail Price, by T. B. Peterson & Brothers, Philadelphia, Pa.**

T. B. PETERSON & BROTHERS' PUBLICATIONS. 7

NEW AND GOOD BOOKS BY BEST AUTHORS.

Beautiful Snow, and Other Poems. *New Illustrated Edition.* By J. W. Watson, author of "The Outcast and Other Poems." With Original Illustrations by Edward L. Henry. One volume, green morocco cloth, gilt top, side, and back, price $2.00; or in maroon morocco cloth, full gilt edges, full gilt back, full gilt sides, etc.,....... $3 00

The Outcast, and Other Poems. By J. W. Watson, author of "Beautiful Snow and Other Poems." One volume, green morocco cloth, gilt top, side and back, price $2.00; or in maroon morocco cloth, full gilt edges, full gilt back, full gilt sides, etc.,............. 3 00

Hans Breitmann's Ballads. By Charles G. Leland. *Volume One.* Containing "Hans Breitmann's Party, with Other Ballads," "Hans Breitmann About Town, and Other Ballads," and "Hans Breitmann In Church, and Other New Ballads," being the "*First*," "*Second*," and "*Third Series*" of the "*Breitmann Ballads*," bound in morocco cloth, gilt, beveled boards,... 3 00

Hans Breitmann's Ballads. By Charles G. Leland. *Volume Two.* Containing "Hans Breitmann as an Uhlan, with other New Ballads," and "Hans Breitmann's Travels in Europe, with Other New Ballads," being the "*Fourth*" and "*Fifth Series*" of the "*Breitmann Ballads*," bound in morocco cloth, gilt, beveled boards,.............. 2 00

Hans Breitmann's Ballads. By Charles G. Leland. Being the above two volumes complete in one. Containing all the Ballads written by "Hans Breitmann." Complete in one large volume, bound in morocco cloth, gilt side, gilt top, and full gilt back, with beveled boards. With a full and complete Glossary to the whole work,..... 4 00

Meister Karl's Sketch Book. By Charles G. Leland. (Hans Breitmann.) Complete in one volume, green morocco cloth, gilt side, gilt top, gilt back, with beveled boards, price $2.50, or in maroon morocco cloth, full gilt edges, full gilt back, full gilt sides, etc.,....... 3 50

John Jasper's Secret. A Sequel to Charles Dickens' "Mystery of Edwin Drood." With 18 Illustrations. Bound in cloth,........... 2 00

The Last Athenian. From the Swedish of Victor Rydberg. Highly recommended by Fredrika Bremer. Paper $1.50, or in cloth,...... 2 00

Across the Atlantic. Letters from France, Switzerland, Germany, Italy, and England. By C. H. Haeseler, M.D. Bound in cloth.... 2 00

The Ladies' Guide to True Politeness and Perfect Manners. By Miss Leslie. Every lady should have it. Cloth, full gilt back.... 1 75

The Ladies' Complete Guide to Needlework and Embroidery. With 113 illustrations. By Miss Lambert. Cloth, full gilt back,......... 1 75

The Ladies' Work Table Book. With 27 illustrations. Cloth, gilt,. 1 50

The Story of Elizabeth. By Miss Thackeray, paper $1.00, or cloth,... 1 50

Dow's Short Patent Sermons. By Dow, Jr. In 4 vols., cloth, each.... 1 50

Wild Oats Sown Abroad. A Spicy Book. By T. B. Witmer, cloth,.... 1 50

Aunt Patty's Scrap Bag. By Mrs. Caroline Lee Hentz, author of "Linda," etc. Full of Illustrations, and bound in cloth,............ 1 50

Hollick's Anatomy and Physiology of the Human Figure. Illustrated by a perfect dissected plate of the Human Organization, and by other separate plates of the Human Skeleton, such as Arteries, Veins, the Heart, Lungs, Trachea, etc. Illustrated. Bound,........ 2 00

Life and Adventures of Don Quixote and his Squire Sancho Panza, complete in one large volume, paper cover, for $1.00, or in cloth,.. 1 75

The Laws and Practice of the Game of Euchre. By a Professor. This is the book of the "Laws of Euchre," adopted and got up by the Euchre Club of Washington, D. C. Bound in cloth,............ 1 00

☞ Above Books will be sent, postage paid, on receipt of Retail Price, by T. B. Peterson & Brothers, Philadelphia, Pa.

8 T. B. PETERSON & BROTHERS' PUBLICATIONS.

NEW AND GOOD BOOKS BY BEST AUTHORS.

Treason at Home. A Novel. By Mrs. Greenough, cloth,	$1 75
Letters from Europe. By Colonel John W. Forney. Bound in cloth,	1 75
Moore's Life of Hon. Schuyler Colfax, with a Portrait on steel, cloth,	1 50
Whitefriars; or, The Days of Charles the Second. Illustrated,	1 00
Tan-go-ru-a. An Historical Drama, in Prose. By Mr. Moorhead,	1 00
The Impeachment Trial of President Andrew Johnson. Cloth,	1 50
Trial of the Assassins for the Murder of Abraham Lincoln. Cloth,	1 50
Lives of Jack Sheppard and Guy Fawkes. Illustrated. One vol., cloth,	1 75
Consuelo, and Countess of Rudolstadt. One volume, cloth,	2 00
Monsieur Antoine. By George Sand. Illustrated. One vol., cloth,	1 60
Frank Fairleigh. By author of "Lewis Arundel," cloth,	1 75
Lewis Arundel. By author of "Frank Fairleigh," cloth,	1 75
Aurora Floyd. By Miss Braddon. One vol., paper 75 cents, cloth,	1 00
Christy and White's Complete Ethiopian Melodies, bound in cloth,	1 00
The Life of Charles Dickens. By R. Shelton Mackenzie, cloth,	2 00
Poetical Works of Sir Walter Scott. One 8vo. volume, fine binding,	5 00
Life of Sir Walter Scott. By John G. Lockhart. With Portrait,	2 50
The Shakspeare Novels. Complete in one large octavo volume, cloth,	4 00
Miss Pardoe's Choice Novels. In one large octavo volume, cloth,	4 00
The Waverley Novels. *National Edition.* Five large 8vo. vols., cloth,	15 00
Charles Dickens' Works. *People's 12mo. Edition.* 21 vols., cloth,	32 00
Charles Dickens' Works. *Green Cloth 12mo. Edition.* 21 vols., cloth,	40 00
Charles Dickens' Works. *Illustrated 12mo. Edition.* 34 vols., cloth,	50 00
Charles Dickens' Works. *Illustrated 8vo. Edition.* 18 vols., cloth,	31 50
Charles Dickens' Works. *New National Edition.* 7 volumes, cloth,	20 00

HUMOROUS ILLUSTRATED WORKS.

Each one is full of Illustrations, by Felix O. C. Darley, and bound in Cloth.

Major Jones' Courtship and Travels. With 21 Illustrations,	$1 75
Major Jones' Scenes in Georgia. With 16 Illustrations,	1 75
Simon Suggs' Adventures and Travels. With 17 Illustrations,	1 75
Swamp Doctor's Adventures in the South-West. 14 Illustrations,	1 75
Col. Thorpe's Scenes in Arkansaw. With 16 Illustrations,	1 75
The Big Bear's Adventures and Travels. With 18 Illustrations,	1 75
High Life in New York, by Jonathan Slick. With Illustrations,	1 75
Judge Haliburton's Yankee Stories. Illustrated,	1 75
Harry Coverdale's Courtship and Marriage. Illustrated,	1 75
Piney Wood's Tavern; or, Sam Slick in Texas. Illustrated,	1 75
Sam Slick, the Clockmaker. By Judge Haliburton. Illustrated,	1 75
Humors of Falconbridge. By J. F. Kelley. With Illustrations,	1 75
Modern Chivalry. By Judge Breckenridge. Two vols., each	1 75
Neal's Charcoal Sketches. By Joseph C. Neal. 21 Illustrations,	2 50

CHARLES LEVER'S BEST WORKS.

Charles O'Malley,	75	Arthur O'Leary,	75
Harry Lorrequer,	75	Con Cregan,	75
Jack Hinton,	75	Davenport Dunn,	75
Tom Burke of Ours,	75	Horace Templeton,	75
Knight of Gwynne,	75	Kate O'Donoghue,	75

Above are in paper cover, or a fine edition in cloth at $2.00 each.

A Rent in a Cloud, 50	St. Patrick's Eve, 50

Ten Thousand a Year, in one volume, paper cover, $1.50; or in cloth, 2 00
The Diary of a Medical Student, by author "Ten Thousand a Year," 75

☞ Above Books will be sent, postage paid, on receipt of Retail Price, by T. B. Peterson & Brothers, Philadelphia, Pa.

DUMAS', REYNOLDS', AND OTHER BOOKS IN CLOTH.

The following are cloth editions of the following good books, and they are each issued in one large volume, bound in cloth, price $1.75 each.

The Three Guardsmen; or, The Three Mousquetaires. By A. Dumas,	$1 75
Twenty Years After; or the "*Second Series of Three Guardsmen,*"...	1 75
Bragelonno; Son of Athos; or "*Third Series of Three Guardsmen,*"	1 75
The Iron Mask; or the "*Fourth Series of The Three Guardsmen,*"....	1 75
Louise La Valliere; or the "*Fifth Series and End of the Three Guardsmen Series,*"	1 75
The Memoirs of a Physician. By Alexander Dumas. Illustrated,....	1 75
Queen's Necklace; or "*Second Series of Memoirs of a Physician,*"	1 75
Six Years Later; or the "*Third Series of Memoirs of a Physician,*"	1 75
Countess of Charny; or "*Fourth Series of Memoirs of a Physician,*"	1 75
Andree De Taverney; or "*Fifth Series of Memoirs of a Physician,*"	1 75
The Chevalier; or the "*Sixth Series and End of the Memoirs of a Physician Series,*"	1 75
The Adventures of a Marquis. By Alexander Dumas..	1 75
Edmond Dantes. A Sequel to the "Count of Monte-Cristo,".........	1 75
The Forty-Five Guardsmen. By Alexander Dumas. Illustrated,...	1 75
Diana of Meridor, or Lady of Monsoreau. By Alexander Dumas,...	1 75
The Iron Hand. By Alex. Dumas, author of "Count of Monte-Cristo,"	1 75
The Mysteries of the Court of London. By George W. M. Reynolds,	1 75
Rose Foster; or the "*Second Series of Mysteries of Court of London,*"	1 75
Caroline of Brunswick; or the "*Third Series of the Court of London,*"	1 75
Venetia Trelawney; or "*End of the Mysteries of the Court of London,*"	1 75
Lord Saxondale; or the Court of Queen Victoria. By Reynolds,.....	1 75
Count Christoval. Sequel to "Lord Saxondale." By Reynolds,......	1 75
Rosa Lambert; or Memoirs of an Unfortunate Woman. By Reynolds,	1 75
Mary Price; or the Adventures of a Servant Maid. By Reynolds,...	1 75
Eustace Quentin. Sequel to "Mary Price." By G. W. M. Reynolds,	1 75
Joseph Wilmot; or the Memoirs of a Man Servant. By Reynolds,...	1 75
Banker's Daughter. Sequel to "Joseph Wilmot." By Reynolds,......	1 75
Kenneth. A Romance of the Highlands. By G. W. M. Reynolds,..	1 75
Rye-House Plot; or the Conspirator's Daughter. By Reynolds,......	1 75
Necromancer; or the Times of Henry the Eighth. By Reynolds,.....	1 75
Within the Maze. By Mrs. Henry Wood, author of "East Lynne,".	1 75
Dene Hollow. By Mrs. Henry Wood, author of "Within the Maze,"	1 75
Bessy Rane. By Mrs. Henry Wood, author of "The Channings,"....	1 75
George Canterbury's Will. By Mrs. Wood, author of "Oswald Cray,"	1 75
The Channings. By Mrs. Henry Wood, author of "Dene Hollow,"...	1 75
Roland Yorke. A Sequel to "The Channings." By Mrs. Wood,......	1 75
Shadow of Ashlydyatt. By Mrs. Wood, author of "Bessy Rane,".....	1 75
Lord Oakburn's Daughters; or The Earl's Heirs. By Mrs. Wood,...	1 75
Verner's Pride. By Mrs. Henry Wood, author of "The Channings,"	1 75
The Castle's Heir; or Lady Adelaide's Oath. By Mrs. Henry Wood,	1 75
Oswald Cray. By Mrs. Henry Wood, author of "Roland Yorke,"....	1 75
Squire Trevlyn's Heir; or Trevlyn Hold. By Mrs. Henry Wood,.....	1 75
The Red Court Farm. By Mrs. Wood, author of "Verner's Pride,"...	1 75
Lister's Folly. By Mrs. Henry Wood, author of "Castle's Heir,"....	1 75
St. Martin's Eve. By Mrs. Henry Wood, author of "Dene Hollow,"	1 75
Mildred Arkell. By Mrs. Henry Wood, author of "East Lynne,"....	1 75
Cyrilla; or the Mysterious Engagement. By author of "Initials,"	1 75
The Miser's Daughter. By William Harrison Ainsworth, ...	1 75
The Mysteries of Florence. By Geo. Lippard, author "Quaker City,"	1 75

☞ Above Books will be sent, postage paid, on receipt of Retail Price, by T. B. Peterson & Brothers, Philadelphia, Pa.

CHARLES DICKENS' WORKS.
GREAT REDUCTION IN THEIR PRICES.

PEOPLE'S DUODECIMO EDITION. ILLUSTRATED.
Reduced in price from $2.50 to $1.50 a volume.
This edition is printed on fine paper, from large, clear type, leaded, that all can read, containing Two Hundred Illustrations on tinted paper.

Our Mutual Friend,......Cloth, $1.50	Little Dorrit,............Cloth, $1.50
Pickwick Papers,.........Cloth, 1.50	Dombey and Son,........Cloth, 1.50
Nicholas Nickleby,......Cloth, 1.50	Christmas Stories,......Cloth, 1.50
Great Expectations,.....Cloth, 1.50	Sketches by "Boz,".....Cloth, 1.50
David Copperfield,......Cloth, 1.50	Barnaby Rudge,.........Cloth, 1.50
Oliver Twist,............Cloth, 1.50	Martin Chuzzlewit,......Cloth, 1.50
Bleak House,............Cloth, 1.50	Old Curiosity Shop,.....Cloth, 1.50
A Tale of Two Cities,...Cloth, 1.50	Dickens' New Stories,..Cloth, 1.50

Mystery of Edwin Drood; and Master Humphrey's Clock,......Cloth, 1.50
American Notes; and the Uncommercial Traveller,............Cloth, 1.50
Hunted Down; and other Reprinted Pieces,....................Cloth, 1.50
The Holly-Tree Inn; and other Stories,......................Cloth, 1.50
The Life and Writings of Charles Dickens,...................Cloth, 2.00
Price of a set, in Black cloth, in twenty-one volumes,..............$32.00
   "   "   Full sheep, Library style,.............................. 42.50
   "   "   Half calf, sprinkled edges,............................ 53.00
   "   "   Half calf, marbled edges,.............................. 58.00
   "   "   Half calf, antique, or half calf, full gilt backs, etc. 63.00

GREEN MOROCCO CLOTH, DUODECIMO EDITION.
This is the "People's Duodecimo Edition" in a new style of Binding, in Green Morocco Cloth, Bevelled Boards, Full Gilt descriptive back, and Medallion Portrait on sides in gilt, in Twenty-one handy volumes, 12mo., fine paper, large clear type, and Two Hundred Illustrations on tinted paper. Price $40 a set, and each set put up in a neat and strong box. This is the handsomest and best edition ever published for the price.

ILLUSTRATED DUODECIMO EDITION.
Reduced in price from $2.00 to $1.50 a volume.
This edition is printed on the finest paper, from large, clear type, leaded, that all can read, containing Six Hundred full page Illustrations, on tinted paper, from designs by Cruikshank, Phiz, Browne, Maclise, McLenan, and other artists. This is the only edition published that contains all the original illustrations, as selected by Mr. Charles Dickens.

The following are each contained in two volumes.

Our Mutual Friend,......Cloth, $3.00	Bleak House,............Cloth, $3.00
Pickwick Papers,.........Cloth, 3.00	Sketches by "Boz,".....Cloth, 3.00
Tale of Two Cities,......Cloth, 3.00	Barnaby Rudge,.........Cloth, 3.00
Nicholas Nickleby,......Cloth, 3.00	Martin Chuzzlewit,......Cloth, 3.00
David Copperfield,......Cloth, 3.00	Old Curiosity Shop,.....Cloth, 3.00
Oliver Twist,............Cloth, 3.00	Little Dorrit,............Cloth, 3.00
Christmas Stories,......Cloth, 3.00	Dombey and Son.........Cloth, 3.00

The following are each complete in one volume.

Great Expectations..............$1.50 | Dickens' New Stories,...Cloth, $1.50
Mystery of Edwin Drood; and Master Humphrey's Clock,....Cloth, 1.50
American Notes; and the Uncommercial Traveller,..........Cloth, 1.50
Hunted Down; and other Reprinted Pieces,..................Cloth, 1.50
The Holly-Tree Inn; and other Stories,....................Cloth, 1.50
The Life and Writings of Charles Dickens,.................Cloth, 2.00
Price of a set, in thirty-five volumes, bound in cloth,............$50.00
   "   "   Full sheep, Library style,.............................. 68.00
   "   "   Half calf, antique, or half calf, full gilt backs, etc. 100.00

CHARLES DICKENS' WORKS.
GREAT REDUCTION IN THEIR PRICES.

ILLUSTRATED OCTAVO EDITION.
Reduced in price from $2.50 to $1.75 a volume.

This edition is printed from large type, double column, octavo page, each book being complete in one volume, the whole containing near Six Hundred Illustrations, by Cruikshank, Phiz, Browne, Maclise, and other artists.

Our Mutual Friend,......Cloth, $1.75	David Copperfield,.......Cloth, $1.75
Pickwick Papers,..........Cloth, 1.75	Barnaby Rudge,...........Cloth, 1.75
Nicholas Nickleby,......Cloth, 1.75	Martin Chuzzlewit,......Cloth, 1.75
Great Expectations,......Cloth, 1.75	Old Curiosity Shop,......Cloth, 1.75
Lamplighter's Story,....Cloth, 1.75	Christmas Stories,.......Cloth, 1.75
Oliver Twist,..............Cloth, 1.75	Dickens' New Stories,...Cloth, 1.75
Bleak House,..............Cloth, 1.75	A Tale of Two Cities,....Cloth, 1.75
Little Dorrit,...............Cloth, 1.75	American Notes and
Dombey and Son,........Cloth, 1.75	Pic-Nic Papers,........Cloth, 1.75
Sketches by "Boz,".....Cloth, 1.75	

Price of a set, in Black cloth, in eighteen volumes,.....................$31.50
    "   "   Full sheep, Library style,................................ 40.00
    "   "   Half calf, sprinkled edges,............................. 48.00
    "   "   Half calf, marbled edges,............................... 54.00
    "   "   Half calf, antique, or Half calf, full gilt backs,... 60.00

"NEW NATIONAL EDITION" OF DICKENS' WORKS.

This is the cheapest bound edition of the works of Charles Dickens, published, all his writings being contained in *seven large octavo volumes*, with a portrait of Charles Dickens, and other illustrations.

Price of a set, in Black cloth, in seven volumes,.....................$20.00
    "   "   Full sheep, Library style,................................ 25.00
    "   "   Half calf, antique, or Half calf, full gilt backs,... 30.00

CHEAP PAPER COVER EDITION.
Each book being complete in one large octavo volume.

Pickwick Papers,............................	35	Our Mutual Friend,................	35
Nicholas Nickleby,.........................	35	Bleak House,.......................	35
Dombey and Son,...........................	35	Little Dorrit,........................	35
David Copperfield,..........................	25	Christmas Stories,.................	25
Martin Chuzzlewit,..........................	35	The Haunted House,...............	25
Old Curiosity Shop,.........................	25	Uncommercial Traveller,..........	25
Oliver Twist,...................................	25	A House to Let,.....................	25
American Notes,.............................	25	Perils of English Prisoners,......	25
Great Expectations,........................	25	Wreck of the Golden Mary,......	25
Hard Times,...................................	25	Tom Tiddler's Ground,.............	25
A Tale of Two Cities,.......................	25	Joseph Grimaldi,...................	50
Somebody's Luggage,.....................	25	The Pic-Nic Papers,................	50
Message from the Sea,...................	25	Hunted Down,......................	25
Barnaby Rudge,.............................	25	The Holly-Tree Inn,................	25
Sketches by "Boz,".........................	25	No Thoroughfare....................	25

Mystery of Edwin Drood. Charles Dickens' last work,..................... 25
Mrs. Lirriper's Lodgings and Mrs. Lirriper's Legacy,....................... 25
Mugby Junction and Dr. Marigold's Prescriptions,......................... 25

THE LIFE AND WRITINGS OF CHARLES DICKENS.

THE LIFE OF CHARLES DICKENS. By *Dr. R. Shelton Mackenzie*, containing a full history of his Life, his Uncollected Pieces, in Prose and Verse; Personal Recollections and Anecdotes; His Last Will in full; and Letters from Mr. Dickens never before published. With a Portrait and Autograph of Charles Dickens. Price Two Dollars.

ALEXANDER DUMAS' WORKS.

Count of Monte-Cristo,	$1 50	Memoirs of a Physician,	$1 00
Edmond Dantes,	75	Queen's Necklace,	1 00
The Three Guardsmen,	75	Six Years Later,	1 00
Twenty Years After,	75	Countess of Charny,	1 00
Bragelonne,	75	Andree de Taverney,	1 00
The Iron Mask,	1 00	The Chevalier,	1 00
Louise La Valliere,	1 00	Forty-five Guardsmen,	1 00
Diana of Meridor,	1 00	The Iron Hand,	75
Adventures of a Marquis,	1 00	The Conscript,	1 50
Love and Liberty,	1 50	Countess of Monte-Cristo,	1 00
Camille; or, The Fate of a Coquette, (La Dame Aux Camelias,)			1 50

The above are each in paper cover, or in cloth, price $1.75 each.

The Fallen Angel,	75	The Black Tulip,	50
Felina de Chambure,	75	The Corsican Brothers,	50
The Horrors of Paris,	75	The Count of Moret,	50
Sketches in France,	75	Mohicans of Paris,	50
Isabel of Bavaria,	75	The Marriage Verdict,	50
Twin Lieutenants,	75	Buried Alive,	25
Man with Five Wives,	75	Annette; or, Lady of Pearls,	50
George; or, The Planter of the Isle of France,			50

GEORGE W. M. REYNOLDS' WORKS.

Mysteries Court of London,	$1 00	Mary Price,	$1 00
Rose Foster,	1 50	Eustace Quentin,	1 00
Caroline of Brunswick,	1 00	Joseph Wilmot,	1 00
Venetia Trelawney,	1 00	Banker's Daughter,	1 00
Lord Saxondale,	1 00	Kenneth,	1 00
Count Christoval,	1 00	The Rye-House Plot,	1 00
Rosa Lambert,	1 00	The Necromancer,	1 00

The above are each in paper cover, or in cloth, price $1.75 each.

The Opera Dancer,	75	The Soldier's Wife,	75
Child of Waterloo,	75	May Middleton,	75
Robert Bruce,	75	Ellen Percy,	75
The Gipsy Chief,	75	Agnes Evelyn,	75
Mary Stuart, Queen of Scots,	75	Pickwick Abroad,	75
Wallace, Hero of Scotland,	1 00	Parricide,	75
Isabella Vincent,	75	Discarded Queen,	75
Vivian Bertram,	75	Life in Paris,	50
Countess of Lascelles,	75	Countess and the Page,	50
Duke of Marchmont,	75	Edgar Montrose,	50
Massacre of Glencoe,	75	The Ruined Gamester,	50
Loves of the Harem,	75	Clifford and the Actress,	50
Queen Joanna; or the Mysteries of the Court of Naples,			75
Ciprina; or, the Secrets of a Picture Gallery,			50

MISS PARDOE'S POPULAR WORKS.

Confessions of a Pretty Woman,	75	The Rival Beauties,	75
The Wife's Trials,	75	Romance of the Harem,	75
The Jealous Wife,	50		

The five above books are also bound in one volume, cloth, for $4.00.

The Adopted Heir. One volume, paper, $1.50; or in cloth, $1 75
The Earl's Secret. One volume, paper, $1.50; or in cloth, 1 75

☞ Above books will be sent, postage paid, on receipt of Retail Price, by T. B. Peterson & Brothers, Philadelphia, Pa.

MRS. HENRY WOOD'S BEST BOOKS.

Within the Maze,	$1 50	Shadow of Ashlydyat,	$1 50
Dene Hollow,	1 50	Oswald Cray,	1 50
Bessy Rane,	1 50	Mildred Arkell,	1 50
George Canterbury's Will,	1 50	Red Court Farm,	1 50
Verner's Pride,	1 50	Elster's Folly,	1 50
The Channings,	1 50	St. Martin's Eve,	1 50
Roland Yorke. A Sequel to "The Channings,"			1 50
Lord Oakburn's Daughters; or, The Earl's Heirs,			1 50
The Castle's Heir; or, Lady Adelaide's Oath,			1 50
Squire Trevlyn's Heir; or, Trevlyn Hold,			1 50.

The above are each in paper cover, or in cloth, price $1.75 each.

The Mystery,	75	A Life's Secret,	50
The Lost Bank Note,	75	The Haunted Tower,	50
The Lost Will,	50	The Runaway Match,	50
Orville College,	50	Foggy Night at Offord,	25
A Light and a Dark Christmas,	25	William Allair,	25

EUGENE SUE'S GREAT WORKS.

Wandering Jew,	$1 50	First Love,	50
Mysteries of Paris,	1 50	Woman's Love,	50
Martin, the Foundling,	1 50	Female Bluebeard,	50
Above are in cloth at $2.00 each.		Man-of-War's-Man,	50
Life and Adventures of Raoul de Surville. A Tale of the Empire,			25

MADAME GEORGE SAND'S WORKS.

Consuelo, 12mo., cloth,	$1 50	Jealousy, 12mo. cloth,	$1 50
Countess of Rudolstadt,	1 50	Indiana, 12mo., cloth,	1 50

Above are only published in 12mo., cloth, gilt side and back.

Fanchon, the Cricket, price $1.00 in paper, or in cloth,			1 50
First and True Love,	75	The Corsair,	50
Simon. A Love Story,	50	The Last Aldini,	50
Monsieur Antoine. With 11 Illustrations. Paper, 75 cents; cloth,			1 00
Consuelo and Countess of Rudolstadt, octavo, cloth,			2 00

CHARLES J. PETERSON'S WORKS.

The Old Stone Mansion,	$1 50	Kate Aylesford,	$1 50

The above are each in paper cover, or in cloth, price $1.75 each.

Cruising in the Last War,	75	Grace Dudley; or, Arnold at	
Valley Farm,	25	Saratoga,	50

WILLIAM H. MAXWELL'S WORKS.

Wild Sports of the West,	75	Brian O'Lynn,	75
Stories of Waterloo,	75	Life of Grace O'Malley,	50

MISS BRADDON'S WORKS.

Aurora Floyd,	75	The Lawyer's Secret,	25
Aurora Floyd, cloth	1 00	For Better, For Worse,	75

D'ISRAELI'S WORKS.

Henrietta Temple,	50	Contarini Fleming,	50
Miriam Alroy,	50		

☞ Above books will be sent, postage paid, on receipt of Retail Price, by T. B. Peterson & Brothers, Philadelphia, Pa.

HUMOROUS AMERICAN WORKS.
Beautifully Illustrated by Felix O. C. Darley.

Major Jones' Courtship,	75	Drama in Pokerville,	75
Major Jones' Travels,	75	The Quorndon Hounds,	75
Simon Suggs' Adventures and Travels,	75	My Shooting Box,	75
		Warwick Woodlands,	75
Major Jones' Chronicles of Pineville,	75	The Deer Stalkers,	75
		Peter Ploddy,	75
Polly Peablossom's Wedding,	75	Adventures of Captain Farrago,	75
Mysteries of the Backwoods,	75	Major O'Regan's Adventures,	75
Widow Rugby's Husband,	75	Sol. Smith's Theatrical Apprenticeship,	75
Big Bear of Arkansas,	75		
Western Scenes; or, Life on the Prairie,	75	Sol. Smith's Theatrical Journey-Work,	75
Streaks of Squatter Life,	75	The Quarter Race in Kentucky,	75
Pickings from the Picayune,	75	Aunt Patty's Scrap Bag,	75
Stray Subjects, Arrested and Bound Over,	75	Percival Mayberry's Adventures and Travels,	75
Louisiana Swamp Doctor,	75	Sam Slick's Yankee Yarns and Yankee Letters,	75
Charcoal Sketches,	75		
Misfortunes of Peter Faber,	75	Adventures of Fudge Fumble,	75
Yankee among the Mermaids,	75	American Joe Miller,	50
New Orleans Sketch Book,	75	Following the Drum,	50

FRANK FAIRLEGH'S WORKS.

Frank Fairlegh,	75	Harry Racket Scapegrace,	75
Lewis Arundel,	75	Tom Racquet,	75

Finer editions of the above are also issued in cloth, at $1.75 each.

Harry Coverdale's Courtship, 1 50 | Lorrimer Littlegood, 1 50
The above are each in paper cover, or in cloth, price $1.75 each.

WILLIAM HARRISON AINSWORTH'S WORKS.

Life of Jack Sheppard,	50	Tower of London,	$1 50
Life of Guy Fawkes,	75	Miser's Daughter,	1 00
Court of the Stuarts,	75	Above are in cloth, at $1.75 each.	
Windsor Castle,	75	Life of Grace O'Malley,	50
The Star Chamber,	75	Desperadoes of the New World,	50
Old St. Paul's,	75	Life of Henry Thomas,	25
Court of Queen Anne,	50	Life of Ninon De L'Enclos,	25
Life of Dick Turpin,	50	Life of Arthur Spring,	25
Life of Davy Crockett,	50	Life of Mrs. Whipple,	25

Lives of Jack Sheppard and Guy Fawkes, in one volume, cloth, 1 75

MISS ELLEN PICKERING'S WORKS.

The Grumbler,	75	Who Shall be Heir?,	38
Marrying for Money,	75	The Squire,	38
Poor Cousin,	50	Ellen Wareham,	38
Kate Walsingham,	50	Nan Darrel,	38
Orphan Niece,	50		

SAMUEL WARREN'S BEST BOOKS.

Ten Thousand a Year, paper, $1 50 | The Diary of a Medical Student, 75
Ten Thousand a Year, cloth, 2 00 |

☞ Above Books will be sent, postage paid, on receipt of Retail Price, by T. B. Peterson & Brothers, Philadelphia, Pa.

T. B. PETERSON & BROTHERS' PUBLICATIONS. 15

T. S. ARTHUR'S HOUSEHOLD NOVELS.

The Lost Bride,	50	The Divorced Wife,	50
The Two Brides,	50	Pride and Prudence,	50
Love in a Cottage,	50	Agnes; or, the Possessed,	50
Love in High Life,	50	Lucy Sandford,	50
Year after Marriage,	50	The Banker's Wife,	50
The Lady at Home,	50	The Two Merchants,	50
Cecilia Howard,	50	Trial and Triumph,	50
Orphan Children,	50	The Iron Rule,	50
Debtor's Daughter,	50	Insubordination; or, the Shoe-	
Mary Moreton,	50	maker's Daughters,	50

Six Nights with the Washingtonians; and other Temperance Tales. By T. S. Arthur. With original Illustrations, by George Cruikshank. One large octavo volume, bound in beveled boards, price...$3.50
Lizzy Glenn; or, the Trials of a Seamstress. Cloth $1.75; or paper, 1.50

MRS. GREY'S CELEBRATED NOVELS.

Cousin Harry, ...$1 50 | The Little Beauty, ...$1 50
The above are each in paper cover, or in cloth, price $1.75 each.

A Marriage in High Life,	50	The Baronet's Daughters,	50
Gipsy's Daughter,	50	Young Prima Donna	50
Old Dower House,	50	Hyacinthe,	25
Belle of the Family,	50	Alice Seymour,	25
Duke and Cousin,	50	Mary Seaham,	75
The Little Wife,	50	Passion and Principle,	75
Lena Cameron,	50	The Flirt,	75
Sybil Lennard,	50	Good Society,	75
Manœuvring Mother	50	Lion-Hearted,	75

G. P. R. JAMES'S BEST BOOKS.

Lord Montague's Page, ...$1 50 | The Cavalier $1 50
The above are each in paper cover, or in cloth, price $1.75 each.

The Man in Black,	75	Arrah Neil,	75
Mary of Burgundy,	75	Eva St. Clair,	50

CAPTAIN MARRYATT'S WORKS.

Jacob Faithful,	50	Newton Forster,	50
Japhet in Search of a Father,	50	King's Own,	50
Phantom Ship,	50	Pirate and Three Cutters,	50
Midshipman Easy,	50	Peter Simple,	50
Pacha of Many Tales,	50	Percival Keene,	50
Frank Mildmay, Naval Officer,	50	Poor Jack,	50
Snarleyow,	50	Sea King,	50

REVOLUTIONARY TALES.

The Brigand,	50	Old Put; or, Days of 1776,	50
Ralph Runnion,	50	Legends of Mexico,	50
Seven Brothers of Wyoming,	50	Grace Dudley,	50
The Rebel Bride,	50	The Guerilla Chief,	75
The Flying Artillerist,	50	The Quaker Soldier, paper,	1 50
Wau-nan-gee,	50	do. do. cloth,	1 75

J. F. SMITH'S WORKS.

The Usurer's Victim; or, Thomas Balscombe,	75	Adelaide Waldegrave; or, the Trials of a Governess,	75

☞ Above books will be sent, postage paid, on Receipt of Retail Price, by T. B. Peterson & Brothers, Philadelphia, Pa.

GEORGE LIPPARD'S GREAT BOOKS.

The Quaker City,	$1 50	The Empire City,	75
Paul Ardenheim,	1 50	Memoirs of a Preacher,	75
Blanche of Brandywine,	1 50	The Nazarene,	75
Washington and his Generals; or, Legends of the American Revolution,	1 50	Washington and his Men, Legends of Mexico, The Entranced,	75 50 25
Mysteries of Florence,	1 00	The Robbers,	25
Above in cloth at $2.00 each.		The Bank Director's Son,	25

EXCITING SEA TALES.

Adventures of Ben Brace,	75	Gallant Tom,	50
Jack Adams, the Mutineer,	75	Harry Helm,	50
Jack Ariel's Adventures,	75	Harry Tempest,	50
Petrel; or, Life on the Ocean,	75	Rebel and Rover,	50
Life of Paul Periwinkle,	75	Man-of-War's-Man,	50
Life of Tom Bowling,	75	Dark Shades of City Life,	25
Percy Effingham,	75	The Rats of the Seine,	25
Cruising in the Last War,	75	Charles Ransford,	25
Red King,	50	The Iron Cross,	25
The Corsair,	50	The River Pirates,	25
The Doomed Ship,	50	The Pirate's Son,	25
The Three Pirates,	50	Jacob Faithful,	50
The Flying Dutchman,	50	Phantom Ship,	50
The Flying Yankee,	50	Midshipman Easy,	50
The Yankee Middy,	50	Pacha of Many Tales,	50
The Gold Seekers,	50	Naval Officer,	50
The King's Cruisers,	50	Snarleyow,	50
Life of Alexander Tardy,	50	Newton Forster,	50
Red Wing,	50	King's Own,	50
Yankee Jack,	50	Japhet,	50
Yankees in Japan,	50	Pirate and Three Cutters,	50
Morgan, the Buccaneer,	50	Peter Simple,	50
Jack Junk,	50	Percival Keene,	50
Davis, the Pirate,	50	Poor Jack,	50
Valdez, the Pirate,	50	Sea King,	50

MILITARY NOVELS. BY BEST AUTHORS.
With Illuminated Military Covers, in five Colors.

Charles O'Malley,	75	The Three Guardsmen,	75
Jack Hinton, the Guardsman,	75	Twenty Years After,	75
The Knight of Gwynne,	75	Bragelonne, Son of Athos,	75
Harry Lorrequer,	75	Tom Bowling's Adventures,	75
Tom Burke of Ours,	75	Life of Robert Bruce,	75
Arthur O'Leary,	75	The Gipsy Chief,	75
Con Cregan,	75	Massacre of Glencoe,	75
Kate O'Donoghue,	75	Life of Guy Fawkes,	75
Horace Templeton,	75	Child of Waterloo,	75
Davenport Dunn,	75	Adventures of Ben Brace,	75
Jack Adams' Adventures,	75	Life of Jack Ariel,	75
Valentine Vox,	75	Forty-five Guardsmen,	1 00
Twin Lieutenants,	75	Wallace, the Hero of Scotland,	1 00
Stories of Waterloo,	75	Following the Drum,	50
The Soldier's Wife,	75	The Conscript, a Tale of War.	
Guerilla Chief,	75	By Alexander Dumas,	1 50

☞ Above Books will be sent, postage paid, on receipt of Retail Price, by T. B. Peterson & Brothers, Philadelphia, Pa.

HARRY COCKTON'S WORKS.

Valentine Vox, Ventriloquist,...	75	The Fatal Marriage,..............	75
Valentine Vox, cloth,.............	2 00	The Steward,......................	75
Sylvester Sound,..................	75	Percy Effingham,.................	75
The Love Match,..................	75	The Prince,.......................	75

GUSTAVE AIMARD'S WORKS.

The Prairie Flower,...............	75	Trapper's Daughter,.............	75
The Indian Scout,.................	75	The Tiger Slayer,................	75
The Trail Hunter,.................	75	The Gold Seekers,...............	75
The Indian Chief,.................	75	The Rebel Chief,................	75
The Red Track,...................	75	The Border Rifles,..............	75
The White Scalper,...............	50	Pirates of the Prairies,.........	75
The Freebooters,.................	50		

HENRY MORFORD'S AMERICAN NOVELS.

Shoulder-Straps,...........	$1 50	The Days of Shoddy. A History of the late War,......	$1 50
The Coward,................	1 50		

Above are each in paper cover, or each one is in cloth, price $1.75 each.

LIVES OF NOTED HIGHWAYMEN, ETC.

Life of John A. Murrel,........	50	Life of Davy Crockett,...........	50
Life of Joseph T. Hare,........	50	Life of Sybil Grey................	50
Life of Col. Monroe Edwards,	50	Life of Jonathan Wild,...........	25
Life of Jack Sheppard,.........	50	Life of Henry Thomas,...........	25
Life of Jack Rann,.............	50	Life of Arthur Spring,...........	25
Life of Dick Turpin,...........	50	Life of Jack Ketch,..............	25
Life of Helen Jewett,..........	50	Life of Ninon De L'Enclos,.....	25
Desperadoes of the New World,	50	Lives of the Felons,.............	25
Mysteries of New Orleans,.....	50	Life of Mrs. Whipple,............	25
The Robber's Wife,.............	50	Life of Biddy Woodhull,........	25
Obi; or, Three Fingered Jack,	50	Life of Mother Brownrigg,......	25
Kit Clayton,...................	50	Dick Parker, the Pirate,.........	25
Life of Tom Waters,............	50	Life of Mary Bateman,...........	25
Nat Blake,.....................	50	Life of Captain Blood...........	25
Bill Horton,...................	50	Capt. Blood and the Beagles,...	25
Galloping Gus,.................	50	Sixteen-Stringed Jack's Fight for Life,.......................	25
Life & Trial of Antoine Probst,	50		
Ned Hastings,..................	50	Highwayman's Avenger,.........	25
Eveleen Wilson,................	50	Life of Raoul De Surville.......	25
Diary of a Pawnbroker,.........	50	Life of Rody the Rover.........	25
Silver and Pewter,.............	50	Life of Galloping Dick,.........	25
Sweeney Todd,..................	50	Life of Guy Fawkes,............	75
Life of Grace O'Malley,........	50	Life and Adventures of Vidocq,	1 50

LIEBIG'S WORKS ON CHEMISTRY.

Agricultural Chemistry,........	25	Liebig's celebrated Letters on the Potato Disease,............	25
Animal Chemistry,.............	25		

Liebig's Complete Works on Chemistry, is also issued in one large octavo volume, bound in cloth. Price Two Dollars.

MILITARY AND ARMY BOOKS.

Ellsworth's Zouave Drill,......	25	U. S. Light Infantry Drill,.....	25
U. S. Government Infantry & Rifle Tactics,..................	25	The Soldier's Companion,......	25
		The Soldier's Guide,...........	25

☞ Above Books will be sent, postage paid, on Receipt of Retail Price, by T. B. Peterson & Brothers, Philadelphia, Pa.

18 T. B. PETERSON & BROTHERS' PUBLICATIONS.

WORKS AT 75 CENTS. BY BEST AUTHORS.

The Brigand; or, the Demon of the North. By Victor Hugo,..........	75
Cyrilla; or, The Mysterious Engagement. By the author of "The Initials." Cloth, $1.75; or bound in paper cover, for.....	75
The Red Indians of Newfoundland. Illustrated,..........................	75
Webster and Hayne's Speeches in Reply to Colonel Foote,............	75
Roanoke; or, Where is Utopia? By C. H. Wiley. Illustrated,......	75

The Banditti of the Prairie,...	75	Flirtations in America............	75
Tom Racquet,.....................	75	The Coquette,.....................	75
Salathiel, by Croly,..............	75	Thackeray's Irish Sketch Book,	75
Corinne; or, Italy,................	75	Whitehall,........................	75
Ned Musgrave.....................	75	The Beautiful Nun,...............	75
Aristocracy, ...	75	Mysteries of Three Cities,......	75
Popping the Question,..........	75	Genevra. By Miss Fairfield,..	75
Paul Periwinkle,..................	75	Crock of Gold. By Tupper,...	75
The Inquisition in Spain,.......	75	Twins and Heart. By Tupper,	75
Elsie's Married Life,.............	75	New Hope; or, the Rescue,.....	75
Leyton Hall. By Mark Lemon,	75	Nothing to Say,...................	75

Hans Breitmann's Party. With other Ballads. By Charles G. Leland,	75
Hans Breitmann In Church, with other Ballads. By C. G. Leland,	75
Hans Breitmann about Town, with other Ballads. By C. G. Leland,	75
Hans Breitmann as an Uhlan, and other New Ballads,..............	75
Hans Breitmann In Europe with other New Ballads,................	75

WORKS AT 50 CENTS. BY BEST AUTHORS.

Leah; or the Forsaken,.........	50	Kate Kennedy,...................	50
The Greatest Plague of Life,..	50	The Admiral's Daughter,......	50
Clifford and the Actress,........	50	The American Joe Miller,......	50
The Two Lovers,.................	50	Ella Stratford,...................	50
The Orphans and Caleb Field,.	50	Josephine, by Grace Aguilar,..	50
Moreton Hall,.....................	50	The Fortune Hunter,...........	50
Bell Brandon,.....................	50	The Orphan Sisters,.............	50
Sybil Grey,........................	50	Abednego, the Money Lender,.	50
Female Life in New York,......	50	Jenny Ambrose,..................	50
Agnes Grey,.......................	50	Train's Union Speeches,........	50
Diary of a Physician,............	50	The Romish Confessional,......	50
The Emigrant Squire,...........	50	Victims of Amusements,.......	50
The Monk, by Lewis,............	50	Ladies' Work Table Book,.....	50
The Beautiful French Girl,...	50	Life of Antoine Probst,.........	50
Father Clement, paper,.........	50	Alieford, a Family History,.. .	50
do. do. cloth,........	75	General Scott's $5 Portrait,...	1 00
Miser's Heir, paper,.............	50	Henry Clay's $5 Portrait,.....	1 00
do. do. cloth, ...	75	Portrait of Schuyler Colfax,...	50

The Woman in Red. A Companion to the "Woman in Black,".......	50
Twelve Months of Matrimony. By Emelie F. Carlen,................	50
Ryan's Mysteries of Love, Courtship, and Marriage,................	50
Robert Oaklands; or, the Outcast Orphan,............	50
Father Tom and the Pope, in cloth gilt, 75 cents, or paper,........	50

REV. CHARLES WADSWORTH'S SERMONS.

America's Mission,................	25	A Thanksgiving Sermon,.......	15
Thankfulness and Character,..	25	Politics in Religion,.............	12

Henry Ward Beecher on War and Emancipation,....................	15
Rev. William T. Brantley's Union Sermon,............	15

☞ **Above Books will be sent, postage paid, on receipt of Retail Price, by T. B. Peterson & Brothers, Philadelphia, Pa.**

T. B. PETERSON & BROTHERS' PUBLICATIONS.

WORKS AT 25 CENTS. BY BEST AUTHORS.

Aunt Margaret's Trouble,	25	The Nobleman's Daughter,	25
The Grey Woman,	25	Ghost Stories. Illustrated,	25
The Deformed,	25	Ladies' Science of Etiquette,	25
Two Prima Donnas,	25	The Abbey of Innismoyle,	25
The Mysterious Marriage,	25	Gliddon's Ancient Egypt.	25
Jack Downing's Letters,	25	Philip in Search of a Wife,	25
The Mysteries of a Convent,	25	Rifle Shots,	25
Rose Warrington,	25	Rody the Rover,	25
The Iron Cross,	25	The Sower's Reward,	25
Charles Ransford,	25	The Courtier,	25
The Mysteries of Bedlam,	25	G. F. Train and the Fenians,	25
Madison's Exposition of Odd Fellowship. Illustrated,			25
The Iniquities and Barbarities Practiced at Rome,			25
Comic Life of Billy Vidkins, with 32 Illustrations,			25

THE SHAKSPEARE NOVELS.

Shakspeare and his Friends,	$1 00	The Secret Passion,	$1 00
The Youth of Shakspeare,	1 00		

Above three Books are also in one volume, cloth. Price Four Dollars.

WAVERLEY NOVELS. BY SIR WALTER SCOTT.

Ivanhoe,	20	The Betrothed,	20
Rob Roy,	20	Peveril of the Peak,	20
Guy Mannering,	20	Quentin Durward,	20
The Antiquary,	20	Red Gauntlet,	20
Old Mortality	20	The Talisman,	20
Heart of Mid Lothian,	20	Woodstock,	20
Bride of Lammermoor,	20	Highland Widow, etc.	20
Waverley,	20	The Fair Maid of Perth,	20
St. Ronan's Well,	20	Anne of Geierstein,	20
Kenilworth,	20	Count Robert of Paris,	20
The Pirate,	20	The Black Dwarf and Legend	
The Monastery,	20	of Montrose,	20
The Abbot,	20	Castle Dangerous, and Sur-	
The Fortunes of Nigel,	20	geon's Daughter,	20

Above edition is the cheapest in the world, and is complete in twenty-six volumes, price Twenty cents each, or Five Dollars for the complete set.

A finer edition is also published of each of the above, complete in twenty-six volumes, price Fifty cents each, or Ten Dollars for the complete set.

Moredun. A Tale of 1210,	50	Scott's Poetical Works,	5 00
Tales of a Grandfather,	25	Life of Scott, cloth,	2 50

"NEW NATIONAL EDITION" OF WAVERLEY NOVELS.

This edition of the Waverley Novels is contained in *five large octavo volumes*, with a portrait of Sir Walter Scott, making *four thousand very large double columned pages*, in good type, and handsomely printed on the finest of white paper, and bound in the strongest and most substantial manner.

Price of a set, in Black cloth, in five volumes,	$15 00
" " Full sheep, Library style,	17 50
" " Half calf, antique, or Half calf, gilt,	25 00

The Complete Prose and Poetical Works of Sir Walter Scott, are also published in ten volumes, bound in half calf, for.................$60 00

SIR E. L. BULWER'S NOVELS.

The Roue,	50	The Courtier,	25
The Oxonians,	50	Falkland,	25

☞ Above Books will be sent, postage paid, on receipt of Retail Price, by T. B. Peterson & Brothers, Philadelphia, Pa.

☞ EVERY LADY SHOULD HAVE IT. ☜

PETERSON'S MAGAZINE

Prospectus for 1873!!

THE CHEAPEST AND BEST.

PETERSON'S MAGAZINE has the best Original Stories of any of the lady's books, the best Colored Fashion Plates, the best Receipts, the best Steel Engravings, &c., &c. Every family ought to take it. *It gives more for the money than any in the world.* It will contain, next year, in its twelve numbers—

ONE THOUSAND PAGES!
 FOURTEEN SPLENDID STEEL PLATES!
  TWELVE COLORED BERLIN PATTERNS!
TWELVE MAMMOTH COLORED FASHIONS!
 NINE HUNDRED WOOD CUTS!
  TWENTY-FOUR PAGES OF MUSIC!

It will also give FIVE ORIGINAL COPYRIGHT NOVELETS, by Mrs. Ann S. Stephens, Frank Lee Benedict, and others of the best authors of America. Also, *nearly a hundred shorter stories,* ALL ORIGINAL. Its superb

MAMMOTH COLORED FASHION PLATES

are ahead of all others. These plates are engraved on steel, TWICE THE USUAL SIZE.

TERMS (Always in Advance) $2.00 A YEAR.
GREAT REDUCTIONS TO CLUBS.

2 Copies for $3.50
3   "   "   4.50
} With a copy of the superb mezzotint (20 x 16) "CHRIST WEEPING OVER JERUSALEM" to the person getting up the Club.

4 Copies for $6.50
6   "   "   9.00
10 "   "   14.00
} With an extra copy of the Magazine for the year 1873, as a premium, to the person getting up the Club.

8 Copies for $12.00
12 "   "   17.00
} With both an extra copy of the Magazine, and the premium mezzotint, to the person getting up the Club.

Address, post-paid,

CHARLES J. PETERSON,
306 Chestnut St., Philadelphia, Pa.

☞ Specimens sent gratis if written for.

www.ingramcontent.com/pod-product-compliance
Lightning Source LLC
Chambersburg PA
CBHW030735230426
43667CB00007B/725